SEVEN DECADES OF KOREAN ECONOMIC SUCCESS:
ISSUES FOR THE NEXT GENERATIONS

SEVEN DECADES OF KOREAN ECONOMIC SUCCESS : ISSUES FOR THE NEXT GENERATIONS

Chang Dae-whan

매일경제신문사

PREFACE

THE REPUBLIC OF KOREA THAT WE DON'T KNOW: A 70-YEAR MIRACLE

In the fall of 2015, Paul Kennedy, a professor at Yale University and leading historian who wrote The Rise and Fall of the Great Powers, was invited to speak at the World Knowledge Forum, which was hosted by Maeil Business Newspaper. Before the event, I reached out to him because I had a request. I asked him to study Korean history before giving his speech, because, even though he was a prominent historian, I thought he might not be familiar enough with the history of Korea.

Then in his speech, he said,

"The Republic of Korea is really a puzzling case. It seems to me that the country should have been wiped out from map a long time ago, but it wasn't. It is a miracle that Korea continued for 5,000 years while surrounded by such powers as China, Japan, and Russia and has even thrived."

That is so true. We talk about the growth of Korea in a matter-of-fact manner, but the erudite foreign scholar perceived the history of the Republic of Korea as a miracle. Paul Kennedy is not alone. People from around the world have been giving indiscriminate praise to the accomplishments of Koreans, made with sweat and tears for the last 70 years since the end of the devastating Korean War. Korea transformed itself from a country that depended on food aid to survive to a country that boasts the 12th largest economy in the world. The world defines this remarkable growth of Korea as the "Miracle on the Han River."

The driving force of that miracle owes much to "Made in Korea." Samsung Electronics has been selling more than 300 million units of mobile phones annually to the global market, making Samsung the global industry leader for seven consecutive years. When Samsung Electronics and LG Electronics are combined, sales of Korean products account for 46% of the global TV market. It was also in Korea that 15 out of the 20 world's largest marine vessels were built, and Korean-made semiconductors --- dubbed "industrial rice" in the era of the fourth industrial revolution --- account for 23% of global sales. Korea started exporting nuclear power plants, submarines and helicopters, and Korea is the first in the world to start the mass production of hydrogen cars and to commercialize 5G mobile communication service. Behind these remarkable achievements are countless touching stories that have undisclosed us.

The popularity and success of products marked with "Made in Korea" have been the foundation upon which numerous Koreans have demonstrated remarkable performance in diplomatic, cultural, and sports circles as well. Some of these Korean global leaders include Lee Jong-wook who was appointed Secretary General of the World Health Organization (WHO), Ban Ki-moon, the UN Secretary-General, Kim Yong, the President of the World Bank, and Kim Jong-yang, the current President of Interpol, all of whom gave a bigger voice to Korea on the international stage. And since the 2008 global financial crisis, Korea has also been taking the leading role at the G20 summit, which is an international forum for 20 major countries of the world. Korean pop music, drama, and movie stars are fanning the Hallyu (Korean-wave) fever that sweeps global stages, screens and households around the world, and Korea hosted the four major international sports events including the Summer Olympics and the Winter Olympics sooner than the United States and China did. As of 2016, Korea was hosting more international conferences than any other country. Korea has been proactively contributing to the promotion of peace and prosperity during the same time by sending more than 65,000 volunteers to regions hit by poverty and disasters, as well as more than 47,000 UN peacekeepers and multinational forces to resolve international disputes and help people recover from wars.

In his speech at the National Assembly during his visit to Korea in November 2017, US President Donald Trump said, "Something miraculous happened on the southern half of this peninsula. In less than one lifetime, South Korea climbed from total devastation to being among the wealthiest nations on Earth. Your economy is 350 times larger than what it was in 1960. Trade has increased 1,900 times. Your economic transformation was linked to a political one. What South Koreans have achieved on this peninsula is more than a victory for your nation. It is a victory for every nation that believes in human spirit."

When the Prime Minister of India, Narendra Damodardas Modi, visited Korea in February 2019, I had the honor of meeting him for a short time. During the meeting, he told me, "I respect Korea and the Korean people for having achieved an economic miracle in such a short time," and he said he wished India could learn from Korea. Prime Minister Modi also said, "The success of Korea, which stands tall as the global leader in economy and technology fields, is a great inspiration to India."

As we can see by their remarks, the national image of today's Korea is wonderous, successful, and respectful in the eyes of people in the international community. However, we Koreans often overlook or downplay the significance of such achievements. Sometimes we even degrade them. Movies about the modern history of Korea, such as "Ode to My Father" and "Taxi Driver" attracted an audience of over 10 million people. The life of Koreans has changed so much in just a few decades that even a TV series like "Reply 1988" that described ordinary Koreans' lives from just 30-40 years back became a sensational hit because it was considered a "retro" drama.

While a majority of people are impressed and touched by the remarkable achievements we have made despite turbulent times, there are people who choose to focus on the history of conflict and division instead. There are angry young Koreans who define Korea as "hell Joseon" and there are groups of people who attack and destroy our own assets that we've worked so hard to build with blood and sweat. Perhaps it is due to the grudge and conflict between social classes, generations, labor and management and political groups that have been left unresolved while Korea was focused on intensive growth. If we fail to keep accumulating momentum from the efforts of the past, the power to move us forward to the future is bound to grow weak. Just as we need to build responsiveness of the private sector for the future, private assets and knowledge must be allowed to accumulate in the private sector, and the efforts to make it happen should not be condemned. The older generation of Koreans once marched together to explore markets around the world as kindred spirits with shared commitment and belief in ourselves and our capabilities. But if they turn on each other, fight, and end up hindering further forward progress as some of them are doing right now, and if the future generation who witnesses the deplorable situation ends up losing confidence and hope for the future, that surely will be a misfortune for all of us.

There are many ways to look at history and analyze what has taken place. Objective evaluation can be difficult if our interests are entangled with the interests of our neighbors. But statistics can be the key we need. In Part 1 of this book, which is about "The Korean Miracle That Surprised the World", I tried to look at the accomplishments Koreans have made over the 70 years since the establishment of the Republic of Korean government with the support of various statistics. I tried to examine how those accomplishments are perceived in the eyes of the people in the international community. In Part 2, Strength and Power Behind the Making of a Miracle, I reflected on the strength of Koreans that made such globally unprecedented accomplishments possible, and in Part 3, Miracle-undermining Enemies Within, I identified weaknesses that we need to overcome for a better future. In Part 4, For Yet Another Miracle, I identified the issues that we have to resolve before we can build a better country based on these reflections.

Koreans have enthusiasm for education and dynamism unrivaled by any other nationals. It means that Koreans have what it takes to take another leap of growth in the era of the Fourth Industrial Revolution where innovation becomes more important than ever, but that doesn't guarantee that Korea will naturally become a better place to live. We have to overcome the challenges that can wipe out we've worked so hard for, just like we have done throughout the past 70 years laden with endless challenges and crises. We must solve the problem of a low birthrate and aging population, and we have to prepare for the era of a unified Korea. Forgiveness and reconciliation must be an integral part in the process of Korea's second leap. With a warm heart, we must turn the energy of conflict into energy of positivity and unity. Freedom has to overflow in schools and workplaces, and government interference and intervention should remain at a minimum. Only then will Korea's creative juices flow and entrepreneurship flourish and make it ready to move forward toward a knowledge-based society.

What is needed as we stand at the starting point of all these endeavors will be objective reflection on our society. Many numbers and graphs that I present in this book may look complicated, but these are the statistic and graphics that I collected whenever I came upon them while reading newspapers and books or surfing the Internet and believed to be good references to reflect on our society. I compiled them and present them in this book, but I'm afraid I was not able to update some statistics during the process of writing and editing. Nevertheless, it is my wish that the graphics and statistics I present in this book might serve as guideposts for our society to move forward in a better direction. And it is my hope that the Republic of Korea will continue to be perceived as the miracle country to people from around the world, not to mention Koreans themselves.

Chang Dae-whan
Chairman of Maeil Business Newspaper

CONTENTS

4   Preface

PART 1   The Korean Miracle That Surprised the World

16   Korea Emerges as the Beacon of Hope for the Economic Development of the Global Village

37   Strength and Peace Built on the Ruins of the Korean War

60   Koreans to the World, the World to Korea

82   "Made-in-Korea" Reigns in the Global Markets

103   The Power of Koreans Behind the Construction of the World's Landmark Buildings

123   Hallyu Fever Heating Up in Music, Drama, and Game Markets

144   From the Seoul 1988 Summer Olympics to the 2018 Winter Olympics

PART 2   Strength and Power Behind the Making of a Miracle

168   Passion for Education and Brainpower

184   Research and Development, the Foundation of Innovation

203   A Long History and Tradition Reflected in the World's Cultural Heritage

219   Solidly Laid Social Infrastructures

235   Dynamism of Koreans and the Global Network of Koreans

PART 3 Miracle-undermining Enemies Within

250   A Sharply Declining Birth Rate and Aging Population

277   Startup Data Shows Weakening Spirit of Challenge Among Young Adults

297   Underdeveloped Financial Industry, Increasing Household Debt, and Overheated Real Estate Investments

319   Resistance from the Groups with Vested Rights including Doctors, Pharmacists, Taxi Drivers and Labor Union

337   The Government and Political Circles are Losing the Public Trust

358   Shortage of Raw Materials and Insufficient Foreign Suppliers

PART 4 For Yet Another Miracle

376   Economic Freedom Should be Expanded to Maximize Creativity

401   Demographic Cliff, Search for a New Growth Engine for the Era of 100 Years of Life Expectancy

421   The Need for Taxation and Regulation Systems That Respect Entrepreneurship

442   Labor Market Reform is the Answer to the Polarization and Low Productivity Problems

467   Korea Has to Foster Hallyu Content, Tourism, Finance, and Service Industries

487   Social Infrastructure is Based on Competitiveness and Most be Constantly Reformed

509   Pursuing a Vision of Unified Korea Despite the G2 Competition

527   Epilogue

PART 1

THE KOREAN MIRACLE THAT SURPRISED THE WORLD

KOREA EMERGES AS THE BEACON OF HOPE FOR THE ECONOMIC DEVELOPMENT OF THE GLOBAL VILLAGE

After the Korean War ended, General Douglas MacArthur, the Commander of the U.N. Forces in Korea, said "It will take at least 100 years before this country can be rebuilt." But the Republic of Korea rose from the ruins of war and made a remarkable transformation from a country whose survival was dependent on foreign aid to a global economic power in just 50 years. With such unprecedented fast economic growth that is admiringly dubbed "the Miracle on the Han River" by the world, Korea became the only country to have transformed itself from a foreign aid recipient to a foreign aid provider. Now, Korea is emerging as the beacon that spreads hope to the world, as testified to by numerous countries rushing to Korea to study the Korean development model.

KOREA BECOMES THE 7TH MEMBER TO JOIN THE 30-50 CLUB

Korea is an advanced country by every standards. Korea's per

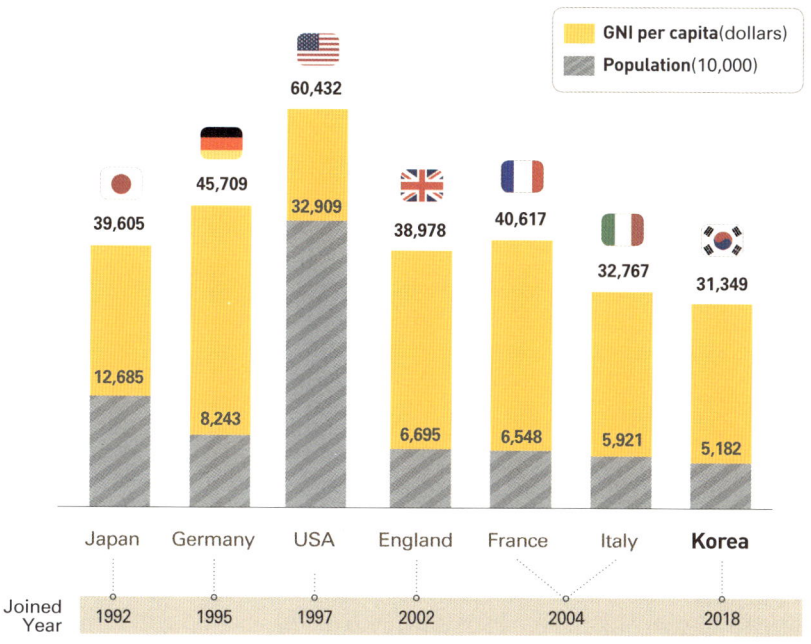

*National income is based on the per capita GNI (Gross National Income)/ As of 2018 for Korea, and as of 2017 for other countries

Source: OECD, Bank of Korea

capita income surpassed $20,000 in 2006 and then the $30,000 mark soon after in 2018. It is not a small country either, even though it may look comparatively small because of the great powers such as the United States, China, Russia, and Japan that surround it.

Korea joined the "20-50 Club" in 2012 and then the "30-50 Club" in 2018. The moniker refers to a small group of large and wealthy countries of the world, as compared to the "30-30 Club" in baseball which refers to baseball players who can hit and run better than

THE KOREAN MIRACLE THAT SURPRISED THE WORLD 17

others and therefore record a higher power/speed number (PSN). Even though the Club does not have an exclusive conference or a secretariat office, it symbolically refers to countries that have per capita income of more than $30,000 and a population of more than 50 million.

When Britain became the sixth member of the 20-50 Club after Japan, the United States, France, Italy, and Germany in 1996, the international community thought it would be unlikely to see any more new members for quite some time. China, India, Brazil and Russia are big countries with large populations, but they don't meet the per capita income requirement. Canada and Australia have a large territory and high per capita income, but their populations are not big enough. There were numerous impressive candidate countries, but they did not have exactly what it takes to become a member of the Club when Korea became a proud member. In fact, Korea was the only country to join the Club out of all the countries that became independent after the end of World War II. It was a feat that signaled to people around the world that Korea was no longer a poor or a weak country anymore.

Korea upgraded itself by reaching the $30,000 mark of per capita income and becoming a member of the 30-50 Club. Earlier, Korea had joined the Organization for Economic Cooperation and Development (OECD), a so-called developed country club in 1996, but recently its meaning has waned considerably after OECD started accepting even developing countries as its members. Therefore, the

30-50 Club is a true club of large and wealthy countries because only seven countries in the world are qualified to become its members.

THE MIRACLE ON THE HAN RIVER: KOREA STANDS TALL AS THE WORLD'S 12TH LARGEST ECONOMIC POWER

We call it a miracle when something great but very unlikely to happen, happens. That's the reason the world dubbed the economic growth Koreans have accomplished "the miracle on the Han River." In 1961, which was the year before Korea's economic development began, Korea's per capita income was a mere $82, which ranked 101st in the world. That means Koreans' per capita income was just half of Ghana in Africa whose per capita income was $179 at the time. Korea was also heavily dependent on aid from the United States. Even in 1969 when industrialization kicked off in Korea, overseas aid accounted for as much as 25% of the annual national budget.

That's how Korean the economy looked when Korea started to flourish and eventually accomplished a wondrous compressed growth in just half a century, a record which cannot be found anywhere in the history of the world. As of 2017, Korea's gross domestic product (GDP) was the 12th largest in the world, after Canada and Russia. It rallied to become the world's 10th largest in 2005 before it slowed down a little, but still, Korea boasts an economy that is larger than that of Australia or Spain.

The size of Korea's economy has grown 400 times since 1960.

THE WORLD'S LARGEST ECONOMIES

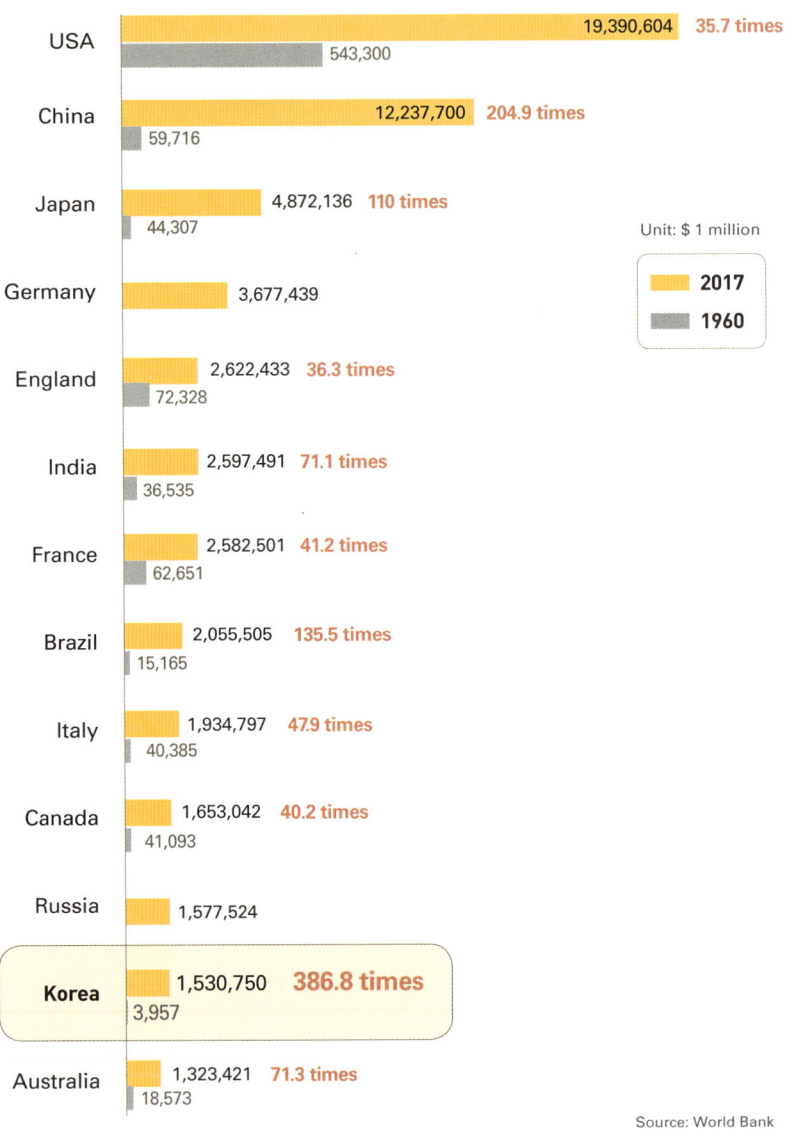

Source: World Bank

No other country in the world has ever recorded such fast economic growth, not even Spain that built a powerful empire in the 16th century through colonization and left a mark on world history; or the Netherlands that became a super power in the 16-17th centuries with maritime trade; or Great Britain that became a hegemonic country with the industrial revolution in the 18th century; or the United States and Japan. It was an achievement Koreans should feel proud of particularly because they accomplished something close to a miracle while still an impoverished country with little in natural resources. China achieved explosive economic growth which some people compared to "the opening of heaven and earth" since Deng Xiaoping's open-door and reform policies, but their economic growth was 200 times more than that of the 1960s. It also makes a huge contrast to the economy of North Korea whose per capita income ranked 50th in the world at the time but which has fallen considerably and is now one of the poorest countries in the world.

KOREA EXPORTS MORE TO THE GLOBAL MARKETS THAN FRANCE OR BRITAIN

Britain and France once built colonies throughout the world and used them as markets that consumed the majority of their goods. Korea, however, is now exporting more "made in Korea" goods to markets around the world than Britain and France without having to employ that kind of imperialistic approach. Korean products such as semiconductors, smart phones, automobiles, and ships offer such high quality and variety that they are a big source of growing pride for Koreans. Korea's exports exceeded $600 billion in 2018, ranking Korea 6th in the world for two years in a row. There are only a handful of countries in the world --- China, the US, Germany, the Netherlands and Japan --- that export more than Korea.

The World's Top 10 Exporters

ranking	2008	2014	2015	2018
1	Germany	China	China	China
2	China	United States of America	United States of America	United States of America
3	United States of America	Germany	Germany	Germany
4	Japan	Japan	Japan	Netherlands
5	Netherlands	Netherlands	Netherlands	Japan
6	France	France	**Korea**	**Korea**
7	Italy	**Korea**	Hong Kong	Hong Kong
8	Belgium	Italy	France	France
9	England	Hong Kong	England	Italy
10	Russia	England	Italy	England
11	Canada			
12	**Korea**			

Source: WTO

In the early 1960s, Korea had only a few limited items to export to foreign markets, including minerals such as tungsten, iron ore, graphite, and marine products such as squid and seaweed. Korea sold the majority of minerals to the United States and marine products, to Japan. At the time, President Park Chung-hee encouraged the export of more, claiming, "Exporting is the only way to keep us alive. Sell everything that can be sold," but the situation was that just one Korean company, Korea Tungsten, was responsible for about 60% of all national exports. That explains why President Park appointed Park Tae-joon the president of Korea Tungsten before putting him in charge of the construction of POSCO: He wanted to test and verify his business management skills first.

It was in 1964, a year after Korea started exporting an agricultural product --- raw silk extracted from silkworms to be specific --- that Korea reached the $100 million mark of annual exports. Korea was so thrilled about this accomplishment that the government designated an "Export Day" and held a grand ceremony to celebrate the milestone. But today, the trade volume of Korea is an astonishing $1.14 trillion. Korea ranks 4th in the world in terms of trade surplus, after Germany, Japan and China, and has been recording a surplus for 20 consecutive years since 1998. The surplus is about half the size of China's, but the popularity of 'Made in Korea' products in the world market far outstrips 'Made in China' products.

KOREA RECEIVES A HIGHER SOVEREIGN CREDIT RATING THAN JAPAN AND CHINA

A sovereign credit rating is an independent assessment of the creditworthiness and stability of a country or sovereign entity, determined by comprehensively evaluating all areas including politics, economy, culture, and the military of the country or sovereign entity. Korea had experienced a crisis when it was bailed out by the International Monetary Fund (IMF) in the wake of the 1997 financial crisis, but that scathing experience resulted in strengthening Korea's capability to respond to a crisis.

Korea's foreign reserves are more than $400 billion. It is the world's 8th largest amount after China, Japan, Switzerland, Saudi Arabia, Russia, Taiwan and Hong Kong. Thanks to a good credit history and the large-scale foreign exchange reserves that Korea has been accumulating through trade despite North Korea's threat, Korea was granted the highest credit rating by the world's top three credit rating agencies, namely, Pitch, Standard & Poor (S&P) and Moody's.

Korea received an AA rating from S&P and Aa2 from Moody's, both of which is the third highest rating from both agencies. They are lower than that of the United States, Germany and Switzerland, but on par with the United Kingdom, France and Kuwait. They are one level higher than that of Taiwan, and two levels higher than Japan and China, the country that has the largest foreign exchange reserves in the world.

Korea's Sovereign Credit Ratings Before and After the Foreign Exchange Crisis

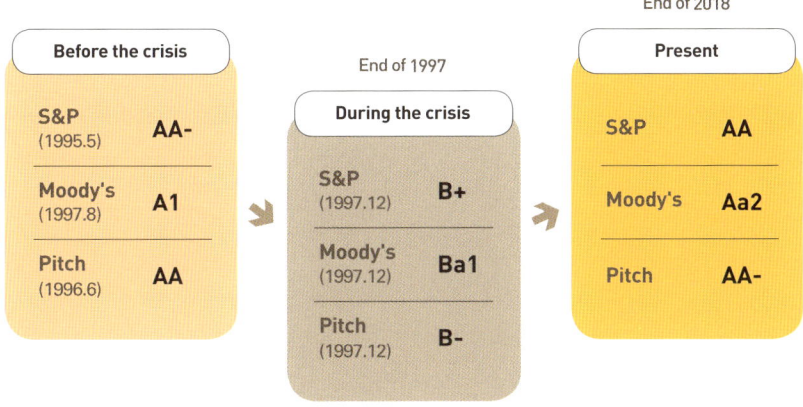

Source: Ministry of Strategy and Finance

Fitch has granted Korea its fourth highest AA- rating, which is one level higher than China, and two levels higher than Japan. During the foreign exchange crisis, S&P downgraded Korea's rating to B+ and Moody's to Ba1, but Korea's ratings recovered at an unprecedented speed. Since the sovereign credit rating has a significant impact on interest rates when borrowing dollars in the international financial market in addition to trade transactions and winning construction orders, Korea's sovereign credit rating being higher than that of Japan and China should be considered an important asset Koreans have built.

KOREA JOINS THE G20, WITH AN EYE TO JOINING THE G8

In 2008, when bankruptcy of the US investment bank Lehman Brothers triggered a wide-spread global financial crisis, the US government held a G20 summit with 20 member countries in Washington DC. It was the US government's move to find a solution to the crisis by including countries that were emerging as economic powers after realizing the limitation of G7 in solving global trade and financial problems.

The G20 countries were selected by taking the size of the economy including GDP and international trade volume into consideration, and Korea was naturally included. Korea hosted the fifth G20 Summit in Seoul in 2010. The first and third summits were held in the United States, and Korea became the fourth country to host the G20 summit following the United States, Britain, and Canada. When the decision was made to hold the G20 summit in Korea, leaders from member countries greeted then-President Lee Myung-bak by telling him, "You are a big man," which is a good example that shows how influential Korea was on the global stage.

Although it is a cause of concern that Korea's economic growth is slowing down, there are constant positive outlook on Korea side. It might be because analysts are recognizing the potential of Korea, a country that transformed itself from one of the most impoverished countries to a world economic power. In its report released towards the end of 2017, UK's leading economics consultancy CEBR (Centre

Previous G20 Summits

Host Country	Host City	Date
Argentina	Buenos Aires	Nov. 2018
Germany	Hamburg	Jul. 2017
China	Hangzhou	Sept. 2016
Turkey	Antalya	Nov. 2015
Australia	Brisbane	Nov. 2014
Russia	Saint Petersburg	Sept. 2013
Mexico	Los Cabos	Jun. 2012
France	Cannes	Nov. 2011
Republic of Korea	**Seoul**	**Nov. 2010**
Canada	Toronto	Jun. 2010
USA	Pittsburgh	Sept. 2009
England	London	Apr. 2009
USA	Washington	Nov. 2008

for Economics and Business Research) predicted that the Korean economy would rank 8th in the world in 2032. That means Korea will be an economic power preceded only by China, the United States, India, Japan, Germany, Brazil, and Britain. Considering that this report is not based on the assumption of a unified Korea, the status of Korea could become even higher if South and North Korea become united. Korea will continue to take a leap if Koreans add innovation to their determination and commitment that made the miracle on the Han River possible.

THE ASCENT FROM AID RECIPIENT TO AID DONOR

An Indian delegation to the United Nations Korean Reconstruction Agency (UNKRA), which was established by the UN shortly after the end of the Korean War, reportedly said, "Expecting the economy to recover in Korea is like expecting a rose to bloom in a trash can." From 1953 to 1961, Korea received $2.3 billion in aid from the United States and others. You get an idea of how heavily Korea was dependent on foreign aid when you consider Korea's exports in 1962 were about $50 million.

Then the tables turned starting in the mid-1980s when Korea began recording a trade surplus and became capable of providing aid to other countries. In 1987, Korea established the Economic Development Cooperation Fund (EDCF) and in 1991, Korean International Cooperation Agency (KOICA), through which Korea has been providing official development assistance (ODA). The United Nations Development Program (UNDP) closed its office in Korea --- which had served as the channel of delivering aid to Korea for 46 years --- and replaced it with the UNDP Seoul Policy Center which handles contributions to a joint trust fund and supports worldwide development campaigns and projects. In 2010, Korea joined the Development Assistance Committee (DAC), which is part of OECD and consists of advanced countries that provide assistance to developing countries. It is an exclusive group of wealthy countries whose ODA is over $100 million or ODA-to-GNI (gross national

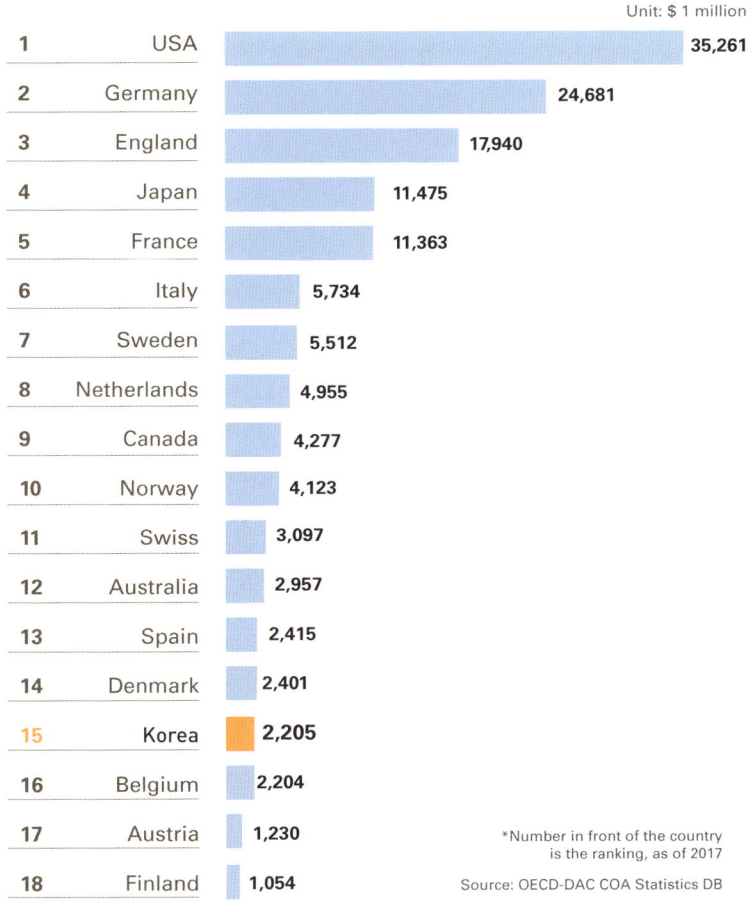

income) ratio is more than 0.3% which qualifies them to join after review.

That is how Korea became the world's first and only country that has raised itself from an aid recipient to an aid donor. There was a time in the past when concerns were growing among advanced countries that international aid was not working. Believing that aid provided to developing countries was not returning any results due to inefficiency and corruption, a growing number of countries became less enthusiastic about participating. It was in this atmosphere that Korea turned into an aid donor and gave hope to developing countries and inspired advanced countries to keep reaching out to help them.

TAKING THE LEAD ON FREE TRADE BY SIGNING FTAS WITH OVER 50 COUNTRIES

"If we don't diligently earn foreign currency from exports and repay our debts, Korea will be bankrupt for real this time when the IMF loans mature." --- This is a quote from a Maeil Business Newspaper headline article dated January 1, 1998. The importance of "earning foreign currency from exports" became clear once again when Korea was hit by a foreign currency crisis. It was around this time that the IMF suggested that Korea sign free trade agreements with countries like Japan, Chile, Singapore, and New Zealand, and subsequently, the Office of the Minister for Trade was established in March 1998. Korea initiated the first FTA negotiations with Chile and managed to strike an agreement four years and three months later. It was a bumpy road until an agreement was reached, but it was another uphill struggle until the agreement was ratified by the

Korea's FTA Map

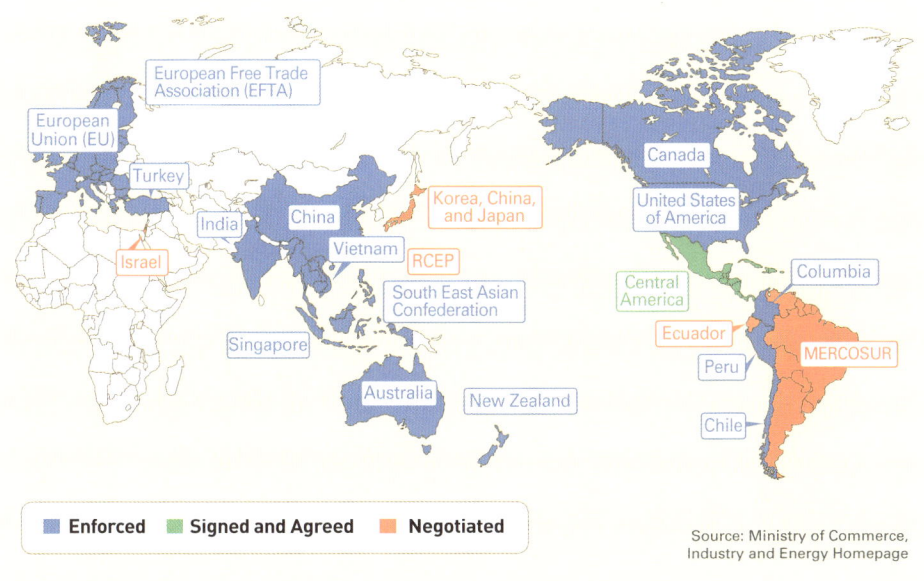

Source: Ministry of Commerce, Industry and Energy Homepage

National Assembly. With grape growers and fishermen carrying out fierce protests against it, the National Assembly failed to approve the FTA bill three times before it was ratified almost a year later.

When Korea's first FTA with Chile came into effect in 2004, it quickly proved that free trade was mutually beneficial. The rate of increase in exports to Chile was 9.6% before the FTA, but it jumped to 58% in the first year and 53% in the second year after the FTA went into effect.

Korea's export-to-GDP ratio is the world's third highest after the Netherlands and Germany. That means Korea is in need of a vast market to export to and a stable supply of raw materials. Confirming that the FTA is a powerful means of expanding economic territory, Korea went on to initiate 15 negotiations and signed FTAs with 54 countries by the end of 2018. When the Korea-China FTA was signed at the end of 2014, Korea had succeeded in signing FTAs with the world's three largest economic blocs --- the EU, China and the US --- and became the third fastest country to expand their free trade agreements after Chile and Peru.

Recently, the so-called 'Mega FTA' has been on the rise. A few examples of mega-FTAs include the Comprehensive and Progressive Agreement for Trans-Pacific Partnership (CPTPP), which is a mega free trade agreement among 11 countries including Japan that entered into force at the end of 2018, and the Regional Comprehensive Economic Partnership (RCEP), which is another proposed multilateral free trade agreement among 16 countries including China and ASEAN that is being negotiated and making fast progress at the moment. Korea should take a leading role in free trade agreements and use them as a stage to expand its economic territory.

TURNING TO A NET CREDITOR IN 2014, SNOWBALLING OVERSEAS FINANCIAL ASSETS

Korea's trade balance has been continuously recording a surplus, fattening national coffers from 2009 until 2014, when Korea became a net creditor country. It means that the amount of financial assets Koreans own in foreign countries in the form of stocks, bonds and loans, surpassed the amount of financial assets own by foreigners in Korea. It also means Korea became an awe-inspiring case of a debtor-turned-creditor, because just a few years earlier when Korea was hit by the foreign exchange crisis toward the end of 1997, the Korean government was drowning in a staggering $63.7 billion net debt. This caused the entire nation to rise up and join in the gold-collection campaign to help the government repay it.

Korea's Net Foreign Assets

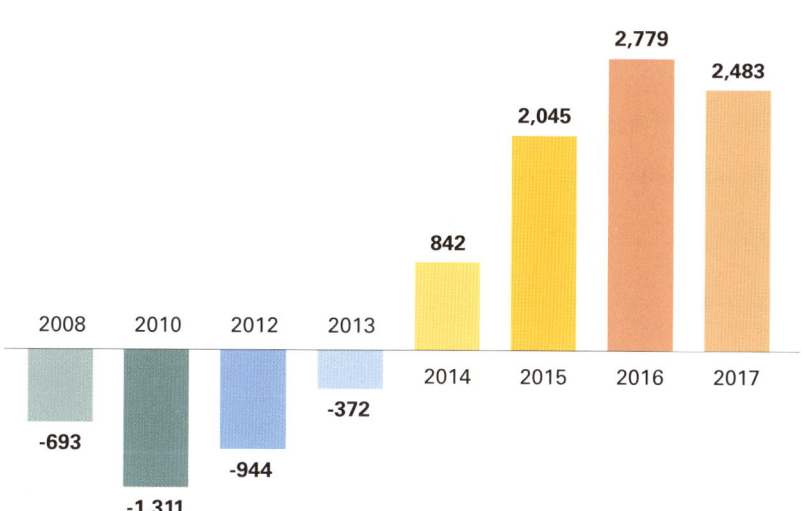

* Net foreign assets = sum of foreign assets − foreign liabilities
Source: Bank of Korea

Korea's financial assets in foreign countries exceeded $1.5 trillion as of 2018. This amount is $340 billion more than the financial assets foreigners have in Korea. Korea's foreign assets include $450 billion worth of stocks and bonds purchased by the Korean Investment Corporation (KIC) and other financial and investment companies. The increased amount of overseas investment means Korean financial companies are subject to bigger losses or gains when the international money markets fluctuate. But it also means Korea is better prepared to respond to economic crisis because there are more foreign assets that can be cashed out and brought into Korea at any time. Trade balance surplus and the subsequent increase in foreign currency deposits in domestic banks brought about a significantly improved borrowing structure in the financial sector as well. Domestic banks are borrowing much less foreign currency, and the short-term foreign currency loans, which once triggered a foreign currency crisis, have also dropped significantly.

Japan's net balance of its external assets totaled $2.9 trillion as of the end of 2017. Japan has remained the world's largest net creditor for 27 years in a row. However, Japan is also the world's largest debtor whose national debt is 240% of its GDP. Nevertheless, the Japanese currency, the yen, is treated as a safe asset in international money markets because of its overseas assets. Germany and China record the largest net external assets after Japan.

KOREA'S NATION BRAND VALUE RANKS 10TH, MAKING IT A WORLD-CLASS BRAND

Korea's nation brand value is rising rapidly with the Korean Wave (Hallyu) is spreading to the world and Samsung competing in the top5 category. While automobiles, smartphones and TVs made by Korean companies such as Samsung, LG and Hyundai Motors have cemented their reputations as World-class brands in the global market, Korea itself is making a stellar ascent into a luxury nation brand.

In its annual report of 2018, the British branding consultancy company Brand Finance estimated Korea's brand value at $2 trillion and ranked Korea 10th in the world in terms of its nation brand value. In this same report, the nation brand value was the highest in the order of the United States, China, Germany, the United Kingdom, Japan and France. Korea ranked 16th in 2013, but it moved up the rank fast by outpacing Australia, Russia, the Netherlands, Switzerland and Mexico in just a few years.

A nation's brand value is calculated from a number of factors including people's awareness, likability, and credibility of the nation, and it is perceived as an important asset instead of just representing the nation's image. It is because it can affect overall activities of the nation comprehensively, beginning from attracting tourists and investors to adding value to its export products and building political alliances.

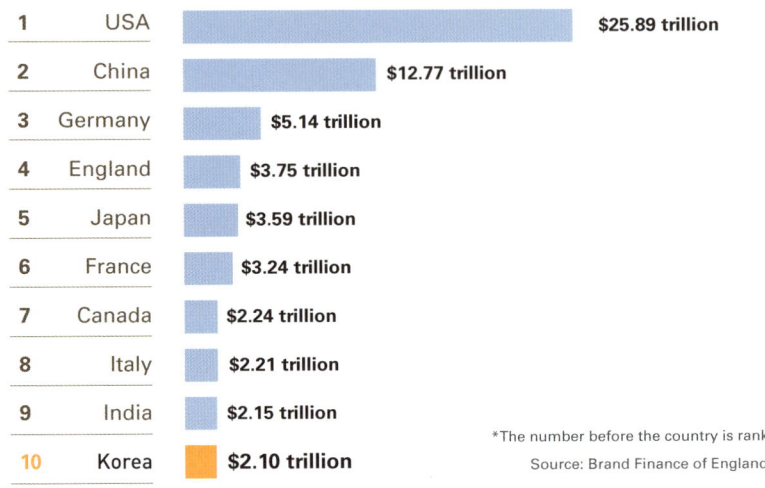

However, a nation's brand value is calculated from different factors using different methods depending on the institutions that study and measure it. For example, Germany's Anholt-GfK Roper Nation Brands Index released a list of nation brand values of 50 countries of the world in 2017. On this list, Korea was not included in the top 10, and Germany was placed at the top. It is hard to say that the absolute standard for the assessment of nation brand value has yet been established, but if the "made in Korea" products continue to perform as well as they do now in the global markets and the Korean Wave fever continues to spread, Koreans will be able to enjoy higher self-esteem and greater pride in being Korean on the global stage.

STRENGTH AND PEACE BUILT ON THE RUINS OF THE KOREAN WAR

The Korean peninsula is not only surrounded by the world's superpowers such as the United States, China, Russia, and Japan, it is also divided into the North and the South. In all four directions, Korea is faced with neighbors none of which can be taken lightly. Squeezed among these neighbors, Korea is destined to walk a diplomatic tightrope, but that doesn't mean Korea is just an international pushover. When you turn your eyes to the broader global village, you can see how Korea is a strong power in terms of the economy and military. Korea is also a country that is contributing to the resolution of global conflicts by sending peacekeepers to various parts of the world.

KOREA MILITARY OUTPACES JAPAN AND BECOMES THE WORLD'S 7TH STRONGEST

The military strength rankings of Korea and Japan are in a neck-

Military Power by Country

ranking	2015	2016	2017	2018
1	USA	USA	USA	USA
2	Russia	Russia	Russia	Russia
3	China	China	China	China
4	India	India	India	India
5	England	France	France	France
6	France	England	England	England
7	**Korea**	Japan	Japan	**Korea**
8	Germany	Turkey	Turkey	Japan
9	Japan	Germany	Germany	Turkey
10	Turkey	Italy	Italy	Germany
11	Israel	**Korea**	**Korea**	Italy

Source: GFP(Global Firepower)

and-neck race just like France and Britain. The US-based online group Global Firepower (GFP) compares the military powers of countries around the world each year and releases the list of their rankings. In the 2018 GFP review, Korea outpaced Japan and ranked 7th. The Korean military had been evaluated to be stronger than that of Japan and ranked 7th-9th each year up until 2015, but it was outpaced by Japan in 2016 and moved down the ranking to11th place before it sprung back again in 2018.

In this analysis, the United States, Russia, China, and India remain the unchanged top 4 in the global military powers ranking. France and Britain are in a longstanding race over 5th place. Britain ranked 5th up until 2015, but it was outpaced by France beginning in 2016. Having fought against each other in the 100 Year War, the ranking race between Britain and Franc is attracting attention just as much as the race between Korea and Japan.

Among the six countries which rank higher than Korea on the military powers list, five countries except India are permanent members of the UN Security Council entitled to use the veto power. That means Korea's military power is almost on a par with those of the world's superpowers.

The final GFP rankings are based on over 55 different factors --- not including such asymmetrical power as nuclear weapons that are not likely to be used in reality --- such as total population, military personnel, available manpower, finance, and defense budget. The index numbers may be different from actual military strength because military powers are difficult to compare simply by numbers, and geographical factors must be taken into consideration as well. Nevertheless, when you consider North Korea having jumped in the ranking from 23rd to 18th, no country can take South and North Korea lightly. If any country attempts to use military force in this region, they should be ready to sustain a fatal blow themselves because it would be comparable to setting a powder keg on fire.

KOREA RANKS 7TH IN MILITARY STRENGTH AND 10TH IN MILITARY SPENDING

The imposing power of Korea's military manifests itself in its number of soldiers, which is supported and maintained by a compulsory draft system. According to the 2018 GFP index, the Korean military has 625,000 soldiers, which puts Korea in 7th place in the world. China has the most at 2.18 million troops, followed by India, the United States and Russia. North Korea ranks 5th in the world with 945,000 troops. Since four out of six countries that have a larger number of troops than Korea --- not including India and Pakistan --- are located close to the Korean Peninsula, Korea is not in a good position to boast of its impressive military power even though it ranks 7th in the world. Japan is in 21st place in the ranking with 247,000 troops.

There is another factor which, along with the number of troops, is critical in determining a nation's military power: money. According to the GFP index, Korea's military expenditure is the world's 10th largest, and it ranks 10th in military budget statistics as released by the Stockholm International Peace Institute (SIPRI) as well.

According to the SIPRI analysis, total world military expenditure jumped and reached its highest amount in 2017 after the collapse of the Soviet Union in 1991. It is largely due to the heated arms race in the Middle East while the US and China are also locking horns

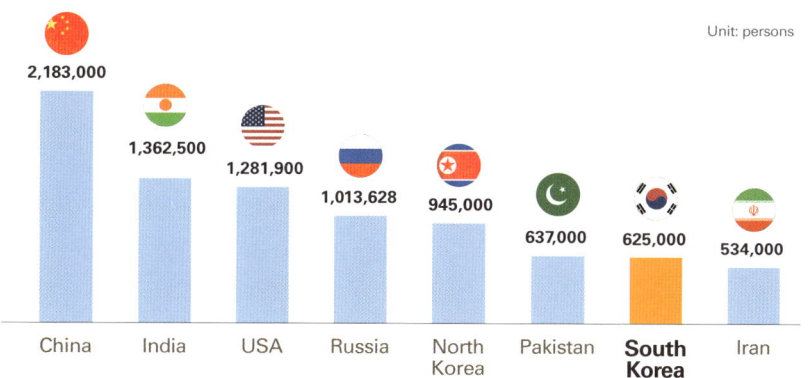

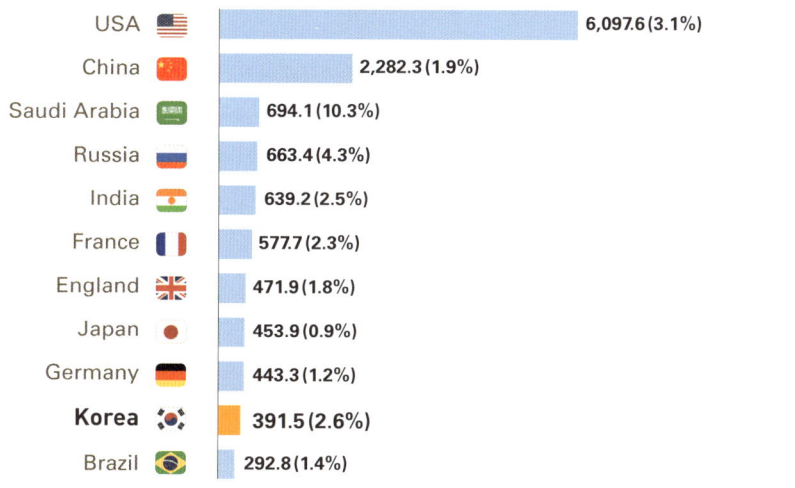

THE KOREAN MIRACLE THAT SURPRISED THE WORLD 41

in their own arms race. With 2.6 times greater military expenditure than China, the United States continues to remain unrivaled at the top, but China is on a continuous, fast-upward trend in spending as well.

Saudi Arabia's military spending continues to rank 3rd after the United States and China. Saudi Arabia spent $69.4 billion, which accounts for 10.3% of their gross domestic production in 2017. Saudi's military spending is higher than Russia, India, France, or Britain. North Korea ranks number one in the world for military expenditures relative to its gross domestic product, but the Middle Eastern counterparts are also allocating a significantly high percentage of the GDP to military spending.

KOREA IS CONSIDERED A BIG BUYER IN THE GLOBAL ARMS SUPPLY CHAINS

The global arms import market goes through significant changes depending on the political landscape of the world. According to the SIPRI analysis, India was the world's largest arms importer for five years until 2017. India imported 12% of all arms imports of the world, and India is followed by Saudi Arabia that imported 10% of the total imports. The world's five largest arms importers including Egypt, UAE and China accounted for 35% of the total arms trade volume.

The rankings of the importers were quite different for the five

The World's Five Biggest Weapons Importers

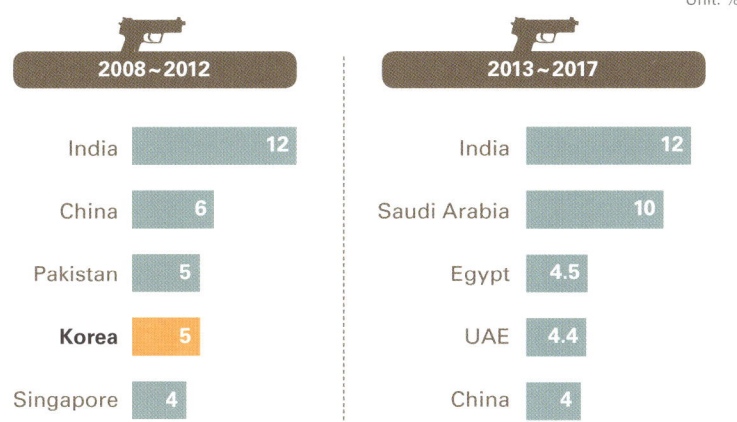

Unit: %

2008~2012
- India: 12
- China: 6
- Pakistan: 5
- **Korea**: 5
- Singapore: 4

2013~2017
- India: 12
- Saudi Arabia: 10
- Egypt: 4.5
- UAE: 4.4
- China: 4

* Numbers indicate the share in the weapons import market
Source: Stockholm International Peace Research Institute

The World's Biggest Weapons Importers in 2017

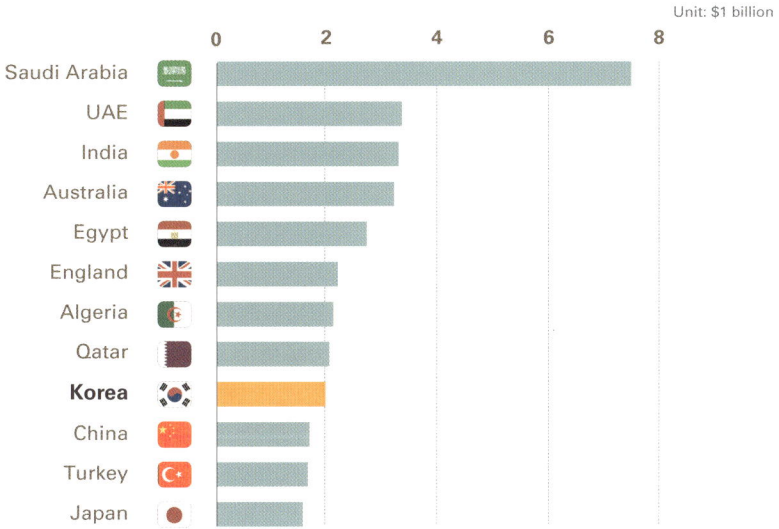

Unit: $1 billion

Source: HIS Markit Financial Times

THE KOREAN MIRACLE THAT SURPRISED THE WORLD

years prior to 2017.

During this period, five Asian countries, namely, India, China, Pakistan, Korea and Singapore, were the largest arms importers. These five countries imported 32% of the total arms trade worldwide, and Korea was once the 4th largest importer with 5% of the total weapons trade. Statistics show that the weapons that were headed to Asia at the time have recently been routed to the Middle East.

Unlike the arms import market, there is little change in the country rankings in the export market. The United States and Russia remain responsible for supplying more than half of the world's weapons. The United States accounted for 34 percent of world arms exports for the five years prior to 2017, while Russia accounted for 22 percent during the same period. They are followed by France, Germany, and China. There has been little change in the rankings of these five largest arms exporters, who collectively account for 74% of all arms exports. Korea ranks around 15th.

There is a clear difference in the markets to which the United States and Russia have been exporting weapons during the span of five years up to 2017. The United States sold weapons to 98 countries, 49% of which were shipped to the Middle East. Saudi Arabia and UAE were the first and the second largest importers, and Korea was the fourth largest importer of US-made weapons after Australia. By comparison, Russian-made weapons were mostly exported to India, China, and Vietnam, and Chinese-made weapons were mostly bought by Pakistan, Algeria, and Bangladesh.

FOUR KOREAN COMPANIES ON THE LIST OF THE WORLD'S TOP 100 ARMS MANUFACTURERS

The global defense industry is spearheaded by US companies such as Lockheed Martin, Boeing, and Raytheon. Among the world's 100 largest companies in the defense industry identified by the Stockholm International Peace Research Institute, 42 of them were

The World's Leading Defense Companies

ranking		company	country
2016	2017		
1	1	Lockheed Martin	USA
2	2	Boeing	USA
3	3	Raytheon	USA
4	4	BAE Systems	USA
5	5	Northrop Grumman	USA
6	6	General Dynamics	USA
7	7	Airbus	European Union
9	8	Thales	France
8	9	Leonardo	Italy
13	10	Almaz-Antey	Russia
40	49	Hanwha Techwin	Korea
56	60	LIG Nex1	Korea
72	85	Daewoo Shipbuilding & Marine Engineering	Korea
50	98	Korea Aerospace Industries	Korea

Source: Stockholm International Peace Research Institute

US companies whose total sales accounted for 57% of the grand total of sales for the 100 companies. There were ten Russian companies included in the list, including Almaz-Antey. SIPRI did not include Chinese companies, claiming that their statistics were not reliable, but the British think tank International Institute for Strategic Studies (IISS) suggests that eight Chinese companies would be among the world's top 30 largest defense companies.

There were four Korean companies among the world's top 100 defense companies as of 2017. They included Hanwha Techwin (49th), LIG Nex1 (60th), Daewoo Shipbuilding & Marine Engineering (85th), and Korea Aerospace Industries (98th). The number and ranks went down compared to 2015 when seven Korean companies were among the top 100 defense companies, including LIG Nex1 (52nd), Korea Aerospace Industries (54th), Hanwha Techwin (65th), Daewoo Shipbuilding & Marine Engineering (67th), Hanhwa (71st) Poongsan Protech (96th) And Hanhwa Thales (100th place).

Even though the government investigation into corruption scandals has put a temporary brake on it at the moment, Korea's defense industry has been continuously evolving and exporting more advanced weapons beginning with military rifles and ammunition in the 1970s to armored vehicles and guided missiles in the 1980s, self-propelled artillery in 1990s and jet trainers, mobile helicopters, submarines and Aegis destroyers in the 2000s. The Korean-made K-9 self-propelled howitzers and T-50 advanced jet trainers are highly competitive export items in the global market. Korea began to export K-9 self-propelled howitzers to Turkey in 2001 and has been selling them to Poland, Finland, Estonia, India, and Norway, seizing half of the global self-propelled howitzers market. Korea Aerospace Industries sold KT-1 (Woongbi) basic training aircraft to Indonesia, Turkey, Peru and Senegal, and the company also exported T-50 supersonic advanced trainers, co-developed by Korea Aerospace Industries and Lockheed Martin, to Indonesia, Iraq, the Philippines and Thailand.

THE THIRD TO FIELD STEALTH FIGHTER IN ASIA

The Republic of Korea Air Force now has the capability to fly freely in North Korean airspace, because the stealth multirole fighter F-35A was introduced and entered service in Korea as of 2019 with the Taegeuk mark on it. North Korea has created the world's tightest defense network near Pyongyang, but it is only an old-fashioned system built with equipment and technology from the pre-1980s. During the Gulf War in 1990, the Iraqi air defense network was reduced to ruins by the US Air Forces, and a similar change in military power is taking place in the Korean peninsula.

In 2014, Korea decided to invest KRW7.4 trillion to purchase 40 F-35A stealth fighters developed by Lockheed Martin, with the final delivery due by 2021. Korea has been sending pilots to the United States since the end of 2017 to receive pilot training, and the first

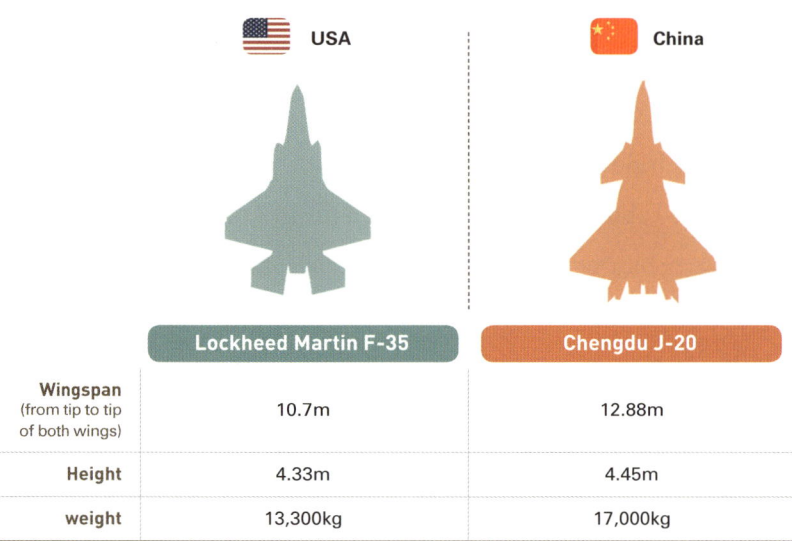

Source: Inputs from the Defense Industries in the US and China

batch of the stealth fighter jets was delivered and fielded in Korea in March 2019. With this purchase, Korea became one of the three Asian countries along with China and Japan to own stealth aircraft.

F-35A stealth fighters can fly 2,200 km at a maximum speed of Mach 1.8 while carrying more than 8 tons of missiles and precision guided bombs. In Japan, F-35A fighters were first introduced and fielded in February 2018 at a Japanese Air Self Defense Forces base in Aomori Prefecture. Japan had agreed to purchase 42 F-35A fighters, and there is also speculation that Japan will eventually purchase up to 100 units. China also announced that they had developed Chengdu J-20 stealth fighters and they entered service in Shangdong Peninsula in early 2018. Russia is in the process of developing a new fifth generation stealth fighter, Sukhoi Su-57, ramping up the stealth aircraft development competition in Northeast Asia.

Ascent from the Coastal Navy to the Blue Ocean Navy

The vessel that symbolizes the ROK Navy is a 14,000-ton-class Dokdo that was commissioned in 2007. It is a large landing ship drew suspicion from China and Japan who thought it was a light aircraft carrier (LAC) at its launch ceremony in 2005. The misperception is understanding because Dokdo is 199 meters long and 31 meters wide, but it is not built for the landing and taking off of fighters. Instead, it can carry a battalion of marines and helicopters and carry out amphibious assault operations. The ROK Navy has named its large landing ships after Korea's outermost islands, such as Dokdo and another ship of the same class, Marado. Marado had its launch ceremony in May 2018 after Dokdo. Slated to be delivered to the Navy in 2020, Marado has the same displacement, length, width, and maximum speed as Dokdo, but it boasts advanced features: The flight deck is adapted to accommodate two aircraft with both vertical takeoff and landing.

There are three types of naval vessels: aircraft carrier, cruiser, and destroyer. They have different operational purposes, a cruiser is of the15,000-ton class whose purpose is assault, while a destroyer is a vessel mostly intended to escort larger vessels in a fleet and defend them against attackers. The ROKN does not have aircraft carriers or cruisers, but it has been evolving into the "blue ocean navy" while acquiring several large landing ships through the three-phased Korean Destroyer eXperimental (KDX) program.

The first phase of the KDX program gave birth to three 3,000-ton-class destroyers in the 1990s: Gwanggaeto the Great, Eulji Mundeok, and Yang Manchun. The second phase of KDX in the 2000s produced six destroyers including the 4,000-ton-class Chungmugong Yi Sun-shin destroyer. A 7,000-ton-class Sejong the Great destroyer with built-in Aegis Combat System was commissioned in 2007 during the third phase of KDX. Foreign observers have categoried as part of the cruiser class instead of a destroyer class. The ROKN has named destroyers after heroes from the Goguryeo period as a manifestation of its commitment to realizing the vision of "a blue ocean navy" by taking on the spirit and legacy of the Goguryeo kingdom that occupied the largest territory in our history.

The ROKN has been holding an International Fleet Review (IFR) once every ten years since 1998 when the first Korean-made destroyer was born. An International Fleet Review was held in Busan in 2008 to commemorate Korea having become the fifth country in the world to build an Aegis-equipped destroyer. In 2018, an International Fleet Review was held in the waters off Jeju Island with a total of 22 Korean vessels and 17 vessels from 12 countries including US aircraft carriers and Russian cruisers.

FIFTH COUNTRY TO EXPORT SUBMARINES, AND THE TOP SHIPBUILDING TECHNOLOGY

Korea is the fifth country in the world to export submarines after Britain, France, Germany and Russia. It was in 1987 that the ROKN first decided to purchase submarines and signed a contract with the German company Howaldtswerke-Deutsche Werft (HDW) to purchase three 1,200-ton submarines. Subsequently, the first German-made submarine was delivered to the ROKN in 1992. By 2001, the Korean company Daewoo Shipping and Marine Engineering (DSME) was able to domestically produce eight 1,200-ton submarines with technical assistance from HDW. DSME continued to work with the German company and built nine additional 1,800-ton submarines by 2018.

Since 2008, Korea has pushed forward with a project to develop Korean-made submarines to improve the nation's self-defense capabilities and secure a future industry. In 2011, DSME competed with HDW --- the very German company that had provided DSME with technological assistance --- over an order to export submarines to Indonesia and won the contract. It was an order for three 1,400-ton submarines, and the first submarine was delivered to Indonesia in 2017. It was a remarkable feat that happened 30 years

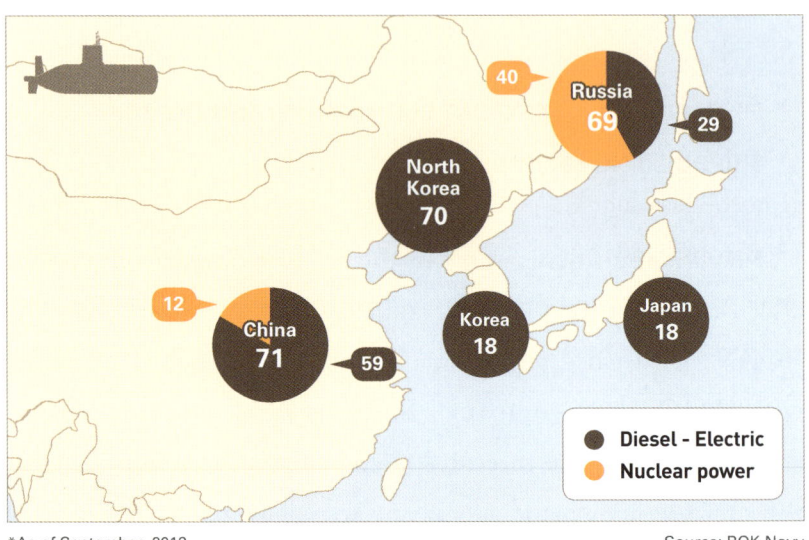

Submarine Fleets in Countries Around the Korean Peninsula
(no. of vessels)

*As of September, 2018

Source: ROK Navy

after submarines were introduced to Korea for the first time.

Korea went one step further to independently develop 3,000-ton submarines, and the first submarine, Dosan Ahn Chang-ho, had its launch ceremony in 2018. When the submarine goes into service in 2020 after testing in the ocean, Korea will become the world's 13th country to have indigenous fleet of submarines. In the meantime, Korea has been increasing the localization ratio for the 1,200-ton submarines to 33 percent, 1,800-ton submarines to 36 percent, and 3,000-ton to 76 percent. When the displacement of a submarine exceeds 3,000 tons, its significance as a strategic weapon increases because it is capable of launching submarine-launched ballistic missiles (SLBM).

The ROKN established its Submarine Force Command in 2015, but since South Korea is currently fielding 18 submarines, it is outnumbered by North Korea that has about 70 subs in service. North Korea may have more submarines --- approximately 20 Romeo-class submarines (1,800 tons), 40 Sang-O-class submarines (300 tons) and 10 midget submarines including the Yono-class submarines (130 tons) --- but the performance of those submarines is far behind the South Korean's. Japan currently fields 18 submarines --- nine Oyashio-class (4,000 tons) and nine Soryu-class (4,200 tons) submarines. Japan has similar number of submarines as Korea, but their submarine force is more powerful than that of Korea.

KOREAN-MADE ROCKET TO BE LAUNCHED INTO SPACE IN 2021

The race to put the national flag ahead of others on the moon or on Mars may be over, but the rockets to launch satellites into space is opening up a new contest in the aerospace business. Korea has only a 30-year history of aerospace research and development because it started in 1989 when KAIST opened its Satellite Technology Research Lab. Nevertheless, Korea owns advanced satellite technology that is among the world's top five and boasts price competitiveness as well. In 1992, Korea launched its first domestically produced satellite, Uribyol-1, and in 1999, Korean launched Uribyol-3, whose entire production process right from

Brief History of The Korea Space Launch Vehicle Project (2010-2022)

Date	Event
2010	Project Launching
2015	Developed 7-ton liquid engine
Nov. 2018	Launched a single-stage test vehicle rocke
Feb-Oct, 2021 (scheduled)	Scheduled to launch a three-stage space launch vehicle

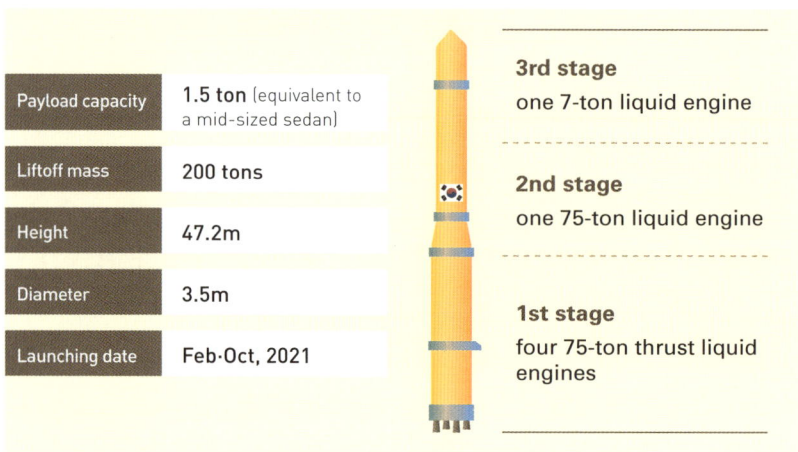

Specifications of the KSLV-II (a/k/a Nuri)

Payload capacity	1.5 ton (equivalent to a mid-sized sedan)
Liftoff mass	200 tons
Height	47.2m
Diameter	3.5m
Launching date	Feb-Oct, 2021

3rd stage one 7-ton liquid engine

2nd stage one 75-ton liquid engine

1st stage four 75-ton thrust liquid engines

Source: Ministry of Science and ICT(MSIT)

design and assembly was done in Korea. With these achievements, Korea became a country with its own satellite developing capability.

However, there are still mountains to climb for the development of a space launch vehicle. Korea successfully test-launched the first stage of its orbital rocket known as Nuri, which was entirely developed by Koreans, and is scheduled to be launched into space in 2021. The Korean-made rocket development kicked off in 1990. The first domestic single-stage unguided solid-propellant scientific rocket KSR-1 was launched in 1993, followed by a two-stage rocket in 1997. KSR-III, which is an orbital launch vehicle powered by a liquid propellant engine that offers more accurate control than a solid propellant engine, was successfully launched in 2002. Up until this point, there were only small science rockets that could not carry a payload on board.

The development of Naro, the first launch vehicle capable of launching a satellite into space, began in 2002 in partnership with Russia. The launching of Naro, which could place a small 100kg satellite into orbit, failed twice before it succeeded in January 2013. It was half a success because the first stage rocket, which is the essential part of a launch vehicle, was developed by Russia, while Korea was responsible of the second-stage rocket that is used to place a satellite into low earth orbit (LEO).

Once Nuri is launched successfully in 2021, it means Nuri can take a 1.5-ton payload to a 600-800km Low Earth Orbit. In this case, Korea will become the 7th country in the world that can launch its own satellite from its own space center with over a ton of payload on board. It is a feat accomplished after the United States, Russia, China, Japan, France, and India. There is still a long way to go compared to the rockets made by the United States and Japan, but these achievements alone allow Korea to do business in the global mid-to-small satellite launch market.

SCIENCE TECHNOLOGY IS THE POWER: DAWNING OF THE ERA OF AI WEAPONS MORE DESTRUCTIVE THAN NUCLEAR WARFARE

An era of new weapons, such as killer robots and bombing drones, is dawning. President of Venezuela Nicolas Maduro was attacked by terrorists who used drones in 2018. At that time, President Maduro avoided being assassinated, but the drones detonated explosives in the air and seriously wounded seven soldiers.

The ongoing developments in science and technology have introduced novel concept weapons such as machine gun armed artificial intelligent (AI) infantry and unmanned submarines, all of which can leave even aircraft carriers helpless. If ten thousand drones carrying 100-500kg of explosives each launch an attack, it will be too overwhelming even for aircraft carriers to handle. The threat of AI becomes all the more serious when you consider how it can disrupt the communication network and software to disable a counterpart's cutting-edge strategic weapons.

In 2015, more than 1,000 tech experts, scientists and researchers warned that the development of killer robot technology would lead to "a third revolution in warfare" after the revolutions of gun powder and nuclear weapons. A potential ban on the military use of killer robots has also been discussed by UN committees. But throughout history, there have been precedent cases in which new warfare such as the crossbow, machine gun, and submarines raised moral issues but eventually were accepted as "modern warfare." Similarly, while effective measures to ban the use of AI weapons have yet to be taken, more than 50 of the world's leading AI and robotics experts released an open letter in 2018 criticizing the KAIST and Hanhwa System for researching AI weapons. They boycotted KAIST claiming that KAIST was developing an AI-based intelligent object tracking and recognizing technology, which could lead to "killer robots".

KAIST's president had to step out and release a statement, explaining, "KAIST does not have any intention of engaging in development of killer robots." The whole episode demonstrated how the technological power of Korea has advanced to a level that draws attention and fear from the world.

KOREA CONTRIBUTES TO PEACE IN 27 COUNTRIES AS A PART OF UN PEACEKEEPING OPERATIONS

In terms of finance, Korea has turned itself from a country that received aid from others to a country that provides aid to others. In terms of military power, Korea has also raised itself from a country that received military assistance from UN forces to a country that is now part of the UN forces for peacekeeping operations.

Korea joined the UN in 1991, and Korea dispatched Sangnoksu unit to Somalia for peace keeping operations (PKO) for the first time in 1993.

It was the beginning of Korea's repayment for the 36,940 American soldiers and over 40,000 UN soldiers from 16 countries who sacrificed their lives while fighting for freedom and democracy during the Korean War.

Starting with Somalia, Korea has deployed 47,000 Korean soldiers to 27 countries over the years including a medical support unit to the Western Sahara, the Sangnoksu Unit to East Timor, and the Danbi Unit to Haiti. The Dongmyeong Unit deployed to Lebanon in 2007 and the Hanbit Unit deployed to Sudan are still participating in UN peacekeeping activities. The Cheonghae Anti-piracy Unit is also

Korean Troops Deployed to Overseas

Haiti
Danbi Unit

Lebanon
Dongmyung Unit

Angola
Engineer Unit

Somalia waters
Cheonghae Unit

Western Sahara
ROK Armed Forces Medical Assistance Team

South Sudan
Hanbit Unit

Somalia
Sangroksu Unit

Iraq
Seohee Unit, Jema Unit, Zaytun Division
Daiman unit, Cheonghae Unit

UAE
Akh Unit

Philippines
Arang Unit

East Timor
Sangroksu Unit

Afghanistan
Haeseong Unit, Cheongma Unit
Dongui Unit, Dasan Unit
Ashena Unit

Source: Joint Chiefs of Staff website

deployed to Somalia to participate in operations in the Gulf of Aden under a Combined Task Force upon request from allied countries.

Currently, about 1,100 Korean soldiers are deployed to 13 countries to participate in operations as part of the UN's peacekeeping forces or combined task forces, or in military exchange activities. They are mostly engaged in surveillance activities in disputed areas, but they are also playing a role as diplomatic missions through medical support and social reconstruction activities. The Korean Akh Unit that has been deployed to Abu Dhabi in UAE since 2011 as a part of the military exchange activities contributed to the spread of hallyu as well when a TV drama series "Descendants of the Sun" was produced based on their activities.

KOREANS TO THE WORLD, THE WORLD TO KOREA

In 1882, when Korea was a country largely unknown to the West, an American named William Elliott Griffis wrote a history of Korea titled "The Hermit Nation, Corea". Another American, Percival Lowell, was commissioned by King Gojong and wrote an introduction to Korea titled "Choson, the Land of the Morning Calm" in 1885. Back in those days, Korea was introduced to the world as a calm, hermit country, but today's Korea is anything but a calm hermit: Korea is known to the world as one of the most dynamic countries.

KOREA HOSTS MORE INTERNATIONAL CONFERENCES THAN ANY OTHER COUNTRY IN THE WORLD

Korea is the country that hosts more international conferences than any other in the world. The Union of International Associations (UIA) analyzed 10,000 international conferences held in 2017

Top International Meeting Destinations of 2017

Ranking	Country	Number
1	Korea	1297
2	Singapore	877
3	Belgium	810
4	Austria	591
5	USA	575
6	Japan	523
7	Spain	440
8	France	422
9	Germany	374
10	Thailand	312

Source: Union of International Associations (UIA)

throughout the world and found that 1,297 of them were held in Korea, ranking Korea as the number one host country for two years in a row. It meant 12 percent of the international conferences were held in Korea with a daily average of 3.5 new international conferences being held.

Singapore, a country that was the focus of global attention when US President Donald Trump and the North Korean leader Kim Jong-un had their first summit meeting, hosted 877 international conferences and ranked number two on the list, but Korea outnumbered Singapore by a large margin. That means Korea is a country that offers excellent transportation, lodging, and conference facilities, not to mention the capabilities to host and run international conferences. According to the UIA analysis, the number of international conferences that were held in 166 countries in 2017 showed a slight decline compared to 2016. Even then, the number of international conferences that were held in Korea and Austria went up significantly during the same period, which is worthy of our attention in connection with geopolitical changes such as the emergence of China.

Back in 2000, Korea ranked 24th in the world and 4th in Asia on the list of international conference destinations. But a remarkable change started to happen when, after gaining confidence from the successful hosting of the Seoul Olympics, Korea went on to host the 2000 Asia–Europe Meeting (ASEM). The so-called MICE (meetings, incentives, conferences and exhibitions) industry started to grow rapidly after the ASEM convention center was opened in Seoul followed by the opening of the Incheon International Airport. It was from this point on that Korea hosted numerous international events such as the Korea-Japan world cup tournament in 2002, G20 summit in 2010, Nuclear Security Summit in 2012, and PyeongChang 2018 Olympic Winter Games in 2018, and one after another international convention centers were constructed and opened in cities like Busan and Daegu, catapulting Korea into a major venue for global events and conventions. As of now, the United States and Japan are hosting less than half of the number of international conferences hosted by Korea.

FIVE KOREAN CITIES AMONG THE TOP 40 INTERNATIONAL MEETING CITIES

Seoul is the venue of about half of the international conferences held in Korea. In the 2017 global meetings ranking, Seoul came in third after Singapore and Brussels with 688 international conferences. Seoul has remained in third place for three years straight since 2015.

Brussels remains as the top European venue for international meetings on the ranking possibly because it is home to the European

Top International Meeting Cities in 2017

Ranking	Country	Number
1	Singapore	877
2	Brussels	763
3	Seoul	688
4	Vienna	515
5	Tokyo	269
6	Paris	268
7	Bangkok	232
8	Busan	212
9	Berlin	198
10	Barcelona	193
15	Jeju	139
24	Incheon	66
32	Daegu	43

Source: Union of International Associations (UIA)

Union (EU) headquarters, but it is noteworthy that the number of international conferences held in other European cities, such as Paris in France and Berlin in Germany, continues to decline. Instead, Asian cities such as Seoul, Tokyo in Japan, and Bangkok in Thailand are witnessing an increasing number of international conferences. When broken down by city, Korea has five cities --- Seoul, Busan, Jeju, Incheon, Daegu --- on the list of 40 cities around the world that had hosted the largest numbers of international conferences. Busan outpaced Berlin of Germany and ranked 8th at 212, while Jeju ranked 15th at 139 international conferences.

As the venue for international conferences expands to other cities such as Incheon and Daegu, visitors from foreign countries naturally stay longer in Korea and their itineraries become more diversified. That means people from around the world will get to know about Korea and Koreans more intimately. The Union of International Associations (UIA) defines an international conference as a meeting of 50 people or more hosted or organized by an international organization. Even if a meeting is hosted by a domestic organization, it qualifies as an international conference if 40 percent or more participants are from five countries and over.

KOREA IS HOME TO 60 INTERNATIONAL ORGANIZATION HEADQUARTERS

Today, Korea is not only plays an active host to international conferences, it is a permanent home to offices and liaisons for international organizations. There were only five international organizations that were based in Korea in 1955, but the number has gone up to 60 today.

Before 2000, most of the international organizations that had offices in Korea had limited functions, such as the United Nations Memorial Cemetery in Korea (UNMCK) whose main duty was the maintenance of the UN memorial cemetery. The only exception was the headquarters of the International Vaccine Institute (IVI) that was founded within the Seoul National University property in 1997 and has about 140 employees.

There have been significant changes in the type and size of international organizations that have been set up in Korea since 2000, and these changes are largely attributed to the rising economic status of Korea and the worldwide popularity of the hallyu (Korean Wave). Another factor that accelerated these changes is many Koreans who took active parts in international organizations such as Ban Ki-moon who was appointed the eighth Secretary-General of the United Nations in 2007.

In 2012, Korea successfully became the host of the Green Climate Fund (GCF), which is an international financial organization dedicated to helping developing countries to adjust to climate change, and Korea also took the leading role in launching of the Global Green Growth Institute (GGGI) as well. In 2018, Asian Forest Cooperation Organization (AFoCO), an intergovernmental

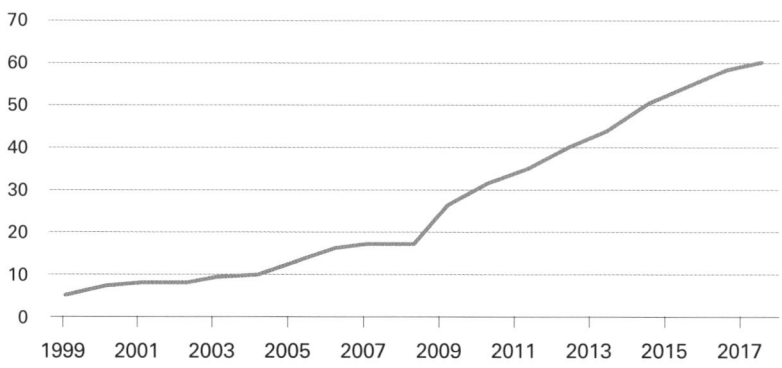

Source: Ministry of Foreign Affairs

organization proposed and spearheaded by Korea to respond to the forest destruction in developing countries and desertification in East Asian regions, was officially launched in Korea.

International organizations other than the above-mentioned ones have Korean branch offices or UN organizations in Korea instead of their headquarters. Regardless of the nature of the office or size, more international organizations in Korea means more opportunities for young Koreans who wish to work in global settings. Korea being an aid recipient-turned-donor, there is no question that Korea has a variety of roles to play as a bridge between advanced and developing countries.

KOREA RANKS 2ND IN PASSPORT POWER AND HAS VISA-FREE ACCESS TO 165 COUNTRIES

Koreans can travel to 165 out of 198 countries in the world without a visa. That means Koreans have the world's third biggest level of travel freedom after UAE and Germany. This is what people call the world's third biggest "passport power."

A global financial adviser Aton Capital collects, reviews, and ranks the passports of the world and regularly releases the "Passport Index" that shows the travel freedom of passport holders. As of January 2019, Korea ranks 3rd in the Passport Index and ties with the United States, Singapore and France. Korea has visa-free access to 122 countries and visa on arrival access to 43 countries, which means Korean citizens will have a visa issued automatically upon arrival in 43 countries. Japan, Britain, and Canada ranked 4th after

Global Passport Power Rank in 2019

Ranking	Country	Visa-free Access Country & Region
1	Japan	190
2	**Korea**, Singapore	**189**
3	France, Germany	188
4	Denmark, Finland, Italy, Spain	187
5	Luxembourg, Spain	186
6	Australia, Netherlands, Norway, Portugal	185

Source: Henley & Partners website, 2019 Henley Passport Index

Korea, because citizens of those countries have visa-free or visa on arrival access to 164 countries.

The London-based global citizenship and residence advisory firm Henley & Partners has also released its Henley Passport Index. The rankings of the countries are slightly different in this index, because it is based on the analysis of 227 possible travel destinations including autonomous nations and micro-states in addition to countries. As of January 2019, Japan ranks number one because Japanese citizens have the freedom to travel to 190 countries and regions without a visa, and Korea and Singapore tied and ranked 2nd, followed by France and Germany that tied in rank at 3rd. China ranked 69th because the Chinese can enter 74 countries and regions without a visa, and North Korea ranked 96th because North Koreans can travel to only 42 countries and regions without a visa.

INCHEON INT'L AIRPORT SERVES MORE PASSENGERS THAN CHARLES DE GAULLE AIRPORT AND RANKS 5TH

The global ranking of Incheon International Airport, the biggest gateway to Korea, jumped to fifth in terms of international passenger traffic in 2018. The airport carried the largest number of international passengers followed by Dubai Airport in UAE, London Heathrow Airport, Hong Kong Airport and Amsterdam Schiphol Airport in the Netherlands. As of 2018, 67.76 million international passengers used Incheon International Airport, a 10.5% increase over the

Top 10 Busiest Airports in the World by Passenger Volume

Ranking	Airport
1	Dubai
2	London Heathrow
3	Hong Kong Chek Lap Kok
4	Amsterdam
5	Incheon
6	Paris Charles de Gaulle
7	Singapore Changi
8	Frankfurt
9	Bangkok Suramabhumi
10	Istanbul Ataturk

Source: Incheon International Airport Corporation

previous year. Incheon International Airport had ranked seventh in 2017 but jumped two ranks to the fifth place by surpassing Charles de Gaulle Airport in Paris and Changi Airport in Singapore. Incheon Airport also handled 2.95 million tons of air cargo, the third largest cargo volume in the world after Hong Kong Airport and Shanghai Pudong Airport.

Incheon airport's rapid growth is attributed to a few factors including the increased demand for overseas travel and flights by low cost carriers (LCC), expansion of air routes departing from Incheon, and the Pyeongchang Winter Olympics. Incheon International Airport, which opened in 2001, operates 188 flight routes as of the end of 2017, and the regional split shows 28.2% of the routes are for destinations in Southeast Asia, 19.8% in Japan, 17.9% in China, and 8.7% in Europe.

Considering how UAI Dubai Airport has 254 flight routes and Turkey Istanbul Airport has 290, Incheon International Airport could aim to add more air routes in the future.

When international and domestic passenger traffic figures are combined, airports in the US and China stand out. The Atlanta International Airport in the US is the busiest airport in the world and served 104 million passengers in 2017. Beijing Capital International Airport was the second busiest airport with 96 million passengers, followed by the third busiest Dubai Airport, fourth Los Angeles Airport, fifth Tokyo Airport, sixth O'Hare Airport in Chicago, eighth Hong Kong Airport and ninth Shanghai Pudong Airport. Incheon International Airport ranked 19th in this category.

A 30 TIMES INCREASE OF OUTBOUND KOREANS WITHIN 30 YEARS

Korea is the world's 7th biggest spender in travel abroad after China, the United States and a few others. Korea's balance of trade from tourism has been in deficit for 18 years straight. Depending on the perspective, the overseas travel fever might be either criticized as excessive consumption or an ideal trend geared towards improved quality of life, but whatever the case is, overseas travel was available only to a few privileged Koreans as recently as 30 years ago. At the time, the Korean government issued a single passport only when the

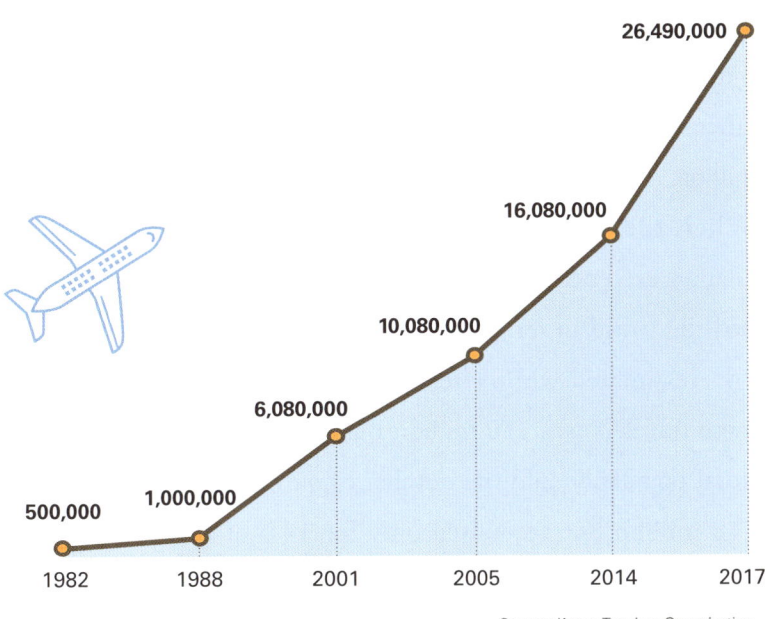

Outbound Korean Travelers by the Year

Source: Korea Tourism Organization

traveler has a clear reason such as official business duty, in order to prevent the outflow of foreign currency and also to keep its citizens from exposure to communism.

When it became inevitable to open to the world after winning the bid to host the 1988 Seoul Olympic and the 1986 Asian Games, the Korean government started issuing a limited "tourism passport" only to citizens over the age of 50 beginning in 1983. It was not until 1989 that the government approved the full liberalization of overseas travel. Consequently, outbound Korean travelers increased from just about 500,000 in 1982 to over one million as of 1988, and in 1989, the first year of the full liberalization of overseas travel, the number jumped to 1.52 million. The number of outbound Korean travelers kept increasing rapidly until it passed the 10 million mark in 2005 and then 20 million mark in 2016. As of 2018, the number is pushing 30 million.

When the ratio of outbound travelers to the total Korean population exceeded 50% in 2017, some people claimed that Korea topped the world in terms of overseas travel, but this is not true. It was overestimated while stressing how the number of outbound Chinese travelers was 150 million but accounted only for 11.5% of the total population and the number of outbound Japanese travelers was 18 million but accounted only for 14% of the total Japanese population. According to the World Bank statistics on outbound travelers from 105 countries, the ratio of outbound travelers to the total Korean population was 43.6% in 2016, placing Korea 46th in the ranking. Considering how 82% of the citizens of EU member countries travel overseas because they border with neighbors on land and therefore can easily travel to other countries either by car or train, it is difficult to compare overseas travel fever simply based on the number of outbound travelers.

KOREA SENDS 3.5 TIMES MORE OVERSEAS VOLUNTEERS THAN JAPAN

Korea is a model for many countries in terms of overseas

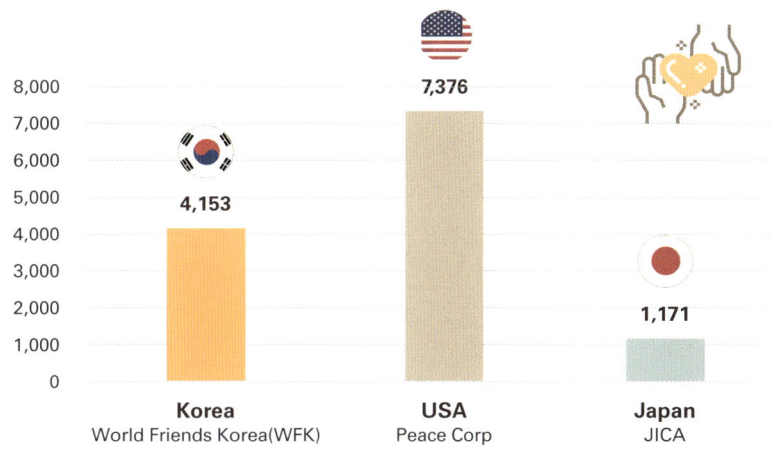

New Overseas Volunteers in 2017

Source: Korea International Cooperation Agency (KOICA)

volunteer activities. As of 2017, Korea sent 4,153 members of the World Friends Korea to countries around the world for volunteer services. It is far less than the United States Peace Corp that sent 7,376 volunteers during the same year, but it is 3.5 times more than the Japan International Cooperation Agency (JICA) that sent 1,171 volunteers.

If the members of the World Friends Korea who were already overseas for volunteer activities were included, there were 5,259 Koreans overseas who offered their volunteer services in computer, automobile repair, farming, cooking and Korean language teaching programs as of 2017.

The Korean government integrated several overseas volunteer teams that had been divided into five organizations ---Korea International Cooperation Agency (KOICA), College Student Volunteers Corps under the Ministry of Education, and the IT Youth Volunteers Corps under the Ministry of Science, ICT and Future Planning --- into one single volunteer service group called the World Friends Korea. In the case of the United States, President John F. Kennedy spearheaded the creation of the Peace Corps in 1961 and sent 230,000 Peace Corps volunteers to all parts of the world and contributed to fighting poverty and recovering from disasters. The Peace Corps members started coming to Korea beginning in 1965 as well, and about 2,000 young American Peace Corps members sweated while providing volunteer services in English teaching, public health, and job training activities. It is a proud achievement considering how Korea was once a country that needed those same volunteer services from the United States but now has grown to become a country that can offer them to others on an equal footing with the United States.

The Japan International Cooperation Agency (JICA) has been sending overseas volunteer groups since 1965, and Korea has since 1990, but as of 2017, the cumulative number of dispatched Korean volunteers is 64,726, which exceeds the 44,143 Japanese volunteers by far. However, it is regretful that the enthusiasm of young Koreans for overseas volunteer service is cooling down lately. Many young Koreans applied to be a part of overseas volunteer service programs up until the 1990s when overseas travel was not as easy and affordable as it is today, but lately, there is less enthusiasm because young Koreans are struggling under the worst unemployment crisis. Instead, the number of older generation Koreans who wish to find happiness and a sense of fulfillment from overseas volunteer activities has been showing a rapid increase, and as of 2017, Koreans over the ages of 50 are accounting for 30.5% of the total overseas volunteer groups.

FEVER FOR LEARNING KOREAN SPREADS WORLDWIDE

Supported by the increasing presence of Koreans in the international community and the wide-spreading hallyu fever, Korean is emerging as a global language. Visitors to famous tourist attractions around the world can hear greetings in Korean more often than ever, and when K-pop stars have concerts in foreign cities, it is common to hear non-Korean audiences singing along in Korean as well.

According to a report released in 2018 by the US-based Modern Language Association (MLA), enrollments in most foreign language programs in US colleges had declined during the period between 2009 and 2016 --- Chinese by 11%, German by 16% and Japanese by 5% --- but only the enrollment in Korean language programs showed an increase of 65%. The British broadcasting company BBC also reported that "Korean uptake in US universities rose by almost

14% between 2013 and 2016, while overall language enrollment was in decline." As of 2016, there are 14,000 students who are enrolled in Korean language programs in US colleges. In terms of enrollment, the Korean language ranks ninth after Spanish, French, German, Italian, Chinese, Arabic, Latin and Russian.

According to the US-based Christian organization SIL International that is dedicated to studying and documenting languages of the world, there are 7,097 living languages. Of those thousands of languages, Korean is the 13th most-widely spoken language. Chinese is the world's most widely spoken language at 1.3 billion, followed by Spanish, English, Arabic, Hindi (India), Bengali (Bangladesh), Portuguese, Russian, Japanese, Landa (Pakistan), Javanese (Indonesia), and Turkish. The Korean speaking population is 77.2 million, which is more than French and German.

Aside from the population, Korean is the world's 10th most frequently used language on the Internet. Throughout the world, there is a growing Korean language learning fever as well. The Korean language school known as the King Sejong Institute Foundation, which was founded in 2007, currently operates 174 Korean language centers in 57 countries, and an increasing number of colleges in the US and Europe are also offering Korean language or literature programs, all of which attest to the rising popularity of the Korean language.

PEOPLE COMING TO KOREA TO STUDY HAS DOUBLED IN FOUR YEARS

Although Korea's study-abroad boom is showing signs of slowing down, the number of students coming to Korea to learn Korean language and about Korea itself continues to rise. This is a phenomenon created by the race among Korean colleges to bring in more foreign students in addition to the hallyu fever. Korean companies expanding their overseas business is another factor that contributes to the increasing number of foreign students coming to Korea. For example, there are about 6,000 Korean companies that have made inroads into Vietnam, and the Vietnamese who are hired by these Korean companies can get better salaries. As a result, the number of Vietnamese students coming to Korea to study went from 3,200 in 2012 to 27,500 in 2017.

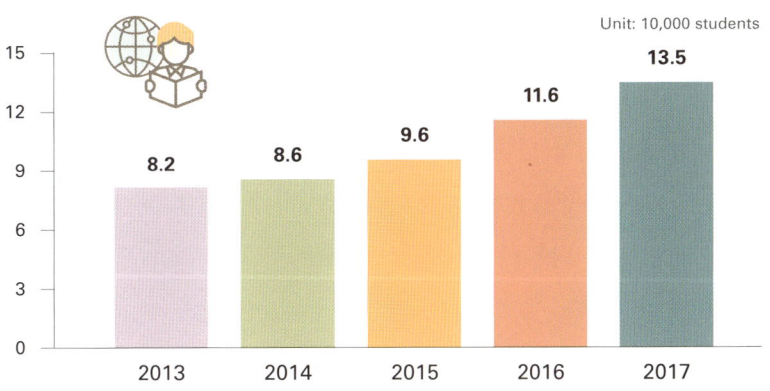

Enrollment of foreign students in Korean colleges

Unit: 10,000 students

2013	2014	2015	2016	2017
8.2	8.6	9.6	11.6	13.5

Source: Minister of Justice

According to the 2017 International Migration Outlook, which is a statistic by the Korean Statistical Information Service that collected and analyzed emigrants and immigrants who visited and stayed in Korea for over 91 days, 453,000 people entered Korea in 2017, up 50,000 from 2016. The net migration population, which is the number that excludes those who left the country, was a total 104,000, which was also an increase of 24,000.

Among the foreign visitors who stayed in Korea for more than 91 days, the largest age group was those in their 20s whose number was recorded as 154,000. The number of students and others who came to Korea to study was 58,000, which was the highest since the beginning of the statistics. The number of people who came to Korea to learn Korean was 30,000, which was more than the 28,000 foreigners who came to Korea for various academic degrees.

As of 2014, the number of enrolled foreign students in Korea was 86,000, but it doubled in about four years and recorded 160,000 in 2018. According to the UNESCO statistics for enrollments in colleges and graduate schools in 2016, the United States had 970,000 foreign students from around the world, making it the unrivaled top in the rankings. The United States was followed by Britain (430,000), Australia (330,000), and France (240,000). Korea ranked 18th on the list, but the number of foreign students coming to Korea to study is growing rapidly.

FOREIGNERS WHO WISH TO BECOME KOREAN CITIZENS

In 2018, about 500 Yemenis arrived on Jeju Island by taking advantage of the island's visa-free tourism policy and applied for asylum. They fled their war-torn country and traveled a great distance until they arrived on the Korean island, but there are still about 20,000 more foreign refugees besides the Yemenis, who came to Korea and applied for asylum. The issue of these refugees is a case that testifies to Korea's elevated status in the international community.

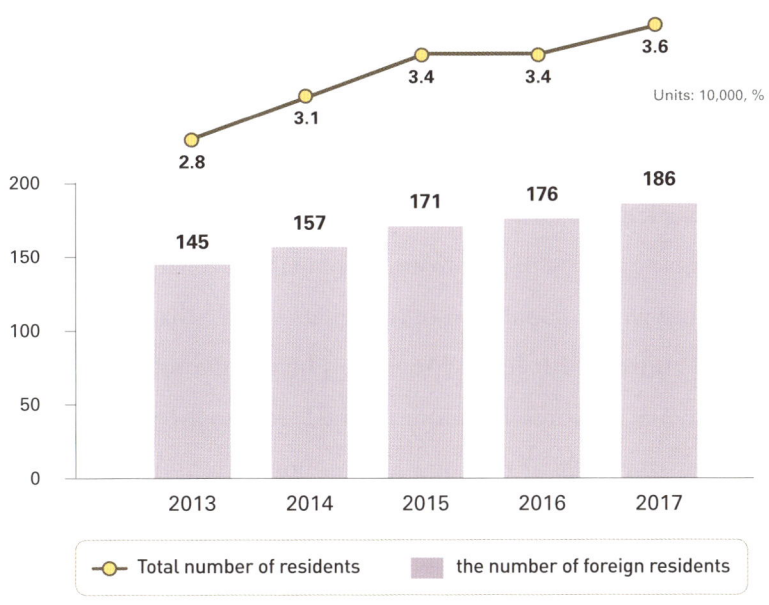

Source: Statistics Korea

While an increasing number of Koreans are tapping into the global arena with about 20,000-30,000 Koreans losing their Korean citizenship each year, there were 11,556 foreigners who were naturalized into Korean citizens as of 2018. Between 2000 and 2015, 32,565 new family clans or family names --- such as the Changwon Kim clan, the Yeongdeungpo Kim clan, and the Taekguk Kim clan --- were created in Korea, all of them created by people who were naturalized and became Korean citizens. According to the statistics by the Ministry of Justice, there were 133,206 people who were naturalized and received Korean citizenship within a span of ten years beginning in 2008, and many of them created their own clan families and surnames by using the names of Korean cities such as Youngdeungpo and Guro. That's the reason there are the Guro Kim clan and the Yeongdeungpo Kim clan whose population is around 100 each.

The population of foreigners in Korea, including short-term visitors such as tourists, was 2.36 million at the end of 2018, which accounts for 4.6% of the Korean population. That means Koreans are living with a population of foreigners greater than the population of the entire North Jeolla Province. The number of foreigners who are staying in Korea for more than 91 days is 1.68 million, which accounts for 3.3% of the total Korean population. Among the long-term stay foreigners, the largest ethnic group is Chinese at 1.07 million, followed by Vietnamese, Thai, and Americans. And among the foreigners who are staying in Korea, about 140,000 of them are qualified to apply for permanent residency. The number of foreigners who receive permanent residency by making a big investment or special contribution or proving themselves to have outstanding talent is rapidly growing.

"MADE-IN-KOREA" REIGNS IN THE GLOBAL MARKETS

Korea's annual exports surpassed $600 billion for the first time in 2018. Today, smart phones, TVs, and automobiles made by Samsung, LG, Hyundai, and other Korean companies can be easily found in any country. It's been a long while since Korean brand signboards started popping up and were put on display in major international airports and streets, and Korean products often make appearances in Hollywood movies as well. For example, Hyundai EF Sonata appeared in the popular movie "The Bourne Supremacy" in 2004, "War of the Worlds" in 2005 and "The Hurt Locker" in 2008. These Korean brands that stand out in the global market are important national assets as well as pride.

"MADE-IN-KOREA" BRAND RANKS 21ST AND SAMSUNG, 5TH

There is a difference in satisfaction that consumers in the global market get from a label marked as "made in Korea" and the satisfaction they get from brand names such as Samsung, Hyundai, and LG.

2017 World's Most Favored "Made in" Labels Ranking

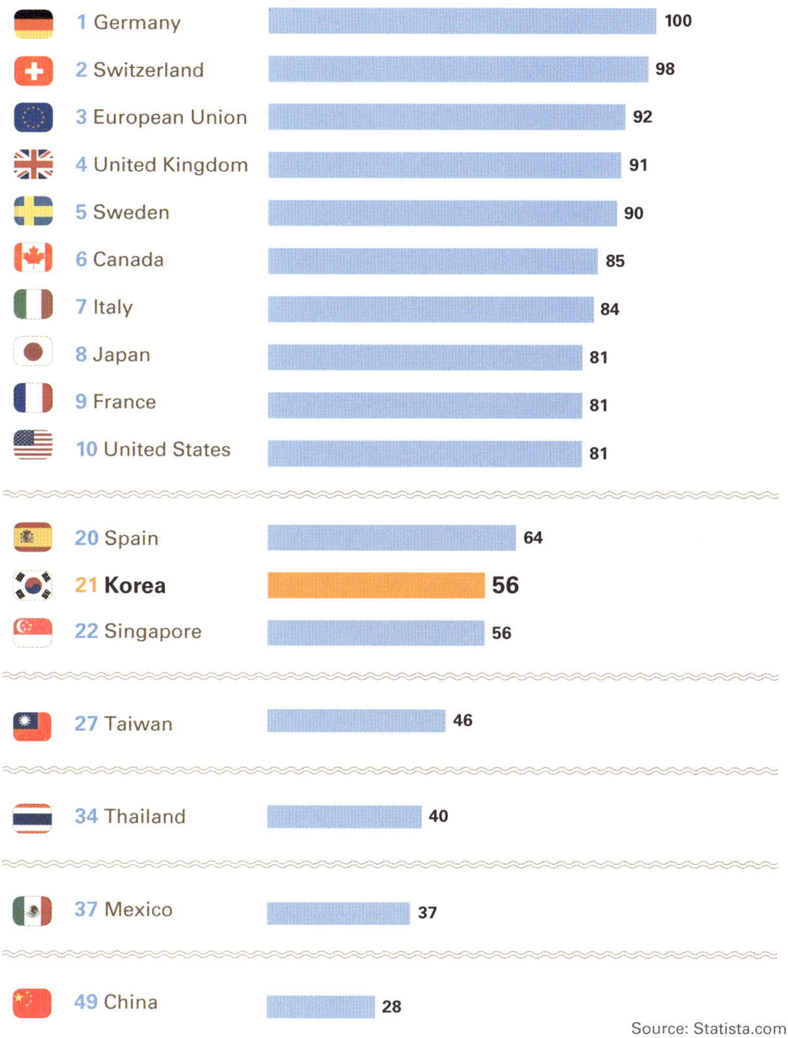

Rank	Country	Score
1	Germany	100
2	Switzerland	98
3	European Union	92
4	United Kingdom	91
5	Sweden	90
6	Canada	85
7	Italy	84
8	Japan	81
9	France	81
10	United States	81
20	Spain	64
21	**Korea**	**56**
22	Singapore	56
27	Taiwan	46
34	Thailand	40
37	Mexico	37
49	China	28

Source: Statista.com

A German-based online portal for statistics, Statista (statista.com), surveyed about 40,000 consumers in 52 countries and created "the World's most favored made-in labels ranking of 2017." In the 'made-in' country index, "made in German" ranked #1 on the list of the most favored labels in the world, and Korea ranked 21st. Switzerland, the European Union, and Britain ranked from second to fourth, and Japan ranked eighth, followed by United States at 10th, and Spain, 20th. European countries with a long manufacturing tradition were among the top group on the list, while emerging Asian countries --- Singapore (22nd), Taiwan (27th), Thailand (34th), China (49th) --- did not get high marks.

But it is a whole different story when it comes to individual company brands such as Samsung. In the ranking of the Best Global Brands of 2018 compiled by the US-based brand consultant company, Interbrand, Samsung ranked 6th out of the 100 brands. That means Samsung was considered the best global brand only after the five US-based companies of Apple, Google, Amazon, Microsoft, and Coca Cola. Samsung was followed by Toyota, Mercedes-Benz, Facebook, and McDonald's in the top 10 group, while Hyundai Motors ranked 36th, and Kia Motors, 71st.

The London-based branded business valuation and strategy consultancy firm, Brand Finance, released the Brand Finance Global 500, where Samsung Group ranked 5th with a brand value at $91.2 billion after Amazon, Apple, Google, and Microsoft. Hyundai Motor Company ranked 79th, and LG Group, 91st. Other Korean

2018 World's Best Global Brands Ranking

Unit: $

Rank	Company	Value
1	Apple	214.48 billion
2	Google	155.56 billion
3	Amazon	100,764 million
4	Microsoft	92.715 billion
5	Coca Cola	66.341 billion
6	**Samsung Elec.**	**59.89 billion**
7	Toyota	53.4 billion
8	Mercedes Benz	48.6 billion
9	Facebook	45.168 billion
10	McDonald's	43.417 billion
36	**Hyundai Motor**	**13.53 billion**
71	**Kia Motors**	**6,925 million**

Source: Interbrand

companies listed on the Brand Finance Global 500 included SK Holdings (158th), SK Hynix (215th), KEPCO (302nd), CJ (444th), Doosan (465th), Shinhan Financial Group (474th), Lotte (479th) and KB Financial Group (496th).

EXPORTS DRIVEN BY SEMICONDUCTOR, PETROLEUM PRODUCTS AND AUTOMOBILES

In 50 years of the industrialization process, there have been some

Top Global Export Market Shares by Country and Item

Country	2016 Rank	2016 No. of Item
China	1	1,693
Germany	2	675
United States	3	572
Italy	4	209
Japan	5	178
India	6	156
Netherlands	7	144
France	8	98
Belgium	9	87
Canada	10	82
Korea	**13**	**71**

Source: Institute for International Trade at the Korea International Trade Association

astonishing changes in Korea's major export items. Semiconductors emerged as Korea's largest export item since 1992 and accounted for 21% of total exports in 2018 when semiconductors totaled $126.7 billion in exports. It is not easy to find similar cases in the history of world trade in which a single item totals $100 billion in exports a year. In fact, Korea was the sixth in the world to make it happen after the German automobile (2004), Japanese automobile (2007), Chinese computer (2008), Chinese wired and wireless communication device (2010) and American aircraft (2013). Major export items other than the semiconductor include petroleum products, automobiles, flat panel displays, and synthetic resins.

In the 1980s, clothing was Korea's biggest export item. Korea's apparel exports totaled $2.7 billion in 1980, which accounted for 16% of the total exports from Korea. Other major export items at this time included steel plates, shoes, ships, audio equipment, and rubber products while in the 1960s, major export items were iron ore, tungsten, raw silk, anthracite, squid, fresh fish and graphite. But Korean corporations and hard-working Koreans brought about astonishing changes in exports in just 50 years after the industrialization began in Korea.

As of today, there are 71 Korean-made products that rank at the top in global export markets. According to the "Competitiveness of Korean Exports Based on the Top Items in Export Markets" which was released by the Institute for International Trade of the Korea International Trade Association, Korea ranks 13th in terms of the number of top export items. China has been the unrivaled number one since 2005 with 1,693 top-selling items, followed by Germany, the United States, Italy, Japan and India. Among Korea's top-selling items, more than half are chemical products (25 items) and steel products (15 items).

SAMSUNG AND SK HYNIX DOMINATE WITH A 23% SHARE OF THE "INDUSTRIAL RICE" SEMICONDUCTOR MARKET

In the era of the Fourth Industrial Revolution, the market for semiconductors --- often referred to as "industrial rice" --- is rapidly

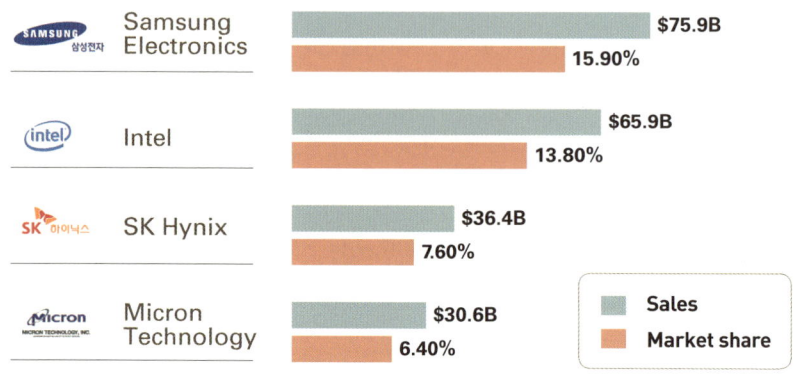

expanding. Worldwide semiconductor revenue grew 13.4% in 2018 to $476.7 billion, which is 13.4% increase from 2017.

In this global semiconductor market, Samsung Electronics remains the top with a market share of 15.9% and total sales of $75.9 billion. The US-based company Intel was top for 25 years starting in 1992, but Samsung Electronics broke that record when it edged out Intel in 2017. Samsung Electronics' market share was just 0.25 in 2018, but the gap was 2.1% in 2018 and it keeps widening.

Intel is followed by SK Hynix, which ranks third in the semiconductor market with sales of $36.4 billion and a market share of 7.6%. When combined, the two Korean companies --- Samsung Electronics and SK Hynix --- are dominating the market with a combined market share of 23.5%, cementing the reputation of Korean-made semiconductors in the world. The memory semiconductor market is reigned over by Korean companies as well. Samsung Electronics boasts a whopping 43.4% market share in the D-ram market, and SK Hynix, 29.1%. That means, when combined, these two Korean companies are dominating the market with a combined market share of 72.5%. These two companies also dominate the NAND flash market with a combined market share of 52.1% --- Samsung with 40.8% and SK Hynix with 11.3%.

Driven by a surging demand for semiconductors following the introduction of AI-based self-driving vehicles, Samsung Electronics recorded a 26.9% operating profit to sales ratio in the Q3 2018. It is difficult to find any other manufacturing company that recorded such an astonishing operating profit to sales ratio other than the US-based cell phone company, Apple. Looking back, the "February 8 Tokyo Declaration" made by Samsung founder Lee Byung-cheol in 1983 with the vision of tapping into the semiconductor industry turned out to have been a great decision that has been supporting and feeding Korea for several decades.

THE WORLD'S SMART PHONE LEADER SAMSUNG SHIPS 300 MILLION UNITS TO THE WORLD EACH YEAR

If Apple restructured the cell phone market when it introduced the iPhone in 2007, it was Samsung that began to expand the smart phone market in earnest. Samsung launched the cell phone business in 1988, and it beat Apple in the third quarter of 2011 and became

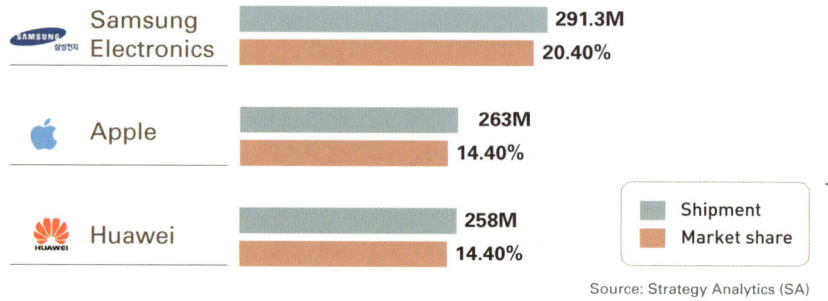

the top in the smart phone market. The company went on to beat Nokia --- which seemed an impregnable fortress in the market at the time --- in 2012 to become number one in the entire global mobile phone market.

In 2012, Samsung sold 215.8 million smart phone units, up 129% from the previous year, and its market share in the mobile phone market recorded 40%. The total sales of mobile phones were 477 million units, which accounted for a 23.7% market share in the mobile phone market.

The global smartphone market kept rapidly increasing from 1 billion units in sales in 2013 to 1.5 billion in 2017 until it started to curve in 2018. The smart phone shipments totaled 1,424.7 million units, a decrease of 5% from 2017, and the Chinese smart phone companies such as Huawei began to show remarkable growth. The combined market share of Chinese companies such as Huawei, Oppo, and Bibo surpassed 30%, and China beat Korea and emerged as the top smart phone manufacturing country in the world.

Despite such market changes, Samsung Electronics sold about 300 million smartphones in 2018, solidifying its perch atop the ranking with a 20.4% market share. According to the US-based strategic market research service provider Strategy Analytics (SA), Apple and Huawei ranked second and third with annual sales of a little over 200 million units and market share of 14.4%, respectively, but Huawei's sales volume is growing rapidly. Samsung Electronics performed strongly in European and South American markets, while Apple performed well in the North American market with a 38% market share, and Chinese smartphones continuously increased its share in Asian markets.

SAMSUNG AND LG DOMINATES HALF OF THE GLOBAL TV MARKET

There is one item that helped Samsung and LG beat Japanese makers such as Sony and Panasonic and engraved the reputation of Korean brands in the minds of global consumers: TV. Samsung Electronics has been the number one in the global TV market for 13 consecutive years since 2006, and LG Electronics is second.

According to the London-based global information provider IHS Markit, the global TV market expanded from $85.2 billion in 2017 to $115.5 billion in 2018, and during this period, Samsung Electronics accounted for a 29% share of the global TV market and LG Electronics,16.4%. It means Korean brands grabbed a 45.5%

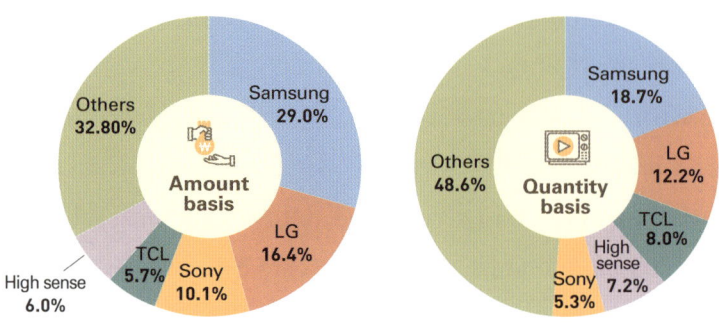

Source: IHS Market

share of the global TV market, which is close to half of the entire market. The combined market shares of Japanese TV makers --- including Sonic, Sharp, and Sony whose share was 10.15 --- was 16.3%, while the combined shares of Chinese TV makers such as TLC, Hisense and Skyworth, was 17.3%.

In 2018, about 220 million TV units were sold in the global market. In terms of the number of units, it is a 0.1% increase, but the sales total in the same period increased 36%. The big increase in the sales figure is attributed to Samsung Electronics and LG Electronics' strategical push to increase the sales of extra-large, high resolution TVs built with QLED and OLED technology. Since its first introduction of QLED TV in 2016, Samsung Electronics has increased its share to 57% in the market of TVs bigger than 75. Samsung can be considered as an unchallenged leader in this market, considering how the runner-up, Sony's market share is only 25%.

Samsung also accounted for 48% of sales of premium TVs that are priced at over $2,500 per unit.

Chinese electronics company Haier has been ranked number one in terms of sales volume of appliances such as refrigerator and washing machines in the global market since 2009, but in terms of sales amount, Samsung and LG are taking the lead in the premium appliances market while also the top sellers of premium refrigerators and washing machines.

HYUNDAI AND KIA BECOME THE WORLD'S FIFTH TO SELL 8 MILLION CARS IN A YEAR

The Pony, which Hyundai developed as its own car model, enjoyed a wild popularity as soon as it went on sale in 1976. With this model, Hyundai moved on from the days when the company imported parts and technology from Ford in the United States and assembled units in Korea, becoming the second in Asia and the 16th in the world to develop its own car model. Hyundai sold 10,000 units of the Pony in the first year after launching and instantly grabbed a 44% share of the entire domestic automobile market. The company also exported six units of Pony to Ecuador for the first time in 1976 and went on to export 1,042 units more to 13 countries within the same year. In 1986, Hyundai exported 300,000 units to 66 countries.

Korea made a remarkable ascent to become the world's fifth largest automaker in 2005, thirty years after Hyundai introduced the

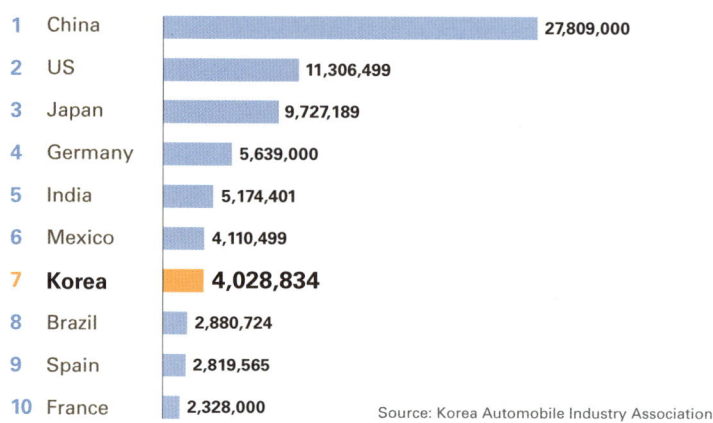

Pony. Korea remained the world's fifth automaker for 11 years, until 2015 after China, the United States, Japan and Germany, except in 2012, when it became the world's fourth largest auto exporter by shipping out a record-breaking 3.17 million units. In 2014, Hyundai Motor Group's two auto units - Hyundai Motors and Kia Motors - became the world's fifth largest in the automotive industry after Toyota, GM, Volkswagen and Renault-Nissan in 2014 when they sold 8 million units in just a year. The automobile industry has a significant impact on the economy as a whole, including employment and production, and it also has a significant effect on making Koreans feel proud when they see "made in Korea" cars in the world market. Given that, it is regretful that Korea's automobile production was outpaced by India and dropped to sixth on the ranking in 2016 and was again outpaced by Mexico and dropped to seventh in 2018. Hyundai Motor and Kia Motors made inroads into the US market in 1985, and by 2018, the two Korean automakers recorded a 7.5% of market share by selling 12 million units in total. In the European market, the Korean automakers recorded a 6.6% market share as of 2018 and reached annual sales of one-million-units for the first time.

KOREA BUILDS 15 OUT OF THE WORLD'S 20 LARGEST VESSELS

People often think of aircraft carriers when talking about the world's largest vessels, but in reality, it is not true. The world's largest aircraft carrier is the USS Gerald R. Ford, which was commissioned in 2017 and boasts a length of 337 meters. In contrast, the world's largest container ship is OOCL Germany, which is owned by the Chinese state-owned shipping company COSCO and boasts a length of 399.87 meters and width of 58.8 meters. This ship was built by Samsung Heavy Industries in 2017, and it can transport 21,413 containers.

The world's shipping industry is racing to build super-sized container ships that can carry more cargo and lower the freight cost. Samsung Heavy Industries has built all of the world's first to sixth largest container ships and Daewoo Shipbuilding & Marine Shipping has constructed the 12th to 20th largest container ships. It means that 15 of the world's 20 largest container ships were built by Korean shipbuilding companies. There is a lot of debate as to

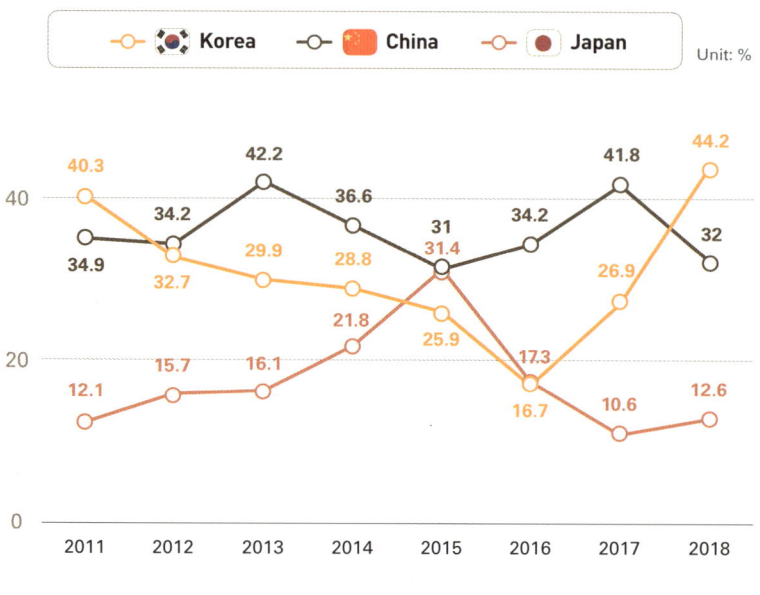

whether floating LNG production vessels --- a type of offshore plant --- should be regarded as ships. If they are, "Prelude FLNG" is the world's largest floating LNG gas platform as well as the largest offshore facility ever constructed. It is 488 meters long, 74 meters wide and 110 meters high, and this vessel was also built by Samsung Heavy Industries in 2017. In terms of the unit, the Korean shipbuilding industry is making four to five out of every ten vessels that sail oceans around the world.

The beginning of the Korean shipbuilding industry was rather reckless in a sense. Chung Ju-yung, the late founder of the

Hyundai Group, decided to become a shipbuilder in 1972 and created Hyundai Heavy Industries shipbuilding division. While the shipbuilding yard was under construction, he took a photo of the coast of Mipo Bay and with the design of an oil tanker borrowed from a British shipbuilder, he traveled around the world to get orders. When a foreign buyer kept refusing to give him an order, he showed him a 500-won Korean bill that had a picture of the Turtle Ship, and won him over by telling him, "Look, we built this kind of armored battleship in the 1500s" and successfully won an order of two large oil tankers according to a now-famous anecdote.

In 1983, Hyundai Heavy Industries beat Japan's Mitsubishi Heavy Industries to become the world's number one shipbuilding company in terms of shipbuilding orders and units. In 1999, the shipbuilding industry in Korea surpassed Japan in terms of shipbuilding orders. It was a miraculous feat that happened in less than 30 years since a shipbuilding dock was constructed on a sandy coast. Korea was outpaced by ambitiously chasing China and lost the honor of being the world's top shipbuilding country to China as of 2012, but in 2018, Korea virtually monopolized the world's orders of LNG facilities and reemerged as the world's number one in terms of global shipbuilding orders again.

WORLD'S FIFTH LARGEST CRUDE OIL IMPORTER, MORE THAN HALF RECOVERED WITH PETROLEUM PRODUCT EXPORTS

Being a country who relies on imports for the majority of their energy consumption, Korea is the world's fifth largest oil importer. Although Korea cannot drill the ground and pump up oil from it, Korea has been growing export industries by making petroleum and petrochemical products with imported oil. Korean-made petrochemical and petroleum products ranked number three and four on the list of Korea's largest export items in2018, after semiconductors and general machinery.

Korean oil companies exported a record-breaking 493.22 million barrels of petroleum products, such as gasoline, air fuel and diesel in 2018. The volume of the petroleum products that were exported mostly to China, Taiwan and Japan is enough to fill the 63-story building in Seoul 206 times, and the value totals $40 billion. Korea imports an annual average of 1,120 million barrels of crude oil, 55% of which are used to make petroleum products for export. Korea's oil refiners boast the world's sixth largest capacity after the United States, China, Russia, India, and Japan. Korea is followed by Saudi Arabia, Brazil and Iran.

The petrochemical industry, which processes refined petroleum products one step further, has long been a major export industry in Korea as well. Ethylene is the basic material for the petrochemical industry to produce synthetic resins, synthetic fibers, and synthetic

Petroleum Refining Capacity

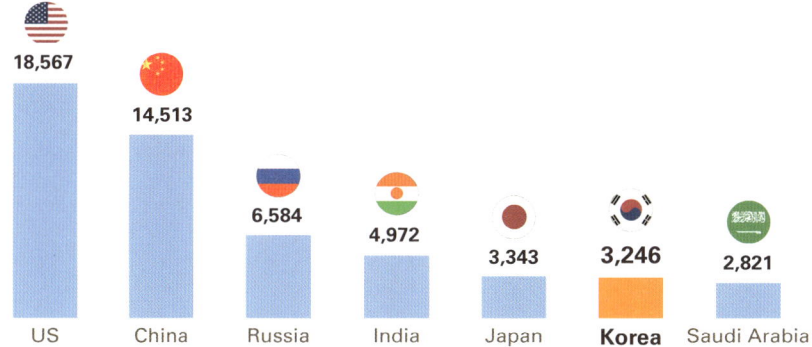

Units: 1,000 barrels

*As of 2017

Source: Korea Petroleum Association

Ethylene Production Capacity by Country

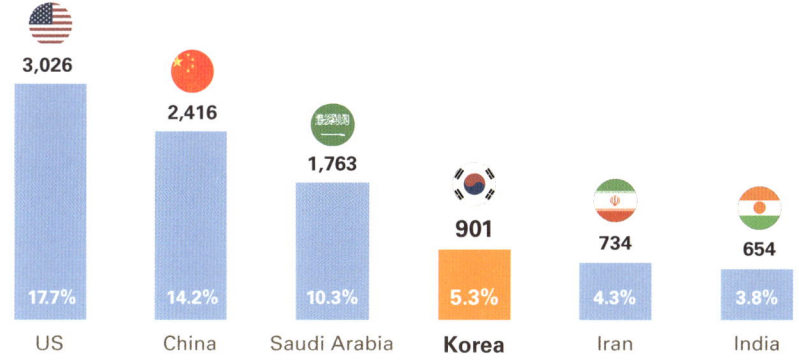

Units: 10,000 tons

*Numbers inside bar are market share, As of 2017

Source: Korea Petroleum Association

rubber. Ethylene production capacity is a measure by which the size of the country's petrochemical industry is determined. In this capacity, Korea passed Japan to rank fourth in the world in 2012, and even today, Korea has the world's fourth largest ethylene production capacity after the United States, China and Saudi Arabia. Korea exports 51.2% of its petrochemical products to China. However, China's ambitious push to promote its petrochemical industry is expected to become a variable in the current situation.

THE STEEL INDUSTRY STANDS TALL, RANKED FIFTH IN THE WORLD DESPITE INITIAL SKEPTICISM ABOUT INVESTMENT

Steel used to be called "industrial rice" ahead of the semiconductor, because it is the base material for all industries, including automobiles, shipbuilding and machinery. Being a large-scale equipment industry, 11 steel companies such as Hanbo Steel and Kia Specialty Steel were hit particularly hard during the 1997 foreign currency crisis and went bankrupt, consequently shutting down production facilities that turned out five million tons of crude steel .

When the Korean government decided to build Pohang Iron and Steel Company (POSCO), it was met by significant objection from inside and outside of the country because the project required a tremendous investment. The international financial institution International Bank for Reconstruction and Development (IBRD)

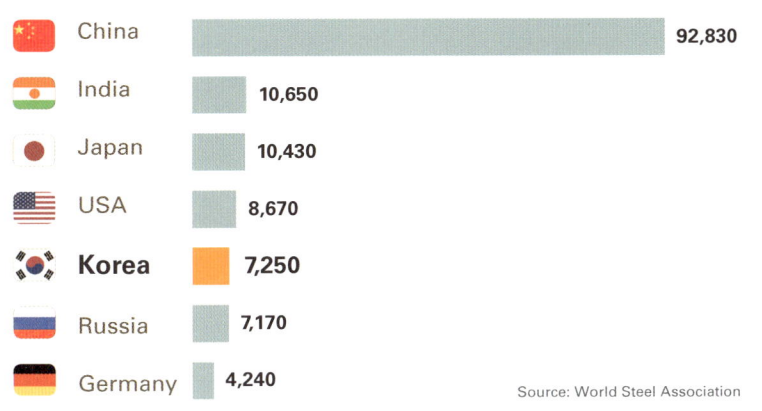

released a report titled "Korea-Current Economic Position and Prospects," and warned that it was too early for Korea to enter the capital and technology-intensive steel industry, and that higher production costs in steel would offset Korea's advantage of cheap labor and diminish its global competitiveness. As a result, the project to build POSCO failed to get foreign loans, and it was eventually constructed with the reparation awards that the Korean government received from a claim against Japan for war damages.

POSCO celebrated its 50th anniversary in 2018, and today, Korea is capable of producing 72.5 million tons of crude steel as the world's fifth largest crude steel producer after China, India, Japan and the United States. Korea had accounted for 8.6% of world crude steel production in 1980, but it dropped to 4.0% as the result of fast-rising China. As of 2018, China produces 51.3% of the entire global crude steel supply.

The conversation that the Chinese leader Deng Xiaoping had with the CEO of Nippon Steel Corporation in 1978 is worth considering at this point. Deng Xioping asked Yoshihiro Inayama, then-CEO of Nippon Steel, "Can you build a steel plant like POSCO in China, too?" Yoshihiro Inayama replied, "But there is no Park Tae-jun in China, is there?"

Later on, China made a thorough study of Park Tae-jun for a while, and the Chinese steel industry started making drastic growth.

Japan was shocked when the amount of Korean steel exported to Japan had begun to exceed the amount imported from Japan in 1981, calling it "the first year of the boomerang effect", but Korea was able to build stronger competitiveness of domestic industries including automobile and shipbuilding thanks to domestically produced quality crude steel.

THE POWER OF KOREANS BEHIND THE CONSTRUCTION OF THE WORLD'S LANDMARK BUILDINGS

Dubai is called the "miracle of the desert." Burj Khalifa, the highest building found in this city which has transformed itself into the world's greatest hub of logistics and tourism, is unquestionably a landmark that attracts attention from people. Some other landmark buildings of the world include Petronas Twin Towers in Malaysia and Marina Bay Sands Hotel in Singapore. A landmark that represents a region is created when society's best innovative minds and capital are matched with the best architectural technology of the time. Therefore, it is a great pride of Koreans that all those above-mentioned landmark buildings were constructed purely by Koreans.

KOREAN CONSTRUCTION COMPANIES REWRITE THE HISTORY OF GLOBAL SKYSCRAPERS

Skyscrapers have been changing skylines across the world. Stories about tall and gigantic buildings date back to the Tower of

Babel in the Bible, but the modern skyscraper construction boom kicked off in full swing in 1871 after the Great Fire of Chicago. The word "skyscraper" comes from the 55-meter-high, 12-story Home Insurance Building that was constructed in 1885 in Chicago, and since then it has been widely used to define high-rising buildings. Beginning in the 1900s, New York has been the leadenetr in the construction of skyscrapers. Indeed, New York was home to most of the world's tallest skyscrapers beginning with the Metropolitan Life Tower (213.4m) built in 1909 to the Empire State Building (381m) built in 1931 and the World Trade Center Building (417m) built in 1972.

Then in 1998, the United States lost the honor of being home to the world's tallest buildings when the 451.9-meter-tall Petronas Twin Towers were constructed in Malaysia, and never recovered the honor again. The building that pushed the Petronas Twin Towers down to second place in the ranking was Taipei 101 Building that was completed in Taiwan in 2003. The record for the world's tallest building was broken again when Burj Khalifa was constructed in Dubai, United Arab Emirates, and it remains as the tallest building in the world ever since with a total height of 828 meters.

The changing history of the world's tallest buildings has been written by Korean construction companies: Burj Khalifa was built by Samsung C&T, the Petronas Twin Towers by Samsung Construction and Kukdong E&C, and Taipei 101 by Samsung C&T.

In Korea, the 63 Building that was constructed on Yeouido in

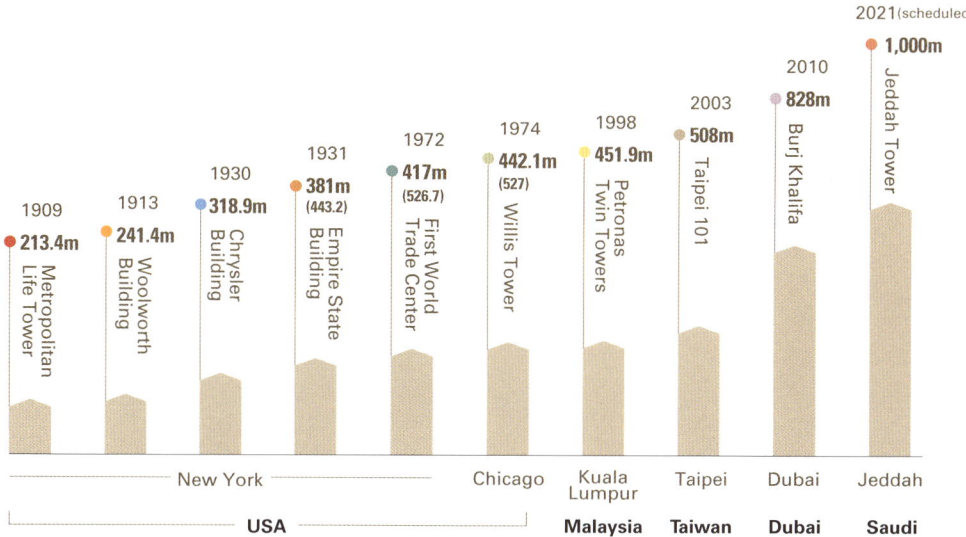

Changing Records of the World's Tallest Buildings

*The numbers within parentheses are the heights including antennas and others.

1985 opened the era of skyscrapers, and the 123-story high Lotte World Tower that was constructed by Lotte Construction in 2017 holds the record of being Korea's tallest building. With a total height of 555 meters, the building is the world's fifth tallest building after Burj Khalifa, Shanghai Tower (632 meters), the Abraj Al Bait Tower (601 meters) in Mecca, Saudi Arabia, and the Ping An Finance Center in Shenzhen, China (599 meters). It is the building that showcased Korea's advanced architectural engineering technology to the world.

KOREA RANKS SIXTH IN WORLD OVERSEAS CONSTRUCTION AND STANDS BETWEEN GERMANY AND JAPAN

The cumulative total amount of contracts won by Korean companies for overseas construction projects reached $800 billion in 2018. This amount is the sum of 12,771 contracts for construction projects in 156 countries for the past 53 years since Hyundai E&C won the bid to build the Pattani-Narathiwat highway in Thailand in 1965.

The contract to build the Patani-Narathiwat Expressway in Thailand was significant not just because it was the first construction contract Hyundai E&C received from a foreign country but also because it was the highway that a Korean construction company had built in accordance with international standards. Having started with insufficient experience and equipment, Hyundai lost about KRW300 million won by the time it managed to complete the construction --- whose original estimate was about KRW1.5 billion won --- in February 1968. Hyundai lost a significant sum of money, but the experience was priceless. The costly experience paid off when Hyundai was able to participate and spearhead the construction of the Gyeongbu Expressway that began in February 1968 with confidence, despite heated debates over the pros and cons of the construction project.

The construction of the Al Ula-Kaiba expressway in Saudi Arabia that Sam Hwan Enterprise began in 1973 was another significant

Global Ranking of Overseas Construction by Country

2016		2017	
Country	Share	Country	Share
China	21.1%	China	23.7%
Spain	12.6%	Spain	13.9%
US	9%	France	7.6%
France	8.9%	US	6.9%
Korea	**7.3%**	Germany	6.3%
Italy	5.7%	**Korea**	**5.3%**
Turkey	5.5%	Japan	5.3%
Japan	5.2%	Turkey	4.8%
Germany	5%	England	4.6%
Sweden	3.2%	Italy	3.8%
Austria	3%	Austria	3.7%
England	1.9%	Sweden	3.3%
Australia	1.9%	Australia	1.8%
Netherlands	1.8%	India	1.5%
Greece	1.4%	Netherlands	1.4%

*Total by country based on sales of the world's top 250 construction companies
Source: ENR(Engineering News-Record)

case because it was the first construction project to blaze a trail for Korean construction companies to tap into the Middle Eastern market. It was followed by the construction of the Jubayl Industrial Port in Saudi Arabia that Hyundai E&C won in 1976 and stunned Koreans because the cost was equivalent to about 25% of Korea's national budget. Supported by this Middle East boom, in the early 1980s the Korean construction industry ascended to rank second in the world in terms of the worth of construction contracts after the US.

Lately, China, Spain, France, and the United States have remained solidly, top four contractor countries in the overseas construction market, and Korea has remained in fifth place for many years. It is unfortunate that Korea was pushed down to sixth place by Germany in 2017 but still, Korea remains a construction country stronger than Japan, Turkey, the UK and Italy.

BURJ KHALIFA, THE FLOWER IN DESERT THAT KOREA MADE BLOOM

The Burj Khalifa building in Dubai, UAE, is considered a global landmark like the Eiffel Tower in France, the pyramid in Egypt, and the Great Wall of China. The total height of this world's tallest building that can serve as a landmark from all four directions is 828 meters, which is similar to the height of the tallest mountain in Seoul, Mt. Bukhan, that stands 836 meters. One of the most popular tourist destinations of Dubai, the building is well known as the filming location for the movie "Mission: Impossible 4".

Several multinational corporations took part in this monumental construction project that proceeded while weathering sandstorms. Burj Khalifa was designed by a US-based company Skidmore, Owings & Merrill (SOM), funded by a joint venture with BESIX

Burj Khalifa

from Belgium and Arabtec from the UAE, and the US-based construction company Turner was the project manager on the main construction contract. As the primary contractor of the project, Samsung C&T oversaw the entire construction process, and the building was finally opened on January 2, 2010 to rave acclaim by the press around the world as "the desert flower that Korea made bloom."

The construction of the building, which started in September 2004, included a crew of technicians and workers from 40 countries including Korea. At the peak of construction, 12,000 workers worked on the building simultaneously, every day. The five-year construction project took over 8.5 million man-days, all of which are new world records. The fact that over 10,000 people worked on the construction day and night for five years without any major accident is considered a miracle even by today's standard. The construction brought about advanced construction technology as well. It was built with a method that blitzed through three stories per day, and GPS technology that measured the building using a satellite, a technique adopted for the first time as well. When building a super high-rise building, the pumping technology that can transport quick-dry concrete to a higher point without delay is very important. In the construction of Burj Khalifa, specially developed concrete pumps transported concrete to the height of 601.7 meters, which was a new world record.

WAR BETWEEN KOREA AND JAPAN OVER THE CONSTRUCTION OF PETRONAS TWIN TOWERS

The Petronas Twin Towers, built in 1998 in the heart of Kuala Lumpur, the capital of Malaysia, is the first building in the world to beat the United States as home of the world's tallest building. The

Petronas Twin Towers

east tower of the 88-story twin buildings that stand 452 meters high was built by Korea, and the west tower, by Japan.

The project specified that bidders for the construction were required to have experience of building 50-story or higher buildings with reinforced concrete. Samsung C&T had no experience of building anything taller than 25-stories at the time, but the company managed to win the bid by creating a consortium with Kukdong E&C. Samsung was in charge of building the east tower, while Kukdong was in charge of building the sky bridge that connected the twin buildings. The west tower was constructed by Hazama, the Japanese construction company that had built Gyeongbu Line and the Supung gravity dam during the Japanese colonial period.

In a competition comparable to psychological warfare between Korea and Japan, a new engineering technique that could shorten the construction period was adopted. Samsung used the method of directly pumping the concrete to 380m and broke the world record of the time, then broke it again when the company was building Burj Khalifa. With these engineering methods, Samsung and Kukdong completed the building six days earlier than Japan even though the two companies started the construction 35 days later than Japan. The 59m long, 4.3m wide sky bridge that connects the twin buildings between the 41st and 42 floors is supported by a pair of "two-hinge arches" springing from supports at the 29th floor. The construction of the sky bridge attracted such interest around the world that the US-based broadcasting company CNN live aired broadcast when the sky bridge was pulled up to its location.

Supported by the experience of building the super-rise skyscraper Petronas Twin Towers, Samsung C&T was able to win the bid to construct the 508m high Taipei 101 building as the main contractor, followed by the construction of Burj Khalifa in Dubai as the primary contractor.

KOREA BECOMES THE WORLD'S SIXTH NUCLEAR POWER PLANT EXPORTER WITH THE CONSTRUCTION OF THE BARAKAH NUCLEAR POWER PLANT

In 2009, Korea successfully won the contract to export four

Barakah Nuclear Power Plant

Korean-made APR-1400 reactors to the United Arab Emirates. It was a feat accomplished 30 years after Korea's first commercial Reactor-1 at Gori Nuclear Power Plant was turned on in 1977. With this contract to build a nuclear power plant in Barakah, United Arab Emirates, Korea became the world's sixth country to export nuclear power plants after the United States, France, Russia, Canada and Japan. It is indeed a remarkable change considering how on May 14, 1948, North Korea who was supplying 92% of electric power used in the entire Korean Peninsula at the time suddenly cut electric power supply to South Korea without prior notice and plunged South Korea into utter darkness. South Korea had to rely on the power ships the United States urgently deployed to Incheon and Busan.

The Barakah nuclear power plant, which is the first to be built in the Middle East, is a $19.1 billion deal lead by the consortium between Korean Electric Power Corporation (KEPCO), Korea Hydro and Nuclear Power (KHNP), Samsung C&T and Hyundai E&C. The Ministry of Commerce, Industry and Energy estimated that the economic effect of the export of Barakah nuclear power would be equivalent to the export of one million units of NF Sonata or 180 units of 300,000-ton-class oil tankers. The construction of the Korean-made nuclear power plant Unit 1 began in 2011 in Barakah, which means "the blessing of God" in Arabic, and the ceremony that marked the completion of the unit was held in March 2018 with President Moon Jae-in attending. Each unit in the power plant has the capacity of 1,400 MW, and all four reactors are slated to be completed by 2020. Once the nuclear power plant is built completely, it will supply 25% of the electricity needs in the United Arab Emirates.

In 2018, the Korean-built nuclear power plant received Standard Design Approval from the US-based Nuclear Regulatory Commission (NRC), which is the world's largest nuclear safety regulator. Once approved by NRC, the nuclear power plant is internationally acknowledged for its safety. As of now, only five US-built nuclear reactors have received the Standard Design Approval, including ABWR built by General Electric and AP1000 built by Westinghouse. Since the Korean-built nuclear plant is the first to receive the NRC approval outside the United States, it can be considered as proof of the quality of Korean technology and safety of the nuclear power plant.

HANWHA CONSTRUCTION BUILDS AN ENTIRE NEW CITY IN BISMAYAH, IRAQ

The construction of the Bismayah New City is a symbol of Iraq's national reconstruction, the largest single project in the history of overseas construction in Korea. The project, which Hanwha Construction won in 2011, is a total $10.1 billion deal if the construction cost of new infrastructure is added in addition to the construction of residential buildings that costs $8 billion.

Bismayah New City is a project that builds 100,000 housing units that can accommodate 600,000 occupants in addition to schools, police stations, fire stations, clinics, parks, transmission and distribution facilities and all other social infrastructures in an area that is about 10 kilometers southeast of the capital city of Baghdad. The total area of the Bundang-level new city is six times the size of Yeouido in Seoul.

The city is constructed under a "design-build" contract, in which Hanwha alone carries out planning, design, procurement and construction. Hanwha designed the Bismayah New City based on the company's accumulated experience of having carried out major urban development and new city construction projects in Korea, such as the urban development in Sorae and Nonhyeon in Incheon and Techno Valley in Daedeok. The company realized the first advanced telegraph-pole-less apartment complex in Iraq by installing all the cables underground, and schools, police stations, clinics and other

Bismayah New City

facilities are placed at the best locations by taking population and the locals' cultural activities into consideration.

The construction of the new city is carried out using a "PC" method, in which the exterior and interior walls and flooring materials are pre-made at thea "precast concrete plant" built next to the city and transported to the construction site. The construction of housing units kicked off in 2014 and occupation is being phased in, but the construction of the entire city is slated to be completed by 2021. When the Sunni militants with Islamic State of Iraq and the Levant (ISIS) seized northern Iraq in 2014, the majority of foreign companies left Iraq, but Hanwha remained and continued the construction while relying on an accurate local information network. Consequently, the Bismayah New City construction project brought about the effect of elevating Korea's image as representing "trust and loyalty" as well.

ÇANAKKALE BRIDGE IN TURKEY REWRITES THE HISTORY OF BRIDGES

Currently, the longest suspension bridge in the world is the Akashi-Kaikyo Bridge located in Kobe, Japan. But in March 2022, the record will be broken by the Çanakkale Bridge that is under construction in Turkey by two Korean contractors: Daelim Industrial and SK E&C.

The 3.7 km long suspension bridge that is being built over the Dardanelles Strait in the Çanakkale province of Turkey was designed to have thea main span of 2,023m. It was designed this way to commemorate the year 2023, the centennial of the Turkish Republic. This is the first time that a bridge with a span more than 2km has been built in the history of bridge construction.

A team made up of Daelim Industrial and SK E&C beat the Japanese consortium that included Itochu and won this KRW3.5 trillion won project in 2016. The competition over this contract between Korea and Japan was so fierce that the Japanese Prime Minister Shinzo Abe even mentioned this project at the summit meeting with the Turkish president Recep Tayyip Erdogan. Daelim and SK succeeded in winning the contract largely because of their experience of having built Korea's longest Yi Sun-sin Bridge (1,545m)

A bird's-eye view of the Çanakkale Bridge

and the local network SK had built while constructing the Eurasia Tunnel in Istanbul, Turkey, that crosses underneath the Bosphorus Strait.

SK E&C had capabilities to carry out development project as well as to design, procure and construct in Turkey when it built and opened the Eurasia underwater tunnel that crosses the Bosphorus Straight at the end of 2016. The Eurasia Tunnel is the world's first double-deck tunnel exclusively for automobiles. The tunnel is 5.4km, but the total length is 14.6 km when the tunnel approach roads are included. SK was lauded for the successful construction of the tunnel because the company made it possible despite several unfavorable conditions such as the seabed of the Bosphorus Strait that is -106m at a maximum depth, some unstable alluvium formations such as the sand and the clay and gravel, as well as ancient relics and sites to be protected. With this construction of the tunnel, the Korean construction company set a new record of connecting the Bosphorus Straight and the Dardanelles Strait that are found between the Black Sea and Mediterranean Sea both under and above the water.

MIRACLE OF MODERN ARCHITECTURE, MARINA BAY SANDS HOTEL IN SINGAPORE

The Singapore Marina Bay Sands Hotel, which is shaped like a giant ship resting on three tall towers, is lauded as "a Miracle of 21st Century Architecture." Built with highly innovative and sophisticated Korean technologies, the hotel became the focus of attention when the United States and North Korea had their first summit there in June 2018. Considered by many to be "the most difficult project to carry out in the whole world", this hotel was built by a Korean contractor, Ssangyong, in March 2010.

The hotel is characterized by the concave shape of each tower, which is nearly 10 times more inclined than the Leaning Tower of Pisa (5.5 degrees). Each tower of the building has two asymmetric legs, with a curved eastern leg leaning against the others until they join at the height of 70m (23rd floor) and rise in parallel, straight up all the way to the 55th floor, creating a shape that resembles two playing cards leaning against each other. The bid for the integrated resort fronting Marina Bay in Singapore began in 2006, but it took as long as 14 months until the contractor was selected, largely because majority of contractors decided it was too complicated to carry out a project marked by such a unique and challenging design. A Hong Kong-based contractor that competed with Ssangyong till the last minute also claimed it would be difficult to build the hotel while faithfully following the original design, but Ssangyong won

Marina Bay Sands Hotel, Singapore

the bid by presenting a plan that followed the original design even though the company did not submit the lowest bid. And Ssangyong completed the $980 million construction project in just 27 months.

To construct a building that was inclined at 52 degrees at its highest, Ssangyong applied the "Vertical Post Tension" method that involved installing a fixing anchor on the floor of the building's bottom level and connecting a steel strand to it. Made by weaving seven wires, the steel strand is pulled like the strings on a guitar and the tighter it is pulled, the more upright the building stands. Sky Park, which connects the top floors of the three towers, is 343 meters long and 38 meters wide. It is twice the size of a soccer field. In order to build this Sky Park, which has a swimming pool, observation deck, garden, walkway, restaurant, and other facilities, 7,000 tons of steel structures were assembled from the ground and lifted up to 200m in what is known as the "Heavy Lifting" method. The methodology used for building the sloping structure of the Marina Bay Sands Hotel was registered as New Construction Technology No. 608 by the Ministry of Land, Transport and Maritime Affairs --- the first time that a technique used on an overseas project took such an honor. If this technique is used in similar projects, the company will be paid about 15% of the construction cost as a royalty.

WATERWAY CONSTRUCTION IN LIBYA TO TURN A REGION, SIX TIMES THE SIZE OF YEOUIDO, INTO FERTILE LAND

In 1983, Dong Ah Construction won the bid to construct an underground waterway system in Libya. Commonly called the "Great Man-Made River Project", it was arguably the world's largest-scale nature reforming civil engineering project. Also dubbed a "green revolution in the desert", the project was designed to turn a region --- six times the size of Yeouido in Seoul --- into fertile land by carrying underground fresh water from Sahara Desert aquifers in southern Libya to cities and farms throughout the country.

It all started decades earlier when efforts to find oil in southern Libya led to the discovery of large quantities of liquid --- 35 trillion tons, 200m underground --- which later turned out to be fresh water. Equivalent to the volume of water flowing down the Nile River for two hundred years, the water was more than enough for Libya to use for a thousand years.

The four-phased construction project involved connecting regions throughout Libya with pipes --- 75 tons each with a radius of 4m and length of 7.5m. In 1983, Dong Ah beat 72 companies from 21 countries to win the bid for the first phase of the construction at $3.752 billion. The first phase of the construction for an 1,895 km waterway began in 1984 and was completed in 1991. Dong Ah won the bid for the second phase of the project at $6,459,000,000 as well. The second phase of construction for a 1,652km waterway started in 1990 and the first water was delivered to the capital, Tripoli, in 1996 during a ceremony.

The third and fourth phases of the project for a 1,720 km waterway was undertaken by ANC, which was a joint venture established by Dong Ah and the Great Man-Made River Authority (GMMRA), in 1993. But when Dong Ah was subject to the government's workout programs in 2000 due to a financial crisis, the company turned over the majority of its shares to Libya. Then Libya entered a state of civil war following the Jasmine Revolution, or the Arab Spring, in 2011, and the Korean government imposed a travel ban to Libya in 2014, effectively cutting Korea's ties to the Great Man-made River project.

HALLYU FEVER HEATING UP IN MUSIC, DRAMA, AND GAME MARKETS

Hallyu (Korean Wave) fever is spreading all over the world including the United States, Europe, and Latin America. When the President of the Republic of Indonesia, Joko Widodo, made a state visit to Korea in 2018, he was seen dancing with members of the popular Korean boy band, Super Junior, thereby giving birth to a new trending term, "Super Junior diplomacy." Koreans have much to thank for hallyu, because, fueled by Korean dramas, games, and cuisine along with others, hallyu is helping people around the world to become more familiar with Korea, and it also causes a significant economic ripple effect.

BTS CONQUERS THE US BILLBOARD CHARTS

BTS became the first K-pop band to debut at number one on the Billboard chart in the United States, the home of pop music, in 2018. In the past, there were people who claimed K-pop fever was only

BTS on the cover of the 2018 October edition of the US-based Time Magazine

a storm restricted to Asian regions, but BTS debunked the theory of regional restriction and proved it can make it big even in the American music market.

It was the first time in 12 years that a foreign language album made it to the Billboard chart, which is based on the sales of albums in the United States. The US weekly magazine Time included BTS as one of the 25 most influential people on the Internet.

BTS was also the first Korean singers to be invited to an event in New York hosted by the United Nations Children's Fund (UNICEF) and where they gave a speech in September 2018, while the 73rd General Assembly of the United Nations was in session. It was a good example that testified to the popularity of BTS and the elevated status of K-pop in the international community. Soon after, BTS became the first K-pop singers to have their own concert in Citi

Field, which is the home stadium of the pro baseball team, the New York Mets. It was a venue available only to top pop stars such as Paul McCartney, Beyoncé and Lady Gaga. During the BTS concert, the New York city government had to add additional subway trains running to the venue to prevent traffic congestion. BTS had 15 concerts on its North American tour, and all 220,000 seats were sold out almost instantly.

BTS is listed in the 2018 edition of the Guinness World Records because the band has the world record for most Twitter engagements with the most retweets in the world. Before BTS there was Psy and his Gangnam Style that rocked the world in 2012. The unique horse dancing he introduced in his Gangnam Style music video became widely popular throughout the world, and the music video itself was listed in the 2012 edition of the Guinness World Records as the most viewed (over 1.5 billion views) and the most liked (2.14 million likes) video in YouTube history.

ECONOMIC EFFECT OF BTS EQUIVALENT TO A LARGE CONGLOMERATE AT 4 TRILLION WON

The incident that happened in January 2019 when the fabric softener, Downy Adorable, completely sold out and ran out of stock for a while is a good example that shows the economic effect of BTS. It all started when one of the BTS members was chatting with a fan club and mentioned the fabric softener when he said he was going

Annual Average Economic Effect of BTS

Category	Incremental and economic effects	Numerical comparison
the number of foreign tourists	Annual average of 79.6 million a year	About 7.6% of the total number of foreign tourists
The Effects of Export of Consumer Goods on the Korean Economy	Annual average of $1.11 billion	Approximately 1.7% of total consumer goods exports
Economic Effects of the Increase of Foreigners and the Export of Consumer Goods Exports	Annual average production inducement effect: 4.14 trillion won	26 times of average sales of a midsized company
	Average annual value-added inducement effect: 1.42 trillion won	8.9 times of average sales of a midsized company

Source: Hyundai Research Institute, Federation of Middle Market Enterprise of Korea

to do laundry before going to bed. Immediately, the fabric softener started selling off the shelves and soon it was sold out in many online shopping malls. Other BTS-themed merchandise such as T-shirts and caps are also hot in the market. Mattel, a company known as the Barbie doll maker, came up with BTS dolls, and Netmarble developed a BTS-themed online game, BTS World, all of which are examples that show how BTS's economic effect is spreading in all directions.

An analysis showed that the combined value of these direct and indirect economic effects of BTS, a Korean boy band that is writing a new history of K-pop, is estimated to be KRW5,560 billion won a year. In a report titled "Economic Effects of BTS" released in 2018, the Hyundai Economic Research Institute estimated BTS is worth KRW4,140 billion won in production inducement effect and KRW1,420 billion won of value inducement effect a year. Considering how the average annual sales of companies registered in the Federation of Middle Market Enterprise of Korea is KRW160 billion won as of 2016, the production inducement effect of BTS is 26 times higher than an average Korean company. That means it is equivalent to the birth of a large conglomerate named BTS.

Hyundai Research Institute estimates that the export effect of BTS will be $1,117,000,000: $233.98 million in clothing, $426.4 million in cosmetics and $ 456.49 million in food. That means BTU is credited for 1.7% of Korea's total consumer goods exports.

REVERSAL OF TRADE IN 20 YEARS AFTER OPENING DOOR TO JAPANESE CULTURE

When the Korean government announced that the ban on Japanese cultural products such as movies and manga was lifted, many people were concerned that the open import policy would make Korea a cultural colony of Japan. Fast forward 20 years in 2006, the Korean market was open even to the imports of Japanese broadcasting content, music, game and animation, but the reality turned out to be the opposite of what people had worried about. As of 2016, Korea's exports of cultural products to Japan recorded $1,376 million, which is nine times more than $150 million worth of Japanese cultural products imported to Korea.

Cultural Product Trade Between Korea and Japan

2016	Exported from Korea to Japan	$ 1,376 million
	Imported from Japan to Korea	$ 150 million
game	Export	$ 600 million
	Import	$ 51.6 million
manga	Export	$ 9.15 million
	Import	$ 5.95 million
Pop music	Export	$ 277.29 million
	Import	$2.91 million
broadcast	Export	$ 79.9 million
	Import	$ 6.7 million
movie	Export	$ 431 million
	Import	$ 4.4 million

Source: Ministry of Culture, Sports and Tourism

The reversal of trade is most clearly noticed in music. While Korea imported $2.91 million worth of Japanese music in 2016, Korea exported $277.29 million worth of Korean music to Japan. The difference is almost a hundred times. Even in the game industry, Korea exported $600 million worth of games to Japan, which is more than ten times the $51.6 million worth of imports from Japan.

The Japanese press identifies three stages of the hallyu boom in Japan. The first stage hallyu boom started in 2002 when the Japanese media heated up World Cup fever in preparation for the upcoming Korea-Japan match, followed by the Korean drama "Winter Sonata" that was aired on NHK in 2003. It was the beginning of the drama hallyu, largely spearheaded by the Korean actor Bae Yong-joon, who was catapulted into super-star fame in Japan where he was affectionately dubbed Yonsama. The second stage hallyu boom was started by K-pop groups including Girls' Generation, Kara, and Dongbangshinki, but the fever cooled off quickly when then-President Lee Myung-bak visited Dokdo in 2012.

Now the hallyu boom in Japan is in its third stage. In 2018, Korea-Japan relations were in a very bad state but the BTS concert at the Tokyo Dome attracted an audience of more than 100,000 people, demonstrating the power of hallyu transcending politics. This phenomenon is credited with the changed music consumption pattern on YouTube and social media. Now, Japanese K-pop fans can enjoy new releases by K-pop groups such as BTS, Wanna One, TWICE, and IZ*ONE without having to turn to Japanese production or broadcasting, because they can listen to them through various social media channels and share and spread them even with instantly translated lyrics.

K-POP, THE FIRST IMAGE TO COME TO MIND WHEN THINKING OF KOREA

It is reported that, when foreigners hear the word "Korea", the first image that comes to their minds is "K-pop". The Ministry of Culture, Sports and Tourism and the Korean Foundation for International Cultural Exchange (KOFICE) have been conducting a survey on the status of overseas hallyu each year since 2012 to understand

Images Foreigners Associated with Korea the Most

Rank	2008	2017
1	Technology (12.0%)	K-POP (16.6%)
2	Korean food (10.7%)	North Korean nuclear threat (8.5%)
3	Drama (10.3%)	IT industry (7.7%)
4	Korean people (9.4%)	Drama (7.6%)
5	Economic growth (6.2%)	Korean food (7.5%)

*Based on a 2008 KOTRA survey of 4,214 people in 25 countries
*2017 data is based on the Korea International Culture Promotion Agency survey of 7,800 people in 16 countries

foreigners' perception of Korea.

In a 2017 survey, 7,800 foreigners from 16 countries were asked what came to their minds first when they thought of Korea. The top answer was K-pop at 16.6%, and it was followed by North Korean nuclear danger at 8.5%, IT industry at 7.7%, drama at 7.6% and Korean food at 7.5% . In the survey conducted by KOTRA in 2008, the images foreigners associated with Korea were mostly technology, Korean food, drama, Korean people, and economic growth. The two survey results show that there was a significant increase of foreigners who gave K-pop and North Korean nuclear issue as their top answer.

The answers to the question about Korean image showed significant difference among countries. The highest number of respondents picked K-pop for their answer in Malaysia, Indonesia, Thailand and Australia. K-pop was also the top answer among the respondents from the United States, Brazil, France and the United Kingdom. Japanese respondents picked Korean cuisine as their top answer, followed by K-pop and drama, while the Chinese respondents picked cosmetics as their top answer, followed by plastic surgery, drama, and Korean stars. In Taiwan, the top answer was hallyu stars, while Russians and Turkish made their top answers automobiles and the Korean War respectively as the first images that came to their minds when they thought of Korea.

When asked if they agreed Korea was an economically advanced country, 66.3% of the respondent foreigners answered they agreed, 26.1% expressed reservations, and only 7.0% gave negative answers.

WHAT IS LOVE, WINTER SONATA AND DAEJANGGEUM, FUEL K-DRAMA FEVER

The wide-spreading hallyu fever is credited just as much to Korean dramas as to K-pop. Export of dramas took a new turn in 1997 when the foreign currency crisis shook the very foundation of the Korean manufacturing industry. It was in that year that the Korean drama, What is Love, debuted on China's national China Central Television (CCTV) and recorded 3.9 million viewer ratings, consequently changing the Chinese perception of Koreans.

It was followed by a wave of Korean dramas making their way into Chinese channels, until the Chinese press started using the term "Hallyu" to indicate the K-drama fever in 2000. In 2004, six out of the top ten foreign dramas with the highest ratings in China were Korean dramas. Some of the most popular Korean dramas that spread hallyu throughout the world include Daejanggeum, Winter Sonata, My Love from the Star, and the Descendants of the Sun.

Since dramas cover a wide variety of elements relating to food, tourism, fashion and household items, they can have far-reaching effects on related industries. For example, Daejanggeum, a 2003 drama whose main theme was court cuisine, was exported to 91 countries and introduced traditional Korean cuisine, dresses, and Korean herbal medicines throughout the world. The view ratings of the drama recorded 47% in Hong Kong, 86% in Iran and 90% in Sri Lanka, and in 2005, it was viewed by 160 million people in China. Even Hu Jintao, the then-General Secretary of the Communist Party of China, stated that he was a Daejanggeum fan. The drama grossed KRW13 billion won in exports, but the effect of improving the Korean image in the world cannot be compared to that monetary gain. In the case of the drama My Love from the Star, the female character had a line that said, "Chicken with beer is best when the first snow of the winter falls." This line made "chicken with beer" fever sweep throughout China.

In Japan, Winter Sonata, a drama that was first aired in 2003 and was rerun in 2004 in response to its explosive popularity, generated KRW100 billion won from the soundtrack music and KRW35 billion won from merchandise relating to the main actor Bae Yong-jun, in addition to the license fees. The drama created a sharp increase in the production and sales of Winter Sonata-related photos, DVD and character products, until the phenomenon gave birth to a new

Images Associated with Korea

Unit: %

	Asia									Americas			Europe					Middle East	Africa
	Asia	China	Japan	Taiwan	Thailand	Malaysia	Indonesia	India	Australia	The americas	USA	Brazil	Europe	France	England	Russia	Turkey	UAE	South America
K-POP	18.7	8.2	16.8	7.8	18.3	33.8	31	10	27.3	22.6	15.4	26.6	11.4	23	20.5	5.3	5.6	15	7
North Korea / North Korea Threat / War Danger	4.4	2.2	5.8	2.8	2.5	0.8	2.5	8.3	10.3	12.8	14	12.1	11.5	14	18.3	11	8.1	5	15.5
IT industry	5.2	2.2	1.8	6	3.3	4	8	12	6	9.4	6.4	11.1	9.4	10.8	9.5	10.5	8.4	9.3	11
Drama	12.3	16.8	9.6	15	8.8	17	17.8	8.8	4.5	1.4	2.6	0.7	5	2	2	2.3	8.5	8.8	1.8
Korean food	9.5	4.6	21.8	14.8	7.3	6.8	3.8	2.8	12.5	6.6	12.4	3.3	5.4	6	6.3	11	2.5	7.5	4.8
Hallyu stars	10.9	15.6	7.8	17.3	11.8	12.3	11	7	4	3.2	4.2	2.7	3.3	1.3	2.8	3.3	4.4	6.3	2.8
Beauty (Cosmetics and molding)	8.8	17.8	9	14	10	5.5	5	3.5	3	2.6	3	2.4	4	2	3.8	7.8	3.4	4.8	1.5
Korean War	1.5	1.8	1.2	1.3	1.3	0.8	0.5	1.8	3.8	3.6	5.8	2.4	9.5	3.5	2.5	2.5	17.5	2.5	2.8
Movie	3.1	2	1.4	2	5.3	1.8	3	7.3	2.5	2.7	2.4	2.9	3.9	3.3	3	2	5.2	6.3	4.5
Tourist destination	3.4	4.8	2.6	2.8	3.3	4.3	2.3	3.8	3	3.1	4.4	2.3	2.8	4.3	3.3	4.3	1.5	4.3	4.8
Car	1.3	1.4	0.4		0.5	1.5	0.3	3.8	2.5	3.3	4	2.9	5.2	2.8	1.3	13.3	4.5	5	6.8
Economic growth	1.5	1.6	0.8	0.5	0.5	1.3	0.8	5.3	1.5	5.2	1.2	7.4	4	3.5	3.5	3.3	4.7	2.5	5.5
Taekwondo	2.1	0.6	0.8	0.8	3	1.5	3	5.5	2.5	3.9	3.6	4	4.2	5	1.5	6	4.2	2.3	3.8
Hangul	2.6	2.8	6.4	1.3	3.8	1	2.3	1	1.8	2.3	2.4	2.2	2	0.3	2.8	2.5	2.2	3.8	3.8
Animation	1.1	0.8	0.8	0.3	1.5	1	0.8	2.5	1.8	3.6	4	3.4	2.8	2.3	2.3	4.3	2.7	1.8	5.8

Source: Korea Institute for International Cultural Exchange Promotion.
A survey of 7,800 foreigners from 16 foreign countries.

term called YonGel's Coefficient, which is coined by adding Yonsama --- the Japanese pseudo name of the main character Bae Yong-jun ---to Engel's Coefficient. The effect of the drama went beyond anybody's imagination as testified to by the fact that the actors and actresses of the drama became global celebrities, and the filming location Nami Island became a hot tourist attraction.

KOREAN CULTURE SPREADS BY 90 MILLION HALLYU FAN CLUB MEMBERS

In 2018, the number of global hallyu fans was estimated to near 90 million. The Korea Foundation's global hallyu data from 2018 revealed that there are 1,843 Korean hallyu fan clubs in 113 countries with the total number of members recorded at 89.19 million.

A hallyu club is defined as a club for people who love or are interested in Korean singers, actors, actresses, culture, cuisine, or Taekwondo, as well as a Korean culture club found at colleges. The number of people who belong to hallyu clubs increased by 14 million in 2017, and again 16.07 million in 2018. At this pace, the number is estimated to reach 100 million by 2020, which is nearly double the number of the entire Korean population. By continents, the number of hallyu club members surpassed 70 million in Asia and Oceania, and over 11 million in the American continent. There are 6.57 million in Europe and 230 thousand in Africa and the Middle East who are enjoying hallyu and contribute to the spread of hallyu as well. Even in Japan, where there is a likelihood of an anti-hallyu atmosphere, the number of hallyu fans tripled to around 300,000.

These hallyu fans are growing their influence through their activities on social media. One example is the BTS Thai fans who gave birth to a new fandom culture by running a blood donation drive campaign in commemoration of the fifth anniversary of BTS in 2018 and donated 200,000 cc of blood. It was an example that

Hallyu Clubs Around the World

Source: 2018 Global Hallyu (Korea Foundation)

showed how the growth of hallyu is resulting in the evolution of the culture of hallyu fans.

While Japanese idol groups rested on the laurels of being successful in Japan, which is the world's second largest music market, Korean idol groups sharpened their foreign language skills with an eye to the global market from the very start. As a result, when K-pop singers have concerts, it is not difficult to find foreign fans singing along with them in Korean.

HALLYU CREATES JOBS FOR 120,000 PEOPLE WITH KOREAN CUISINE, TOURISM AND EXPORTS

The popularity of Korean dramas in China and Southeast Asian countries resulted in the growing interest in Korean food and plastic surgery for people who wish to look like Korean celebrities. It is also likely to result in growing demands for cell phones, dresses and appliances that are featured in Korean dramas.

Korean Foundation for International Cultural Exchange (KOFICE) analyzed these economic effects of hallyu and presented the results in its "2017 Hallyu Ripple Effect Research Report."

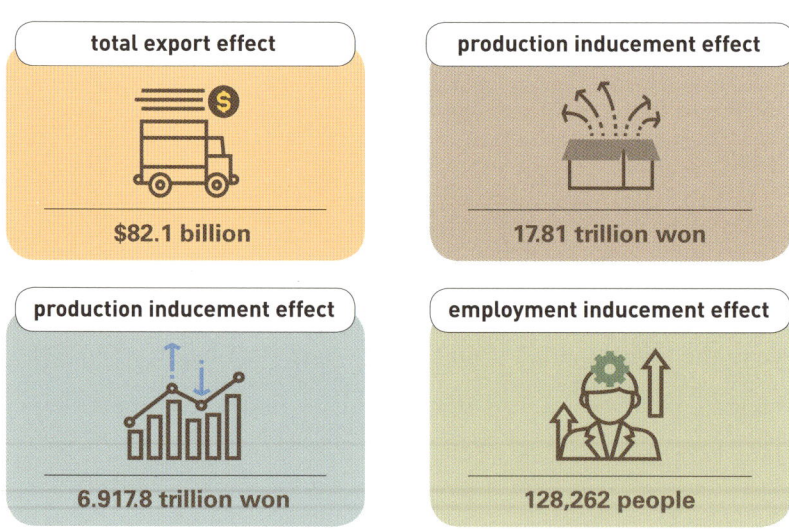

The Effects of Hallyu on the Economy in 2017

- total export effect: $82.1 billion
- production inducement effect: 17.81 trillion won
- production inducement effect: 6,917.8 trillion won
- employment inducement effect: 128,262 people

Source: 2017 Hallyu Wave Effectiveness Study (Korea Institute for International Cultural Exchange Promotion)

According to the report, hallyu fans in Thailand and Indonesia spent the most time enjoying hallyu content. They spent 100 hours on average a month, each. Hallyu fans around the world spent the most time enjoying Korean games (monthly average of 12.4 hrs.), followed by K-pop (11.8 hrs.) and drama (11.5 hrs.).

Hallyu fans overseas were more likely to visit Korea as tourists as well. Of the 13.3 million foreign tourists who visited Korea in 2017, 7.9% of them, or 1.05 million, were tourists who came to visit Korea because of hallyu. They spent over one billion dollars while visiting Korea. Consumer products that benefited most from hallyu were food and beverage, cosmetics, mobile phones, clothing, accessories, household appliances, and automobiles. Korea recorded $4.8 billion in food exports, and $800 million of this amount was attributed to having been influenced by hallyu. Korea also exported $5 billion worth of cosmetics the same year, and about $800 million worth of that amount was also believed to have been influenced by hallyu.

Shipments of cultural content products reached $6.2 billion in 2017, $3.8 billion of which is estimated to be shipments of hallyu-related cultural products. Games accounted for the largest percentage at $2.3 billion, and the exports of broadcasting content and music also showed an increase of $500 million each as the result of hallyu.

KOFICE analyzed the consumption trends of overseas consumers and concluded that in 2017, hallyu was attributed with having generated KRW17.8 trillion won's worth of production and KRW8.8 trillion won's worth of exports. KOFICE also estimated that hallyu created 128,262 new jobs.

HALLYU AND DIGITAL POWERHOUSE KOREA RANKS SEVENTH IN THE CONTENT MARKET

The age of the internet and smartphone has accelerated the spread of online contents. This is an age where well-made online content can dominate and even monopolize a market. With the fast growth and proliferation of various online services and content, such as webtoons, web novels and video-on-demand (VOD) streaming, the content industry is emerging as a promising industry that can make up for stagnant growth in the manufacturing industry. Consequently, the war is heating up over content to seize its distribution channels (platforms) and intellectual property rights.

According to the "2017 Overseas Content Market Trends Report" released by the Korea Creative Content Agency (KOCCA), Korea is the world's 7th largest content market after the United States, China, Japan, Germany, England and France. In 2009, the Organization for Economic Co-operation and Development (OECD) defined content industry as "an industry that produces, publishes, and distributes informational, cultural and entertainment products to deliver organized messages to people." Comparison of global content markets is based on ten categories of publication, cartoon, music, game, movie, animation, broadcasting, advertisement, character license, and intellectual information. Analytic data in 2016 showed

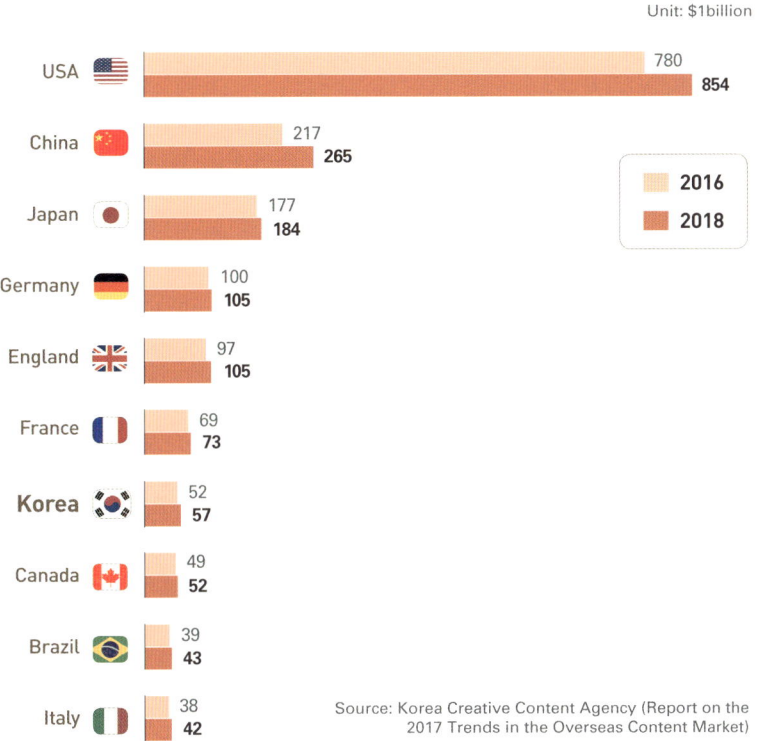

that the global market was expected to grow at an annual rate of 4.2% for the following five years.

The United States is the world's strongest powerhouse with a 37.5% share of the global content market. China used to rank third after the United States and Japan, but it moved up the second in 2014. Being a country that is growing rapidly in all sectors, China has been increasing its share in the content market as well until it recorded 10% share in the global market in 2016. Korea ranks higher than Canada, Brazil and Italy at seventh, but its market share is only 2.5%. In the game category, Korea is performing relatively well and ranks fourth after the United States, China and Japan. In the movie category, India is strong and ranked fifth, while Korea was eighth in the world. Korea should continuously build its competitiveness in digital content category by taking good advantage of its smart phone distribution rate and the internet access and speed that are considered the best in the world.

HALLYU FEVER IN THE GAME MARKET RESULTS IN SIX TRILLION WON OF TRADE SURPLUS

Supported by the spread of hallyu in the global game market, Korea recorded close to KRW6.7 trillion won in game exports in 2017. It means the trade surplus in game trade is KRW6.4 billion won, because Korea imported only KRS300 billion won's worth of games from overseas. According to the "2018 Korea Game Industry White Paper" released by KOCCA, Korea's game industry shipped $5.9 billion worth of game products in 2017, a year-on-year increase of 80%.

Korea ranked third in PC games and fourth in mobile games. In the PC game sector, Korea had ranked second in terms of market share for several years after China, until it was overtaken by the United States in 2017 and dropped to third in the ranking (12.1%

market share.) In the mobile game sector, Korea ranked second in 2015 but dropped to fourth in 2017 after China (20.7%), Japan (16.4%) and the US (15.6%).

In the entire game market, Korea's share was 6.2%, which put Korea in fourth place after the US, China and Japan. Korea was followed by England, France, Germany, Italy, Canada and Spain. Korea shiped 60.5% of game exports to China, and the rest to Southeast Asia (12.6%), Japan (12.2%), North America (6.6%) and Europe (3.8%).

While the global game market showed 12% year-on-year growth in 2017, the Korean game market recorded 20% growth to KRW13 trillion won. One noticeable change during this period was the

Korea's Game Imports and Exports by Year

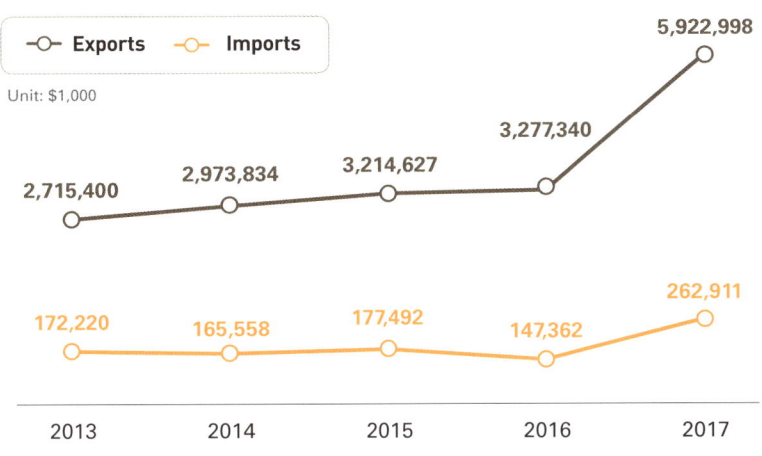

Source: Korea Creative Content Agency. 2018 White paper on Korean games

mobile game sales that made a sharp increase to account for 47.3% of the total sales and surpassed a 34.6% share of PC games for the first time.

ESPORTS PLAYERS COMING TO KOREA FOR FIELD TRAINING

Korea is a superpower in the eSports market, thanks to its nationwide super-speed internet access that has been available for the last 20 years, not to mention over 10,000 PC cafes that sparked the development of a dynamic online game culture. Korea is the five-time champion of the world's largest eSports match, League of Legends World Championship, which is better known as the "Lold Cup."

League of Legends is an online battle game released in 2009. The total amount of prizes paid to the winners of this championship game in 2018 was KRW7.2 billion won, and the final match that took place in Incheon Munhak Stadium was aired on over 30 TV channels and internet platforms in 19 languages to 100 million people.

Lee Sang-hyeok, the world's top League of Legends gamer whose nickname is Faker, is the icon of Korean eSports. His global fans compare Faker to Michael Jordan and Lionel Messi in eSports. He is credited with bringing three championships to SK Telecom T1, which is the eSports team that he belongs to as a mid laner. How much the 7-year gamer earns a year is unknown, but he is projected to rake in minimum KRW5 billion won a year in prize money and bonuses.

Being a leader unmatched by any other country in eSports, Koreans account for 30% of the eSports coaches around the world, and eSports gamers are coming to Korea for field training every year. Korea established the Korea e-Sports Association in 2001, launched the eSports, Star Craft Pro League in 2003, and operates the world's first broadcasting channel dedicated to gaming. There are more than 20 eSports teams run by large Korean corporations such as SK Telecom, KT, and Hanwha.

FROM THE SEOUL 1988 SUMMER OLYMPICS TO THE 2018 WINTER OLYMPICS

It is always inspiring to watch sports players who demonstrate their wholehearted commitment to their games. Their performance also makes countless people go wild. Mega sports events such as the Olympics and World Cups are a tremendous occasion that excites and inspires people, while at the same time a great opportunity for the host country to introduce their culture and developments to the world. Korea is one of the world's most dynamic sports powers which has produced numerous global sports stars, not to mention having hosted of one after another major world sports event successfully with the full support of the people and their competencies.

KOREA ACHIEVES A SPORTS GLAND SLAM AHEAD OF THE UNITED STATES AND CHINA

In baseball, the term "grand slam" is used when a hitter hits a home run with all three bases occupied, and in golf and tennis, when the player wins all major championship tournaments in the same calendar year. It may seem this glorious sports title is reserved only for the top star athletes, but there are six countries including Korea that are lauded as a country that has achieved the "sports grand slam."

In the sports world, there are four major sports events: Summer Olympic Games, Winter Olympic Games, FIFA World Cup, and IAAF World Championships in Athletics. The Summer Olympic Games organized by the International Olympic Committee (IOC) is the zenith of all sports events in which the world's best star athletes compete. Among the sports of the Olympics, soccer is the most popular sport in the world, while Olympic track and field --- also known as Athletics --- has a symbolic significance because it is a highlight of the games where athletes are competing for 47 gold medals, the most in any discipline.

Korea successfully hosted the 1988 Summer Olympic Games in Seoul, followed by the Korea-Japan World Cup hosted jointly with Japan in 2002, and the IAAF World Championships in Athletics in Daegu in 2011. Then in 2018, Korea successfully hosted the 2018 Winter Olympic Games in Pyeongchang, thereby achieving the "grand slam of four major international sports events."

Korea is the fifth country in the world to have achieved this feat after Italy, Germany, Japan, and France. Korea achieved a grand slam in February 2018 after hosting the Winter Olympic Games, while Russia achieved it a few months later in June 2018 after the successful hosting of the FIFA World Cup. The Grand Slam of

Countries That Have Achieved a Sports Gland Slam

	1st	2nd	3rd	4th	5th	6th
	Italy	Germany	Japan	France	**Korea**	Russia

	Italy	Germany	Japan	France	Korea	Russia
Summer Olympics	1960 Rome Olympics	1936 Berlin Olympics	1964 Tokyo Olympics	1900 Paris Olympics	1988 Seoul Olympics	1980 Moscow Olympics
Winter Olympics	1956 Cortina d'Ampezzo Olympics	1936 Garmisch-Partenkirchen Olympics	1972 Sapporo Olympics	1924 Chamonix Olympics	Feb. 2018 PyeongChang Olympics	2014 Sochi Olympics
International Track and Field	1987 Rome, Italy	1993 Stuttgart, Germany	1991 Tokyo, Japan	2003 French Saint-Denis	2011 Daegu, South Korea	2013 Moscow, Russia
World Cup	1934 Italy World Cup	1974 West Germany World Cup	2002 Korea-Japan World Cup	1938 France World Cup	2002 Korea-Japan World Cup	2018 Russia World Cup

sports is not a record that comes with any special prize, but it is an index that symbolically shows the status of the country. The United States and China are considered the world's top superpowers, but these two countries have yet to make a grand slam in sports. The United States will become the seventh country to accomplish the grand slam of sports when it hosts the IAAF World Championships in Athletics in 2021. China hosted the 2008 Summer Olympic Games in Beijing and IAAF World Championships in Athletics in 2015, and are scheduled to host the Winter Olympic Games in 2022, but with regard to FIFA World Cup, China is only dreaming of hosting it in 2034.

KOREA RANKS FOURTH IN THE SUMMER OLYMPICS AND CONTRIBUTES TO THE FALL OF THE SOVIET UNION

Korea stunned the world when it hosted the 1988 Summer Olympic Games in Seoul just 35 years after the ceasefire of the Korean War. It was a turning point for Korea to enter an age of prosperity while the country was still representing poverty and the ruins of war to the world. It was also from this point that Korea began to develop an IT industry, because the government connected the entire nation with optical networks and laid submarine communication cables in order to live broadcast the Olympic Games to the world.

At that time, the world was still impacted by the Cold War system. When the former Soviet Union hosted the Olympic Games in Moscow in 1980, a majority of Western countries boycotted the event, and the 1984 Los Angeles Olympic Games was just a half-success because communist countries declared a boycott of the Games. North Korea had been demanding to jointly host the Olympic Games in Seoul and Pyongyang from 1985 until January 1988, when it declared that it was not going to participate in the Seoul Olympic games after all. There were sporadic protests in Seoul

Korea's Medal Counts and Rankings in the Summer Olympics

Year	Host Country	Host City	Gold/Silver/Bronze Medals	Rank
1972	West Germany	Munich	0 / 1 / 0	33
1976	Canada	Montreal	1 / 1 / 1	19
1980	Soviet Union	Moscow		N/A
1984	USA	Los Angeles	6 / 6 / 7	10
1988	**Korea**	**Seoul**	**12 / 10 / 11**	**4**
1992	Spain	Barcelona	12 / 5 / 12	7
1996	USA	Atlanta	7 / 15 / 5	10
2000	Australia	Sydney	8 / 10 / 10	12
2004	Greece	Athens	9 / 12 / 9	9
2008	China	Beijing	13 / 10 / 8	7
2012	UK	London	13 / 8 / 7	5
2016	Brazil	Rio de Janeiro	9 / 3 / 9	8

Source: Korean Sport & Olympic Committee

by those who refused to host "a divided Olympic Games" as well. But the Seoul Olympic Games were held in Korea with the participation of a majority of communist countries including China. When Eastern European countries came to Korea for the games, they were shocked to see how advanced Seoul was, because they wondered, "How did Korea develop so much while being exploited by the US imperialists?" That is the reason the Seoul Olympic Games is pointed out as one of the reasons the Soviet Union collapsed a few years later.

Olympic Medal Counts and Rankings for Korea, China and Japan

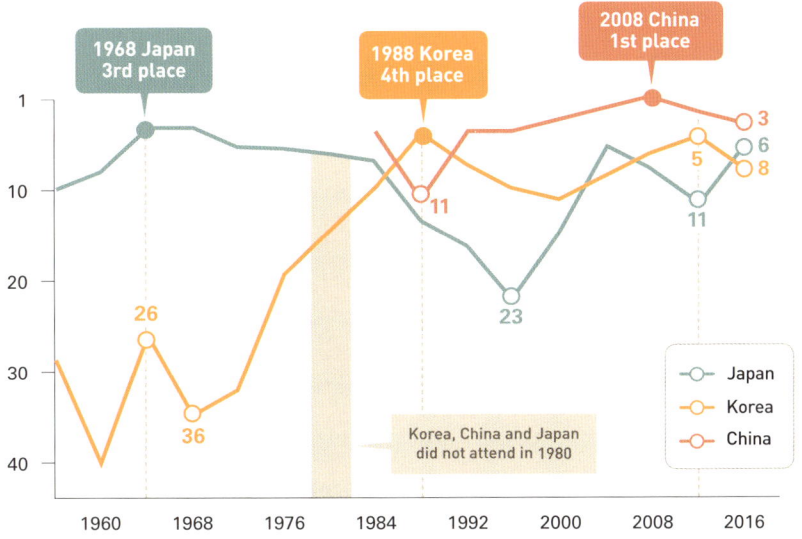

Korea stunned the world again when it won 12 gold, 10 silver, and 11 bronze medals in the Seoul Olympic Games and ranked fourth in the final medal count after the Soviet Union, East Germany and the United States. Korea was followed by West Germany, Hungary, Romania and Bulgaria in the ranking, with China coming in at 11th. Since then, Korea has cemented its reputation as a global sports powerhouse by ranking fifth in the London 2012 Summer Olympics and eighth in the 2016 Summer Olympics in Rio de Janeiro, Brazil.

THE PYEONGCHANG WINTER OLYMPICS SURPRISE, SOUTH-NORTH KOREA MARCHING TOGETHER

In the case of the Pyeongchang Winter Olympics, it was a bumpy road from the very beginning because it took Korea three failed attempts until finally winning the bid to host the games in PyeongChang. Then in 2017, North Korea launched one after another nuclear weapons and missile tests, raising tension in the Korean peninsula and causing grave concerns in the international community. But the situation took a drastic turn with just a month left before the opening of the games: North Korea, which had refused to participate in the Seoul Summer Olympics declared that it had decided to participate in the Pyeongchang Winter Olympics in January 2018.

Eventually, the PyeongChang Winter Olympic Games turned into the largest event in the history of the Winter Olympics, where 2,925 athletes from 92 nations including North Korea participated. At the opening ceremony, the entire world watched in awe the performance that created the Olympic flag with 1,218 drones, and at the closing ceremony, the performances of K-pop singers captivated the people. The Winter Olympics generated a lot of talk around the world from the beginning till the end with the South and the North marching together in the opening ceremony, a South-North joint women's field hockey team, and the participation of the North Korean cheering squad.

Medal Count and Ranking of Korea in the Winter Olympics

Year	Host country	Host city	gold/silver/bronze medals	Korea's Ranking
1988	Canada	Calgary		
1992	France	Albertville	2 1 1	10
1994	Norway	Lillehammer	4 1 1	6
1998	Japan	Nagano	3 1 2	9
2002	USA	Salt Lake City	2 2 0	14
2006	Italy	Torino	6 3 2	7
2010	Canada	Vancouver Whistler	6 6 2	5
2014	Russia	Sochi	3 3 2	13
2018	**Korea**	**Pyeongchang**	**5 8 4**	**7**

Source: Korean Sport & Olympic Committee

Thomas Bach, President of the International Olympic Committee (IOC), lavishly praised the event and said, "I have seen nobody who was not happy with the Olympic village and facilities during the Pyeongchang Olympics, which realized a Peace Olympics." Gunilla Lindberg, an elected member of the IOC, also stated, "The PyeongChang Olympics was probably one of the most well-organized ones in the history of the Olympic Winter Games," and added, "The Korean people should be proud of it."

At this Olympics, the Korean team finished seventh in the final medal count by winning five gold, eight silver, and four bronze medals. Korea came out on top among Asian countries, followed by Japan (11th) and China (16th). Up until 1988, Korea had never won any medal in the Winter Olympics. Team Korea started emerging as a strong competitor beginning with the 1992 Winter Olympics in Albertville, France, and eventually ranked fifth in the final medal count at the 2010 Winter Olympics in Vancouver, Canada. In the Pyeongchang Olympics, the Korean team did not win as many gold medals as anticipated, but it was encouraging that Korea won medals in more diverse disciplines such as women's curling, sliding sports (skeleton, bobsleigh) and snow sports (snowboarding).

KIM YUNA, HWANG YOUNG-CHO AND PARK TAE-HWAN GLORIFY THE OLYMPICS

The Olympic stage produced many Korean star players. One such example is Kim Yuna, who is frequently referred to as Queen Yuna by various media named global stardom across the world. She won gold with a world-record score in women's figure skating at the Vancouver 2010 Olympics. It was the moment she took the throne of the Queen in the women's figure skating world after winning the 2009 and 2013 World champion title, the 2009 Four Continents champion and a three-time Grand Prix Final champion.

In marathon, the summer Olympics gave birth to two Korean heroes: Sohn Kee-chung and Hwang Young-cho. Sohn became the first Korean to win a gold after setting a world record in the

KIM YUNA   HWANG YOUNG-CHO   PARK TAE-HWAN

marathon with a time of 2:29:19 at the Berlin 1936 Summer Olympics. Another Korean athlete Hwang Young-cho made the Korean people go wild by winning gold in the marathon with the Taegeukgi on his chest at the Barcelona 1992 Summer Olympics. Korean athletes left a big impression on the world's sports fans at the Olympics in Barcelona by winning both the first and the last gold medals of the entire event: Yeo Kab-soon the first gold in air rifle, and Hwang Young-cho the last gold in the marathon.

In 1976, Korean wrestler Yang Jung-mo earned Korea its first gold medal at the 1976 Montreal Summer Olympics. It was a great feat that came 28 years after Korea made its debut at the 1948 London Summer Olympics.

"Marine Boy" Park Tae-hwan won a gold medal in the 400-meter freestyle at the 2008 Beijing Summer Olympics, earning Korea its first gold medal in swimming. He was the first Asian male to win an Olympic gold in swimming in 72 years since the Japanese swimmer Derada Noboru won gold in the 1,500-meter freestyle at the 1936 Berlin Olympics.

Other Korean athletes that left their mark on Olympic history include Jang Mi-ran who won the gold medal with a new world-record score at the 2008 Beijing Summer Olympics; Yang Hak-seon who became the first Korean gymnast to win Olympic gold in gymnastics at the 2012 London Olympics; Jin Jong-oh who became the first athlete to have won three consecutive gold medals in one event, shooting, at the 2016 Rio de Janeiro Olympics; and Lee Seung-hoon and Lee sang-hwa who won gold in speed skating in the winter Olympic Games.

SUMMER OLYMPICS FOR ARCHERY, WINTER OLYMPICS FOR SHORT TRACK

There are sports games where Korean athletes can be intimidating to athletes from other countries, such as archery and short track. The Korean archery team and short track team can be compared to the American basketball team, Canadian ice hockey team, Chinese table tennis team, and Russian rhythmic gymnastics team.

The Korean archery team won 23 out of 40 gold medals so far since archery was selected as an official sport for the 1972 Munich Olympics. The Korean national team never missed a gold medal from the 1984 Los Angeles Olympics to the 2016 Rio Olympics. Korea's female and male national archery teams swept all four gold medals in the archery championship in the Olympics in Rio de Janeiro, Brazil. With the skills of Korean archers being so advanced, even the process of selecting a national team is so difficult that only those who have participated in Olympics twice in a row are qualified to participate in the national team selection competition. Competition to recruit a Korean archer as a coach is also fierce, understandably because the coaches of the four national teams that made it to the semifinal at the London 2012 Olympics --- Korea, the United States, Italy and Mexico --- were Koreans.

The Korean short track team won its 24th gold in the 2018 PyeongChang Winter Olympic Games, surpassing the total number of gold medals that the Korean archery team won at 23. Korea has won 24 out of the 53 gold medals that had been up for grabs since short track was selected as an official sport in the 1992 Albertville Winter Olympics. This is more than half of the 46 gold medals Korea has won at the Winter Olympics. At the Torino 2006 Winter Olympics, Korea won six out of the total eight gold medals available in short track. But since this Olympics, the Korean short track team's dominating power has slightly weakened because the first-generation players of the Korean short track team have been recruited and

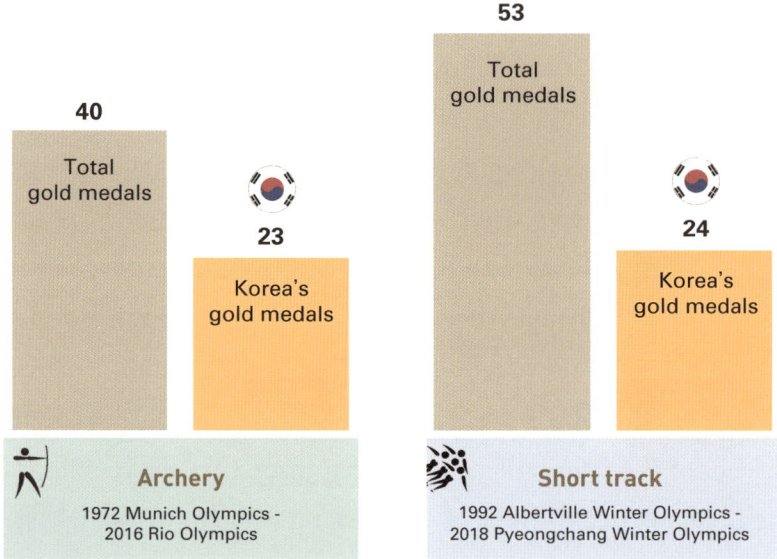

moved to coach national teams of other countries. Other sports that won the most gold medals after short track and archery include Taekwondo at 12 gold and judo and wrestling at 11 gold each.

WORLD CUP SEMIFINALS AND NINE CONSECUTIVE ADVANCEMENTS TO THE WORLD CUP

FIFA World Cup is considered the largest sports festival in the world, because it is an event to select the strongest national team in soccer, which has the most sports fans in the world, as shown by the fact that as many as 211 countries are members of the event organizer, The Fédération Internationale de Football Association (FIFA) and there were cases in which the game of soccer was blamed for causing a war.

Korea surprised the soccer fans of the world when it beat Japan and made it to the semifinal in 2002. Korea failed to reach the round of 16 in the 2018 World Cup in Russia, but left a strong impression by defeating top ranked Germany by 2-0 in the World Cup group stages. The Associated Press picked this Korea-Germany match as one of the eight biggest surprises of the year in 2018.

In soccer games, the more people believe the outcome is subject to luck and surprises, the more people become intrigued by how many times the team made it to the semifinal tournaments, because it is a measure by which the team can prove it has skills good and stable enough to have continuously passed continental preliminaries.

The World Cup started in Uruguay in 1930 when the first World Cup event took place, and the World Cup that was held in Russia in 2018 was its 21st event. Brazil is the only country that has participated in all 21 World Cup tournaments without missing a year. Germany is the second in the number of advancements to the World Cup at 19 times (17 consecutive), followed by Italy at 18 (14 consecutive) because Italy failed to make it to the semifinals at the World Cup in Russia. Argentina ranks fourth at 17 (12 consecutive), and Spain ranks fifth at 15 times (11 consecutive).

Korea ranks sixth because Korea made it to the World Cup

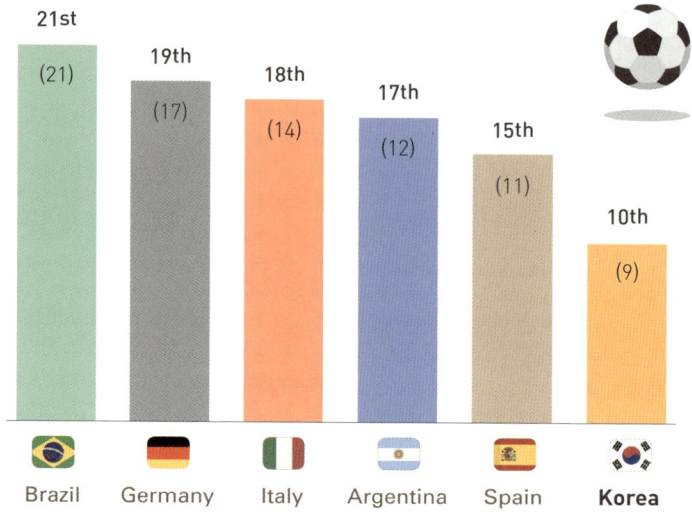

Advance to the World Cup Finals Record

*Continuous advance record in parenthesis
Source: FIFA

semifinals 9 times consecutively beginning with the 1986 World Cup Mexico to the 2018 World Cup Russia. In Asia alone, Korea is perched at the top with a total number of consecutive advancements to the World Cup at 10. In Asia, Japan made it into the semifinals six times consecutively beginning with the 1998 World Cup France, and Saudi Arabia made into semifinals four consecutive times until the 2006 World Cup Germany.

CHA BUM-KUN, PARK JI-SUNG, AND SON HEUNG-MIN SHAKE THE EUROPEAN SOCCER WORLD

Cha Bum-kun, Park Ji-sung, and Son Heung-min are Korea's top soccer players who left a deep impression in Europe, the home of pro soccer. Cha Bum-kun scored goals in three games in a row as soon as he debuted in the West German Bundesliga in 1978. When the political landscape in Korea was in disarray in the wake of the assassination of President Park Chung-hee, Cha rose to international stardom in Germany with such nicknames as the Brown Bomber and Tscha Bum ("Cha Boom") by scoring 98 goals in 308 games in ten years. Even though he debuted in Bundesliga at age 25, he left with the record of most goals scored among foreign players by the time he retired in 1989. Cha was the third highest paid player in the Bundesliga at his peak. All of the 98 goals he scored were field goals and he received only one yellow card during his entire career in Germany, thereby being recognized as a fair player as well.

Park Ji-sung came to sudden prominence when he played in the Korea-Japan World Cup tournament in 2002 and helped the Korean team make it into the World Cup semifinal before joining PSV Eindhoven in the Netherlands towards the end of 2002 at age 21. With tireless physical strength and intuitive game sense, he earned the reputation as "a man with two hearts" while playing a critical role in helping PSV reach the semifinals of the 2004–05 UEFA Champions League. He joined Manchester United in England in

CHA BUM-KUN　　　　PARK JI-SUNG　　　　SON HEUNG-MIN

July 2005 and remained with the team for seven years, during which time Park won the Premier League four times and also won the 2007–08 UEFA Champions League.

Son Heung-min is another star Korean soccer player who is writing a new history of Asian players who have entered Europe. While Cha Bum-kun and Park Ji-sung debuted in Europe at age 25 and 21 respectively, Son Heung-min was different from the very beginning. Son joined Hamburger SV's youth academy before making his debut as a pro in Hamburger in 2010 at age 18, and then he transferred to Bayer Leverkusen before joining the Premier League club Tottenham Hotspur in England in 2015. Son Heung-min is breaking the records set by Cha Bum-kun and Park Ji-sung and is treated as a top player worth more than KRW100 billion won. Another noteworthy Korean soccer player is Lee Kang-in, who became the second youngest player when he made his La Liga debut in Spain in 2019 at age 17.

PARK CHAN-HO, RYU HYUN-JIN AND SUN DONG-YUL SHINES IN THE PRO BASEBALL LEAGUES IN THE US AND JAPAN

Korea has produced a number of baseball star players such as Park Chul-soon, Choi Dong-won and Sun Dong-yul since the official Korea pro baseball league began in 1982. In 1994, Park Chan-ho made his professional debut for the Los Angeles Dodgers and became the first Korean baseball player to play in the US Major League. Before Park Chan-ho, there were Choi Dong-won and Sun Dong-yul who either received a scouting offer or signed a contract with an American professional baseball league, but their dreams of making it into the American major league were foiled because of the Korean military service law.

Park began as a starting pitcher for the Los Angeles Dodgers in 1996 and gave great hope to the Korean people who were in distress because of the foreign exchange crisis that hit Korea towards the end of 1997. Park had a record of 124–98 during the 17 years he played in the Major Leagues, which include more than ten victories for five seasons in a row beginning in 1997 when he sported a 160km/

h fastball. Numerous other Korean baseball players attempted to join the Major Leagues after Park Chan-ho, and currently, there are two Koreans who are playing in the Major Leagues: Choo Shin-soo who a right fielder for the Texas Rangers, and Ryu Hyun-jin who is a starting pitcher for the Los Angeles Dodgers.

The first Korean baseball player to join the professional baseball league in Japan was Baek In-cheon, who signed a contract with Toei Flyers in Nippon Professional Baseball in 1962. He gave stellar performances and became a leading pitcher in the Pacific League in 1975 before returning to Korea when the pro baseball league began here. He was followed by Sun Dong-yul, who is considered the "national treasure-level pitcher." Sun became the first Korean baseball player to join a pro Japanese team at age 34 in 1996 and recorded the most saves before retiring. Sun was followed by other players who joined Japanese pro leagues, such as Lee Jong-beom, Lee Seung-yuop, and Lee Dae-ho. Lee Seung-yuop had a record of 41 home runs and 108 RBIs in 2006, and Lee Dae-ho's record includes winning the 2012 Pacific League Best Nine Award for his best RBI record.

"PAK SE-RI KIDS" REIGN OVER THE LPGA FOR MORE THAN TEN YEARS

Pak Se-ri is another Korean sports hero who uplifted Koreans at tumultuous time in the late 1990s when Korea was hit by a foreign exchange crisis. Pak joined the LPGA Tour in 1998 in America, and in the very first year, she triumphed in two majors --- the McDonald's LPGA Championship and U.S. Women's Open --- and captured the LPGA's Rookie of the Year award. Pak went on to win in the Weetabix Women's British Open in 2001 and the McDonald's LPGA championship in 2002 to join the World Golf Hall of Fame in 2007. Inspired by her success, a wave of kids started playing golf, and these so-called "Pak Se-ri kids" completely took over the LPGA beginning in the mid-2000s.

Within a span of 10 years until 2018, Korean golfers recorded 99 wins on the LPGA tour. The overwhelming power of Korean female golfers is clearly revealed when you consider how the United States ranked second with 66 wins during the same period, followed by New Zealand and Japan who tied in third with 15 wins each. During the same period, Korean female golfers accounted for half the players who were top earners as well: Shin Ji-yai became the LPGA tour money leader in 2009; Choi Na-yeon in 2010; and Park In-bee in 2012 and 2013. In 2017, Park Seong-hyun won the LPGA Rookie of the Year award and also became the LPGA's money leader, thereby setting the record for Korean players to become the money leader five times over 10 seasons.

It was in 2006 when the Women's World Golf Rankings, sanctioned by eight women's golf tours and the organizations, was introduced. Shin Ji-yai was the first Korean woman golfer to make it to the ranking in 2010, and she was followed by Park In-bee, Yoo So-

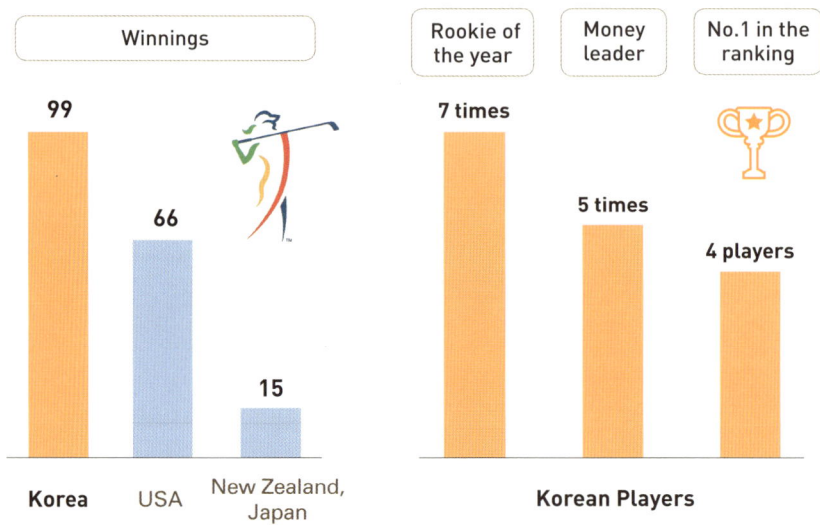

Performance Records of Korean Players in the LPGA for Ten Years Up to 2018

youn and Park Seong-hyun who ranked first as well. When broken down by nationality, Korea ranked first with four top-ranking players, followed by the United States with two, and six other countries including Taiwan, New Zealand and Sweden with only one each.

Korean players have been taking an overwhelming lead in winning the Rookie of the Year award as well. During the span of ten years up to 2018, seven Korean players won the Rookie of the Year Award beginning with Shin Ji-yai in 2009, followed by Seo Hee-kyung, Ryu So-yeon, Kim Sei-young, Chun In-gee, Park Sung-hyun and Ko Jin-young who won the award in 2018. Thanks to their outstanding performance, Korean female golfers took home 20-35% of the total LPGA prize money payout each year, and during the 10-year period, they won over $140 million in prize money. Since there are new Korean golfers with proven records who are following suit, the reign of Korean women golfers is expected to continue for a while.

Korean women golfers Ahn Seok-ju, Chun Mi-jeong and Lee Bo-mi also won the title of money leaders on the LPGA of Japan Tour seven times within a span of nine years since 2010. The top four lowest average round scores in the history of golf in Japan were also recorded by Korean golfers.

THE ORIGIN OF HALLYU, TAEKWONDO EVOLVES BY ADDING MUSIC

Taekwondo is a contemporary creative martial art that originated in Korea. Taekwondo can be considered the origin of hallyu, considering how the World Taekwondo (formerly known as World Taekwondo Federation) headquartered in Seoul has been sending over 3,000 Taekwondo coaches throughout the world and introduced Korea to everyone along with Taekwondo. A Taekwondo exhibition is a presentation that is just as indispensable as a K-pop performance and Korean cuisine tasting in various events intended to introduce Korean culture to foreigners. Taekwondo words and commands such as Charyeot, Sijak, and Jungji, are all in Korean.

Considering that 209 countries are members of the World

Taekwondo as of 2019, it is difficult to find any country in the world where Taekwondo is not taught. In America alone, there are over 10,000 Taekwondo centers where students come not only to build a healthy body but also to discipline themselves both in mind and body. Taekwondo associations have been established in such newly independent countries as East Timor, South Sudan and Kosovo as well as such troubled countries as Afghanistan and Rwanda.

Taekwondo made its debut as a demonstration Olympic sport at the 1988 Seoul Summer Olympic Games and was included as an official sport for the first time at the 2000 Summer Olympics in Sydney. World Taekwondo has been organizing the World Taekwondo Championship every two years since 1973. Korea opened the world's first Taekwondo-specific stadium, Muju Taekwondo-won, in 2014 and used it as the venue for the 23rd World Taekwondo Championship event. The 2017 Muju World Taekwondo Championships that took place in this stadium had 1,763 competitors from 183 countries for the 7-day event.

Taekwondo used to be all about competition, poomsae (form) and breaking, but today, it is evolving into Taekwon dance and other forms of performance by adding music and dance moves to it. It is part of the efforts to reform the original hallyu, Taekwondo, into a new kind of hallyu.

PART 2

STRENGTH AND POWER BEHIND THE MAKING OF A MIRACLE

PASSION FOR EDUCATION AND BRAINPOWER

Education fever is undoubtedly one of biggest drivers behind Korea's rags-to-riches transformation. It is not an overstatement to say that the power that made Korea rise from a destitute stand with a shortage of national resources and become the world's 10th largest economy today came from Koreans' passion for education and learning. Korea has many excellent records in various statistics to prove it: percentage of tertiary education attainment that is higher than advanced countries; the number of students studying overseas; performance at the Mathematical Olympiad and the OECD statistics on educational attainment. Korean students have the world's highest level of mathematics and science skills. Korea faced overcrowded classroom challenges in the past, but as the number of students per teacher keeps going down, the educational environment is also continuously improving.

KOREA RANKS FIRST IN THE WORLD FOR OVER TEN YEARS IN THE TERTIARY EDUCATION ATTAINMENT

Korea has the highest percentage of people who have completed some form of tertiary education out of all advanced countries. Korea boasts a high school and college entrance rate that is higher than countries in Europe, America, and Japan, not to mention developing countries. According to the statistics by the Ministry of Education, 48% of the total population have completed some form of tertiary education as of 2017. When broken down by age group, those between the ages of 24-35 recorded the highest tertiary education at 70%. The number shows a big gap even when compared to the numbers of the United States, England, Japan and France ---

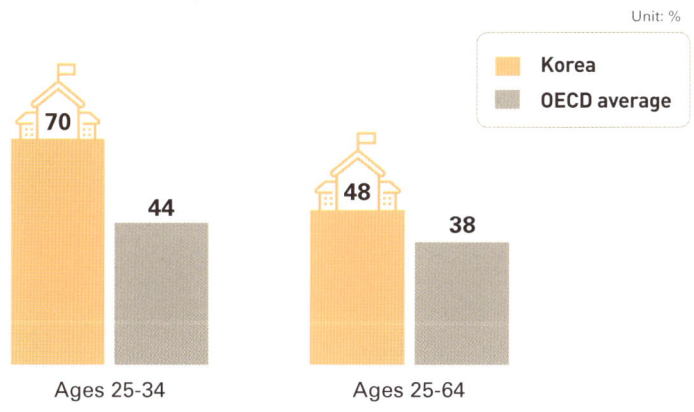

Tertiary Education Attainment by Age Group (2017)

Source: Ministry of Education

countries with relatively good education systems. Korea's tertiary education attainment has been on top since 2008.

In Korea, the percentage of young people with tertiary education has been increasing significantly each year, and this trend is continuing. In 2005, only 51% of the young Korean population turned out to have completed some form of tertiary education, but the number jumped by 19% in just 12 years. This increase is largely credited to the increasing number of students going to college. Of course, quantitative growth alone cannot measure the outcome of higher education. Korea is also facing a limit with regard to lifelong education, which is not up to the level of advanced countries. But it is true that the overall education level of Korea is steadily improving.

KOREA LEADS IN THE INTERNATIONAL MATHEMATICAL OLYMPIAD

The excellence of Korean education is proved by the fact that Korean students rank among the top group each year at the International Mathematical Olympiad (IMO). The first IMO was held in 1959 in Romania, and since then, it has been providing an opportunity for exchanges between mathematicians and mathematically gifted high school students from around the world. Korea has been participating each year since 1988, and Korean students dominated the top scores.

IMO is open for students younger than 20 who have not started university, and the content of the competition includes algebra,

Performance Records of Korean Students at the IMO

Year	Team size			P1	P2	P3	P4	P5	P6	Total	Abs.
	All	M	F								
2017	6	5	1	42	39	1	42	22	24	170	1
2016	6	6		42	41	23	42	33	26	207	2
2015	6	6		42	15	18	42	25	19	161	3
2014	6	6		42	29	23	42	27	9	172	7
2013	6	6		42	38	26	42	36	20	204	2
2012	6	6		42	42	21	39	42	23	209	1

geometry, number theory and functional equations.

At the 58th Mathematical Olympiad that took place in 2017 in Rio de Janeiro, Brazil, all six South Korean students who participated in the competition won gold medals, placing Korea first in the final medal count with 170 points. Korean students have been participating in the IMO for 31 years as of 2017, and 14 out of the 144 participating Korean students received more than two gold medals.

KOREA TOPS IN THE INTERNATIONAL STUDENT ASSESSMENT BY OECD

The mathematics and science skills of Korean students are also proved by the OECD, which evaluates educational systems by measuring students' scholastic performance in mathematics, science and reading. The fact that Korean students excel in the OECD

OECD's PISA 2012 Results by Country

Math			Reading			Science		
Country	Average score	OECD rankings	Country	Average score	OECD rankings	Country	Average score	OECD rankings
Korea	**554**	**1**	Japan	538	1~2	Japan	547	1~3
Japan	536	2~3	**Korea**	**536**	**1~2**	Finland	545	1~3
Switzerland	531	2~3	Finland	524	3~5	Estonia	541	2~4
Netherlands	523	3~7	Ireland	523	3~6	**Korea**	**538**	**2~4**
Estonia	521	4~8	Canada	523	3~6	Poland	526	5~9
Finland	519	4~9	Poland	518	4~9	Canada	525	5~8
Canada	518	5~9	Estonia	516	6~9	Germany	524	5~10

Source: OECD

evaluation despite poor government support for math as a subject can be considered proof of the excellence of Koreans as a people. In the analytic results of the 2012 Program for International Student Assessment (PISA) of about 510,000 students from 65 countries released by the OECD, Korea was among the top group, ranking first in math and second to fourth in science. The average mathematics score of Korean students was 554, which was the highest among OECD member countries. The science score of the Korean students (538) followed Japan (547), Finland (545), and Estonia (541). The average scores of Korean students broken down by subject were 494 in mathematics and 501 in science. In the ranking of all the participating countries including the OECD member countries, Korea ranked third to fifth in math (554), third to fifth in reading

(536), and fifth to eighth in science (538). Korean students excelled in previous PISAs as well.

In 2009, Korean students were among the top group, ranking third to sixth in math (546) and fourth to seventh in science (538). Korean male students demonstrated math skills that were far ahead of the OECD average. The first PISA was carried out in 2000, and the test is conducted every three years by a random sample of 15-year old students around the globe.

In the 2015 PISA test, Korean students excelled in the international "collaborative problem solving" assessment that OECD had added in addition to math. Students from 52 countries competed in the assessment that was designed to evaluate their knowledge, skills, and efforts to solve problems with virtual team members on the computer. In this assessment, Korean students scored an average of 538 points and ranked third to seventh in evaluation categories such as teamwork. For years, Korean education had been criticized for focusing only on the cramming method of teaching instead of developing students' creativity and problem-solving skills, but the PISA results showed that these weaknesses were gradually improving.

KOREA RANKS AMONG THE WORLD'S TOP COUNTRIES IN NATIONAL SCIENCE COMPETITIVENESS

Korea is in the leading group in national science competitiveness as well. In the annual World Competitiveness Yearbook released

The IMD Competitiveness in Science and Technology

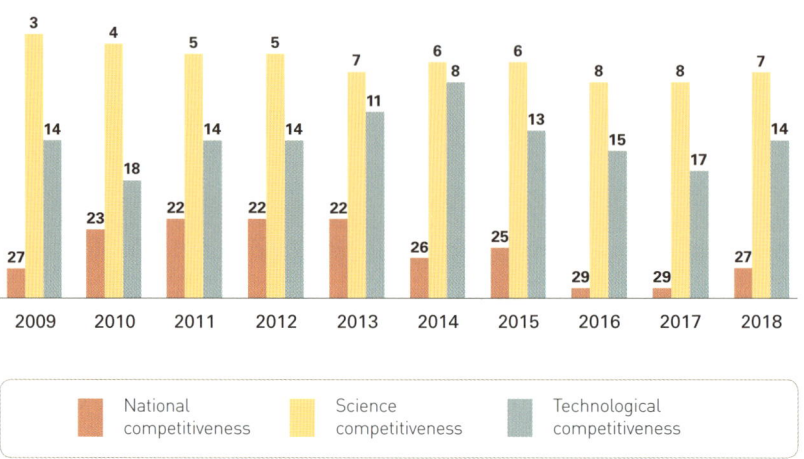

Unit: ranking among the countries reviewed

Source; IMD (The world competitiveness yearbook)

by the Swiss-based International Institute for Management Development (IMD), Korea has remained among the top ten in the science and technology competitiveness category since 2009. IMD analyzes the capacity of over 60 countries and ranks their national competitiveness by country each year and has been releasing the results since 1989. It consists of 20 sub-factors in four key factors and 333 indicators that include national science competitiveness.

In terms of scientific competitiveness, Korea fared well in the investment for R&D, the percentage of R&D investment to GDP, total R&D personnel per capita, number of published science papers, and patent grants. Of course, Korea has weaknesses such as intellectual property rights and security, as well as the legal and systematical environment for the development of science. Satisfaction of researchers, corporate innovation, and cooperation between the industry and the academy also turned out to be in need of further improvement. In the Digital Competitiveness Ranking (DCR) that IMD released for the first time in 2017, Korea ranked rather low at 19th, indicating that close cooperation between the government and public sector is necessary to advance the overall level of science to its highest point.

One concern is the fact that the math and science skills of Korean students are growing less competitive over the years. Their scores in math have been showing a particularly sharp decline. The performance at the International Mathematical Olympiad is not necessarily an accurate indicator of the level of math education. However, the math scores of Korean students, which have been growing farther away from the top group since 2018, calls for a careful look into math education. The decline undeniably reflects the fact that fewer students are up for the challenge of the Olympiad because their performance at the competition is not reflected in their college admission, and also because math education is geared more towards a college entrance exam.

If math skills are shaky, it is difficult to improve national competitiveness through technological innovation. Math skills can also affect the status of the nation when the Fourth Industrial Revolution unfolds in full swing, because new technology developments, such as Big Data and AI, are largely founded upon mathematics and statistics. Therefore, Korea needs to reform the educational environment to ensure Korean students can continue the legacy of their outstanding performance at the Mathematical Olympiad.

DECREASING NUMBER OF STUDENTS PER TEACHER SOLVES THE OVERCROWDED CLASSROOM PROBLEM

Korea's extraordinary passion for education is leading to improvement of school and classroom environments. All Korean baby boomers born between 1946 and 1965 have experienced overcrowded classrooms and they all remember how 60-70 students listened to a teacher while crammed into a small classroom. The seriously overcrowded classroom where a teacher had to deal with dozens of students inevitably took a toll on the quality of education.

Korea used to have a notoriously bad educational environment, but today, it has improved enough to be on a par with that of advanced countries. The overcrowded classroom problem that had plagued Korea since the end of the Korean War up until close to 2000 has been significantly resolved now, and there are statistics that confirm this. According to the "Education at a Glance 2018: OECD Indicators" released by the Ministry of Education and the Korea Education Development Institute, the number of students per teacher in Korea is 16.5 in elementary school, 14.7 in junior high, and 13.8 in high school as of 2016. These numbers show that

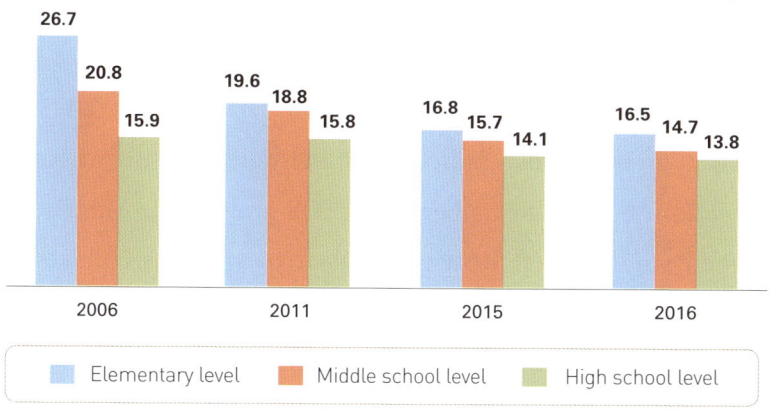

Changing Number of Students per Teacher

Source: Ministry of Education

Korea comes very close to the level of advanced countries because statistically, Korea has an average of only 1.2 more students per teacher that the OECD average.

As recently as 1980, the number of students per teacher was 19.9 in kindergarten, 47.5 in elementary school, 45.1 in middle school, and 33.3 in high school. However, the number of students per classroom is still high: the average number of students in an elementary school classroom is 23.2, and 28.4 in middle schools, which means Korea has up to five students more in a classroom than the OECD average. However, the number of students per classroom and per teacher is expected to decrease to the level of OECD average since the number of students continue to decline as the result of a low birth rate.

OVER 200,000 KOREAN STUDENTS GOING ABROAD TO STUDY EACH YEAR

The number of students going abroad to study advanced knowledge is another indicator of the development of Korean education. For ten years between 2008 and 2017, over 200,000 Korean students left Korea each year to study at colleges and graduate schools overseas. The number has fluctuated slightly up and down each year since 2008 when it recorded 216,867, but it has been steady in general. By country, students going to the United States and China account for about half the total number. But the countries of their choice have been gradually diversifying to include Australia, Japan, the Philippines, Britain, Canada, France, and Germany because of the trend of looking for cultural diversity.

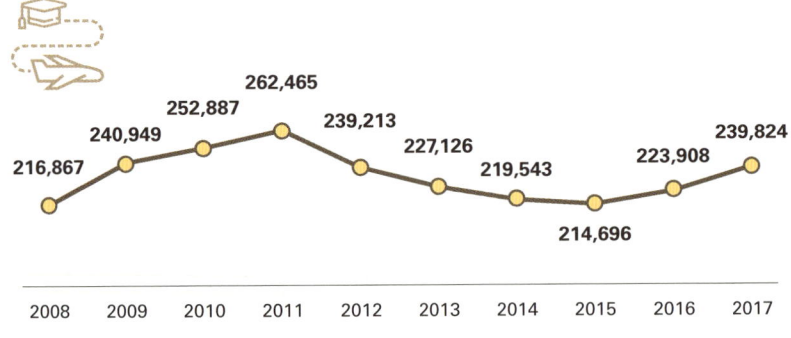

Overview of Korean College Students Studying in Overseas (for degree and training)

2008: 216,867
2009: 240,949
2010: 252,887
2011: 262,465
2012: 239,213
2013: 227,126
2014: 219,543
2015: 214,696
2016: 223,908
2017: 239,824

Source: Ministry of Education

It is noteworthy that the trend of studying abroad is growing more mature. In the past, students from well-to-do families tended to go abroad to study, but now, a growing number of students are going abroad only when they have good reasons to.

That is also the reason the number of students studying abroad starts showing signs of stagnation after a rapid increase. It is a phenomenon resulting from the realization that studying abroad does not guarantee a successful future, but it also results from a growing number of students who choose practical interests. Another factor that contributed to this changing trend is the environment in which students have access to a wide variety of channels such as the internet, social media and YouTube through which they can learn.

People's changing attitude about studying abroad is also helping to eliminate its negative effects such as the students who flee abroad under the pretense of studying, or families sending their kids abroad while they are too young. Eventually, a virtuous cycle is created, where outstanding students who must study abroad go abroad to study, learn advanced knowledge, and return to Korea to contribute to the academic and industrial development of Korea, and eventually contributing to Korea's educational development as well.

KOREA PRODUCES THE MOST WINNERS IN THE WORLDSKILLS COMPETITION

Korea's performance in the WorldSkills Competition (WSC) is

Rankings of the WorldSkills Competition by Year

Year	1st Place	2nd Place	3rd Place
1975	Switzerland	Korea	Spain
1977	Korea	West Germany	Japan
1978	Korea	Japan	Switzerland
1979	Korea	Japan	Switzerland
1981	Korea	Japan	Switzerland
1983	Korea	Taiwan	Austria
1985	Korea	Japan	Switzerland
1988	Korea	Japan	Taiwan
1989	Korea	Taiwan	Austria
1991	Korea	Japan	Austria
1993	Taiwan	Korea	Japan
1995	Korea	Taiwan	Germany
1997	Korea	Switzerland	Taiwan
1999	Korea	Taiwan	Japan
2001	Korea	Germany	Japan
2003	Korea	Switzerland	Japan
2005	Switzerland	Korea	Germany
2007	Korea	Japan	Switzerland
2009	Korea	Switzerland	Japan
2011	Korea	Japan	Switzerland
2013	Korea	Switzerland	Taiwan
2015	Korea	Brazil	China
2017	China	Korea	Switzerland

setting the country apart from countries around the world. WSC started in 1947 as a small regional competition in Spain, but it was in 1950 that the competition was held as an international event. Later on, WorldSkills International (WSI) was established in 1954, and a growing number of countries started participating in the competition. WSC has been held biennially since 1973.

At a time when Korea was in desperate need of developed industrial competitiveness to support the government's ambitious 5-year Economic Development Plan, Korea participated for the first time in the 16th WorldSkills Competition that was held in 1967 in Madrid, Spain. In the following competition, Korea ranked third in the final scores and stunned the world. Then in 1977, Korea became the overall winner of the competition for the first time in ten years and has been in the lead ever since in every competition including winning nine times in a row.

At the 44th competition that took place in Abu Dhabi, UAE, in 2017, the Korean team came second on medal points with 8 golds, 8 silvers, and 8 bronzes. Korea came second after China, which won with 281 points, because Korea earned 279 points when final point scores were counted based on the average points, number of competitors, number of medals, and medallion for excellence released by WSI. But that doesn't mean there is a big difference in the skills between the two countries, because China's victory was largely credited to the heavy investment the Chinese government put forward in preparation for the upcoming 2021 competition in

Shanghai. Korea is rewarding winners with medals and prizes, but the competition is not conjuring as much interest as before. The Korean government should make investments suitable for a country that has won the most in the international skills Olympics if Korea is to keep its reputation as the manufacturing power in the international community.

RAPIDLY INCREASING PRIVATE SECTOR INVESTMENT IN EDUCATION

Korea's education fever is leading to proactive investment in education. Korea has a very high percentage of expenditure on education to GDP ratio. According to the "Education at a Glance 2018: OECD Indicators," total government expenditure on primary to tertiary education was 5.8% in Korea as of 2015, which was 0.8% higher than the OECD average of 5.0%. Koreans were spending $11,143 per student for primary to tertiary education, which was also $500 more than the OECD average of $10,520. Expenditure on tertiary education alone was also slightly higher than the OECD average as well. The problem is that, while the investment in tertiary education is increasing in the private sector, investment from the government has remained at a stalemate. When the Korean government's expenditure on primary to tertiary education was broken down, 87.1% of the total expenditure was for primary schools, and the expenditure on tertiary education was only 36.1%. In the case of the other OECD member countries, their average government

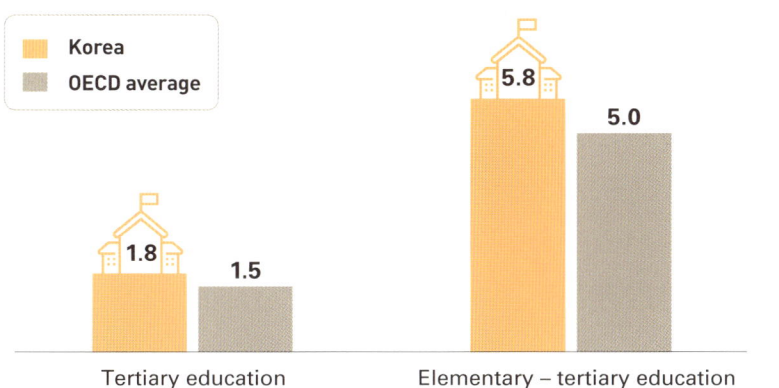

Overview of the Expenditure on Education as a Percentage of GDP

Unit: %

- Korea
- OECD average

Tertiary education: 1.8 / 1.5
Elementary – tertiary education: 5.8 / 5.0

Source: Ministry of education

expenditure on tertiary education was as high as 66.0%.

In Korea, however, the expenditure on education per student is on a steady rise each year. If this trend continues, Korea's expenditure on education is likely to reach the level of advanced countries. This can be expected from the increasing percentage of Koreans with tertiary education. As of 2017, the percentage of Koreans with tertiary attainment among 25-64-year-olds was 48%, which was 10% higher than the OECD average of 38%.

The percentage of tertiary attainment among 25-34-year-olds was 70%, and it has remained the highest among OECD member countries for ten years. As a result, the percentage of children with a higher education level than their parents was also higher than the OECD average. The government budget for education is also on a continuous rise, recording KRW70 trillion in 2019.

RESEARCH AND DEVELOPMENT, THE FOUNDATION OF INNOVATION

National development doesn't happen without a strong desire for change and innovation. Development is possible only if the country has people who dream of a tomorrow that is better than today. Innovation and change don't happen on their own: It is difficult to make anything happen unless there is tireless effort.

The Republic of Korea was one of the poorest countries on Earth when it became independent from Japanese colonial rule, but today, it stands tall and strong as a manufacturing powerhouse. It is not an overstatement to say that Korea is what it is today because there were changes and innovations that fed on the Korean people's strong desire for prosperity. Koreans have been pouring tremendous effort into various fields, such as investing more money in research and development than any other, and applying and acquiring just as many patents, international intellectual property rights and trademarks as any advanced countries like the United States, Japan and Germany. Countless academic papers and patents associated with the Fourth

Industrial Revolution technology are another good example of Korea's innovation capability.

WORLD'S HIGHEST R&D EXPENDITURE TO GDP RATIO

A country's foundation for innovation and growth is determined by how much money the country invests in R&D. The R&D expenditure ratio is an important indicator of how much a country has invested in R&D for a year. With that indicator, one can get a good picture of the national level effort for technological innovation, not to mention the investment trend by sector.

Korea leads the world in terms of the ratio of research and development (R&D) spending to gross domestic product (GDP). According to the OECD economic surveys of 2015, Korea tops the ranking in the total R&D to GDP spending ratio at 4.2%, followed by Japan at 3.3%, Germany at 2.9% and the US at 2.8%. Korea's R&D spending was only 2% of the GDP in 2000 but the percentage kept growing until it reached 4.24% in 2016. By sector, Korean companies recorded a ratio of 3.29%, followed by the government and higher education institutions that recorded 0.56% and 0.39% respectively. In 2000, R&D expenditure by company was only 1.6% of the GDP, but the percentage is continuously growing because large companies such as Samsung Electronics and Hyundai Motors have been spending more on R&D. In particular, Samsung Electronics ranks second among companies around the world in its

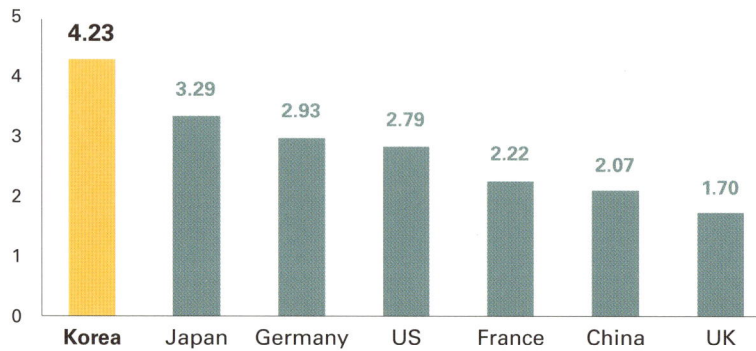

total amount of research and development spending. This trend is likely to continue because, in the age of the Fourth Industrialization Revolution, competitiveness among companies over the latest technology is expected to grow fiercer than ever.

Of course, these statistics are based on the percentage of the national GDP, and there is a wide gap between Korea and big countries such as the United States and China where the absolute amount of R&D expenditure is concerned. In the case of Korea, the total amount of R&D expenditure is about KRW70 trillion won, which is only about one fifth of China's. Korea is continuously increasing expenditure on R&D but still, Korea needs to invest more in research and development if Korea is determined to grow into a technology powerhouse. Korea also needs to become more conscious about improving investment efficiency. In order to become a technologically advanced country, it is necessary for Korea to upgrade the level of research and development itself as well.

KOREA RANKS FOURTH IN THE WORLD AFTER THE US AND JAPAN IN PATENTS APPLICATIONS

The number of patent applications is another indicator of a nation's innovation effort. Korea has been showing a continuously growing number of patent applications since it reached the 100,000 mark in 2000. Since then, the number kept increasing by the thousands and sometimes tens of thousands a year until it reached 200,000 in 2014.

According to the World Intellectual Property Indicators 2017 released by the World Intellectual Property Organization (WIPO), Korea ranked fourth in the world with the number of patent applications standing at 208,330 as of the end of 2016. China ranked first at 1.34 million, showing a big gap between then and the United States, which ranked third at 606,000, and Japan at 318,000. Even though Korea ranked fourth in terms of the number alone, Korea is a leader in patent application in terms of the ratio of patent application to the population and GDP, and it is far ahead of advanced countries such as the United States, Japan and German.

China stands out in international patent applications, but Korea is also among the top group. An analysis of the applications filed under

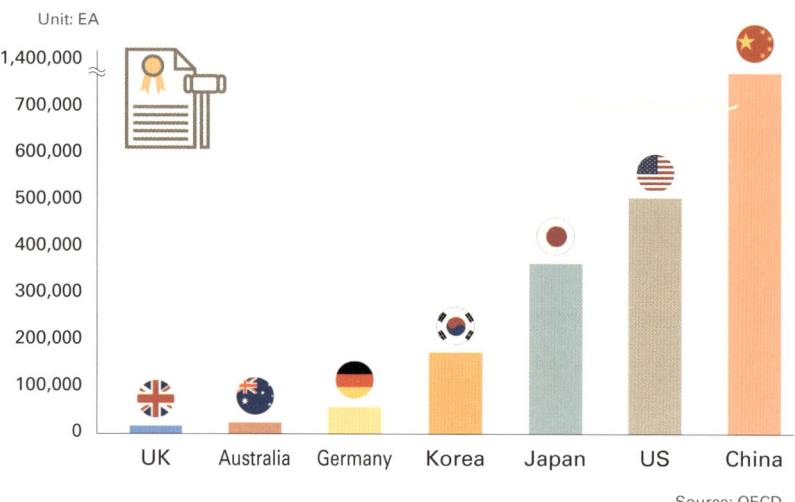

Number of Patent Applications of Major OECD Member Countries

Source: OECD

WIPO's Patent Cooperation Treaty (PCT) in 2017 shows that the United States remains a long-time leader and was followed by China, Japan, Germany and Korea. The record shows that inventors from Korea filed 15,763 international patent applications, which is a 1.3% increase from the previous year.

It is worth noting that the patent applications were heavily concentrated in areas that are associated with the Fourth Industrial Revolution. Analysis of the number of domestic patent applications filed with the Korea Institute of Intellectual Property (KIIP) between 2008 and 2017 showed that patents related to areas of the Fourth Industrial Revolution recorded an annual average 8.7% increase, which exceeds the overall annual average of 1.3% during the same period by a big margin. This spike is believed to be the result of a large number of patents in the areas of artificial intelligence (AI), internet of things (IoI), big data, and autonomous vehicles. Analysis also revealed that Samsung Electronics, Electronics and Telecommunications Research Institute (ETRI), LG Electronics, Hyundai Motor and other large companies and research institutes took the lead in patent applications in the areas of Fourth Industrial Revolution technology.

KOREA SCORES 28.31 OUT OF 35 ON THE GLOBAL INTELLECTUAL PROPERTY INDEX

The Global Intellectual Property Center (GIPC) of the U.S. Chamber of Commerce releases the "Global IP Index" each year by assessing and ranking 45 countries that represent roughly 90% of the global GDP based on 35 indicators under six broad categories. In the 2017 Global IP Index released by GIPC, Korea scored 28.31 out of the total score of 35 and ranked ninth in the world. This was one rank up from 2016. Even though Korea is not the top, being one of the top ten signifies that Korea has a high level of intellectual properties. In comparison, the United States topped the ranking at 32.62, followed by Britain (32.39), Germany (31.92), and Japan (31.29). China ranked 27th at 14.83, and Venezuela ranked last at 6.88.

The Global IP Index shows how a country is protecting its unique

Ranking of the Global Intellectual Property Index

Unit: points, 2017, 45 countries

Ranking	Country	Total scores	Ranking	Country	Total scores
1	USA	32.63	8	Singapore	28.62
2	UK	32.39	9	Korea	28.31
3	Germany	31.92	10	Italy	27.73
4	Japan	31.29	11	Spain	27.48
5	Sweden	30.99	12	Australia	27.07
6	France	30.87	13	Hungary	25.39
7	Switzerland	29.86	27	China	14.83

Perfect score: 35

Source: 2017 GIPC Index

technology and promotes the development of innovative technology. The evaluated indicators include patent and copyright terms of protection, patentability requirements, scope of limitations and exceptions to copyrights and related rights, protection of trade secrets, barriers to market access, digital/online piracy rates, legal measures that provide necessary exclusive rights that prevent infringement of copyrights and related rights, and membership in and ratification of international treaties. It also evaluates the legal measures available that provide necessary exclusive rights to redress unauthorized uses of trademarks, industrial design rights, regulatory and administrative barriers to the commercialization of intellectual property assets, and transparency and public reporting by customs authorities of trade-related intellectual property infringement. It practically covers everything that is related to intellectual property.

WORLD'S HIGHEST LEVEL OF ENFORCEMENT AND PROTECTION OF TRADEMARK-RELATED RIGHTS

Of all the intellectual property assets, Korea came in first place in the protection of trademarks. According to GIPC, Korea was tops in the protection of trademarks and related rights by receiving 6.55 total points out of 7. Korea has been leading in this category, which proves that Korea has the highest level of protection and enforcement for trademarks and related rights.

The scores of indicators in the trademark category are based on analysis of the terms of protection, limitations on the use of brands on packaging, protection of well-known marks and the framework against online sale of counterfeit goods, among many others. Enforcement mechanisms have been growing stronger in response to the increasing added value of the designs of new products. Korea has

Ranking of Trademarks

Unit: points

Ranking	Country	Score	Ranking	Country	Score
1	Korea	**6.55**	8	Spain	5.75
2	Switzerland	6.50		Italy	
	Sweden		10	France	5.50
	Germany		11	Singapore	5.35
5	USA	6.35	12	Canada	4.90
6	Japan	6.30	13	New Zealand	4.85
7	UK	6.00	33	China	3.90

Perfect score: 7

Source: 2017 GIPC Index

also been strengthening the protection of design-related intellectual property rights in response to the level of design skills that keeps going up to meet the demands of Korean consumers whose tastes have been leaning towards the luxurious. The same trend can be witnessed in advanced countries as well.

CONTINUOUS IMPROVEMENT OF COPYRIGHT AND PATENT RIGHTS ENVIRONMENT

Compared to trademark rights, Korea received lower scores in the copyright and patent rights categories, even though in the copyright category, Korea remains among the top five. Korea received the highest scores in: enforcement, which provides necessary exclusive rights to prevent infringement of copyrights and related rights; availability of frameworks that promote cooperative action against online piracy; and digital rights management legislation. Korea also received high scores in the clear implementation of policies and guidelines requiring that any proprietary software used on government ICT systems should be licensed software, in addition to the terms, limitations, and exceptions of copyrights.

Overall scores of indicators in the patent category were relatively low, but the situation is improving as attested to by some indicators that received perfect scores. Korea is on a par with advanced countries such as England, Switzerland, Sweden, Germany and France in patent term of protection; patentability of computer-implemented

Ranking of Copyrights

Unit: points

Ranking	Country	Score	Ranking	Country	Score
1	USA	6.00	8	Australia	4.88
2	UK	5.63	9	Japan	4.53
3	Germany	5.38	10	Sweden	3.85
4	Singapore	5.24	11	Malaysia	3.78
5	Korea	4.99	12	Italy	3.66
5	France	4.99	13	Hungry and 4 others	3.38
7	New Zealand	4.91	22	China	2.28

Perfect score: 6   Source: 2017 GIPC Index

inventions; the use of compulsory licensing of patented products and technologies; and patent term extensions for pharmaceutical products. Korea is expected to move up to the top group in this category by improving scores of indicators that received low scores, such as the pharmaceutical-related patent enforcement and resolution mechanism and the regulatory data protection term.

KOREA IS THE LEADER IN THE BLOOMBERG RANKING OF INNOVATIVE COUNTRIES OF THE WORLD

Bloomberg News analyzes and ranks innovation by country by evaluating dozens of criteria using seven metrics, including a country's R&D spending as a percentage of their GDP, manufacturing value-added, productivity, high-tech dentistry, tertiary efficiency, researcher concentration, and patent applications. In the

Ranking of the World's Most Innovative Countries 2019

Unit: points, 60 countries

Ranking	Country	Total scores	Ranking	Country	Total scores
1	Korea	87.38	6	Singapore	84.49
2	Germany	87.30	7	Sweden	84.15
3	Finland	85.57	8	USA	83.21
4	Switzerland	85.49	9	Japan	81.96
5	Israel	84.78	10	France	81.67

Source: Bloomberg (2019 Bloomberg Innovation Index)

2019 Bloomberg Innovation Index, Korea took first place with an 87.38 score. That means Korea ranked top in the innovation index for six years in a row. Korea was among the top group in the rankings in most metrics except patent activity (20th) and productivity (18th).

The area where Korea stood out most was the spending as a percentage of GDP on R&D intensity. Korea ranked second in both R&D expenditure and manufacturing value-added metrics. Korea ranked fourth in the high-tech companies indicator, and ranked seventh in both the rate of admission to tertiary education and the number of research personnel. But Korea's score in productivity was relatively lower than in other areas. The productivity score is calculated by dividing the GDP by the population in the labor force over the age of 15, and Korea scored the lowest in the service industry in this category.

Germany ranked second with 87.30 points, followed by Finland at 85.57 points. Other countries that made it to the top 10 included Switzerland, Israel, Singapore, Sweden, the United States, Japan, and France. Korea scored slightly less than in 2018 when Korea ranked first with 89.28. Korea is among the leading group in other indexes such as the Global Innovation Index released by the World Intellectual Property Institute (WIPO) as well, and it is largely because Korea scores high in the population with tertiary education and research and development expenditure. The problem is, Korea is not getting enough results from the significant resources that it is putting into innovation. This is largely because of the lack of quality investment. The challenge that faces Korea is to advance the level of research and development so that Korea can get real results.

PERFORMANCE OF KOREA'S LEADING SCIENTISTS ASTONISHES THE WORLD

In the field of science, Korea has not yet produced Nobel Prize winners, but there are a few who have outstanding research achievements. According to a report released by the National Research Foundation of Korea (NRF) in September 2018, there were at least six Korean scientists whose research performance is equivalent to the level of Nobel Prize winners. It was based on the analysis of the number of citations per paper, research productivity and the impact index. According to NRF, an analysis of papers registered in Elsevier's abstract and citation database, Scopus, between 1960-2018,

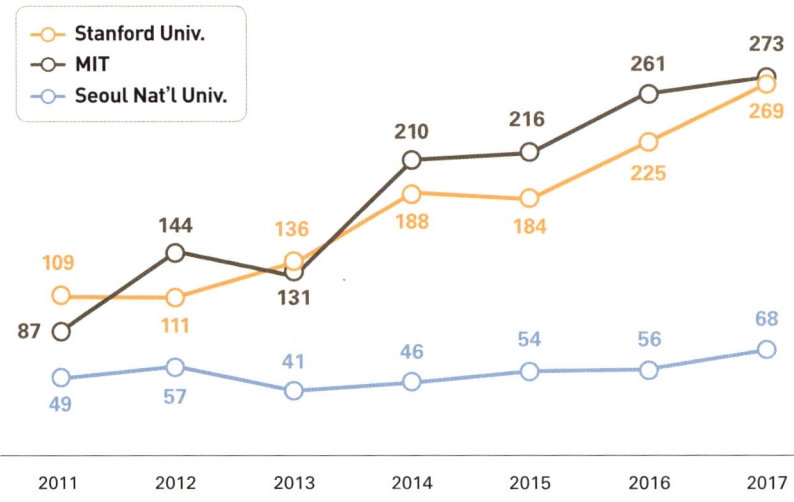

showed that there were six Korean scientists whose papers were cited more than the average of the Nobel Prize winners in the last ten years. There were three additional researchers who were likely to join the list within the next three years as well.

In the field of physics, those scientists included: Philip Kim, a professor at Harvard who is known for his study of quantum transport in carbon nano-tubes; Lee Young-hee, a professor at Sungkyunkwan University and a physicist; and Cheong Sang-wook, a professor at Rutgers University known for his study of enhanced physical functionalities in complex materials. In the field of chemistry, they included: Hyeon Taeg-hwan who pioneered work in chemical synthesis of uniformly sized nano-crystals; and Kim Kwang-soo, a professor at Ulsan National Institute of Science and Technology (UNIST) who developed the technology for the positive and negative electrodes for lithium-based secondary batteries. In the field of physiology, Lee Seo-goo, a professor at Yonsei University, was included for the impact of his discovery of phospholipase involved in the physiological function of eukaryotic cells and its role and functions. Of course, the analysis of NRF is not the criteria for a Nobel Prize. But the fact that Korea produced such internationally acknowledged scientists in the field of science which used to be near barren within such a short time can be explained as the fruit of Korea's passion for education.

KOREA RANKS SECOND IN THE WORLD IN THE WORLD BANK'S HUMAN CAPITAL INDEX

The World Bank published the first edition of the Human Capital Index in October 2008. It is an index that shows how well children born now can realize their potential as productive members of society in scores. In this index, Korea was second only to Singapore among 157 countries, and it means Korean children have good potential for future productivity. Korea's human capital index score was 0.84, which was 0.04 less than Singapore, which ranked first. The closer the score is to 1, the higher the potential of future productivity is.

The HCI has three components: survival as measured by the rate of mortality under the age of 5; expected years of quality-adjusted school, which combined information on the length of education and the level of school performance; and health environment, which measured the survival rate of adults up to the age of 60 and the rate of stunting for children under the age of 5.

According to the World Bank, the children in Korea had 100% of chance to survive until the age of 5 and expected to be in school for 13.6 years. The rate of 15-year old children to survive until the age of 60 was relatively high at 94%. Korea was followed by Japan, Hong Kong, Finland, Ireland, Australia, Sweden, Netherlands, and Canada. The United States ranked 24th, and China, 46th. The country with the lowest score was Chad in Africa at 0.29.

However, in the Global Talent Competitiveness Index (GTCI) that is released at the annual World Economic Forum Annual Meeting, Korea ranks between 20th and 30th. When the index was first released in 2014, Korea ranked 29th, but it dropped to 37th when it was released based on the two years between 2015 and 2016. Korea moved up the rank to 29th in 2017, but it dropped again to 30th in 2018, and remained at the same place in 2019. Countries that belong to the top group include Switzerland, Singapore, the United States, Norway, and Sweden. The GTCI comprehensively indicates the competitiveness of human resources, including what countries are doing to attract, grow and retain talent. It evaluates and indexes 48 indicators in six pillars including research and development,

World Bank Human Capital Index Top 10 Countries

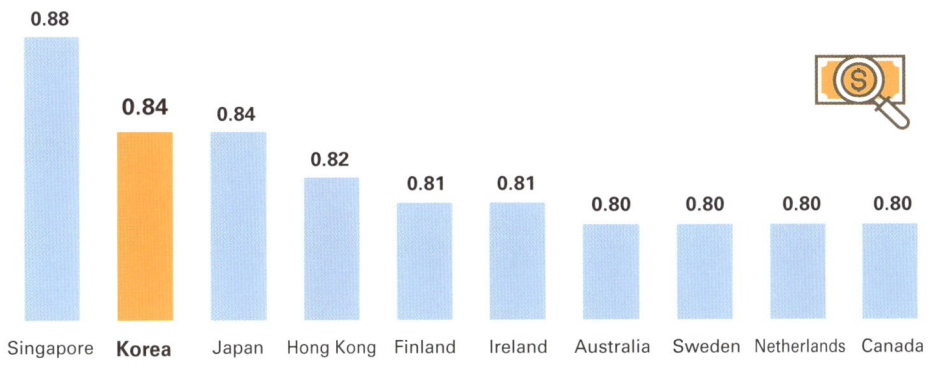

Source: World Bank

tertiary education, flexibility of labor market, and opportunity for women's entrepreneurship. Korea is in the leading group in the IT communication technology infrastructure, but Korea scored very low in management-labor cooperation, income gap between men and women, and women's leadership opportunities. In order to increase the competitiveness of human resources, Korea needs to push forward with a big shift in policy.

KOREA AMONG THE TOP TEN IN FOURTH INDUSTRIAL REVOLUTION-RELATED ACADEMIC PAPERS

It is necessary to pay attention to the number of papers related to new industries as an indicator of a country's innovation capacity. Unfortunately, Korea is falling slightly behind major competitors

Top 5 Companies in the AI Patent Applications

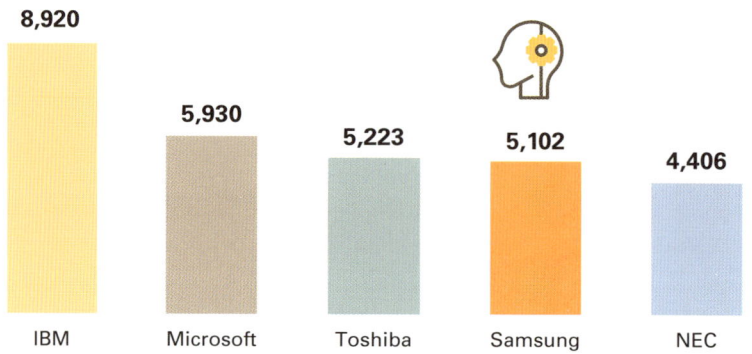

Source: World Intellectual Property Organization (WIPO)

such as the US and China in its capability for core technology research --- such as artificial intelligence (AI) and big data ---- that will lead the Fourth Industrial Revolution. According to the report by Science and Technology Policy Institute (STEPI) that Maeil Business Newspaper obtained, Korea ranked tenth, third, sixth, seventh, eighth, fifth and fourth in the number of papers in seven areas of artificial intelligence, internet of things (IoT), 3D printing, big data, cloud computing, robots, and autonomous vehicles, respectively. These rankings were based on the papers registered in the Scopus database between 2012 and 2017.

However, the gap between Korea and the United States and China was significant in the quality of the papers. In particular, Korea's Field Weighted Citation Impact (FWCI) score in the area of robots was only 0.85, which was less than the 1.0 average score of all countries. Korea's score in artificial intelligence was also only 0.88. In the case of the United States, the FWCI score in the area of artificial intelligence was 1.71. However, Korea scored high in the competitiveness of Korean companies in the areas related to the Fourth Industrial Revolution. WIPI released "Tech Trends – Artificial Intelligence related Technologies" in February 2019, where Samsung ranked fourth with 5,102 AI patent applications. The US-based IBM ranked first with 8,290 AI patent applications followed by U.S.-based Microsoft Corp. with 5,930, Japan-based Toshiba Corp. with 5,223, and Japan-based NEC Group ranked fifth with 4,406 applications.

KOREAN COMPANIES SELECTED TO BE ON FORBES' WORLD'S 100 MOST INNOVATIVE COMPANIES LIST

The US business magazine Forbes announces the "the World's Most Innovative Companies" each year. In 2018, four Korean companies made it to the list including Naver, which ranked 9th. Naver was among the top 10 for two consecutive years, ranking 9th among 100 companies. Naver had ranked only 53rd in 2014 but made a vertical rise afterward until it ranked 21st in 2015, 13th in 2016 and 9th in 2017. Naver received high marks on having continuously created new technology and services.

Never was followed by a bio company Celltrion which ranked

Innovative Companies as Selected by the US-based Magazine Forbes

Ranking	Company
1	ServiceNow
2	Workday
3	SalesForce
4	Tesla
5	Amazon
6	Netflix
7	Insight
8	Hindustan Unilever
9	Naver
10	Facebook
14	Celltrion
18	AmorePacific
27	LG Household & Health Care

*As of 2018

Source: Forbes

14th, Amore Pacific which ranked 18th, and LG Household & Healthcare, 27th. American companies, of course, took over the top spots. The US-based cloud computing company Service Now topped the ranking, followed by Workday, a cloud-based financial management and human capital management software vendor. Other US companies that ranked from third to fifth were Salesforce, Tesla, and Amazon. The number of innovative Korean company is not small considering the size of the national economy, but Korea needs to increase the number through continuous research and development.

A LONG HISTORY AND TRADITION REFLECTED IN THE WORLD'S CULTURAL HERITAGE

National competitiveness is not built overnight. It is the fruit that is borne only after enduring and overcoming numerous challenges and hardships over a long period of time. The longer the history of a country is, the more traces of having overcome hardships and challenges, and these traces are fully reflected in the country's cultural heritage. Korea being a country with a 5,000-year history, there are many cultural heritage and assets that Korea can boast to the world. It is not too much to say that the power that allowed Korea to grow into the world's 12th largest economy in just seventy years and to realize democratization in such a short time despite little land and population came from its history, tradition, and outstanding cultural heritage that is acknowledged by the world.

EACH YEAR AT LEAST ONE CULTURAL ASSET IS REGISTERED AS WORLD CULTURAL HERITAGE

In November 2018, UNESCO registered Korea's traditional wrestling, ssireum, on the list of Intangible Cultural Heritage of Humanity after South and North Korea submitted the bid separately then decided to combine their bids. This became the first case where a cultural asset from two Koreas was jointly listed. Korea listed three cultural heritages on the UNESCO cultural heritage for the first time in 1995: Jongmyo Shrine, Seokguram Grotto and Bulguksa Temple and Haeinsa Temple Janggyeong Panjeon (the Depositories for the Tripitaka Koreana Woodblocks). Two years later, Changdeokgung Palace Complex and Hwaseong Fortress were listed as part of world heritage, and the Veritable Records of the Joseon Dynasty and the Hunminjeongeum manuscript were listed on the UNESCO's Memory of the World registry. In 2001, Seungjeongwon Ilgi (the Diaries of the Royal Secretariat) and Jikji Simche Yojeol (Anthology of Great Buddhist Priests' Zen Teachings) were registered on the list of Memory of the World registry, and the royal ancestral ritual in the Jongmyo shrine and its music were registered on the list of Intangible Cultural Heritage of Humanity. Since 2010, at least one Korean cultural asset has been registered on the UNESCO list each year, making Korea acknowledged in the international community as a country with a rich culture.

UNESCO is classifying world heritage into three types. First,

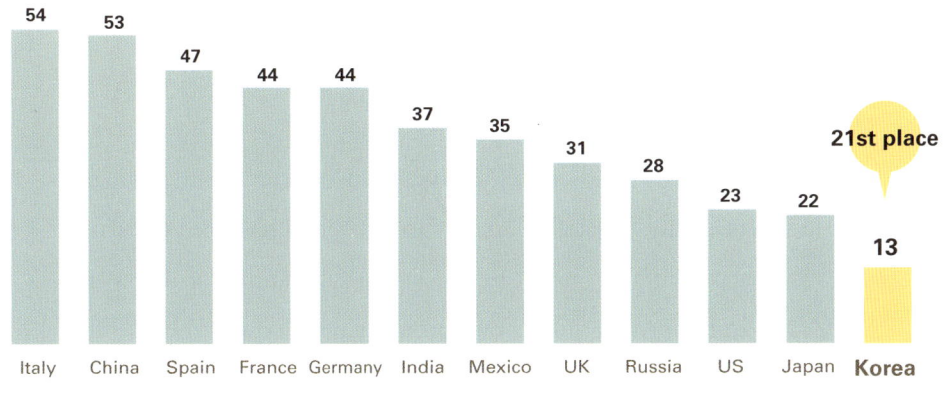

there is "a World Heritage Site" which is a landmark or area which is selected by the UNESCO as having cultural, historical, scientific or other form of significance and is legally protected by the Convention concerning the Protection of the World Cultural and Natural Heritage. The second is the intangible cultural heritage protected by the Convention on the Protection and Promotion of the Diversity of Cultural Expressions. It was created in 2005, and the previous list of oral and intangible heritage of humanity was incorporated into this. Lastly, there is the Memory of the World, which is a program established by UNESCO instead of international treaties such as in the case of a world heritage site and intangible cultural heritage. Korea has a total 48 heritage sites on the UNESCO lists: 12 on the list of UNESCO World Heritage Sites, 16 on the list of the UNESCO Memory of the World, and 20 on the list of the UNESCO Intangible Cultural Heritage of Humanity. Quantitatively, Korea falls short of those from advanced countries such as in Europe, but Korea has more heritages listed with UNESCO than the overall global average.

Korea joined UNESCO's "Convention on the Protection of World Cultural and Natural Heritage" in 1988 and has been carrying out various projects to promote the excellence and originality of Korea's cultural properties to the international community. This is because the world cultural heritage can not only be utilized as a tourism resource but also contributes to raising national trustworthiness.

OVER 170,000 KOREAN CULTURAL ASSETS SCATTERED OVERSEAS

Unfortunately, many Korean cultural assets are scattered across the world. According to the Overseas Korean Cultural Heritage Foundation, 172,316 Korean cultural properties are scattered in 20 countries as of April 2018. By country, Japan accounted for 43.4% of the total with 74,442, followed by the United States with 46,488 (27 percent). There are other, not insignificant numbers of Korean cultural properties in the possession of China, Britain, Germany, and Russia as well.

The Cultural Heritage Administration and the Overseas Korean Cultural Heritage Foundation are trying to bring these cultural assets

Source: Overseas Korean Cultural Heritage Foundation

back to Korea through various channels by working with foreign investigation agencies and owners of those cultural properties.

Their efforts resulted in the returning of 46 Korean cultural assets from overseas in 2015, including an epitaph tablet from the grave of a Joseon-era scholar named Yi Seon-je and a garment belonging to Princess Deokhye, daughter of King Gojong.

But the process of bringing them back is not easy. It requires effort to convince their owners, and it also requires a budget when they have to be purchased instead of being donated. Cooperation of investigation agencies in other countries is also necessary to confirm the source. Finding documents to prove they were illegally taken out of Korea is not a simple job either. But regardless of these difficulties, many Korean cultural assets are coming back to Korea each year. Locating cultural properties that are in foreign countries but not yet discovered is also just as important as bringing back the located ones.

KOREA PUBLISHES THE WORLD'S 10TH LARGEST VOLUME OF BOOKS

Of the books released each year, two economic superpowers, the United States and China, publish almost half of the total. According to the International Publishers Association (IPA), the world's

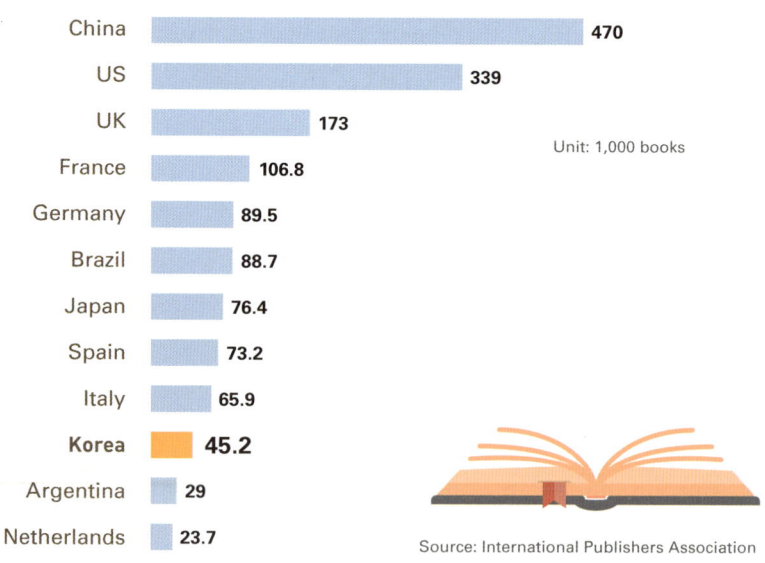

Ranking of the World's Book Publishing by Country

Country	Value
China	470
US	339
UK	173
France	106.8
Germany	89.5
Brazil	88.7
Japan	76.4
Spain	73.2
Italy	65.9
Korea	45.2
Argentina	29
Netherlands	23.7

Unit: 1,000 books

Source: International Publishers Association

publishers collectively put out over 1.6 million books in 2015, out of which 470,000 books were published by China, and 339,000 by the United States, making these two countries first and second in the world in terms of the volume of published books. By percentage, China published 28% of the total, and the US, 20%.

Korea ranked 10th after Britain, France, Germany, Brazil, Japan, Spain and Italy. It is not a bad record considering Korea has a short history of book publishing and a relatively small population. Korea is putting out over 40,000 books a year. It doesn't make Korea a powerhouse in the global book market, but Korea belongs to the upper middle group in the ranking at least. With the declining demand for paper books, it is difficult to get an accurate idea of how much people are reading, but Korean publishers have continued producing books on diverse subjects. This robust publishing culture may very well reflect Koreans' tradition of having high regard for humanities subjects.

KOREA RANKS FIFTH AMONG OECD COUNTRIES IN THE CIRCULATION OF PAID DAILY NEWSPAPERS

Overall print newspaper circulation worldwide continues to decline. But in Korea, the circulation of print newspapers remains relatively high compared to other countries. Even though it is old data, a survey of daily newspaper circulation figures of OECD countries based on 2008 data shows that Korea ranked fifth in the

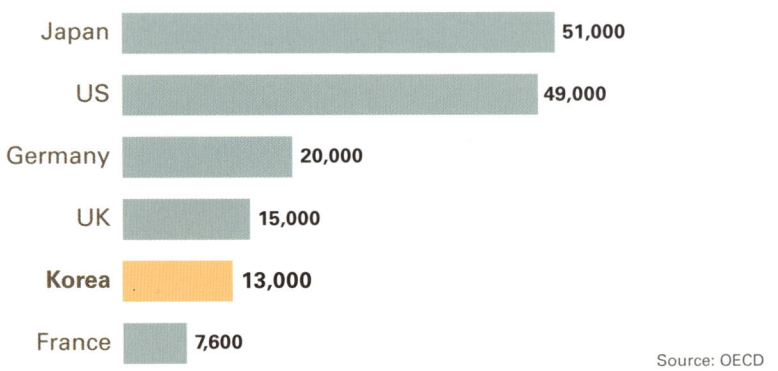

Highest Newspaper Circulation in OECD

Unit: 1,000 copies

- Japan: 51,000
- US: 49,000
- Germany: 20,000
- UK: 15,000
- Korea: 13,000
- France: 7,600

Source: OECD

circulation of paid daily newspapers after Japan, the U.S., Germany and the U.K. By newspaper, the top group was dominated by Japanese newspapers such as Yomiuri Shimbun which ranked first in terms of daily circulation of newspapers among the OECD countries.

In the World Press Trends Report 2012, Korea ranked sixth in terms of the average number of copies printed per 1,000 people after Norway, Japan, Finland, Sweden and Hong Kong. There were only seven countries including Switzerland that recorded more than 300 copies printed per 1,000 people. However, the subscription rate is relatively low compared to the number of circulations in Korea. It is largely because of growing access to the internet. This trend is expected to continue as readers are shifting to mobile news channels. However, that doesn't mean the power of the press is weakening, because the number of people consuming news either in print newspaper or mobile format is continuously growing.

KOREANS READ BOOKS MORE THAN THE AVERAGE OF MAJOR EUROPEAN COUNTRIES

The Korean government released a report on the reading rate of Koreans as compared to OECD and EU countries. It was based on the surveys by OECD's Program for the International Assessment of Adult Competencies (PIAAC), which is a program of assessment and analysis of adult skills. In this report, Koreans' reading rate --- including reading ebooks and cartoons --- was 74.4%, which was not much different from the OECD average of 76.5%. It was lower than Sweden (85.7%), Denmark (84.9%) and Britain (81.1%) but similar to France (74.7%), Belgium (65.5%), Japan (67.0%) and the Netherlands (73.6%).

When compared with the data of EU countries compiled in 2013,

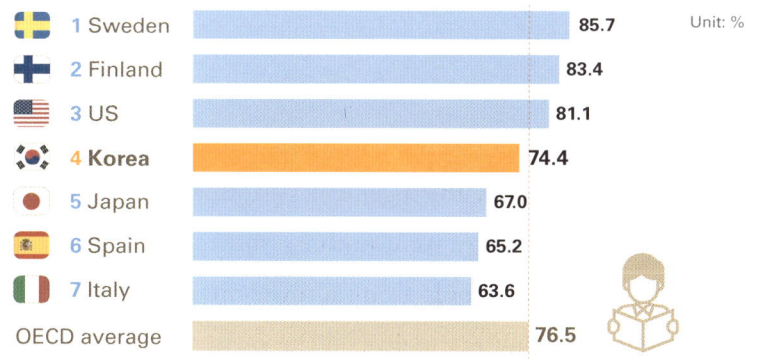

Annual Reading Rate by Country

	Country	Rate
	1 Sweden	85.7
	2 Finland	83.4
	3 US	81.1
	4 Korea	**74.4**
	5 Japan	67.0
	6 Spain	65.2
	7 Italy	63.6
	OECD average	76.5

Unit: %

Source: Ministry of Culture, Sports and Tourism

Koreans' reading rate of 73% was slightly higher than the average EU countries' reading rate of 68.3%. It indicates that Koreans' reading rate is on the same level as the average European advanced country. Of course, the average number of books Korean adults read in a year has been decreasing. A biennial survey on people's reading habits by Statistics Korea shows that Korean adults read an average of 9.1 books a year in 2015, but it went down to 8.3 books a year in 2017. The percentage of reading population (percentage of people who read more than one book in the previous year) is also declining. This may be because they are spending more time watching videos on their smartphones and the internet and therefore have relatively less time to read books.

KOREA'S CULTURE AND ARTS BOAST THE WORLD'S HIGHEST LEVEL

Big events such as the Olympics, the World Cup, and the expos are opportunities to measure a country's level of art and culture. The opening ceremony of the PyeongChang Winter Olympics in February 2018 was an event that showcased s significant level of Korean arts and culture. The ingenious performances that combined pure art with technology were nothing short of a splendid, awe-inspiring experience. People from all over the world applauded at the opening ceremony that delivered the message of peace through performances that visualized the past, present and future by using both analog and digital technologies.

The hallyu fever, largely fueled by K-pop, is already proving the wild popularity of Korean pop culture throughout the world, but Korea on a significant level when it comes to the field of pure art as well. One example is the Korean music artists who have been winning prestigious international competitions. These high achieving Korean music artists and their popular world tours are proof that Korea is not a country on the periphery when it comes to classic music either. Traditional Korean performance arts such as Samulnori and Nanta are also receiving rave feedback from everywhere around the world. It is an undeniable fact that this phenomenon has a lot to do with many talented Korean artists working in the fields of theater and film industries, in addition to classic music and fine arts.

CONTINUOUSLY INCREASING CULTURAL, ART, AND SPORTS EVENT ATTENDANCE RATES

Korea has been able to produce so many world-class artists and sports stars because there was a growing number of Koreans who enjoyed watching cultural, art, and sports events. It is worth paying attention to the cultural and art activities of a country because they reflect the quality of life and the level of the society. In 2000, Koreans who had ever been to a museum, theater, concert, dance performance, theater play, or a sports event within the previous year were only 39.9% of the entire population. But this number shot up to 66.2%

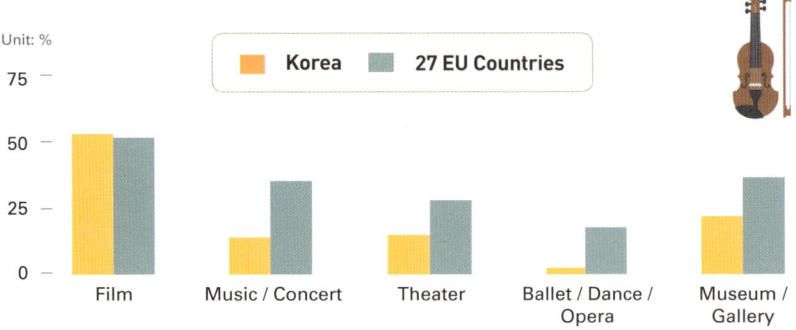

Korea and European Countries' Attendance Rates by Cultural and Art Event

Source: Ministry of Education

in 2015. The number has been continuously growing since then. By genre, the largest percentage of Koreans have been to movies at 88.1%, and those who have been to a museum, concert, gallery, or sports event were also 19-26%. That means at least two out of every ten people in Korea have been to a cultural and art performance, or a sports competition.

The popularity of such events has grown, thanks to Koreans' expenditure on cultural and leisure activities. In 2003, Koreans were spending KRW99,500 won per household on cultural and leisure activities, and it went up to KRW149,700 in 2016. In particular, the amount of money Koreans spent for movies and other cultural and art events went up by 15.7% in 2003 and by 24% in 2016. The increase rate was similar to travel expenditures that went up from 8.8% to 24% during the same period. Of course, this expenditure

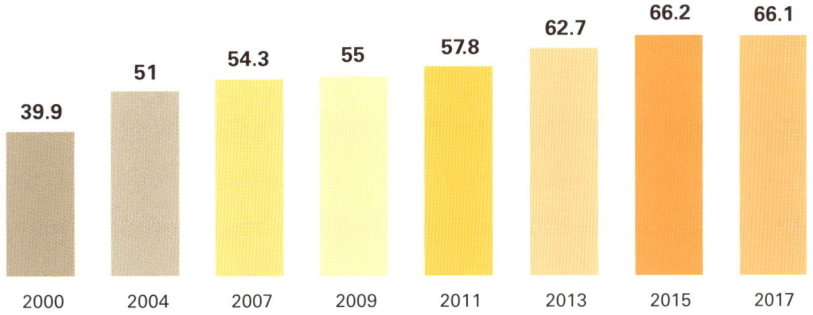

accounted only for 4-5% of the total expenditures, and the percentage remained more or less the same.

The fact that Koreans are spending more money on cultural and art activities and sports events means Koreans are more financially stable than before. It is clear that the cultural art market has been growing in Korea along with economic development, even though there was a period of slowdown in the wake of the global financial crisis in 2008. But still, Korea is falling behind advanced countries. Korea's spending on cultural and leisure activities as a percentage of the GDP is 3.7%, which is just over half that of the US, Japan, Australia and Europe, whose percentage is around 6%. However, Korea is expected to catch up with them as the Korean economy grows, because Koreans' spending has been recording a steady increase.

KOREAN ARTISTS MAKING MARKS IN THE GLOBAL MUSIC, ART, AND FILM COMMUNITIES

Korea is producing distinguished artists in diverse fields such as music, fine arts, and film. One good example is the Chung Trio who have achieved prominence in the international music world since the 1980s. Each of the three siblings ---Chung Myung-whun, Chung Myung-wha and Chung Kyung-wha --- is highly acclaimed as a conductor and pianist, a cellist, and a violinist respectively. Chung Myung-whun graduated from the Julliard School in New York, and during his music career, he conducted virtually all the world's leading orchestras, including the Berliner Philharmoniker and all the major London and Paris Orchestras and explored a new world of music performance. He was also the first Korean to become the music director and conductor of the world's most prestigious opera house, the Opéra de Paris-Bastille. He was appointed music director and conductor of the Seoul Philharmonic Orchestra in 2006, and he is praised to have raised the level of Korean classic music performance.

Chung Myung-wha, a cellist who garnered a lot of attention when she won the Geneva International Music Competition, became famous in Europe before Korea. She made her debut by collaborating with the LA Philharmonic Orchestra under the conduction of Zubin Mehta in 1969 and has performed in numerous historic concerts ever since. Her younger sister, Chung Kyung-wha, shot to fame earlier than her sister did when she won the Edgar Leventritt Competition

Tchaikovsky Competition Major Winners

Name	Year	Category	Prize
Van Cliburn	1958	Piano	First place
Vladimir Ashkenazi, John Ogden	1962	Piano	First place tie
Gidon Kremer	1970	Violin	First place
David Geringas	1970	Cello	First place
Myung-whun Chung	1974	Piano	Second place
Jongmin Park	2011	male vocal music	First place
Sunyoung Seo	2011	female vocal music	First place
Daniil Trifonov	2011	Piano	First place
Yeol Eum Son	2011	Piano	Second place
Seong-Jin Cho	2011	Piano	Third place

Source: Wikipedia

in 1967. Throughout her music career, Chung Kyung-wha demonstrated her skills while working alongside the world's finest conductors such as Daniel Barenboim, and in 1995, she was the only classic musician to be named as one of the "20 Greatest Asians" by Asia Week. Upon the groundwork laid by the Chung Trio in 1995 came numerous Korean artists who rose to fame in the classic music world. They include the pianists Cho Seong-jin and Lim Dong-Hyek and the opera singer Sumi Jo.

The field of art is no exception. There are dozens of Korean artists who received worldwide recognition including: Lee Jung-seob, a painter known for his dynamic depiction of ox; Park Su-geun, the painter known for the masterpiece "the washing place"; world-famous video artist Nam June Paik; Kim Whan-ki, a pioneering avant-garde abstract artist; Cheon Kyeong-ja, who is known as "a painter of flowers and women'"; and Lee Ufan, a Korean minimalist painter acclaimed for his contribution to contemporary art.

In the movie industry, there are directors such as Im Kwon-taek, Park Chan-wook, and Hong Sangsoo who have been in the spotlight at international film festivals. And then there are artists like Kang Sue-jin, who became a world-class ballerina after overcoming a language barrier and the handicap of having an Asian physique.

SOLIDLY LAID SOCIAL INFRASTRUCTURES

One of the biggest criteria that sets developed countries apart from developing countries is their social infrastructure, because that's what determines the quality of life for people. Korea has social infrastructures comparable to those of developed countries, with one of the highest percentages of internet users and smartphone ownership, and Korea also boasts access to affordably priced quality resources such as electricity and tap water. Korea is close to the level of advanced countries in many other social infrastructures including; digitalized government administration system; quality of services in international airports; housing supply rate; recycling of resources; number of registered vehicles; road networks per land area; and the rate of urbanization.

KOREA BECOMES THE WORLD'S FIRST TO ROLL OUT THE 5G COMMERCIAL MOBILE NETWORK SERVICE

On April 3, 2019, Korea launches the world's first nationwide commercial 5G mobile network service. It proved Korea's network technology that is ahead of others. This feat has a lot to do with Korea's smartphone ownership rate and super-fast internet connection.

When Koreans go abroad, they often feel frustrated with the slow internet connection. They experience the same frustration even in advanced countries such as the U.S. and European countries. Perhaps that is because Koreans are used to the fast internet connection available at home, where internet speed is proved to be faster than any other countries by objective statistics.

In 2019, the US-based market research organization, the Pew Research Center, surveyed 39 countries and released a report on their internet usage, smartphone ownership, and social media use. According to the report, 96% of Korean adults are using the internet, placing Korea in first place. Korea was followed by the Netherlands and Australia, and China and Japan ranked 17th and 23rd, respectively.

Korea is boasting the world's fastest internet speed as well. According to the content delivery network and cloud service provider Akamai Korea, the average internet speed in Korea as of Q1 2017 was 28.6 Mbps (megabits/second), making Korea the world's number one for 13 straight quarters. Norway ranked second with 23.5Mbps, followed by Sweden with 22.5Mbps, Hong Kong with 21.9Mbps and Switzerland with 21.7Mbps. Because the internet speed has

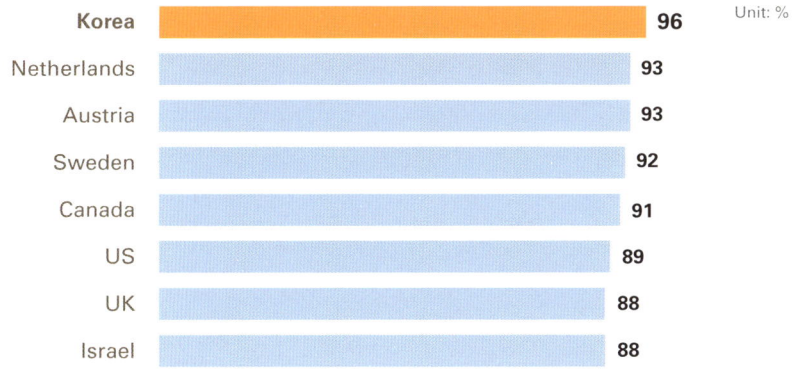

Source: Pew Research Center

been growing faster since then, the numerical values of the speed at a certain point do not mean much. What matters is the fact that the speed is continuously growing.

KOREA NAMED AS THE COUNTRY WITH THE LARGEST SMARTPHONE OWNERSHIP

The Pew Research Center surveyed smartphone ownership in 27 countries, and Korea topped the rank with 95%. If mobile devices are included, virtually all Koreans own mobile phones. Israel ranked second after Korea, but Israel's smartphone ownership was only 88%. The smartphone ownership in most other advanced countries including the Netherlands and Sweden, Australia and the United States, Spain, Germany, the UK, France, Italy, Japan and Canada,

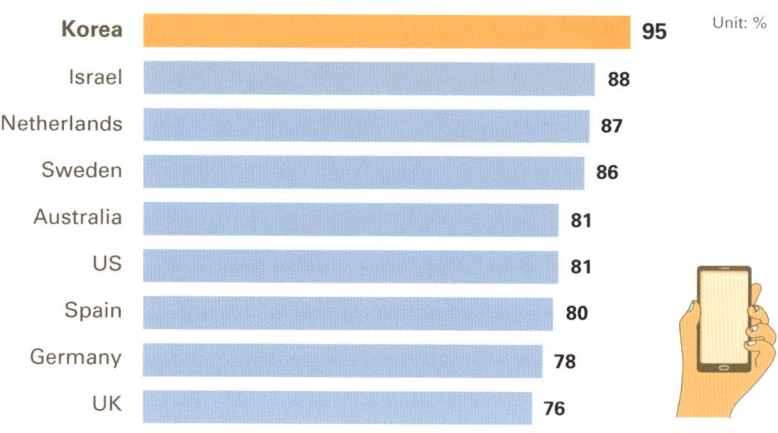

Source: Pew Research Center

recorded only a 60-80% range.

A survey shows that Korea is also tops in terms of the number of apps downloaded on their smartphones. An interesting fact was that in Korea, the use of finance-related apps was comparatively higher than other apps. According to a 2018 survey of mobile market data from Korea, the US, and Japan by a mobile marketing service provider, Mobidays, finance apps were the most popular category among Korean users, while in the US, the most the most popular category was social media, and in Japan, games. Probably it is because easy and simple mobile payment and money transfer services were made available at a time when almost everybody in Korea was using a smartphone.

Another interesting finding was that Korean smartphone users downloaded an average of 102 apps per phone. When measured by the average number of downloads divided by the average monthly number of apps used, Korea ranked first at 38%, followed by the U.S. at 36.3% and Japan, at 31.8%. In this survey, Korea was tops in smartphone ownership with 92% as well.

CHEAPER UTILITY COSTS AND CONVENIENT PUBLIC TRANSPORTATION INCREASES KOREANS' QUALITY OF LIFE

Korea has the advantage of cheaper utilities including electricity and enjoys the convenience of public transportation as well. For example, a household electricity bill in Korea is among the cheapest in the world. According to a report from the Department for Business, Energy and Industrial Strategy (BEIS) of England, Korea's household electricity bill was only 8.47 pence per kWh (about 125 won) in 2017.

When compared with 28 OECD countries, the electricity cost was similar to Canada (8.46 pence) and Norway (8.76 pence) but cheaper than most other advanced countries. It cost as much as 26.68 pence in Germany. Australia was more expensive than Korea at 18.41 pence, and in the case of Japan, the cost was almost twice that of Korea. However, electricity for business was 7.65 pence, which was similar to the OECD average.

Water costs are low in Korea too. According to the OECD reports on water resources management by country, Korea's tap water

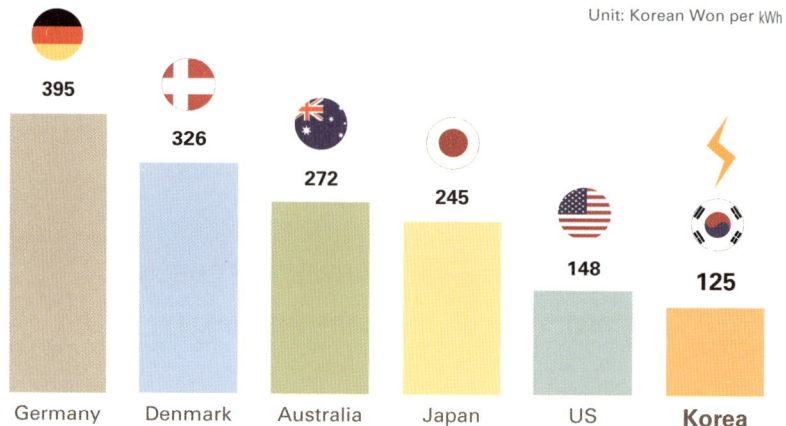

price is $0.34 per ton, the lowest among the OECD countries. The water price in Denmark was $3.18, which was ten times higher than in Korea. However, low water price is blamed for encouraging waste of water. The World Bank also warned that unless Korea implements water management policies, Korea's GDP will be reduced by 6% by 2050.

Korea boasts an excellent public transport system in addition to affordable public utility rates. In particular, the mass transit system that covers the metropolitan area is lauded around the world. According to the Deloitte City Mobility Index (DCMI) released by Deloitte Global, the public transportation system that covers Seoul, Incheon and Gyeonggi Province area ranked seventh among the 46 countries that were evaluated, and third in Asia alone. The analysis shows that Korea scored high because the cost of public transportation was lower than in other countries.

KOREA TOPS IN ONLINE PARTICIPATION FOR E-GOVERNMENT AND MOBILE AND ONLINE ACCESS TO ADMINISTRATIVE SERVICES

Korea proved to have the world's highest level of online participation in e-government, which provides information and administrative services to people through the internet. Korea's e-government provides access to convenient public administrative services such as round-the-clock government, people's petitions, citizen participation budget system and open data portal. In the survey conducted biennially by the UN, Korea has been among the top group for ten straight years.

In the 2018 evaluation, Korea tied for top place with Denmark and Finland in online participation. Stefan Schweinfest, the head of the UN's statistics operation who released the results of the survey, stated "Korea is showing excellent examples of digital innovation, and is credited with having provided good examples to others, such as establishing an e-government cooperation center and inviting developing countries for training and proactively supporting their e-government."

The U.N has been evaluating 193 member states on people's online participation and their e-government development and publishing the U.N. e-Government Survey biennially since 2002.

Top 10 Counties in the e-Participation Index (EPI) 2018

Unit: EA

Ranking	Country	Online Information Providing	Online Policy Participation	Online Policy Decision	2016 Ranking
1	Korea	100	100	100	4
1	Denmark	100	100	100	22
1	Finland	100	100	100	8
4	Netherlands	96.67	100	100	5
5	Australia	100	95.65	100	2
5	Japan	100	95.65	100	3
5	New Zealand	100	95.65	100	5
5	Spain	100	95.65	100	7
5	UK	100	95.65	100	1
5	USA	100	95.65	100	12

Source: UN

Korea ranked top in both categories three straight times in 2010, 2012, and 2014, and ranked fourth and third in 2016, and first and third in 2018, respectively.

KOREA REACHES A 100% NATIONAL HOUSING SUPPLY RATE

The housing supply rate is a key indicator that determines the national living standard of people. Korea reached a 100% national housing supply rate in 2008 and the rate has continued rising to 101.1% in 2012, 102.6% in 2016 and 103.3% in 2017. The housing supply rate is the ratio of the number of housing units divided by the

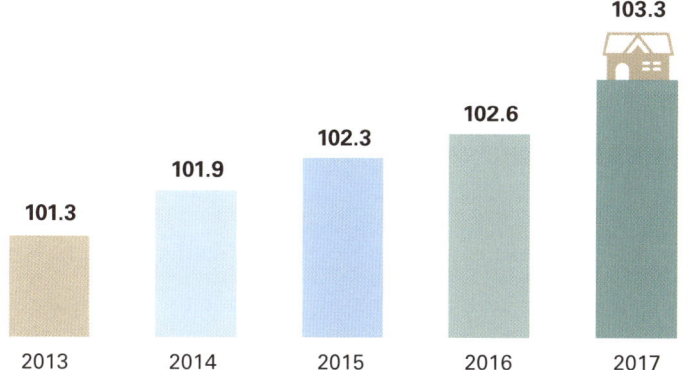

Trend of the Housing Supply Rates

Unit: %

- 2013: 101.3
- 2014: 101.9
- 2015: 102.3
- 2016: 102.6
- 2017: 103.3

Source: Ministry of Land, Infrastructure and Transport

number of households, and is an indicator that shows the housing unit inventory available for households. This indicator alone shows that Korea does not have a housing shortage problem.

However, the housing supply rate in Korea shows a big difference among regions. The rate is comparatively low in regions with a high density of population such as the capital area. While most of the capital areas including Seoul record a less than 100% housing supply rate, some local regions with low density of population are recording over 100% of the housing supply rate. Since there are many people who own more than two houses, the actual ownership and occupancy rate is just about half of the housing supply rate.

The Korean government is using a variety of policies to stabilize the real estate market and to provide more people with an opportunity to own a house. However, since the demand for residence in Seoul and the metropolitan area is high, it is likely that it will take more time to realize a balanced housing supply rate.

KOREA SURPASSES MAJOR ADVANCED COUNTRIES IN EUROPE IN THE RECYCLING RATE

One of the areas in which Korea is ahead of others is waste recycling. Korea is not only among the first to participate in the international treaties on waste management, but it has also been one of the leaders in practicing a volume-rate garbage disposal system ahead of others since the mid-1990s. That means Korea is managing waste in accordance with both Korea's own recycling regulations and international treaties. As a result, Korea's waste recycling rate is close to 60%, contending with Germany for top place in waste recycling. In 2016, Korea beat Germany and topped the waste recycling ranking of the world.

Korean citizens living in major cities regard sorting and recycling garbage as an integral part of their daily activities. They started recycling resources earlier on by adopting a system that has not been introduced even in some advanced countries such as the United States. However, it is a problem that some of the waste collected is not properly managed. As a result, Seoul and other capital areas have experienced garbage crises.

When China stopped importing waste, Korea even had to turn to the Philippines and illegally export and dump waste that has not

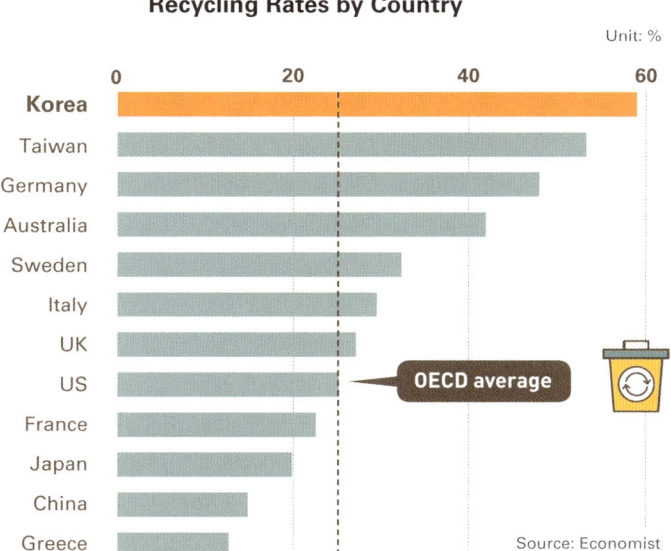

been recycled in that country. It is good to increase the recycling rate, but it is necessary to ensure a proper waste treatment system that surpasses advanced countries. For example, it would be effective to adopt a policy that uses the volume of waste that can be recycled as the standard, and gradually increase the standard. There is also a need to take stronger measures to drastically reduce the amount of waste plastics and the use of plastic bags that are largely responsible for environmental pollution.

ONE REGISTERED MOTOR VEHICLE PER 2.2 PERSONS

Korea is one of the few car makers of the world along with the U.S.,

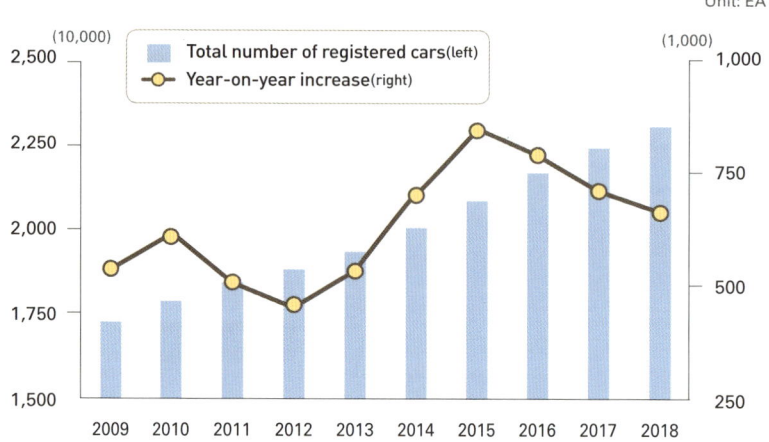

Source: Ministry of Land, Infrastructure and Transport

Japan, and Germany. Data from the Ministry of Land, Infrastructure, and Transport shows that there are 23,202,555 registered motor vehicles in Korea as of the end of 2018, which is a 3.0% increase from the previous year. When divided by the population, it indicates the car ownership rate in Korea is one registered motor vehicle per 2.234 persons.

The number of registered vehicles in Korea has been showing a sharp increase each year since domestic companies started producing cars with their own technology. Even though most Korean households own at least one car, the number of registered vehicles is continuously growing. The increase rate has been slowing down over the years, but there has not been a single year that didn't record any increase at all. Even after 2015, the number has been going up by

3-4% each year. When the era of self-driving cars and car-sharing systems is fully opened, the increase rate of registered vehicles might decline, but general opinion of experts is that there will be a slow yet continuous growth until that time arrives.

One notable fact is that the percentage of eco-friendly vehicles is showing a sharp increase, while the percentage of registered vehicles built on internal combustion engines, such as gasoline and diesel, remains at a standstill. As of the end of 2018, there were more than 460,000 hybrid, electric and hydrogen cars in Korea. Their percentage of the total number of vehicles also went up by 2.0%. Most eco-friendly cars currently running on the streets are hybrid cars, but pure electric cars and hydrogen-cell vehicles are expected to increase significantly when the necessary infrastructure such as electric charging stations is built.

KOREA RANKS SIXTH AMONG THE OECD COUNTRIES IN ROAD DENSITY

No matter how many cars there are, the quality of life for people cannot be improved without a good road environment for driving cars. Korea is among the group of countries with well-maintained roads. Korea Research Institute for Human Settlements (KRIHS) published a research report on the direction of long-term investment in social overhead capital (SOC) in 2016. According to this report, the total extension of roads in Korea was 105,673km as of 2014. That

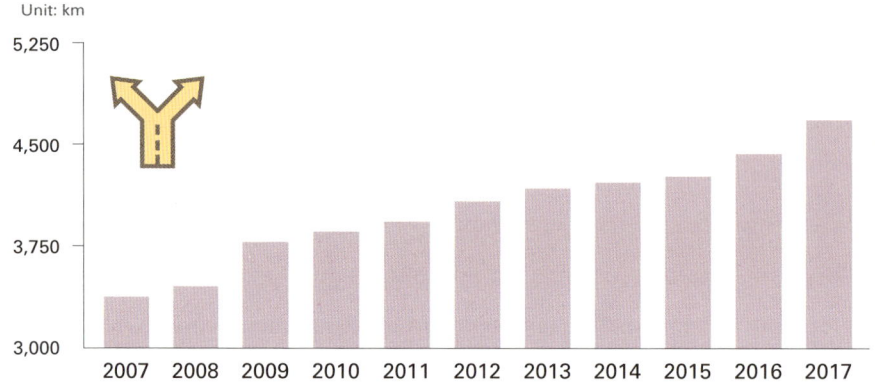

Road Supply Rate By City And Province

Source: Ministry of Land, Infrastructure and Transport (Source: Korea Expressway Corporation Data on expressways and national highways)

ranked Korea 20th among 34 OECD countries and made Korea belong to the lower-middle group.

But the total length of highway network where cars can drive over 100km/hr was 4,139km, which put Korea in 10th place in the ranking, and in terms of the road density --- the ratio of the length of total road network to the country's land area --- Korea ranked sixth among the OECD countries. These numbers signify that Korea has a good highway environment that is comparable to advanced countries. Korea is likely to have moved up the ranking by now, since Korea has been putting forward projects to expand road networks after the release of the report by the KRIHS.

However, the railway environment is not as good as the highway environment. The railroad density of Korea was 3,590km, which put Korea in 17th place and the middle group. It means the railway network is falling behind compared to advanced countries in Europe and the United States and requires more investment in its expansion.

KOREA'S URBANIZATION RATE IS DOUBLE THE AVERAGE OF OECD COUNTRIES

Korea's infrastructures tend to be concentrated in the capital area and major local cities. This tendency is related to Korea's urbanization rate that is exceeding the OECD average.

According to "OECD Urban Policy Reviews: Korea", Korea's urbanization rate is 85.4% as of 2010, twice the average 47.1% of the 34 OECD countries. The figure is higher than Japan (76%) and the United States (84%).

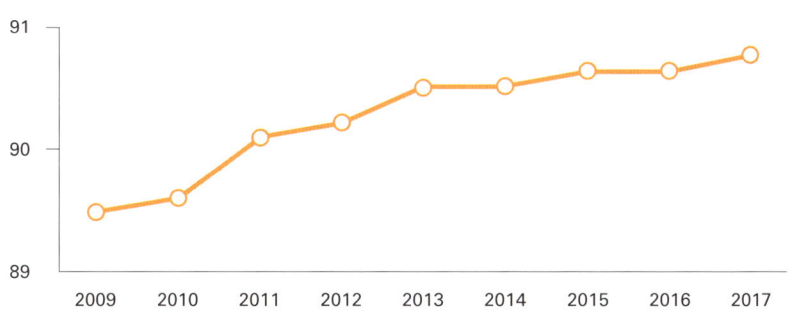

Changing Population Rate in Urban Areas

Unit: %

* the national population since 2005 is based on the census statistics of the Ministry of Security and Public Administration (excluding foreigners)

Source: Ministry of Land Transportation, Korea Land and Housing Corporation (LH) "Statistics of Urban Planning"

The reason for Korea's high urbanization rate can be found in the rapid industrialization that kicked off in the 1960s. Prior to industrialization, most Koreans' lives were built on farming, but urbanization started speeding up once the manufacturing and service industries started to grow. Subsequently, many rural people flocked to cities, and this caused the urbanization rate to go up rapidly within a short period of time. This is corroborated by the figures analyzed in the OECD report. According to the OECD report, the secondary and tertiary industries accounted for slightly over 50% of the total employment in 1970, but it went up to over 90% in the 2000s. The correlation between the two phenomena is clearly revealed in the urbanization rate that doubled from 40% to 80% within the same period. A sharp increase of urban population recorded at a time when Korea was recording over 10% of annual growth rate can be explained within the same context as well.

Rapid urbanization brought about numerous problems, such as the growing gap between cities and local regions and drainage of young people to cities leaving rural areas desolate. The government is putting forward policies intended for balanced regional development, but they are not powerful enough to turn a strong current around. Establishing development strategies customized to fit each region is one way to take advantage of urbanization while minimizing its negative consequences. However, the issue calls for Solomon's wisdom, because it is not easy to achieve those two goals at the same time.

DYNAMISM OF KOREANS AND THE GLOBAL NETWORK OF KOREANS

Koreans are more dynamic than any other people on Earth. This dynamic nature of Koreans became the foundation upon which Korea was able to achieve both a remarkable economic development and democratization within a short period. The mass street-cheering that unfolded thanks to Korean soccer fans during the Korea-Japan World Cup games was an event that demonstrated the dynamic nature of Koreans. Practically every available adult in Korea turned out on streets across the country and rooted for the Korean team with such passion and order that this Korean-style street cheering left deep impressions on sports fans around the world.

The dynamic nature of Koreans can be seen not only within Korea, but abroad as well. There are numerous Korean business leaders making foray into global markets and professionals playing important roles in international organizations, all the while introducing Korea to a broader world and raising the status of Koreans in the international community. Then there are second and even third generations of Koreans who have proved the dynamic nature of Koreans and the strong bond of Korean networks by making it to Capitol Hill in the United States as elected officials

KOREANS BLOOM DEMOCRACY WITHIN A SHORT TIME

The history of democracy in Korea is very dramatic. Korea has successfully achieved both economic growth and democratization within a very short time which is hard to find anywhere in the world. The fact that democratic movements unfolded ceaselessly even at a time when simply remaining alive was such a pressing matter in the aftermath of the Korean War that it was hard to care about such lofty things as individual citizen's rights, which testifies how dynamic Koreans really are. Of course, this dynamism sometimes brought about social disorder, but nobody can deny that democracy had evolved while Korea was going through a period laden with trials and errors. The history of democracy marked by such major incidents as the April 19 Revolution and the May 18 Democratic Uprising are testimonials to the hidden power of the Korean people.

The Economist Intelligence Unit (EIU), which is a British research and analysis unit within the Economist magazine, evaluates and compiles the state of democracy in countries around the world based on analysis of electoral process in addition to five categories: pluralism, function of government, political culture, political participation and civil liberties. In the Democracy Index

2018 published by EUI, Korea ranked 21st among 167 countries by scoring 8 points out of the perfect score of 10. Korea scored the highest 9.17 points in the electoral process and pluralism category, and the lowest 7.22 points in political participation.

The EIU classifies countries that rank in the top 20 in the index as "full democracy." Korea is classified as a "flawed democracy" because Korea is just outside the top 20 group by one rank. But Korea's democracy index was higher than Japan (22nd) and the United States (25th.)

From 2008 to 2014, Korea ranked within the top 20 group and

was classified as a "state of full democracy", but Korea dropped in the ranking after the inauguration of an authoritarian government later on. Although the EIU's assessment is not an absolute indicator, it is a miracle that the Republic of Korea that was once considered a dictatorship had made it to the upper group in the index.

STREET CHEERING DURING THE KOREA-JAPAN WORLD CUP GAMES DEMONSTRATED THE DYNAMISM OF KOREANS

The dynamism of Koreans was most clearly demonstrated by the "street cheering" that unfolded during the 2002 Korea-Japan World Cup games. According to the police and the Organizing Committee for the 2002 FIFA World Cup, over 28 million Koreans took to the streets to root for the Korean team during the event. That means almost half of the entire Korean population came out to the streets for the "street cheering." The area around Gwanghwamun and City Hall Square alone witnessed a cheering crowd of over seven million people, which is an unprecedented record worldwide. It was a case where World Cup event lit the fuse to the hidden power that had guided Koreans to unite and pull through numerous crises throughout history and made it erupt in the dynamic form of street cheering.

The power that made the wind of hallyu sweep through the cheering culture all over the world came from the "Red Devils", a cheering crowd often referred to as "the 12th Taeguk Warrior".

Statistics of the Street Cheering Participants During the 2002 World Cup

Game	Date	Venue	No. of participants
Korea Against Poland	4-Jun	Busan	500,000
Korea Against the US	10-Jun	Daegu	770,000
Korea Against Portugal	14-Jun	Incheon	2,790,000
Korea Against Italy (16 rounds)	18-Jun	Daejeon	42,000,000
Korea Against Spain (16 rounds)	22-Jun	Gwangju	5,000,000
Korea Against Germany (16 rounds)	25-Jun	Seoul	7,000,000
Korea Against Turkey (3rd and 4th place matches)	29-Jun	Daegu	4,000,000
Grand total number of participants			**28,760,000**

Source: Police Agency

Red Devils started as a soccer fan club in 1995, but it evolved into a cheering squad that appeared whenever the Korean national soccer team was playing and passionately rooted for the team chanting its iconic slogan, "Be the Reds." They organized and spearheaded street cheering without exception whenever team Korea had games overseas. Their creative cheering support caught the attention of sports fans around the world and has been benchmarked for street cheering in other countries.

KOREAN BUSINESS LEADERS RAISING REVOLUTION THROUGHOUT THE WORLD

In October 2002, Maeil Business Newspaper and the Overseas

The 17th World Korean Business Convention

Koreans Foundation jointly hosted the first World Korean Business Convention in Lotte Hotel, Seoul. It was from this convention that the term, Hansang, or Korean Businessmen or Korean Traders, began to be used officially. Since then, the annual World Business Convention has been held every October in major cities across the country. Beginning in 2005, the Convention has been jointly hosted with municipal governments with the intention of promoting local economy. The Maeil Business Newspaper that has been organizing the event from the very beginning in partnership with the Overseas Korean Foundation is the only media partner of the World Business Convention.

In earlier days, the Convention had about several hundred Korean participants doing business overseas, but now, the number is over

1,000. When combined with attendees from Korea, the total number of participants is several thousand. For example, the 17th World Business Convention held in Songdo, Incheon, in October 2018 had a total of 3,500 participants including about a thousand Korean businessmen who came from 60 countries. That means it has now grown into Korea's biggest economic festival for the Korean people.

There are a variety of programs at the World Business Convention, an including investment promotion workshop. Through these programs, Korean businessmen build stronger networks and look for new business opportunities. There is also a forum for mid-to-long-term business strategies such as a plan to raise the status of Korean businesses in the world market and a program to foster the next generation of Korean business leaders.

Over 1,000 Korean businessmen who participate in the World Business Convention are demonstrating their entrepreneurship and the creativity of Korean people while engaged in various businesses around the world. These Korean expat businessmen such as Oh Se-young, the chairman of KoLao Holdings, which serves as a major axis of the Lao economy in Laos, are the trailblazers who are expanding the economic territory of the Korean people while overcoming failures in a difficult business environment. Their hard work is contributing to the growing status of Korea and expanding the Korean economic capital in the international community.

THE NUMBER OF KOREANS WORKING IN INTERNATIONAL ORGANIZATIONS EXPERIENCES A SHARP INCREASE EACH YEAR

There are a number of Koreans who made great achievements or who are currently serving as active leaders in international organizations such as the United Nations. There is a significant number of Koreans who have served or are serving in senior positions. One of them is the late Dr. Lee Jong-wook, who met a sudden death in 2006. He was the first Korean to be appointed the head of a specialized agency of the United Nations. A graduate from Seoul National University medical school, his first tie with the UN agency, WHO, started in his mid-30s when he worked with leprosy in Samoa, an island country in the South Pacific.

In 2003, when the then-head of the World Health Organization (WHO), Gro Harlem Brundtland, finished his term, he was elected to the 6th WHO Director-General's post, replacing Brundtland after competing with over 80 candidates. During his term, he contributed to the welfare of humanity with such initiatives as getting 3 million HIV-positive individuals around the world on antiretroviral drugs. In 2004, he was listed as one of the "100 most influential people in the world" by Time magazine, and Scientific American dubbed him the "Vaccine Czar" for his contribution to reducing the polio rate to less than one per 10,000 people worldwide. During the short 3-year term in office, he made his fellow Koreans proud by making great contributions in the prevention and treatment

Statistics on Koreans Working in International Organizations

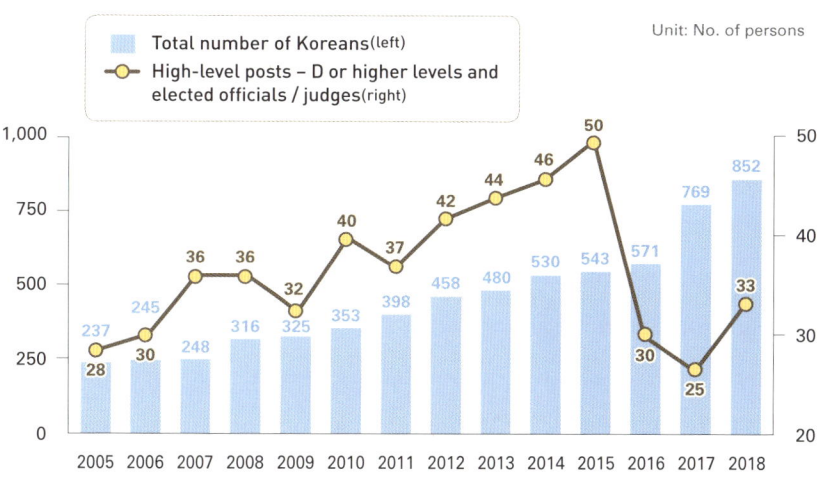

Source: Ministry of Foreign Affairs

of epidemics for people around the world.

Another Korean who served as the head of an international organization is the former UN Secretary General Ban Ki-moon. He was elected to the post of Secretary General of the United Nations in 2006, and he made many great achievements on such global issues as climate change and the proliferation of nuclear weapons until his term expired in December 2012. The chief of the International Maritime Organization (IMO) which oversees shipping safety and security and the prevention of marine pollution, is also a Korean. His name is Lim Ki-tack, and he was inaugurated in 2016 as the 9th Secretary General of IMO. He built experience while serving as a Korean delegate to the IMO since 1986. Kim Jong-yang, the former

Chief of Gyeonggi Provincial Police Agency, is the first Korean to be elected to the post of President of Interpol at the 87th session of the Interpol General Assembly in November 2018.

Kim Yong was appointed President of the World Bank after being nominated for the post by the then-US President Barack Obama and started his five-year term in 2012. He was reappointed to a second five-year term as president before he suddenly announced his resignation three years before the term expired. Lee Yang-hee is the first Korean to be appointed as Special Rapporteur on the state of human rights in Myanmar at an organizational meeting of the UN Human Rights Council in 2014. There are dozens of other Koreans who have served or are currently serving in international organizations, including: Lee Sang-heon, the Director of the Employment Policy Department of the International Labor Organization (ILO); Rhee Chang-yong, the Director of the IMF's Asia and Pacific Department; and Song Sang-hyun, the former President of the International Criminal Court (ICC). Korea was able to produce so many heads of international organizations possibly because there is an increasing number of Koreans who become members of international organizations. According to the Ministry of Foreign Affairs, there are a total of 852 Koreans working in international organizations as of the end of 2018. The number of Koreans who work for international organizations has steadily increased from 200 in 2004 to 300 in 2008, 400 in 2012, 500 in 2014, and 700 in 2017.

REMARKABLE ACTIVITIES OF KOREANS IN US POLITICS

In the US midterm elections held in November 2018, there were two Koreans who became the center of attention: Andy Kim and Young Kim. These two Korean Americans were candidates in the US House of Representatives election. A Middle East specialist, Andy Kim was a national security adviser for the White House under President Barack Obama. Kim ran against the incumbent Republican, Tom MacArthur and won in the tight race. With this victory in the election, he became the first Korean-American Democrat member of the U.S. House of Representatives, and he was also the first to enter the US Congress in 20 years since another Korean-American, Kim Chang-joon, lost the election to the US Congress in 1998.

Another candidate Young Kim was a 1.5 generation Korean who was educated in America after leaving Korea and moving to Guam in 1975 with her family. She worked as a financial analyst before becoming a business owner, and she entered politics on the recommendation of her politician husband while working for him at an NGO in Orange county, California. She defeated a Democratic Assembly member and won the election in 2014. With this victory, she became the first Korean-born Congresswoman from the Republican Party. Unfortunately, she lost the 2018 midterm elections and lost her chance to join the Congress, but she proved her ability to the full extent during her election campaign.

Statistics on Koreans Overseas

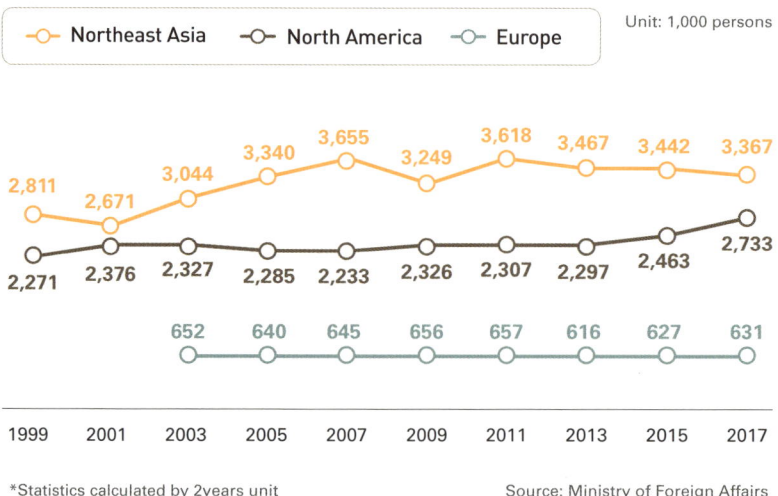

*Statistics calculated by 2years unit Source: Ministry of Foreign Affairs

The Korean American community in the United States began in January 1903 when 102 Koreans arrived in Hawaii. The Korean immigrants settled and took solid root in America while overcoming the difficult situations and sorrow of being an ethnic minority. One generation later, the Korean American community started witnessing fellow Koreans making a foray into US politics, such as Andy Kim and Young Kim. Starting with a Korean who became a member of the Hawaii House of Representatives in 1958, an increasing number of Koreans started entering politics in America, until a Korean American was elected to the US Congress in 1992 for the first time when Kim Chang-joon won the election to become a member of the US House of Representatives from California as a Republican.

Since his defeat in the following election, there has not been another Korean who made it to the US Congress, but many Koreans were elected to become mayors and assembly members and have been playing important roles in American society.

PART 3

MIRACLE-UNDERMINING ENEMIES WITHIN

A SHARPLY DECLINING BIRTH RATE AND AGING POPULATION

Korea has many strengths, but equally many weaknesses. There are two problems that are shaking Korean society from the very foundation: a rapid population decline and aging population. The population is aging faster because people are living longer than before while young Koreans, finding it already hard enough to support themselves, are refusing to have babies. Young people who have a hard time finding a job are putting off getting married, and even those who are married are not having babies. The result is a continuously decreasing fertility rate.

In fact, Korea has the lowest fertility rate among OECD countries. The low birth rate means an eventual decrease of the working age population, as well as weakening of the economic growth engine. Even though the population is declining, the number of elderly people is rapidly growing. The aging population is causing many problems such as draining the state's finances as the result of a sharp increase in the people receiving a government pension, and poverty of the elderly. The government has brought forth diverse policies and increased the budget to tackle the low fertility rate and aging population problems, but a fundamental solution is yet to be found.

KOREA HAS THE LOWEST BIRTH RATE AMONG OECD COUNTRIES

The biggest problem the Republic of Korea is faced with as it stands on the cusp of the rank of advanced countries is the declining fertility rate. If the birth rate continues to decline at its current pace,

Total Fertility Rates of OECD Member Countries in 2016

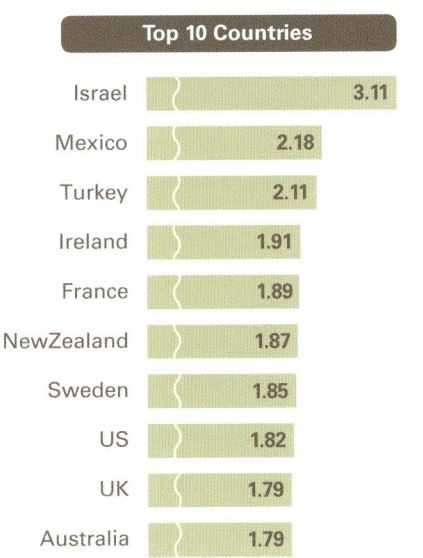
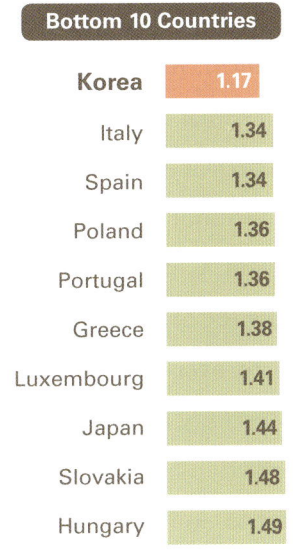

* OECD average is 1.68 babies
* The total fertility rate of Korea in 2018 was 0.98 babies

Source: Statistics Korea

Koreans could become extinct. Low fertility rate is not a problem that affects Korea alone: Most developed countries are sharing the same concern because of young people who refuse to have babies, and their governments are pushing forward with policies to encourage childbirth. Korea is no exception on this.

But the real problem is how strong is their reluctance to have babies. As of 2016, the average total fertility rate of OECD countries is 1.68. Total fertility rate is defined as the average number of children a woman would have assuming that current age-specific birth rates remain constant throughout her childbearing years. Korea ranked the lowest among the major advanced countries with a total fertility rate of 1.17. The rate has kept going down since then until in 2018, the rate went below one child. The rate is low even when compared to some countries in Europe such as Italy and Spain notorious for low childbirth. Korea is literally a country with a super-low birth rate. Korea's total fertility rate has been below 1.3 since 2002.

Korea is the only country among the OECD countries with the dishonor of having failed to resolve the super-low fertility rate problem. Countries such as Portugal were in the same position of having the lowest fertility rate in the past, but their rates are bouncing back to over 1.3 now. Even in the CIA's World Fact Book, Korea's total fertility rate in 2017 ranked 219th among 224 countries and was classified to be among the lowest group. Among the OECD member countries, only a few countries have a rate above 2.1, which is the standard needed to maintain the current size of population. They are

Israel (3.11), Mexico (2.18) and Turkey (2.11). It is time for Korea to think seriously about what we can learn from these countries.

DECLINING CHILDBIRTH RATE REACHES THE LOWEST POINT IN HISTORY

Unfortunately, the declining number of newborns is casting a dark shadow over the prospect of the total fertility rate. According to the "Birth Statistics for 2017" released by Statistics Korea, the number of

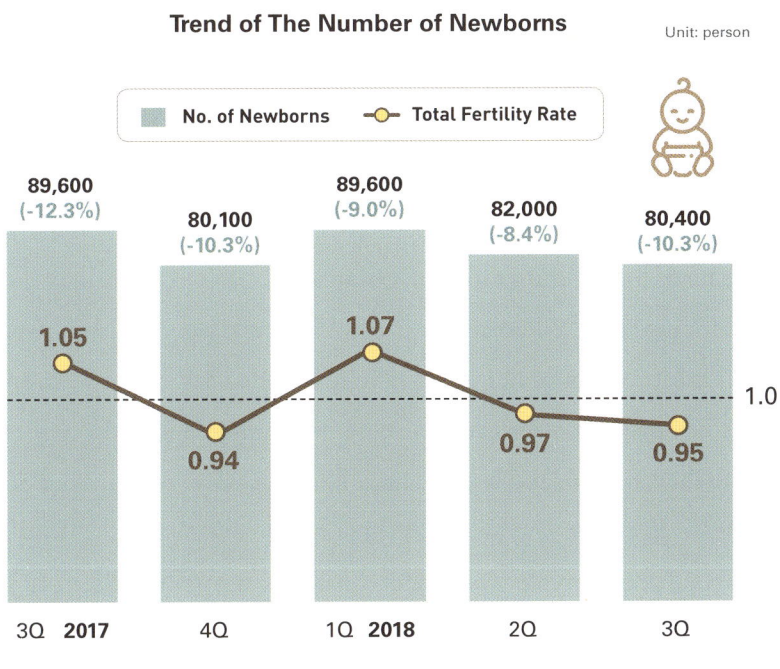

Trend of The Number of Newborns Unit: person

*Number in parenthesis is the year-on-year increase & decrease

Source: Statistics Korea

MIRACLE-UNDERMINING ENEMIES WITHIN

newborns was 357,800, which was the lowest since the government started compiling the data in 1970. The figure shows a decrease of 48,500 newborns, or an 11.9% decrease from the previous year. Korea's birth rate --- the total number of live births per 1,000 in a population in a year or period --- was 70, which was a decrease of 0.9% from the previous year as well. The number of babies born within the first two years of marriage also went down to 65.8%, which was a 2.3% decrease from the previous year. This figure indicates that there is a growing number of couples who are married but are postponing having children for unavoidable reasons.

When broken down by age group, the women in their early 30s showed the highest birth rate of 97.7, but still, this is also a decrease from the previous year's rate of 110.1. The next highest birth rate group was women in their late 20s at 47.9, followed by those in their late 30s at 47.2, and those in their early 20s at 9.6. All across these age groups, their rates recorded a decrease from the previous year. The birth rate of the groups of women who should focus on bearing children is likely to become an obstacle to building a healthy state.

This trend is undeniably related to the fact that the average childbirth age is on a gradual increase. The average age of the first-time mothers was 31.6, and second-time mothers, 33.4, which was a 0.2% increase from the previous year. This trend continued in 2018 when the total fertility rate went below one and recorded 0.95 in Q3. A declining number of babies is bound to result in a declining working age population, which is the backbone of the national economy.

DECLINING BIRTH RATE IS RESULTING IN A RAPID POPULATION DECLINE

The working age population is defined as those aged 15-64 who can reasonably be expected to be economically active. In general, the working age population excludes certain individuals such as those who are doing compulsory military service, but it is data that is used as a quantitative indication of the available labor force of a country. Of course, the working age population includes those who are not economically active in reality, such as housewives and unemployed, but still, the size of the working age population is an important figure from the perspective of national development.

In this sense, the first decline in Korea's working age population that happened in 2017 was a major turning point. According to the 2017 census survey results published by Statistics Korea, the working age population, defined as those aged 15 to 64, was 361,906,000 as of November 2017, which was 116,000 less than the previous year, or a 0.3% decrease. That signifies that the production engine will become weaker by the same amount. It also means the rate of decline is faster than the government had predicted. In the "Future Population Estimates, 2015-2065" report, Statistics Korea had predicted that even though the working age production might decline, the size of a decline would not be that great.

In the meantime, the percentage of the elderly population surged and exceeded 14% of the population for the first time. In 2017, the population over the age of 65 was 7,115,000, an increase of 340,000, or 5.0%, compared with the previous year. As a result, the share of elderly people in the total population has increased from 13.6% to 14.2%. The United Nations define an "aging society" as one in which 7-14% of the population is 65 years or older; an "aged society" as one in which the percentage is bigger than that of the aging society; and a "super-aged society" as one in which more than 20% of the population is 65 years or older. Korea has moved past the "aging society" and is on the cusp of becoming an "aged society". Now, it is only a matter of time before Korea becomes a super-aged society. The percentage of people over the age of 65 was only 7.0% of the total population in 2000, but it doubled in just 17 years.

On the other hand, the number of children aged 0-14 was 6,632,000 as of 2017, a decline of 2.0%, or 137,000 children. The gap has been growing bigger since 2016 when the percentage of people aged over 65 surpassed the percentage of children aged 0-14. The aging index, which is the ratio of the number of elderly persons aged 65 and over to the number of children from 0 to 14 years old also recorded a sharp increase from 100.1 to 107.3. The elderly dependency ratio, which is the ratio of the elderly population (ages 65+) per 100 people of working age (ages 15-64), also shows to have increased by 1.0 points to 19.7. These figures are warning that the economy will grow less dynamic while the social burden will grow heavier. If it is not possible to increase the working age population within a short time, the other alternative will be to improve productivity, but it is not an easy task.

DECLINING BIRTH RATE IS RESULTING IN A RAPID POPULATION DECLINE

The working age population is defined as those aged 15-64 who can reasonably be expected to be economically active. In general, the working age population excludes certain individuals such as those who are doing compulsory military service, but it is data that is used as a quantitative indication of the available labor force of a country. Of course, the working age population includes those who are not economically active in reality, such as housewives and unemployed,

Population Rate Changes by Age Group

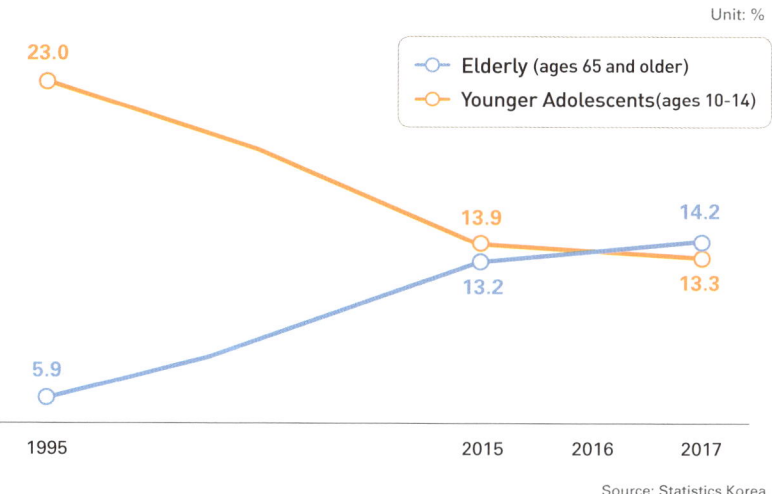

Source: Statistics Korea

but still, the size of the working age population is an important figure from the perspective of national development.

In this sense, the first decline in Korea's working age population that happened in 2017 was a major turning point. According to the 2017 census survey results published by Statistics Korea, the working age population, defined as those aged 15 to 64, was 361,906,000 as of November 2017, which was 116,000 less than the previous year, or a 0.3% decrease. That signifies that the production engine will become weaker by the same amount. It also means the rate of decline is faster than the government had predicted. In the "Future Population Estimates, 2015-2065" report, Statistics Korea had predicted that even though the working age production might decline, the size of a decline would not be that great.

In the meantime, the percentage of the elderly population surged and exceeded 14% of the population for the first time. In 2017, the population over the age of 65 was 7,115,000, an increase of 340,000, or 5.0%, compared with the previous year. As a result, the share of elderly people in the total population has increased from 13.6% to 14.2%. The United Nations define an "aging society" as one in which 7-14% of the population is 65 years or older; an "aged society" as one in which the percentage is bigger than that of the aging society; and a "super-aged society" as one in which more than 20% of the population is 65 years or older. Korea has moved past the "aging society" and is on the cusp of becoming an "aged society". Now, it is only a matter of time before Korea becomes a super-aged society. The percentage of people over the age of 65 was only 7.0% of the total population in 2000, but it doubled in just 17 years.

On the other hand, the number of children aged 0-14 was 6,632,000 as of 2017, a decline of 2.0%, or 137,000 children. The gap has been growing bigger since 2016 when the percentage of people aged over 65 surpassed the percentage of children aged 0-14. The aging index, which is the ratio of the number of elderly persons aged 65 and over to the number of children from 0 to 14 years old also recorded a sharp increase from 100.1 to 107.3. The elderly dependency ratio, which is the ratio of the elderly population (ages 65+) per 100 people of working age (ages 15-64), also shows to have increased by 1.0 points to 19.7. These figures are warning that the economy will grow less dynamic while the social burden will grow heavier. If it is not possible to increase the working age population within a short time, the other alternative will be to improve productivity, but it is not an easy task.

KOREA IS SLATED TO BECOME THE WORLD'S OLDEST COUNTRY BY 2060

The Korea Institute for Health and Social Affairs (KIHASA) presented a shocking report at the forum held in 2018. The main point of the report titled "The Dawning of the Aging Society and the Direction of Responses" was that the population aging rate in Korea will surpass that of Japan in 2060, and that Korea will be a country

Trend of the Aging Rate and Prediction for the Future by Country

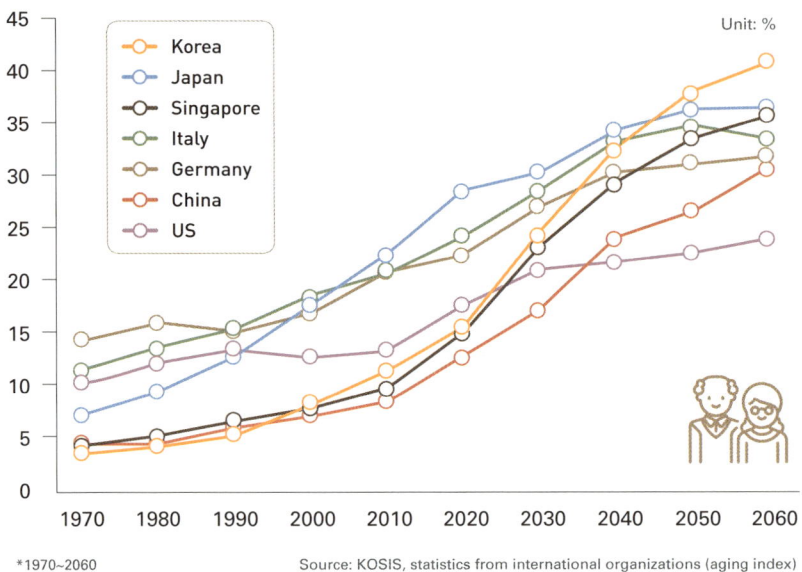

*1970~2060   Source: KOSIS, statistics from international organizations (aging index)

with the highest percentage of aged population in the world as a result. Furthermore, KIHASA predicted in the report that by 2065, four out of every ten Koreans will be classified as elderly.

The turning point is 2025. The report predicted that Korea will experience significant changes throughout society once Korea becomes a super-aged society with an over 20% aging population rate, and that everybody's life --- not to mention elderly people's lives --- will be completely different from what it is today in virtually all areas including politics and the economy.

If this prediction is correct, Korea will go down in history as a country that ages faster than Japan, because while Japan took ten years to move from being an aged society to a super-aged society, Korea is likely to take only 7-8 years. As mentioned previously, the reason for this can be found in the low fertility rate and increasing life expectancy. The total fertility rate continues to decline, but the life expectancy has increased by more than 20 years from 58.8 years in 1970 to 79.5 in 2010. In 2060 when Korea becomes a super-aged society, the life expectancy can go up to 88.5 years, according to the report.

The problem is that the growing number of elderly people is likely to result in a growing poverty rate for elderly people, because a declining working-age population will bring down the potential growth rate. If there is a good system that guarantees a comfortable life for elderly citizens, there should be nothing to worry about, but it is a different story if there are not enough young people who are capable of supporting elderly people. The disaster of the super-aged society will become an unavoidable reality unless the government starts taking appropriate measures as soon as possible.

SHARP INCREASE OF NATIONAL PENSIONERS IS DEPLETING PENSION REVENUE

The data released by the National Pension Service in March 2018 shows how uncertain the future is. According to the released data, the number of national pensioners went up by 330,000 to 4.69 million as of the end of 2017, which is more than twice the figure of 2.11

million in 2007. The number of people who are receiving a pension after making contributions to the pension program for more than 20 years also went up from 13,000 in 2008 to 328,000 in 2017, showing a whopping 25 times increase in nine years. There are also about 300,000 couples who joined the pension program together and are receiving it now, and their number went up by 19% from the previous year as well.

While the number of pension recipients keeps going up the number of people who make contributions keeps going down. As of the end of December 2017, there were 21,824,172 people who had joined the pension program, which is 8,352 less than the previous year. As mentioned previously, the pension revenue remains more or less the same while the pension payout amount is increasing fast due to the rapidly declining birth rate and aging of the population. According to the results of the third fiscal projection announced by the government in 2013, the national pension fund will be depleted in 2060. The pension cost rate, according to the government's calculation, was 17.4% in 2040 and it is likely to reach 21.4% in 2060. The pension cost rate is defined as the contribution rate required to obtain zero current balance for a given total pension. The government is trying to delay the time of the depletion, but there is no fundamental solution other than demanding that people make higher contributions or reducing the payout to pensioners.

These concerns were fully reflected in the Fourth Comprehensive National Pension Management Plan that was passed at a cabinet

Prospect of the Projected Depletion of National Pension by 2058

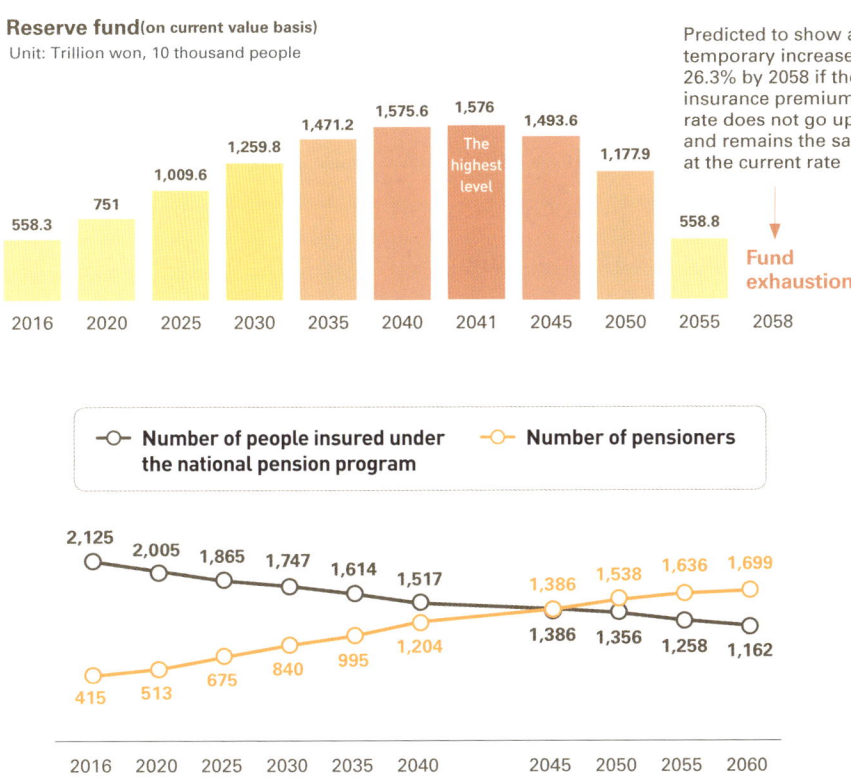

Source: Korea Institute for Health and Social Affairs

meeting on December 14, 2018. The plan took two months longer in process until it was passed, but the plan that included four pension reform proposals was submitted for parliamentary approval. The first proposal was reducing the income replacement rate (the total amount of income in retirement divided by the income earned during the career phase) that was set at 45% by the National Pension Act revised in 2007 by 0.5% each year until it reached 40% in 2028, and setting the insurance premiums at 9% (4.5% for corporate members). The second proposal was about maintaining the current national pension program but raising basic pension to KRW400,000 in 2022 from the current monthly basic pension of KRW250,000. The third proposal was to raise the income replacement rate to 45% beginning in 2021 and raising insurance premiums by 1% every five years from the current 9% until it is increased to 12% in 2031. The fourth plan was to raise the income replacement rate to 50% by 2021 and raising the insurance premiums by 1% every five years until it is increased to 13% in 2036. All four proposals having pros and cons, it will not be difficult to get the general consensus of the people.

Since the national pension program was introduced in 1988, the monthly insurance premium for the pension, which was set at 9% of income at the time, has never been changed. If the government tries to change the rate now, it will be met with strong resistance from the people. An alternative to the raise will be less monthly pension payout, but then people will argue that the national pension is not sufficient to give a sense of security to elderly people. The only solution to this problem will be a grand social compromise.

KOREA'S HEALTH EXPENDITURE INCREASE RATE IS THREE TIMES THAT OF ADVANCED COUNTRIES

One of the biggest threats Korea will face if it becomes a super-

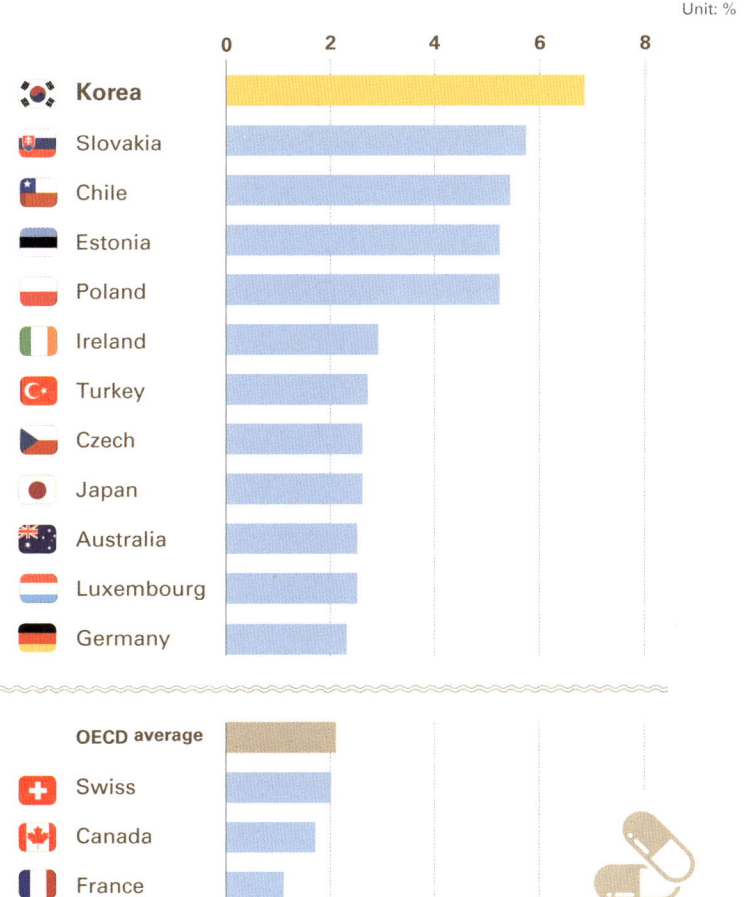

Health Expenditure Increase Rate of Major OECD Countries

*Based on the average annual growth rate of current medical expenses in 2005-2015 for 34 countries
Source: Korea Institute for Health and Social Affairs

aged country without the support of a national pension with adequate income replacement rate is medical expenses. According to the "2017 Report on the Quality of Korean Medical Services" released by the Korea Institute for Health and Social Affairs, the current health expenditure (% of GDP) in Korea recorded an average annual increase of 6.8% between 2005 and 2015, which is three times the average OECD increase rate of 2.1%. Even though major developed countries are facing the same aging population problem, the increase rate of their medical expenses is not as high compared to Korea. During the same period, France recorded an average annual increase rate of 1.1%, Canada recorded 1.7%, and Germany, just 2.3%. Japan is a country with a high percentage of elderly population, but their annual increase rate was 2.6%, which was almost the same as the OECD average.

Data from Statistics Korea shows that the current health expenditure in Korea has increased substantially from KRW7.5 trillion in 1990 to KRW125.2 trillion in 2016. The expenditure as a percentage of the GDP also went up to 7.7% in 2016, narrowing the gap with the OECD average of 9.0%.

Despite the high rate of increase in medical expenses, the number of doctors per 1,000 people was only 2.3, the lowest among OECD member countries. These figures were released by the Ministry of Health and Welfare based on analysis of the "Health Statistics 2018" released by OCED. According to the analytic data, the OECD average was 3.3 doctors per 1,000 people, and Norway ranked first with the highest number of doctors at 4.5, followed by France at 3.1 and the US at 2.6. Fortunately, out-of-pocket medical expenses turned out to be relatively low in Korea. Nevertheless, the government needs to lower the increase rate of medical expenditure in order to maintain a high level of medical standards.

KOREA'S HEALTH EXPENDITURE INCREASE RATE IS THREE TIMES THAT OF ADVANCED COUNTRIES

One of the biggest threats Korea will face if it becomes a super-aged country without the support of a national pension with adequate income replacement rate is medical expenses. According to the "2017 Report on the Quality of Korean Medical Services" released by the Korea Institute for Health and Social Affairs, the current health expenditure (% of GDP) in Korea recorded an average

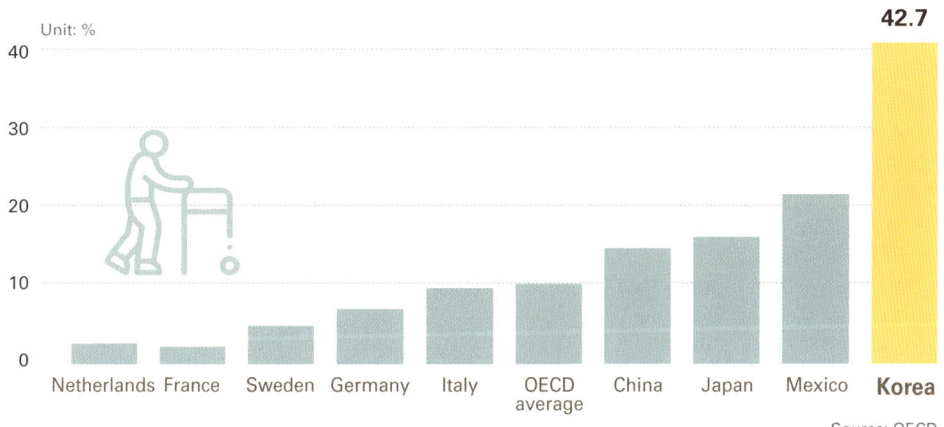

Elderly Poverty Rate of OECD Countries

Source: OECD

annual increase of 6.8% between 2005 and 2015, which is three times the average OECD increase rate of 2.1%. Even though major developed countries are facing the same aging population problem, the increase rate of their medical expenses is not as high compared to Korea. During the same period, France recorded an average annual increase rate of 1.1%, Canada recorded 1.7%, and Germany, just 2.3%. Japan is a country with a high percentage of elderly population, but their annual increase rate was 2.6%, which was almost the same as the OECD average.

Data from Statistics Korea shows that the current health expenditure in Korea has increased substantially from KRW7.5 trillion in 1990 to KRW125.2 trillion in 2016. The expenditure as a percentage of the GDP also went up to 7.7% in 2016, narrowing the gap with the OECD average of 9.0%.

Despite the high rate of increase in medical expenses, the number of doctors per 1,000 people was only 2.3, the lowest among OECD member countries. These figures were released by the Ministry of Health and Welfare based on analysis of the "Health Statistics 2018" released by OCED. According to the analytic data, the OECD average was 3.3 doctors per 1,000 people, and Norway ranked first with the highest number of doctors at 4.5, followed by France at 3.1 and the US at 2.6. Fortunately, out-of-pocket medical expenses turned out to be relatively low in Korea. Nevertheless, the government needs to lower the increase rate of medical expenditure in order to maintain a high level of medical standards.

SIX OUT OF TEN KOREANS ARE CONCERNED ABOUT GENERATION CONFLICT

Life is hard not just for elderly Koreans, but also young Koreans. Young Koreans are faced with a grim reality too: It is difficult to find a job after college, and even if they are hired, it takes forever to become a house owner, because the real estate prices went up so high that it is near impossible to buy a house by saving from their pay checks. The consequence is the creation of a vicious cycle in which they give up on getting married and accelerate the already declining birth rate.

With both young and older generations struggling while dealing with their own issues, there is a growing generation conflict problem. According to a report titled "The Problem of Social Integration and the Measures to Respond (4) - Social Problems and Social Integration", which was published by the Korea Institute for Health and Social Affairs in 2018, roughly 8 out of 10 Koreans think that generation conflicts are serious in Korean society. In a survey of 3,839 men and women aged between 19 and 75 about their perception of social conflict, 80.3% of the respondents answered that the overall level of conflict was "very serious" or "generally serious."

When asked about the type of conflict that they thought was most serious, the largest percentage of 85.2% answered it was the ideological conflict between the progressive and the conservative, followed by the conflict between regular and non-regular employees

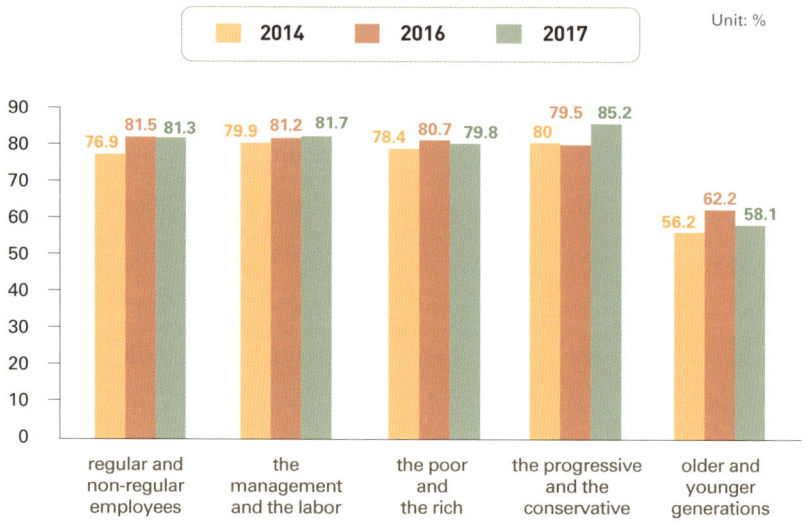

Source: Korea Institute for Health and Social Affairs

(81.9%), conflict between management and labor (81.7%), and conflict between the poor and the rich (79.8%). In addition, 58.1% of the respondents also felt the conflict between the old and the young generation was a serious problem as well.

The Korea Institute for Health and Social Affairs (KIHASA) publishes the same report every year. In 2017, the percentage of the respondents who answered generation conflict was the most serious type of conflict was higher at 62.2%. Considering how the percentage was 56.2% in 2014, there is a steadily growing number of people who are deeply concerned about generation conflict. About this survey result, KIHASA explained, "Generation conflict is emerging as a major type of social conflict, and this is largely attributed to the growing conflict between generations over jobs." Even though generation conflict is not restricted to Korea alone, it is a shameful reality of Korean society that old and young Koreans confront each other over the means of making a living.

GLASS CEILING REMAINS HIGH WITH FEMALE EXECUTIVES ACCOUNTING FOR ONLY 3% IN TOP 500 COMPANIES

Although the role of women in the economy is growing more important as the result of rapid economic growth, gender inequality in the workplace is still a problem that needs to be resolved. Women are getting more educated and skilled, but they are not getting the treatment that they deserve. One good example is the percentage of female executives in the workplace, which is extremely low. The Ministry of Gender Equality and Family commissioned the Korean Women's Development Institute to analyze the 2017 business reports of 500 companies registered in the Data Analysis, Retrieval and Transfer System (DART) run by the Korea Financial Supervisory Service (KFTC) and found out that the number of female executives was only 454, which accounts for just 3%. The result speaks volumes about how high the "glass ceiling" is in the corporate world. A total of 328 firms out of the 500 surveyed, or 65.5%, did not have a single female executive. The finding is shocking because it means six out of ten companies do not have any female executives. The percentage of female executives has been going up by 0.1-0.3% each year from 2.3% in 2014 to 2.45 in 2015 and 2.7% in 2016. But still, the percentage is extremely low compared to the OECD average of over 20%.

By sector, the percentage of female executives was highest in the wholesale and retail sector at 4.1%, followed by the financial and insurance sectors at 3.7%. The figures of these two sectors were slightly higher than the average, but the manufacturing sector had lower than average at only 2.7%. If the top 500 Korean companies are classified by industry, companies that belong to the manufacturing industry account for 50.4%. There are financial companies (14.6%), wholesale and retail companies (7.4%), and construction companies (7.4%), but their percentages are not even comparable to the overwhelming percentage of manufacturing companies. Another problem is that industries with a relatively large number of female executives are concentrated in a few sectors.

Utilization of the female workforce is important because it has direct impact on economic growth. According to the gender equality report released by McKinsey in 2018, advancing women's equality can add 9% growth to Korea's GDP. McKinsey also published a report on research results that showed how companies with a higher number of female workers demonstrate better work performance. The title of the report was "Why Diversity Matters," and the major findings of the research on companies for a span of ten years between 2007 and 2017 showed that those in the top 25% for gender diversity outperformed by an average of 21%, companies in the lowest 25% in

Glass Ceiling Index of Major OECD Countries

Rank	2013	2014	2015	2016	2017
1	New Zealand	Norway	Finland	Iceland	Iceland
2	Norway	Sweden	Norway	Norway	Sweden
3	Sweden	Finland	Sweden	Sweden	Norway
4	Canada	Poland	Poland	Finland	Finland
5	Australia	New Zealand	France	Hungary	Poland
6	Spain	France	Hungary	Poland	France
7	Finland	Denmark	Denmark	France	Denmark
8	Portugal	Hungary	Spain	Denmark	Belgium
9	Poland	Canada	Belgium	New Zealand	Hungary
10	Denmark	Spain	New Zealand	Belgium	Canada
11	France	Israel	Canada	Canada	New Zealand
12	USA	Belgium	Portugal	Portugal	Portugal
13	Belgium	Portugal	Israel	Spain	Spain
14	Hungary	Slovakia	Slovakia	Israel	Australia
15	Ireland	Netherlands	Germany	Slovakia	Slovakia
16	Slovakia	Australia	Australia	Austria	Israel
17	Israel	USA	USA	Germany	Italy
18	England	Germany	Italy	Australia	Austria
19	Austria	Austria	Greece	USA	Germany
20	Germany	Greece	Netherlands	Czech Republic	USA
21	Greece	Italy	Austria	Italy	Greece
22	Italy	England	England	Netherlands	England
23	Czech Republic	Czech Republic	Ireland	Greece	Ireland
24	Swiss	Ireland	Czech Republic	England	Netherlands
25	Japan	Swiss	Swiss	Ireland	Czech Republic
26	Korea	Japan	Turkey	Swiss	Swiss
27		Korea	Japan	Japan	Turkey
28			Korea	Turkey	Japan
29				Korea	Korea

Source: Rep. Shin Yong-hyun of the People's Party,
Ministry of Gender Equality and Family, Economist

terms of the pre-tax operating profit to sales ratio.

Morgan Stanley & Co. International (MSCI) also released a report in 2016 and revealed how companies with female board members showed better financial performance than companies that didn't have any.

AN ALARMING NUMBER OF YOUNG KOREANS BELIEVE MARRIAGE IS NOT NECESSARY

The main cause of the rapidly declining fertility rate is the increasing tendency among young Koreans to avoid marriage. The results of a survey conducted by Statistics Korea in 2018 shocked Korean society because they shattered the conventional idea about marriage being a necessity in life. The findings showed that the percentage of Koreans who believe marriage is a necessity went down to less than half of the population for the first time.

According to the survey of Koreans over 13 years of age by Statistics Korea, the number of respondents who answered that marriage was a necessity was 48.1%, which was a 3.8% decline from 51.9% the previous year. In 2010, 64.7% of respondents answered marriage was a necessity, but the number has been going down continuously each year until there were more people who didn't think marriage was a necessity than those who did. By gender, 52.8% of men answered marriage was a necessity, while only 43.5% of women answered the same. That means women were more negative about

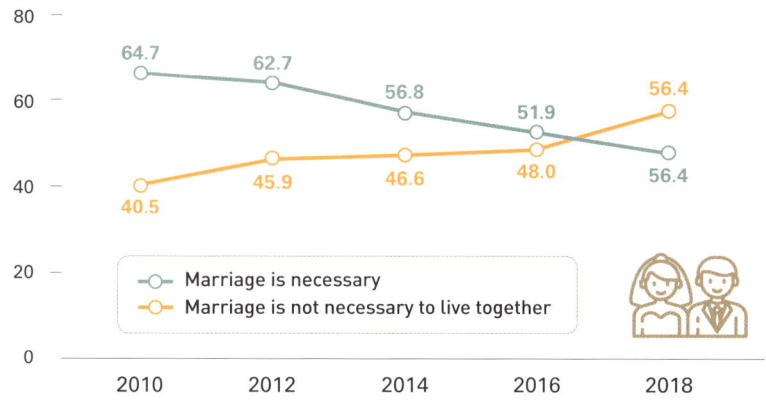

Survey on the Willingness to Get Married

Unit: %

- Marriage is necessary: 64.7 (2010), 62.7 (2012), 56.8 (2014), 51.9 (2016), 56.4 (2018)
- Marriage is not necessary to live together: 40.5 (2010), 45.9 (2012), 46.6 (2014), 48.0 (2016), 56.4 (2018)

Source: Statistics Korea

marriage than men. The survey also showed that more than half of the respondents, or 56.4% of them, answered that a couple could live together without getting married. This figure has been increasing from 40.5% in 2010 to 45.9% in 2012, 46.6% in 2014 and 48.0% in 2016, until it reached more than half of the respondents for the first time in 2018.

Koreans' attitude about divorce has also changed significantly. In 2008, some 58.6% of Koreans answered that divorce was not acceptable, but the figure went down to 33.2% in 2018. It is the result of wide-spreading perception that marriage vows can be broken at any time if it doesn't work out well. Survey results showed that a majority of people were reluctant to get married for financial reasons, such as the excessive cost of a wedding, supporting parents, and the cost to raise children. But the biggest reason to avoid marriage was employment status. Understandably, it is not easy for people to decide to get married when they cannot find a decent job and become financially independent. The survey results remind us how important it is to support companies that will create quality jobs.

STARTUP DATA SHOWS WEAKENING SPIRIT OF CHALLENGE AMONG YOUNG ADULTS

Another factor that casts a dark shadow over the future of the Republic of Korea is the increasingly weakening mentality of young Koreans. The young generation of Koreans tends to prefer settling in their comfort zone than taking a challenge and starting their own business. Instead of dreaming of becoming a global-trotting business leader or a scientist who changes the life of mankind, they are dreaming of becoming a building owner who can rely on stable income from rent. There is also an increasing number of young Koreans who turn away from jobs that require hard work, or even turn to killing themselves or succumbing to the temptation of committing crimes.

However, the young generation of Koreans are solely to be blamed for this reality, because it is the social structure of Korea that is making life harder for young people. As the Korean economy becomes stuck on a plateau of slow growth, jobs become harder to find, and even though the youth unemployment rate is worse than ever, everybody is so fixated on going to college that everybody refers to the competition over college admission as a "hell." Now, let's look at the reality that the youth in Korea is faced with today.

DISAPPEARING JOBS AVAILABLE FOR YOUTHS

The young generation of Koreans is struggling with a sense of crisis that they will be the first generation to live a life that is worse than their parents' generation. The biggest reason for this fear is because the number of good jobs available to them is disappearing. According to a report "Comparative Analysis of Youth Unemployment in Korea and Japan and its Implications" by the Bank of Korea, the youth unemployment rate in Korea recorded 9.5% as of 2017. It is a 3.5% increase from 6.0% in 2000. This finding contrasts with the young unemployment rate in Japan, which went down from 6.2% to 4.1% during the same period. These figures clearly show how the unemployment rates of youths in Korea and Japan --- which used to be similar in the past ---are now headed in different directions: Japan for the better, and Korea, for the worse. Even in 2018, the youth unemployment rate in Korea has remained at its worst level at around between upper 7% and 9% each month.

The trend of the unemployment rate of Korean youth is heading in the opposite direction to OECD member countries. While the average youth unemployment rate in OECD countries is declining after reaching its peak at 10.6% in 2010, the rate has

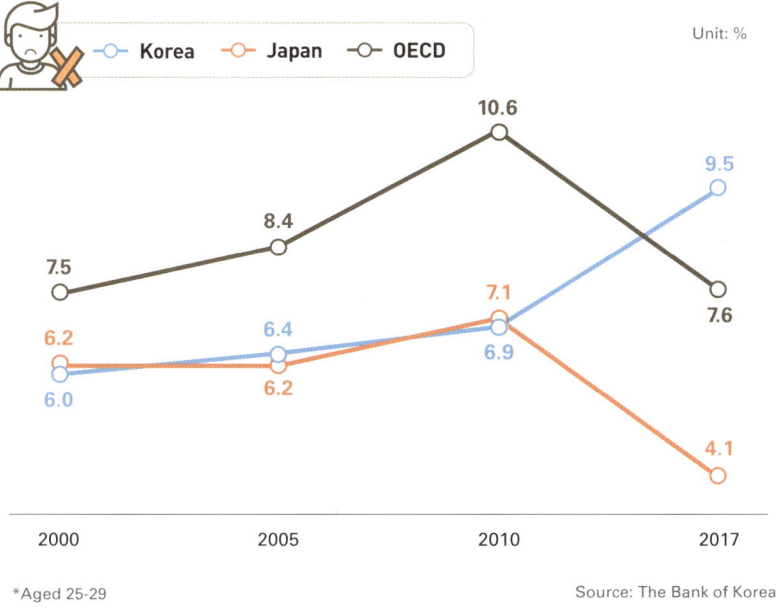

Trend of Youth Unemployment Rates of Korea and Japan

*Aged 25-29

Source: The Bank of Korea

been continuously going up in Korea. There are many reasons for this, but the biggest one is the declining economic growth rate. The labor market polarization and the consequential unbalance in jobs that require different job skills is another factor that cannot be ignored. The wage gap between large corporations and small-to-medium companies is also growing every year. There are many small-to-medium companies whose wage level is less than half of large corporations. In the case of Japan, the wage of small-to-medium companies is around 70-90% of large companies. Small and medium Korean companies are having trouble recruiting people to fill vacancies, but young Koreans are not applying for those jobs because the pay is too low compared to what they can get from large corporations. As a result, there is a wide-spread perception among young Koreans in the job market that they'd rather remain unemployed than work for those small and medium sized companies.

Some other factors that contribute to the worst youth unemployment rate include the increasing number of temporary jobs resulting from the big increase in minimum wage, and the distribution of available jobs resulting from the aging population. The government needs to improve the investment and employment environment, while making the market more flexible through labor reform in order to solve the chronic youth unemployment problem. If the government can improve the economic growth rate through these measures, it will naturally result in the creation of good jobs available to young Koreans.

KOREA'S ENTREPRENEURSHIP INDEX REMAINS IN THE MIDDLE RANK AMONG OECD COUNTRIES

Another factor that overshadows the future of Korea along with the youth unemployment rate is the weakening spirit of challenge. In the "2018 Global Entrepreneurship Index (GEI)" published by the Global Entrepreneurship Development Institute (GEDI), Korea ranked 24th among the 137 economies examined, and belonged to the top class. However, when compared to a smaller number of

Ranking of Korea in the Global Entrepreneurship Index (GEI)

Category	Indicator	2016 Score	2016 Ranking	2017 Score	2017 Ranking	2018 Score	2018 Ranking
Entrepreneurial attitude	Opportunity Recognition	0.26	37/132	0.29	/137	0.46	20/137
	Ability to start a business	0.61		0.46		0.77	
	Risk acceptance	0.58		0.76		0.91	
	Networking	0.70		0.61		0.77	
	Cultural support	0.45		0.33		0.27	
	Subtotal	**47.2**		**45.1**		**55.6**	
Entrepreneurial ability	Opportunity start-up	0.57	27/132	0.56	/137	0.62	29/137
	Technology absorption	0.78		0.78		0.67	
	Human capital	0.81		0.55		0.56	
	Competition	0.23		0.25		0.32	
	Subtotal	**51.8**		**48.2**		**50.1**	
Entrepreneurial aspiration	Product innovation	0.85	20/132	0.91	23/137	0.95	27/137
	Process innovation	0.89		0.95		1.00	
	Rapid growth	0.60		0.38		0.45	
	Globalization	0.47		0.42		0.32	
	Venture capital	0.79		0.77		0.58	
	Subtotal	**61.1**		**58.2**		**56.8**	
GEI average		37.3	-	33.1	-	34.2	
Grand total		**53.4**	**27/132**	**50.5**	**27/137**	**54.2**	**24/137**

Source: Korea Entrepreneurship Foundation

OECD countries alone, Korea ranks 20th among the 35 countries and belongs to the lower-middle class. Korea scored high in the technology sector, such as product and process innovation, but its score hit the bottom in the anti-business sentiment and globalization.

Korean ranked in the lower class as well in the Amway

Entrepreneurial Spirit Index (AESI) released by Amway in March 2018 based on its survey of about 50,000 people including 1,500 Koreans. According to this index, Korea scored 39 points, which was a 9-point drop from the previous year, and ranked only 33rd among 44 countries surveyed. Korea scored less than the average 61 points in Asia, and 47 points worldwide. Vietnam, India, and China ranked first, second and third, and Australia, Hong Kong, and Taiwan ranked fifth, 13th, and 18th respectively. These countries belonged to the middle and top classes and made a big contrast with Korea.

But the bigger concern is that young Korean people's entrepreneurial spirit is among the lowest in the world. In the survey of young people under the age of 35, Korea scored 38 points, a 10-point drop from the previous year. Korea's score showed a big gap with Asia's average score of 61 and the global average score of 52. The findings showed that Korea was behind in almost all categories including the sectors that measured their commitment and willingness to take risks. Perhaps this is due to a social atmosphere that does not tolerate failure. The national economy is bound to lose its vitality if the youths' entrepreneurship spirit is not revived. Korea needs to build a system that promises big rewards for success, and supports recovery from failure as well, just like countries that are known as a haven for start-ups, such as the US and Israel.

KOREA'S CURRENT STARTUP ECOSYSTEM STANDS AT JUST HALF THAT OF THE UNITED STATES

The low entrepreneurship index of young Koreans is also evident in the data of Korea's startups, which is found in the report "Current Status of Korea Start-ups from a Global Perspective" published by the Korea International Trade Association (KITA) in 2018. The report was based on the survey of 128 companies that participated in the "Viva Tech," an annual technology conference dedicated to innovation and startups that was held in Paris, France, and it shows how most of the companies surveyed did not know much about Korean startups. The result was a sharp contrast with the US startups that were highly recognized in the field of artificial intelligence (AI), big data, internet things, bio-health, and renewable energy, and all other areas related to the Fourth Industrial Revolution. Supposing the score of the US startups was 100, the average score of Korea was 55 points. Even when compared with the startup ecosystem, Korea was falling behind them in terms of government regulations, global conference attractiveness, and corporate culture. This means that Korea's startups are just domestic market-centered "big fish in a small pond."

Korea didn't even make it to the top 30 in the ranking of the startup exit, which is about investment return that can indicate if a startup was a success or not. For startups, the two most prominent exit routes are the Initial Public Offering (IPO) and the Merger

Comparison of Major Indexes Between Korea and Silicon Valley in the US

Korea	Category	Silicon Valley
99,720 (20.8 times)	Area(km²)	4,802
51.8 (16.7 times)	Population (million)	3.1
26.6 (16.2 times)	Jobs (million)	1.64
1.693 trillion ('17 IMF)	GDP / total (dollar)	The total value of the big five companies is 3.637.1 trillion won (2.1 times)
32,774('17)	GDP per capita	193,000('17) (5.9 times)

Source: Joint Venture, Silicon Valley Index (2018)

and Acquisition (M&A). According to the KITA report titled "the Economic Contribution and Implications of US Technology-based Startups," the US recorded over 1,600 cases of startup exits, and China, Singapore and Japan were among the top 30 in the number of startup exits. Korea did not make it to this ranking group, because there is no system that can fairly evaluate startups and exit routes are not active. As a result, there are many cases in which promising Korean startups disappear from the scene before finding an opportunity to realize their potential.

YOUNG KOREANS' MOST IDEAL JOB IS BEING A GOVERNMENT EMPLOYEE

Further evidence that young Koreans lack the spirit of challenge is the fact that government employee is the overwhelming number one choice for a career among young Koreans because it is thought to offer the best job security. According to a survey of 1,143 adults in 2018 conducted by a Korea-based online job search portal Saramin, some 26.7% of the respondents (multiple responses allowed) answered government employee or working for public organizations was their number one choice of job. It was twice the second choice of being the owner of a business such as a café and restaurant (16.2%) or office worker (15.0%). The next most popular choices were in the order of artist (11.4%), professionals such as lawyer and doctor (11.4%), engineer and designer (9.9%), one-person broadcasters such as YouTuber (9%), entertainers (7.4%) and webtoon artist. When asked to choose a job that they think was the best, the largest percentage of them picked government employee, and when asked to take into account the real nature of their top choice of job, the largest number of them answered office worker, all of which results are reflecting the reality of today's young Koreans. The survey results were in line with the fact that the most important points for them to consider in a job search were job security and monthly income, in addition to aptitude.

Prior to the Saramin survey, an online job search and HR service provider Incruit and an operator of an internet research company Embrain conducted a survey of 2,153 Korean career men and women about their perception of the relationship between the power group and the no-power group in Korean society. When asked who

Top Ten Dreams Jobs Among Adult Men and Women

Ranking	Desired Occupation	Percentage
1	civil servant, public institution employee	26.7%
2	businesses such as restaurants, cafes, and online markets	16.2%
3	an office worker	15.0%
4	a pure artist, musician	11.4%
5	professionals including lawyer, doctor, etc	11.4%
6	Engineers, designers, etc.	9.9%
7	oe-person broadcaster, such as YouTuber and BJ.	9.0%
8	entertainer	7.4%
9	Creator such as Webtoon Writer	6.4%
10	architect, interior designer, etc	6.3%

*Survey of 1,143 adult males and females. Source: SaramIn

they thought had the most power in Korean society, some 30.1% of the respondents answered government employees have the most power of all occupations. It was followed by chief executives (23.2%) and politicians (19.0%). These findings are in parallel with the survey finding where the largest percentage of respondents picked government employee as the best occupation.

A SOCIETY WHERE EVERYBODY DREAMS OF BECOMING A BUILDING OWNER

It is also shocking that young Koreans are dreaming of becoming a landlord, because it signifies that they prefer settling comfortably in the present instead of taking challenges for a better tomorrow. This finding reflects the increasing number of people who make a fortune without having to work due to the hot real estate market. This is a serious problem facing Korean society because a society cannot be productive if its members don't have the motivation to work.

The fact that their dream is becoming a landlord was confirmed by many other surveys. One such survey was conducted by the job search website, Incruit in 2018. When 801 people were asked what their dream was in the past and what their dream was in the present, the largest number of the respondents (26.3%) answered it was "to have a comfortable life", and the second largest number of respondents answered to become a landlord (16.8%), followed by

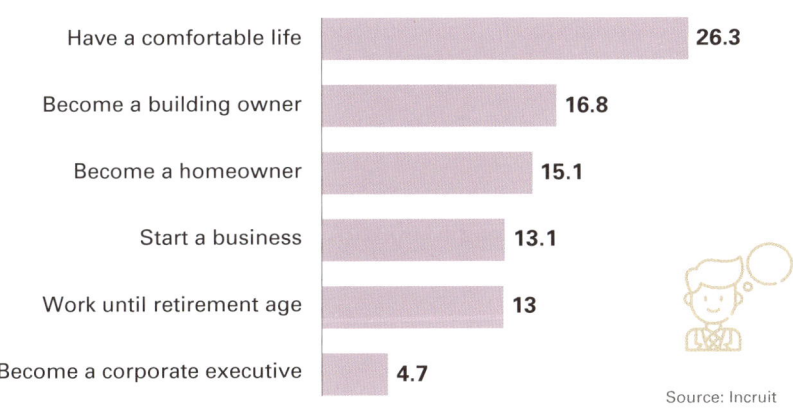

Now that you are a grownup, what is your dream?
Unit: %

Have a comfortable life	26.3
Become a building owner	16.8
Become a homeowner	15.1
Start a business	13.1
Work until retirement age	13
Become a corporate executive	4.7

Source: Incruit

"buy a house" (15.1%). That meant one out of three young adults was dreaming of becoming a landlord. Only a small number of people answered their dream was "startup company" (13.1%) and becoming a corporate executive (47%). These were far from what they dreamt in childhood. Korea has turned into a society where people dream of becoming a teacher, scientist, doctor, singer, or designer when they are little, but once they are grown up, their dreams change to being a building owner. There were less than two out of every ten people who still cherished their childhood dreams.

YOUNG KOREAN ADULTS AVOID JOBS THAT ARE DIRTY, DIFFICULT AND DANGEROUS

At the end of 2017, when the youth unemployment rate had been going up for four years straight, the Korea Development Institute (KDI) published a report that analyzed the reason for the increase. According to the analytic report, the major reason behind the increasing youth unemployment rate was that young Koreans were avoiding jobs in the so-called 3D industries: dirty, difficult and dangerous.

This result has something to do with the fact that young Koreans in the job market have similar levels of skills and competencies. According to the Program for the International Assessment of Adult competencies (PIAAC), which is a worldwide study by OECD, the competencies of the young Korean adults (aged 25-34) are mostly

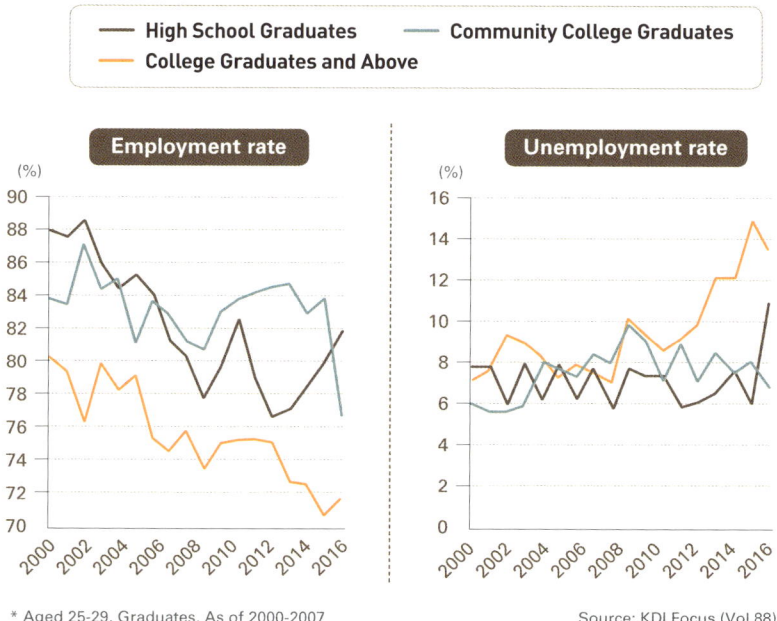

Employment and Unemployment Rates of Men by Educational Level

* Aged 25-29, Graduates, As of 2000-2007 Averages of Jan.-Oct. of each year, a standard error is applied in the 2-year college graduates

Source: KDI Focus (Vol.88)

in the middle levels which means the difference in average levels of competencies was slim. Compared with counterparts in other countries, young Korean adults' language skills were among the top, and math and problem-solving skills were among the middle group.

That is the reason most young Korean adults are searching for middle-level positions in white-collar or blue-collar jobs, while avoiding low-skilled 3D jobs, according to KDI. The problem is the middle-level positions that they prefer are disappearing continuously as the result of automation and other technological innovation. It is important to revitalize the economy and create jobs to bring down the young unemployment rate, but more importantly, the current reality where everybody tries to go to college needs to be changed. It means the education structure has to be reformed from the very earliest stage so that young people can choose a wide variety of jobs depending on their skills and talent.

KOREAN TEENS ARE SUFFOCATING UNDER THE PRESSURE OF COLLEGE ADMISSION

There is another reason Koreans need to change their obsession about college degrees: Korean high school students need to be saved from the crisis resulting from tremendous stress over college admission. Smart Students Uniform, a company specializing in school supplies, conducted a survey through social media about high school students' stress. The results showed that more than half of the respondents said "schoolwork" was their biggest cause of stress. Some answered that friends and family issues were their major source of stress, but their percentages were significantly lower than the stress over college admission.

The result mirrors the fact that Korean students' perceived happiness index is always at the bottom level according to analysis of UNICEF's child well-being report by Yonsei University Institute for Social Development Studies. The happiness index is based on

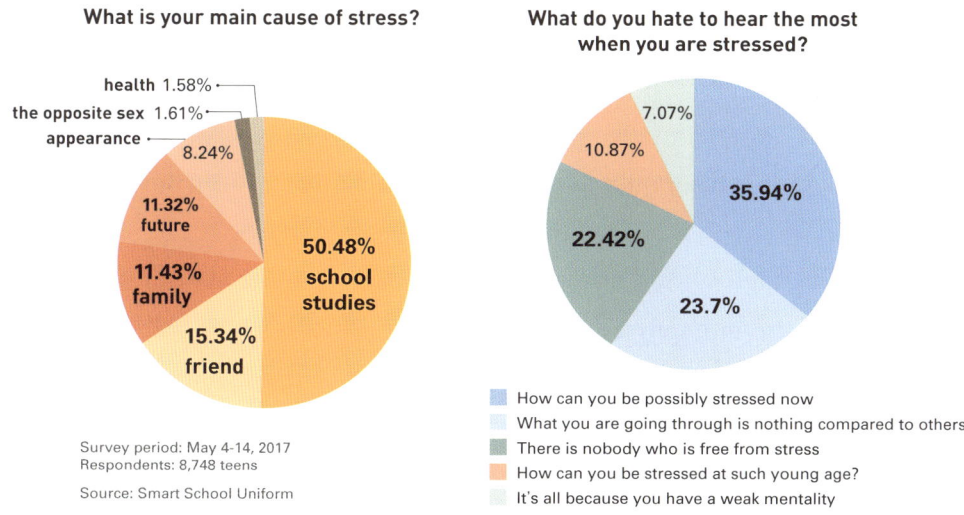

a survey about levels of satisfaction in several aspects of life, school, health, and others. One noteworthy finding was that the higher the students' grade was, the more they experience sleep deprivation. This finding reflects the reality in which students cannot go to bed until very late at night because they have to study for the college entrance exam.

Likewise, the higher the grade was, the bigger the percentage was of students who had experienced suicidal thoughts more than three times and therefore belonged to the suicide risk group. The result signifies that the stress from schoolwork makes Korean youth feel frustrated and helpless until it reaches the point where they develop suicidal thoughts. The level of pressure and frustration students feel over the college admission is so serious that there are even students who declare they refuse to go to college immediately after taking the College Scholastic Ability Test.

Suicide is the Number One Cause of Death Among Young Koreans

The high suicide rate of Korean youth is another statistic that shows the unhappy environment Korean youth are exposed to. According to the Ministry of Gender Equality and Family, suicide has been the number one cause of death among Korean youth for ten years straight since 2007. As of 2016, the suicide rate of Korean youth is 7.8 per 100,000, which is more than double the 3.8 deaths by car accidents per 100,000. Some 2,200 youth are also attempting to commit suicide or harming themselves each year as well. In 2017 alone, 114 Korean juveniles committed suicide. The government estimates that there are about 16,900 Korean adolescents who are at risk of committing suicide or have suicidal thoughts.

The fact that there is no one for the youth to turn to as they go through a difficult time while fiercely competing with others for better school performance is another factor that pushes them to the edge. Many of them are loners who have no sibling or friends. As a result, the number of adolescents who develop mental issues such as depression continues to rise.

According to the "2017 Suicide Prevention White Paper" published by the Ministry of Health and Welfare and the Korea Suicide Prevention Center, the overall suicide rate has been on a

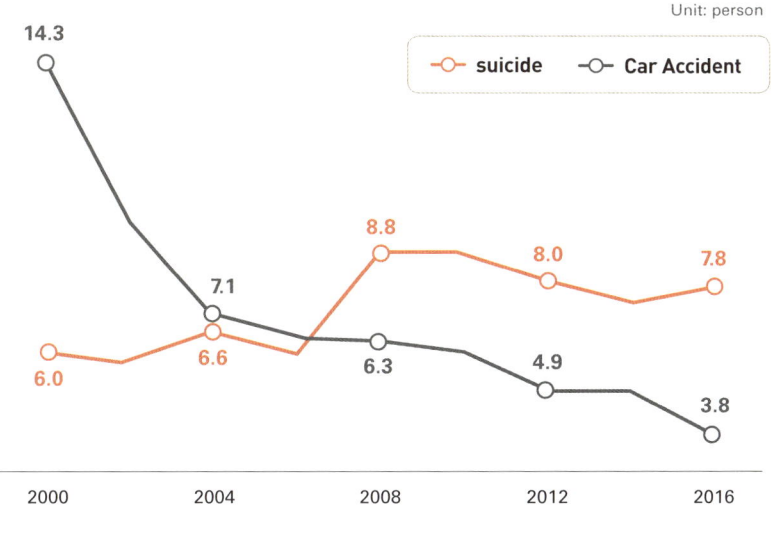

Cause of Death by 100,000 Young Koreans

Source: Statistics Korea

steady decline since 2011, but the suicide rate of teens has increased slightly. Five out of 10 suicides were unemployed or students. The most common cause of suicide was mental problems (36.2%), and the main reason for adolescents to think about committing suicide turned out to be their school record (40.7%).

JUVENILE CRIME RATE THAT CANNOT BE IGNORED ANY MORE

Korean adolescents' stress is contributing to the rising crime rate as well. According to parliamentary inspection reports, a total of 398,917 juvenile offenders were arrested between 2013 and

2017, a daily average of 218 arrests. Theft was the highest with 127,749 offenders, followed by assault at 105,429. There were many adolescents arrested on felony charges, such as rape, aggravated robbery and murder. In the span of five years, 11,200 adolescents were arrested on rape charges, 2,037 on aggravated robbery, and 108, murder. The real concern is that the number of adolescents charged on rape and aggravated assault is continuously going up.

It is a serious problem that school violence and sex offenses are on the rise. According to the National Police Agency, the number of juveniles arrested for school violence went up from 12,495 in 2015 to 12,805 in 2016, and 14,000 in 2017. Sex offenses are increasing at a higher rate. Juvenile delinquency can be attributed to the individual offenders' behavioral problems, but the influence of the social

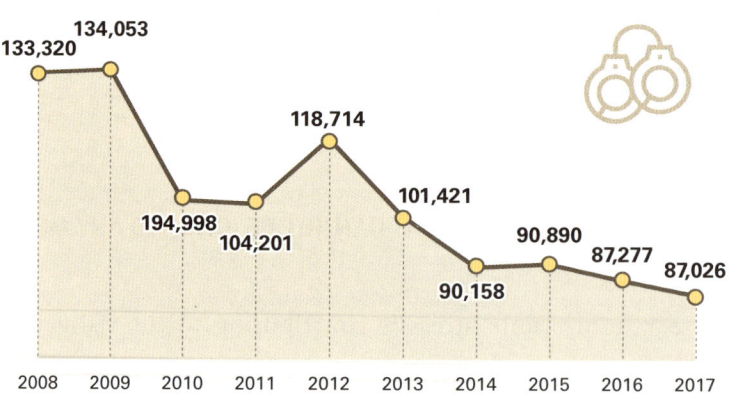

Source: Supreme Public Prosecutor's Office (Prosecution Statistics System)

environment cannot be ignored. There is a need to install systems to prevent crimes before they happen, instead of neglecting students with behavioral problems. Juvenile delinquency is a problem that needs to be resolved by adults. Korean society as a whole should work together to come up with a preemptive measure to solve the juvenile crime problem.

Overview of the Juvenile Crime Offenders by Year / Unit: person / Source: Supreme Prosecutors' Office (Prosecution statistics system)

THE GROWING "KANGAROO TRIBE" POPULATION WHO CANNOT LEAVE THEIR PARENTS' NESTS

The last problem to think about with regard to the weakening Korean youth is the increasing population of the "kangaroo tribe", which is a term for young people who depend on their parents. This problem requires a structural approach since it is a phenomenon resulting from the unemployment crisis and the avoidance of marriage. According to a survey of 3,086 men and women in 2018 by the online job search engine Incruit and the market research agency Duit, 31.0% of the respondents turned out to be the members of the "kangaroo tribe". By age, 45.8% of the respondents in their 20s were members of the kangaroo tribe, and 35.8% of those in their 30s, making them the two largest age groups. Even among people who are in their 40s and 50s, some 20.3% and 15.0% of them were still dependent on their parents, respectively.

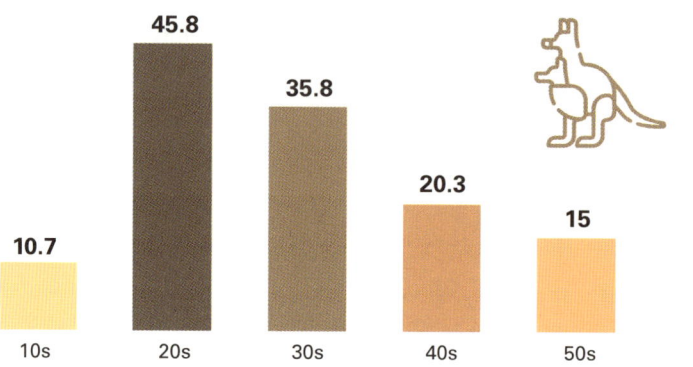

Percentage of People Who Classified Themselves as "kangaroo tribe"

Unit: %

Source: Incruit

Surprisingly, when asked if they had any plan to become independent from their parents anytime soon, one out of ten members of the kangaroo tribe answered they hadn't. Among the respondents who answered that they were going to become independent someday, the majority of them were planning to become independent within three years. Those who answered "within three years" accounted for 30.4% of them, and "within five years", 22.3%. If they are combined with those who planned to become independent "within 10 years", the percentage is pushing 60%. On the other hand, only 19.9% of the respondents answered they would become independent within a year. The growing number of young Koreans cohabitating with parents is not a welcome sign because it can cause conflict among family members and generations, and it also undermines the social dynamic.

UNDERDEVELOPED FINANCIAL INDUSTRY, INCREASING HOUSEHOLD DEBT, AND OVERHEATED REAL ESTATE INVESTMENTS

Real estate and stock markets are the bases on which build their wealth. If these markets are fair and transparent, people can pursue financial stability and a comfortable life after retirement by making investments in real estate and stocks. But that is not reality in Korea. Rapid economic growth caused the skyrocketing increase of real estate prices, and the majority of Koreans are left with no chance to become homeowners. While the housing prices are surging, the government has just been adding more confusion to the real estate market with inconsistent real estate policies, and in the process, contributing to the further polarization of wealth in society.

Rampant urban development projects added another problem to this reality: the overinflated housing prices that are out of reach of most hard-working citizens. Seoul is not among the top group in the ranking of the best cities to live in the world, but the housing prices are among the top in the world. People's belief about real estate never being a losing investment and the government's low-interest rate policy have resulted in ever-increasing household debt as well. The household debt-to-GDP ratio is increasing at the second fastest pace in the world, and the number of "high risk households" that are struggling with heavy household debt continues to grow. The stock market is also stuck in an underdeveloped state where many investors are caught up in the get-rich-quick fever and look for opportunities to make profit from short-term investment. Another problem is the weakening competitiveness of the financial industry, which resulted from a government-controlled finance system.

SIX YEARS OF SAVING ON AVERAGE TO BUY A HOUSE

For Korean people, home ownership has a special significance because Koreans believe true independence means having a house in their names. In areas where housing prices are affordable, people buy a house within a short time after getting married, but in Seoul and the capital area where the majority of apartment units are over a million dollars, it is not easy for people to buy a house.

The "2017 Housing Statistics" released by the Ministry of Land, Infrastructure and Transport shows how long it takes for Koreans to become a homeowner. According to the statistics, it took an average of 6.8 years for Koreans to buy their first house. It means they have to save every penny that they earn for 6.8 years without spending any of it until they have enough money to buy a house. It is two years less compared to the average of 8.5 years in 2010, but the number has

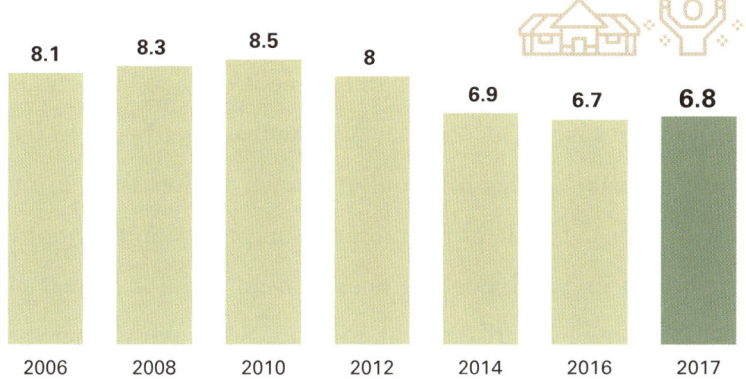

Years It Takes to Buy the First House in Life

Unit: Year

Source: Ministry of Land, Infrastructure and Transport

remained at around 6-7 years consistently since 2014. It takes a lot longer when the region is restricted to the capital area.

Since housing prices are so high, half of the homeowners are feeling burdened by mortgage payments, according to the statistics. Even though the statistics show how difficult it is to be a homeowner in Korea, the home ownership rate is over 60%. This number indicates how much Koreans aspire to be homeowners. The result is in parallel with the results of a survey conducted by the Ministry of Land, Infrastructure and Transport, where eight out of ten Koreans responded that they believe they must buy their own houses.

LIFE GETS HARDER BUT HOUSE PRICES CONTINUE TO SURGE IN SEOUL

Even though the average length of time it takes to buy a house is seven years, it takes a lot longer when purchasing a house in Seoul, because housing prices in Seoul are much higher than in other areas. It is because all infrastructure, companies and schools are concentrated in Seoul, but that doesn't mean Seoul is a great place to live, as show by statistics that compare Seoul with other major international cities.

Mercer, a global management consulting firm , evaluates and ranks 231 cities on 39 factors including political, economic, environmental, personal safety, education and transportation and publishes the results in the Quality of Life Survey. In this survey, Austria's capital Vienna is unrivaled at the top. Vienna has been selected as the best city to live in for eight years straight since 2010. The Economist Intelligence Unit's (EIU), a British business within the Economist Group, also picked Vienna as the world's second most livable city. Zurich of Switzerland, Auckland in New Zealand, Munich in Germany and Vancouver in Canada are some of the cities that ranked high on the survey. Seoul ranked 76th and did not make it to the top group.

However, the ranking of real estate prices was different from the ranking of the best cities to live. According to Numbeo, a global database of cities and countries worldwide, the average price of

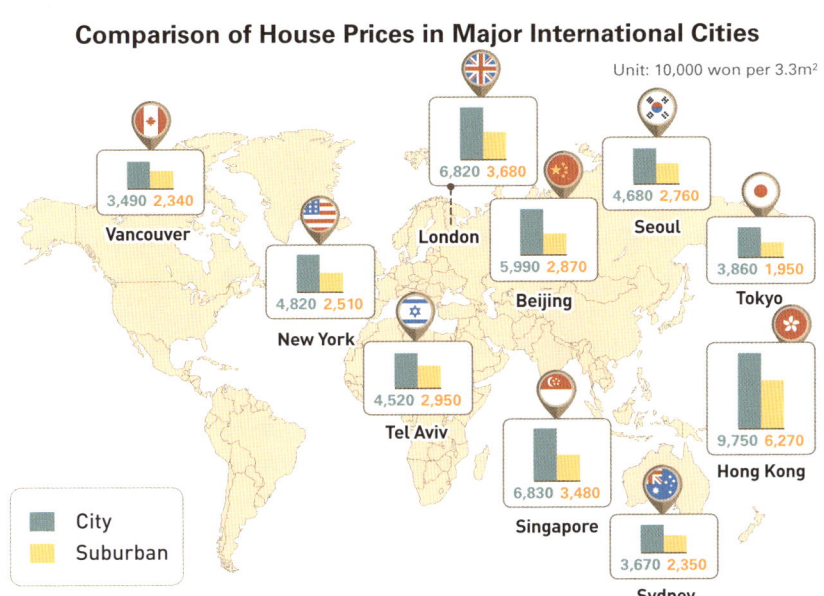

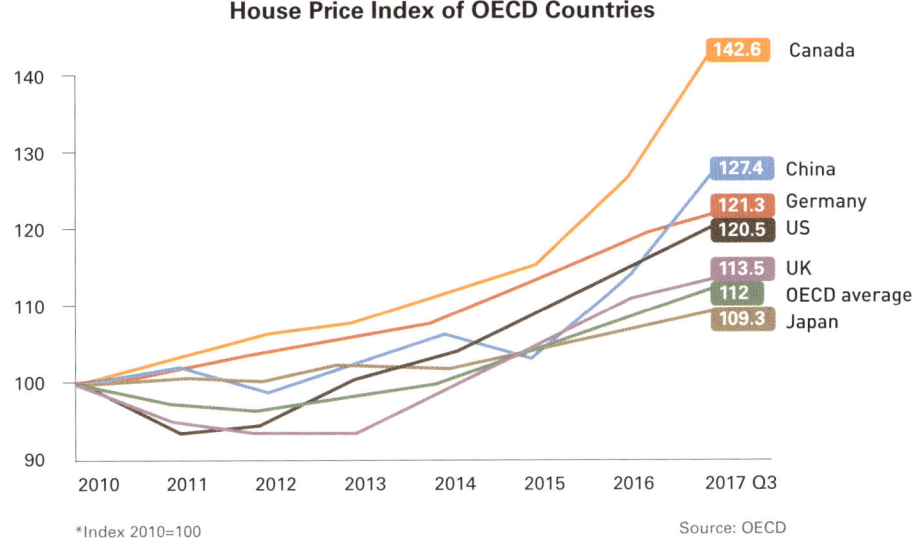

apartments in Vienna was about KRW24.1 million per 3.3 m2 as of February 2017, which was only about half of the average price of KRW46.8 million in Seoul. Housing prices in Seoul were lower than Zurich, but other than that, it was higher than other international cities such as Auckland, Munich and Vancouver. Of course, there are cities like Hong Kong, Shanghai and Bangkok house prices are higher than Seoul even though the living conditions are no better. But in terms of the living conditions for the cost, Seoul cannot be considered as better than those cities.

THE PRICE-TO-INCOME RATIO IS RELATIVELY HIGHER THAN IN MAJOR INTERNATIONAL CITIES

House prices being subject to consumer prices and the income level of different countries, a comparison of absolute amounts might not give an accurate picture of the housing market conditions of each country. That is the reason the price-to-income ratio (PIR) is often used as the standard. Simply put, PIR can be easily understood as "the number of years that it takes to save enough money to buy a house". If the PIR number is ten, it means one can buy a house by saving disposable income for ten years without spending any of it.

Analytic data proved that housing prices in Seoul are overinflated even when compared to other cities based on the PIR data. According to the "Comparative Analysis of House Prices in Cities Worldwide" by NH Investment & Securities, the PIR of Seoul

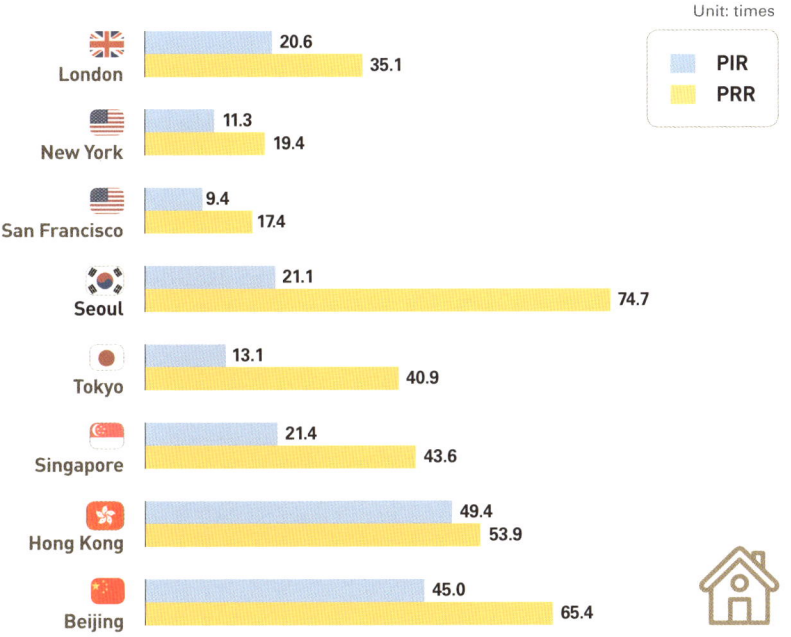

recorded a rather high 21.1 as of the end of 2018. When calculated to get the 10-year average, the PIR went down to 15.7, which is a result of the significant increase in house prices in 2018. The PIR data of major cities around the world shows that Seoul was higher or similar to New York (11.3), Tokyo (13.1) and London (20.6) but was lower than Hong Kong (49.4) and Beijing (45.0).

In the survey by Numbeo, Chinese cities such as Beijing, Shanghai, Hong Kong, and Shenzhen ranked first to fourth. London came in at eightieth, Singapore at ninth, and Bangkok at 15th. Seoul ranked 23rd among all cities evaluated. The PIR of Seoul was no higher than major cities in China and Southeast Asia, but still, it does not belong to the low level in terms of the absolute standard. In the case of Vienna, which was selected as the world's best city to live, its PIR ranked 67th.

DIFFERENCE OF HOUSE PRICES CONTINUES TO GROW BETWEEN SEOUL AND SURROUNDING AREAS

Comparative analysis of house prices in Seoul with those in local cities within Korea also proves how expensive houses in Seoul really are. According to statistics released by the Korea Appraisal Board, the quintile share ratio of the houses sold nationwide has been around 8-11 times since 2012 when the earliest data is available. The quintile share ratio is calculated by dividing the fifth quintile (top 20%) by the first quintile (bottom 20%) prices of houses sold throughout the country. The ratio indicates how many times higher, the most expensive house prices are relative to the least expensive house prices.

For example, if the average house price of the first quintile in the nation is KRW100 million, the house prices of the fifth quintile range between KRW800 million and KRW1100 million. As of 2018, house prices of the first quintile nationwide were within the range of KRW60-70 million. During the same period, the quintile share ratio was slightly over 11, indicating the average house price of the

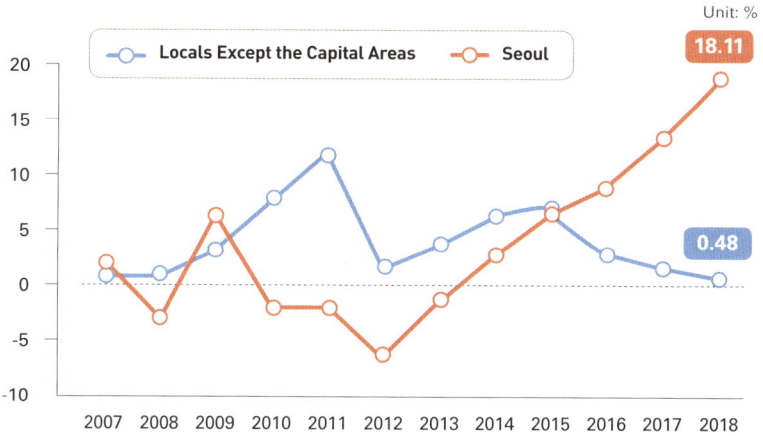

Changes in House Prices in Seoul and Local Areas

*The price for 2018 is based on the cumulative price change as of Dec.14, 2018 compared to the end of 2017

Source: Real Estate 114

fifth quintile was more than KRW700 million. The problem is, the ratio continues to grow over time, because despite the government's strong regulations intended to control the real estate market, the house prices continue to surge in Seoul and the capital area while it continues to drop in local regions.

Sometimes the government introduces measures to curb skyrocketing real estate prices in the capital areas only to create the negative effect of making house prices in local cities drop. The gap in house prices is widening particularly fast between the Gangnam district in Seoul and local cities where the population is rapidly declining. The reason is clear; housing demand is concentrated in regions with well-developed infrastructure such as transportation, education, and companies. All government agencies are raising their pitches for balanced regional development, but the house prices only keep polarizing, primarily because they are all talk and no action.

SERIOUS REAL ESTATE SPECULATION ROBS NON-HOMEOWNERS OF THEIR DREAM

Real estate has been widely popular as a "never-losing" investment in Korea, but this popular investment also brought about some negative consequences, the biggest of which was real estate speculation. Speculators rush in and fuel speculation fever in areas whose property values are likely to increase for various reasons, such as being rezoned for urban development. The National Tax Service carried out undercover investigations in new cities around the capital area and discovered real estate speculators were resorting to truly diverse methods to make money off properties. Sometimes they purchase an apartment building and split it or rezone it into multi-family housing units and split the shares of the building among themselves, and sometimes they get involved in the trading of apartment purchase rights for which they are not qualified. The speculators also raise prices of lots designated for redevelopment by repeatedly purchasing and selling them until they make the final sales when the price is high enough and leave the market all at the cost of the actual end users of the lots.

There are people who fake marriage or make false claims of

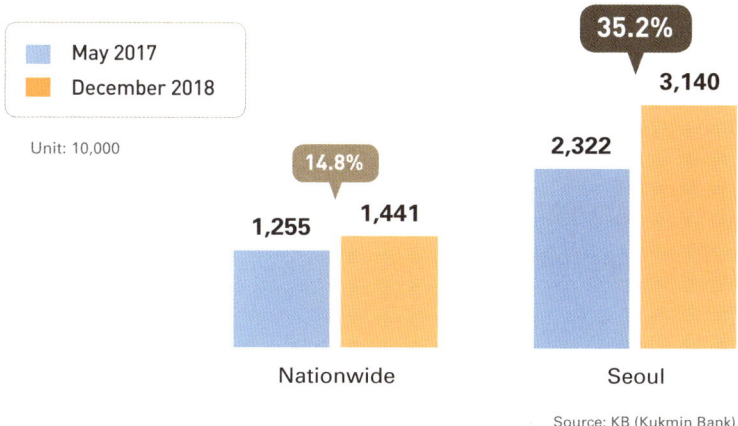

Source: KB (Kukmin Bank)

pregnancy to increase their chance to get the purchase rights of apartment units, and some even doctor papers to make it look like they are caring for aged parents for the same reason. There are even people who file for a fictitious divorce solely for the purpose of speculating on real estate. The situation reached a point where real estate agencies would provide consulting and advice on how to cheat the system in order to speculate on real estate and enjoy a business boom when the housing prices skyrocket. The government has been cracking down on the speculators and introducing preemptive measures to stop those speculative forces, but the government's efforts could not completely eliminate them. It is largely because there are so many people who are hell-bent on getting rich quick on real estate speculation, but it is also because the supply could not meet the demand. Anybody can see the answer to the situation is balanced supply and demand, but the situation remains unresolved because, concerned about the possibility of rapid increase of housing prices and real estate speculation, the government has not been able to introduce a bold and consistent real estate policy.

REAL ESTATE POLICIES THAT CHANGE DIRECTION EACH TIME THE ADMINISTRATION CHANGES

It is the people who don't own a house that get hit the hardest when property prices surge. For that reason, the government pulled out a wide variety of real estate policies whenever the property prices go up. But the government policies only end up making the prices go up more and encouraged more speculations instead of stabilizing the real estate market because the policies keep leading the market astray. Almost all government real estate policies give the impression that they are politically motivated decisions or rash responses to the changes happening in the real estate market, instead of being rational or consistent.

When the oil crisis towards the end of 1970 froze the real estate market, the Chun Doo-hwan administration implemented policies designed to stimulate and revitalize it. But when the housing prices skyrocketed as a result, the government introduced regulatory policies. This approach continued in the following Roh Tae-woo and Kim Young-sam administrations. The first phase of new city

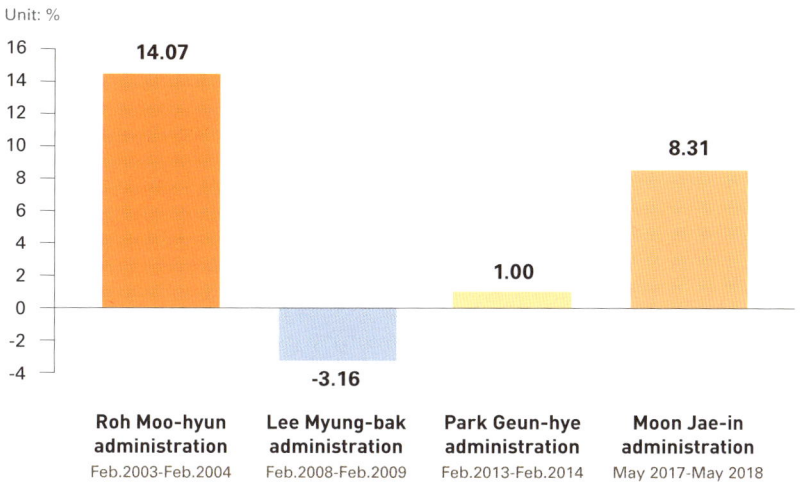

Changes in Apartment Prices Nationwide One Year After a New Administration

Source: Real Estate 114

development that started along with these regulatory policies, played a critical role in stabilizing the real estate market, proving how supply had a more powerful effect than regulation.

When the market was virtually frozen in the wake of the foreign exchange crisis that hit Korea in 1997, the Kim Dae-jung administration turned real estate policies in the opposite direction: The administration implemented virtually every kind of policy that could increase real estate prices such as deregulation of property prices, abolishment of the restriction on purchase right resale, easing up on requirements for apartment applications, reduction of taxes on the transfer, acquisition, and registration of property, and expansion of home loans. These measures resulted in an overheated real estate market. The following Roh Moo-hyun administration introduced debt-to-income ratio (DIT) and lowered the loan-to-value ratio (LIV) to curb real estate speculation. The Roh administration also reintroduced the restriction on the purchase right resale and increased property tax, while trying to supply more housing units through the second phase new city development project. But all these efforts fell short of controlling the skyrocketing house prices.

To overcome the financial crisis that hit Korea, the Lee Myung-bak administration liberalized real estate market regulations, and the succeeding Park Geun-hye administration maintained the same line of real estate policies. Then during the Moon Jae-in administration, housing prices started to go up again, and the government turned to the implementation of strong measures to curb real estate speculation. While the real estate market in Korea continue the cycle of heating up and cooling off, people lost their trust in the market and the government could not eradicate speculating forces.

ALARMING INCREASE IN THE RATE OF HOUSEHOLD DEBT-TO-GDP

The high housing price relative to income has a lot to do with rapidly increasing household debt, which is one of the detonators for the Korean economy. According to the Bank for International Settlements (BIS), Korea's household debt-to-GDP ratio as of

Increase and Decrease of Household Debts to GDP in Major Countries

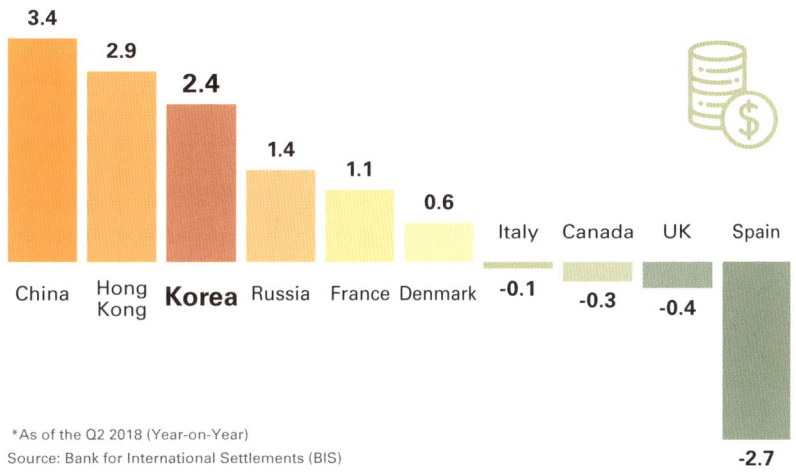

Unit: %P

*As of the Q2 2018 (Year-on-Year)
Source: Bank for International Settlements (BIS)

the end of the second quarter of 2017 reached 96.0%, which made Korea rank seventh among the 43 countries evaluated for statistics. The household debt started to increase sharply after 2014 when the government loosened regulations on loans, until it made a 14.0% increase within a span of four years. At the end of the third quarter of 2017, Korean household debt reached the KRW1,500 trillion mark for the first time ever. The government is implementing stricter regulations to control the situation, but there is no sign of improvement. Instead, the household debt is increasing at a rate faster than other countries. According to the BIS, Korea's household debt is growing at the second fastest pace in the world.

Korea's household debt service ratio (DSR) hit a record high during the same period as well. A household DSR measures the share of disposable household income used for debt repayment during a certain period, and it is often used as an indicator of the risks posed by household loans. The higher the DRS number is, the greater the burden of debt repayment. Korea's DSR was the sixth highest among 17 countries evaluated for statistics. Korea's household debt has continued to grow even after the release of these statistics.

A GROWING NUMBER OF HIGH-RISK HOUSEHOLDS STRUGGLING WITH LOAN REPAYMENT

The mounting household debt is resulting in the growing number of "at risk households." When the percentage of a family's disposable income that goes toward paying debts is over 40%, the family is classified to be "at high risk". Simply put, a family is at high risk if the household income is one million won and 400,000 of that is used to pay debt, and the amount of debts is higher than the amount of assets. According to the Financial Stability Report submitted by the Bank of Korea to the National Assembly, the number of Korea's high-risk households exceeded 340,000 as of the end of March 2017, up 10 percent from the previous year. The number of hig-risk households has continued to grow from 297,000 in 2015 to 312,000 in 2016, and 346,000 in 2017.

This is data from the period marked by low interest rates, and the household debt is sure to grow faster if the interest rate goes up. The

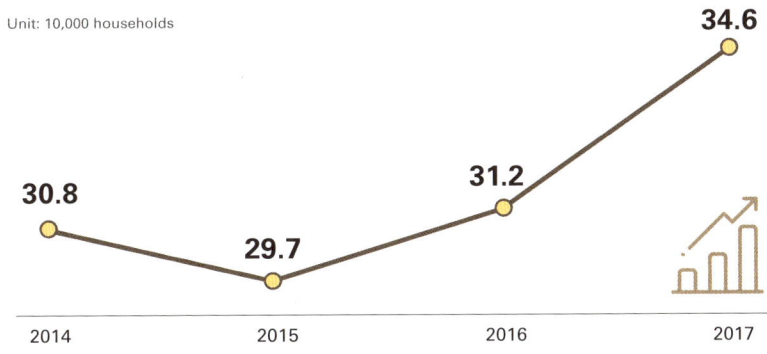

Sharply Growing Number of High-Risk Households

*When the percentage of a family's disposable income that goes toward paying debts is over 40% and the amount of loans is higher than the amount of assets, the family is classified as "high-risk household."

Source: Korea Bank

Bank of Korea conducted a test to find out the impact the interest rate increase has on high-risk households. According to the test results, if the interest rate on loans goes up by one percent, debt ratio of at-risk households increases from 5.9% to 7.5%. If the interest rate on loans increases by two percent, the debt ratio is expected to increase to 9.3%.

The sharply increasing number of high-risk households include the so-called "house poor" people, who own a house but are struggling because they took out a mortgage beyond their means to buy the house. According to the "Financial Report", some of those "house poor" people are spending over 70% of their disposable income to pay loans. Some of the heavy debtors who took out loans from more than three financial institutions were from the bottom 30% of low income households. These are the people with the high risk of turning into delinquent debtors once the interest rate goes up or the economy gets worse.

STOCK MARKET IN KOREA DOMINATED BY GAMBLING-TYPE SHORT-TERM INVESTMENTS

Th real estate market is not the only market that attracts speculative funds. A significant amount of money is streaming into the stock market from those who only look for opportunities to get rich quick. Speculation is more pervasive among small investors. Korea's speculation in the stock market comes in various forms such as direct investment whose ratio is higher than advanced countries, short-term investment, and investing when there are special events. Of course, investment institutions and foreigners who make investments with massive amounts of funds are the main players behind the market fluctuation, but the small investors who make their investments based on rumors are also causing disruption in the stock market.

The fact that there are a significant number of investors who are betting on short-term investment as if they are gambling is indirectly proved by how long the investors hold shares on average. According to the Korea Exchange, the average holding period per stock in the securities market is 180-200 days. In the KOSDAQ market, it is much shorter at 65 days. These figures include investment institutions and foreigners who tend to hold their shares for a relatively long

Average Stock Holding Period and Index Growth Rate by market

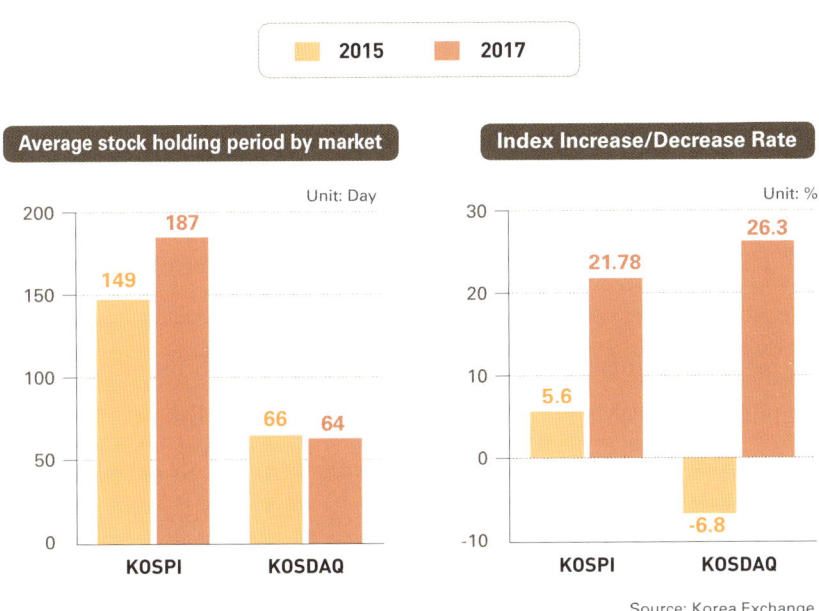

Source: Korea Exchange

period. The number of days is sure to be much shorter if it is calculated based only on individual small investors.

This phenomenon makes a big contrast with stock markets in advanced countries where investors hold stocks for more than six months. The problem is, short-term investment has the higher risk of loss. According to a report by Samsung Asset Management, the odds of losing money when making an investment only for a day in the KOSPI from 1980 to 2016 were 48.8%. On the other hand, the odds of losing was zero if invested for more than 20 years. Ultimately, short-term investment not only contributes to the backwardness of the Korean stock markets, but it also increases the risks for investors to lose money.

COMPETITIVENESS OF A FINANCIAL SECTOR THAT IS SMALLER THAN THOSE OF OTHER INDUSTRIES IS ANOTHER PROBLEM

The competitiveness of theKorean financial industry, including the stock market, is falling far behind in the global market compared to Korea's manufacturing industry. In the Global Competitiveness Report by the World Economic Forum, Korea's financial sector ranked around 80th until 2017. For this reason, Korea used to be mocked as worse than Uganda in Africa. The Korean government raised an objection to its evaluation method, and when it changed the evaluation method that used to heavily lean towards qualitative evaluation, Korea jumped in the ranking to 19th in 2018. By becoming one of the upper-middle group of the top 14% among the 140 countries evaluated, Korea was able to recover its pride to a certain degree. But still, it was below 15th place in the overall ranking. Korea's financial competitiveness is low largely because of the involvement of the government. There has been no major innovation for a long time because financial institutions have been operated in a fashion similar to a bureaucratic society.

Hyundai Research Institute published in 2017 "the Fourth Industrial Revolution and Its Impact on the Financial Market" that included statistics on finance-related patent applications that were

Financial Industry-related Patent Applications Filed Under the PCT

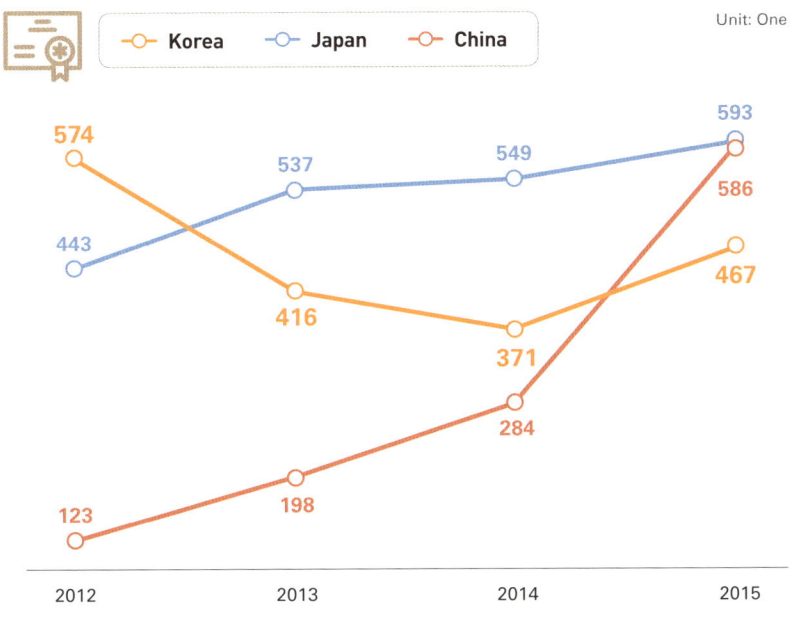

Source: OECD

filed under the PCT (patent cooperation treaty) by OECD countries. According to the statistics, the number of patent applications filed by the US has been continuously growing from 1,651 in 2012 to 1,802 in 2015, while the number has been going down in Korea from 574 to 467 during the same period. This is related to the fact that the R&D-to-sales ratio in the financial and insurance sector is only 0.2%. This number speaks volumes about how underdeveloped the Korean financial industry is, particularly when considering how the number is less than wholesale and retail (0.5%) and construction industries (0.5%) where the need for R&D is not so strong. The data on research and development expenditure in the financial industry by country shows the United States spend over 800 times that which Korea does, and the UK, over 100 times.

RESISTANCE FROM THE GROUPS WITH VESTED RIGHTS INCLUDING DOCTORS, PHARMACISTS, TAXI DRIVERS AND LABOR UNION

In Korea, there are groups that unleash the biggest power in hindering national and social development, and even the economic growth: interest groups. They collude with government employees and hinder government policies intended to promote people's health and welfare and consumer protection and benefits. If these interest groups think newly introduced products and services have even the slightest possibility to undermine their interest, they mobilize all methods and channels to stop them. Consequently, there are a significant number of cases where innovative technologies developed by hard working researchers at schools, laboratories and companies are not utilized properly.

Even though sharing cars, accommodations, and workspaces is becoming a global trend, the shared economy is not working in Korea. There are technologies and telemedicine devices that can be used to diagnose and treat patients remotely, but their use is limited due to the opposition from doctors' organizations. Even though the fintech market is growing at a fast pace, online banking enterprises are held back due to the regulations that mandate the separation of banking and commerce. The labor market is in urgent need to become more flexible for companies to increase productivity, but the labor unions leaders who have vested rights and earn billions of won in annual salary are serving as a stumbling block, while civil and social organizations interfere in politics and block government efforts for labor reform and deregulation policies. The pervasive abuse of power and authority by those who are in superior positions and unfair trading practices in industries are also a malaise that undermines the potential of the Republic of Korea.

THE WORLD'S LARGEST RIDESHARING SERVICE PROVIDER UBER HAS A HARD TIME IN KOREA

According to the London-based multinational professional services network PwC, the global shared economy market has grown at an annual rate of 80 percent since 2010 and is expected to reach $335 billion by 2025. Citing the figures, Hana Institute of Finance identified favorable market conditions, such as the scalability of the internet and responses from younger generation consumers as reasons for the great potential of a shared economy. Uber, which is a ridesharing service provider that is leading the shared economy, and Airbnb, a shared accommodation provider, and WeWork, a shared workspace provider, are supporting such predictions and analyses.

But the situation is different in Korea. These sharing service providers cannot do business in Korea because they are stopped by double and triple regulatory barriers and strong resistance from interest groups. Uber had entered the Korean market in 2014 but had to withdraw in just a year without really having an opportunity to test its services in Korea. Kakao tried the same ridesharing business but met the same fate as Uber did: Kakao had to stop the service just 39 days after it started due to extreme opposition from the taxi industry and the government's lukewarm attitude toward regulatory reform. Various sharing services that took root as ordinary businesses in the United States, China, and even in Southeast Asian countries are not able to make forays into Korean markets because of the resistance of groups with vested rights.

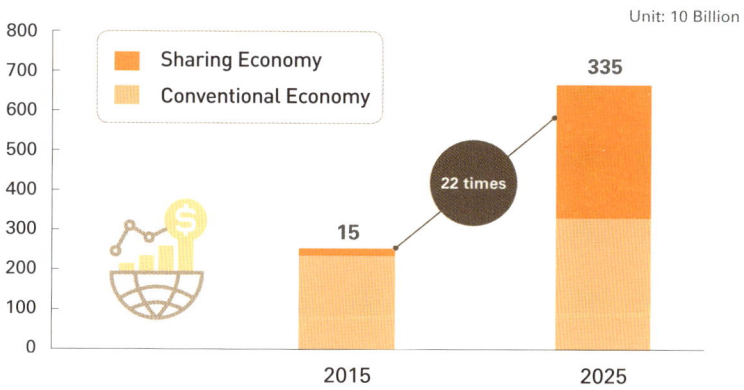

Economic Scale Growth Forecast

Source: Credit Suisse, Hana Institute of Finance

TELEMEDICINE SERVICE IS STOPPED BY THE STRONG POWER OF DOCTORS

Telemedicine is emerging as a new growth engine supported by the development of the information technology industry, but it is also struggling in Korea due to opposition from doctors. Unlike advanced countries that are conducting various telemedicine experiments, the Korean government is allowing it only on a limited basis. In Korea, the first medical examination is mandated to be a face-to-face examination between patient and doctor, and the telemedicine service is allowed only from the second examination. Even this medical practice is allowed under such strict conditions that it is almost as if telemedicine services are prohibited in Korea.

LG Economic Research Institute has published a report that forecasted the future of the medical field in 2003, which was around the time when medical service providers were allowed to practice telemedicine. This report included a scene where a home physician who was available round the clock measured the patient's body temperature and wrote prescription to the patient all through the online application. Twenty years have passed since then, but this has not happened in reality yet.

It is the Korean Medical Association (KMA) that is preventing the growth of the telemedicine industry, citing the need for strong regulations. The KMA has been interfering with telemedicine in every way possible, even to minor details of guidelines in pilot

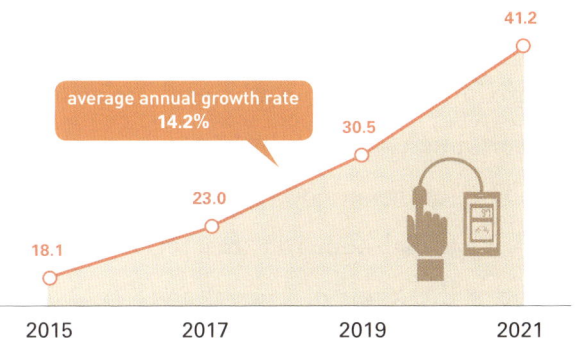

Scale of the Global Telemedicine Market

projects. It is all because they are trying to protect doctors' vested rights. Even though the technology is advanced enough to allow doctors to examine patients and write prescriptions remotely through smartphones or wearable devices, the KMA is blocking the improvement of the system under the premise that they are committed to protecting people's lives and safety. Doctors are such a strong influential group in society that even politicians are taking their sides because they don't want to cross the medical community.

According to statistics portal Statistica, the global telemedicine market is expected to grow from $18 billion in 2015 to more than $41 billion in 2021. It is frustrating that Korea may not be able to grab and take advantage of such a huge opportunity due to resistance from the medical community and government regulations.

EVEN SIMPLE MEDICINES ARE NOT ALLOWED TO BE SOLD AT CONVENIENCE STORES

Another case in which consumer benefits are being held up due to resistance from interest groups is the regulation on sales of over the counter (OTC) drugs at convenience stores. The Ministry of Health and Welfare had numerous meetings trying to complete the adjustment of the kinds of general and OTC drugs allowed to be sold at convenience stores by June 2017 but failed to reach a conclusion in the end. The over-the-counter drugs at issue included antacid drugs that treat stomach pain, antidiarrheal medicines that relieve symptoms of diarrhea, and ointments for burns. The government tried to expand the list of allowed items as much as possible for consumer convenience but failed to reach a conclusion due to opposition from pharmacists' groups including the Korean Pharmaceutical Association. These groups insisted that, while a few slow-selling medicines could be allowed to be sold at convenience stores, Tylenol --- one of the bestselling medicines at convenient stores --- should be excluded from the allowed items, eventually ending further discussion about the issue.

Pharmaceutical companies and consumer groups are criticizing the government that is being led around by the nose by pharmacists and are calling for increasing the number of items allowed to be sold or bought at convenience stores, because, while in the U.S. and other foreign countries, consumers can buy the medicines that they need

Chronicle of Efforts to Expand OTC Medicines Available at Convenience Stores

Nov.2012	Started to sell 13 types of general medicine 24 hours a day at convenience stores
Feb.2017	The Ministry of Health and Welfare started discussion on expanding items (Plan to be completed in June 2017)
March-December 2017	2nd, 3rd, 4th, 5th meetings took place but failed to reach an agreement
Aug.2018	Failed to reach an agreement at the sixth meeting due to opposition from the pharmaceutical community
2019	The 7th meeting has not been scheduled

at nearby convenience stores even at night or on holidays, it is not possible in Korea. If a drug store is closed, consumers have no option other than going to hospital even for minor symptoms that could be relieved by simple medicines. Even then, people in remote, isolated areas don't have that luxury of getting medicines from a hospital because they have very limited access to medical facilities. These are the inconveniences that must be addressed and resolved, but the government cannot do anything about them due to the interference from interest groups.

INTERNET BANKS MANAGE TO OPEN FOR BUSINESS ONLY TO FACE FURTHER OBSTACLES

Internet banking businesses such as K-Bank and Kakao Bank have also been unable to grow due to regulations. These two banks

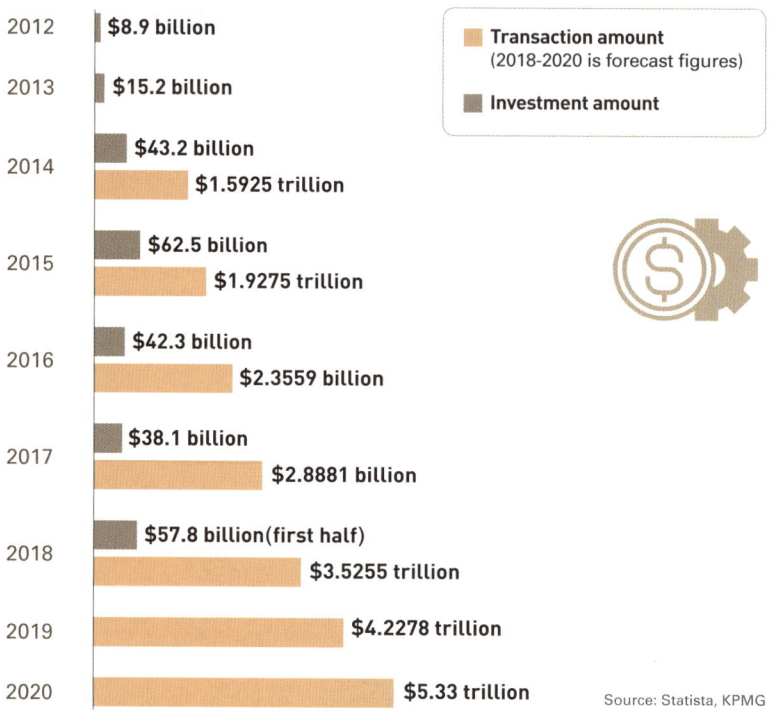

began operations in 2017. It marked the first opening of new banks in 25 years after the establishment of Pyeonghwa Bank. However, it was the first time ever in Korea that fintech-based internet banking businesses were established. There were many sabotage attempts by existing financial institutions with vested interests to stop their establishments, but they managed to open for business after overcoming the many obstacles put in their way. The internet banking services turned out to have many advantages in terms of interest rates and fees, not to mention the convenience of making deposits and payments and taking out loans all through smartphones. Although it might not be able to replace conventional offline banks all together, it was expected that its "catfish effect" would bring innovation and vitality to the financial market.

But reality unfolded differently. The profit structure was poor compared to the high initial investment costs. They suffered significant unnecessary losses during the trial and error stage. On top of that, the regulation regarding the separation of banking and commerce was the biggest stumbling block for internet banking to take a leap forward. Their innovative financial services required IT companies to become the largest shareholders, but the government had put a cap on the shares allowed to them: The existing regulation whose original objective was preventing conglomerates from turning banks into their own private vaults was now holding back the growth of internet banking services. The government has been loosening regulations in accordance with the growing global trend and increasing the limit of shares for IT companies, but still, there are too many restrictions compared to advanced countries.

According to the US-based statistics portal Statista, the size of the global fintech market is expected to surpass $5 trillion in 2020. In Korea, however, eight out of 10 fintech startups are complaining about having trouble when it comes to growth due to excessive regulations, and investment has also been slow as well.

LABOR REFORM IN LIMBO DUE TO THE GREEDY LABOR UNIONS OF LARGE CORPORATIONS WITH VESTED RIGHTS

According to the Ministry of Employment and Labor, Korea's labor union membership rate stood at 10.7% (2.088 million members) as of 2017. It was the highest since 2008 after a small increase from the previous year. Korea's labor union membership rate peaked at 19.8% in 1998 before recovering the 10% level in 2011 after membership to multiple unions was allowed. The two umbrella labor groups, the Federation of Korean Trade Unions and the Korean Confederation of Trade Unions, account for 41.5% and 34.0% of the membership rate respectively. The number of members who belong to individual business unions that do not belong to umbrella organizations accounts for 21.4%. As of 2016, the union membership rates of major advanced countries were mostly higher than that of Korea. The U.S. was comparable to Korea at 10.7%, while Britain (23.5%), Japan (17.3%), Germany (17%), and Australia (14.5%) had higher rates than Korea's union membership rate. The average union membership rate of OECD member countries was 29.1%, which was twice that of Korea. Korea has a low union membership rate, but the impact of labor unions on society is significant. In fact, their impact reaches beyond labor-management issues to politics, society and the economy as a whole.

The Federation of Korean Trade Unions and the Korean Confederation of Trade Unions are mainly led by labor unions of

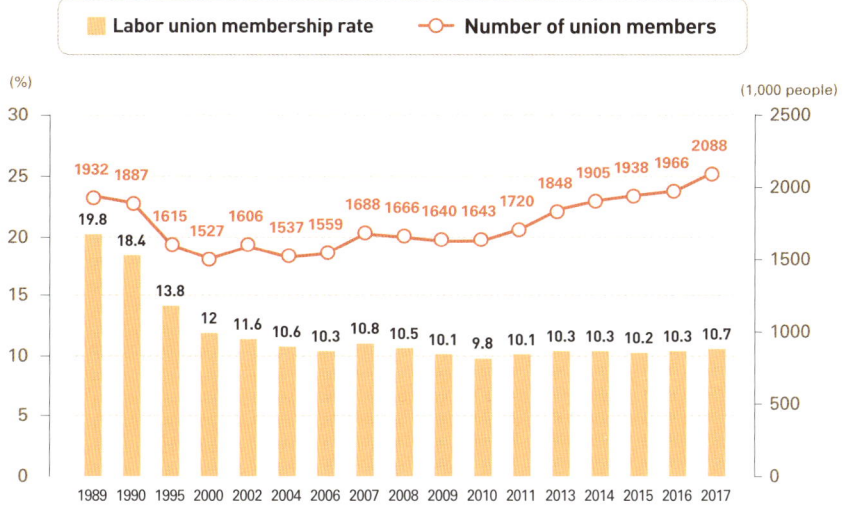

big companies in major industries such as automobiles, shipbuilding and steel. The average annual salary of many of the union leaders exceeds KRW50 million. Nevertheless, they have been demanding wage hikes and excessive bonuses that exceed the inflation rate every year. When their demands are not met, they cause massive damage to companies by going on strike until they get what they want, which they do in the end.

As a result, wages at large companies that belong to the two umbrella labor unions continued to rise, widening the wage gap with temporary hires and employees at small-and-medium-sized companies along the way. That is the main reason behind the solidly established dual structure of the Korean labor markets. The two umbrella labor unions have also been actively intervening in politics, blocking the expansion of the flexible work system which became more needed than ever as a result of the shorter working hour policy, and they've been protesting the "Gangju-style jobs (44 hr./wk., KRW35 million a year jobs)" that the government pursued as a win-win model for both labor and management as well.

Consequently, labor-management relations are becoming the biggest Achilles' heel of the Korean economy. According to the "2019 Global Talent Competitiveness Index (GTCI)" released at the World Economic Davos Forum in January 2019 by INSEAD, a graduate business school with campuses in Europe, and the Adecco Group, a temp staffing firm, Korea's labor-management cooperation ranked 120th out of 125 countries. It was a few ranks drop from 116th place a year earlier. Korea ranks 30th in overall talent competitiveness, largely because of the labor-management relation problem.

SOCIAL ORGANIZATIONS' OVERSTEPPING INTERFERENCE WITH POLITICS

Korea has built a democratized political system within a relatively short time compared to other countries. During the democratization process, many civic and social organizations were born and continuously expanded their influence in various areas, including politics, society, economy and culture. Many people with

Number of Registered Non-Profit Civil Organizations

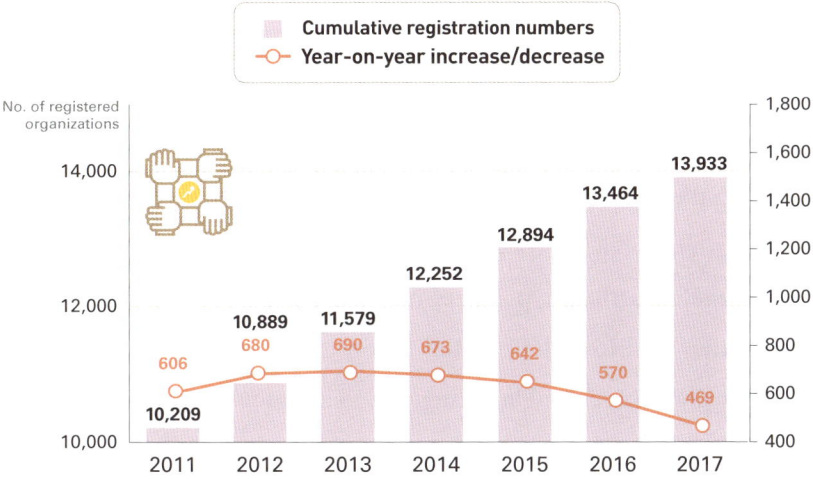

Source: Ministry of Public Administration and Security

a background of working in citizen groups, including the mayor of Seoul, have entered politics and changed the map of Korean politics.

In the early days of democratization, social groups played a big role in developing and advancing Korean society. However, some social groups became the cause of various negative side effects due to their biased political views and radical claims. There are civic groups that are seeking goals different from each other, criticizing each other and dividing public opinion. Of course, civic groups can intervene in politics to some extent for values and policies that are consistent with their aims. The fact that they contribute to the nation's development by presenting the right alternative cannot be ignored either. Even so, they are overstepping their authority when they directly intervene in politics.

If civil and social groups start to interfere with government policies, it could create a situation where too many cooks spoil the broth. Civil and social groups should limit their activities to conveying the needs of citizens to the government and politicians and criticizing fault policies. If they jump into politics and either support or sabotage a particular political party, their actions will backfire, because they will lose their initial vision and only add more chaos and confusion to society. Unfortunately, many social organizations in Korea are engaged in political activities while claiming that they are there to advocate democratization, justice and fairness.

PERVASIVE ABUSE OF AUTHORITY AND POWER DESTROYS INTERPERSONAL RELATIONSHIPS

One of the factors that is promoting and contributing to the division of Korean society is the interpersonal relationships that are clearly divided into the ones who have positions of power and the others who haven't. The abuse of power and authority by those holding superior status emerged as a pervasive and serious phenomenon in Korean society after a few corporate executives, politicians, and high-ranking government employees were accused of having abused their power and authority and enraged the Korean people in what came to be known as the "Gapjil scandals." Gapjil involves two parties: the abuser known as Gap, and the victim known as Eul. Gapjil became so embedded in Korean society that even the Euls who had been abused by the Gaps repeat the same Gapjil once they move up the ladder to acquire the status of a Gap. The consequence is that almost all Koreans are subject to abuse of power and authority in one way or another, except for the small number of people who have the most superior status in society.

There are many reasons that can explain this phenomenon. One of the reasons is the fact that compressed economic growth brought about prosperity in terms of materials, but not in terms of morality. The culture of treating others with respect remains so poor in Korean society that people often look down and belittle others once they grab power in whatever form or scope. Another reason is the rapidly disappearing traditional social order following the Korean War because it resulted in the growing desire among people to become recognized by others. This desire often manifests in the form of Gapjil by those who have the wrong idea about showing off their power and achievement.

According to a survey released in 2015 by the Korea Press Foundation, some 95% of the respondents thought "Gapjil is a problem more serious in Korea than other countries." When asked about the scope of the problem, 77% of respondents answered that it was a problem "widespread at all levels." The number of respondents who considered themselves as the victim of Gapji, or Eul, accounted for 85%. By abuser, the largest number of respondents, or 64% of

Is the Gapjil Problem More Serious in Korea Than in Other Countries?

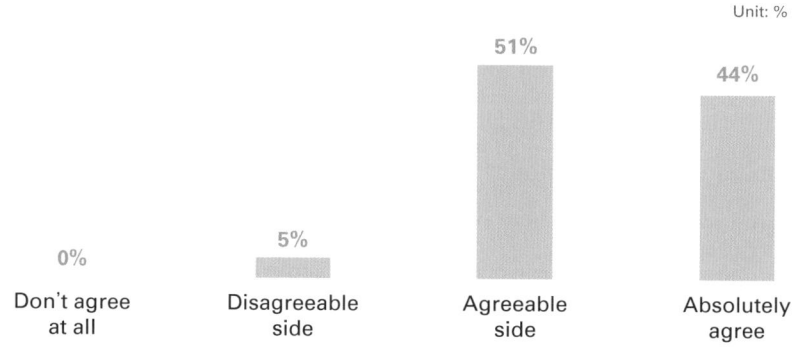

Source: Korean Press Foundation Research Center Online Survey (Jan.14 – 16, 2015)

them, pointed out chaebol as the main abuser, followed by politicians and high-ranking government officials at 57%, employers and bosses at 46%, clients and higher-level institutions at 45%, journalists at 32%, professionals such as professors at 31%, and retail customers at 28%. In short, they all believed Gapjil was taking place virtually in every sector.

DIE-HARD UNFAIR TRADING PRACTICE

The pervasive culture of Gapjil is one of the leading causes of unfair trading practices among companies as well. In Korea, industries are built on structure where small and medium-sized companies are the subcontractors making money from supplying materials and services to larger companies. Under these circumstances, numerous

Percentage of Cases Filed for Violation of Fair Trade Act by Type

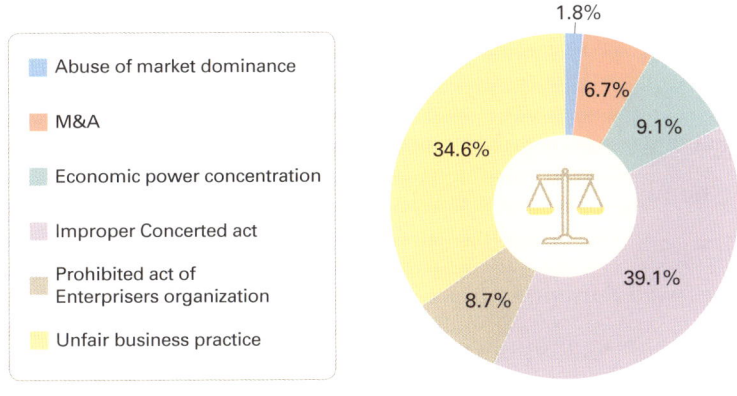

*As of 2017

Source: Fair Trade Commission

subcontracting small-to-medium-sized companies fiercely compete with each other to supply their products to larger companies, during which process the power of the larger companies keeps growing until they became a hotbed of unfair trading practices. The situation is improving little by little as the result of the government's intervention, but still, many small-to-medium-sized companies that are bound by exclusive trade contracts are suffering from unfair trading practices.

This reality was verified by a written survey conducted by the Fair Trade Commission (FTC) in 2018 on 5,000 contractors and 95,000 subcontractors that were heavily engaged in subcontract transactions in manufacturing, construction and service sectors. The

FTC conducts the same survey every year. The result showed that nine out of 10 small-to-medium-sized subcontractors thought their trading practices have improved, but many subtractors who were bound by an exclusive trade contract with contractors or supplying products to large retailers answered that not much have improved. The number of subcontractors who were forced into unfair terms in transactions recorded an increase compared to the previous year as well. Unfair transactions were happening in various ways, including misappropriation of technical data, unfair management interference, and unfair decision on payment amount and discount. The FTC is striving to improve the system by revising related laws and regulations to fix unfair trading practices, but it is not easy to eradicate unfair trading practices as long as the people's awareness of the issue is not raised to the level of advanced countries.

THE GOVERNMENT AND POLITICAL CIRCLES ARE LOSING THE PUBLIC TRUST

In Korea, the government and political circles are at an underdeveloped level unlike the rapid economic development. They fail to present vision and long-term plans for national development because they are too caught up in party politics with the goal of seizing power to worry about anything else. The result is that more than 60% of people have lost their trust in the government. There are other factors that push people to lose their confidence in the government including bureaucratic government employees and civil complaints that take forever to be addressed, in addition to the poor communication between government agencies. It also has a lot to do with the fact that Korea's corruption perceptions index remains in the mid-tier range, even though its economic power has reached almost to an advanced country's level. In the National Assembly, issues that call for immediate measures for the people's livelihoods are pushed aside because the ruling and opposition parties are in an extremely conflicting relationship. In fact, seven out of 10 bills submitted to the National Assembly end up being scrapped after having been left unprocessed for a long period of time. Given that, there is no wonder that people lost their confidence in political circles.

SIX OUT OF TEN KOREANS DISTRUST THE GOVERNMENT

The more advanced a country is, the more people trust their government. It is because the administration is transparent, fair, and efficient. The OECD evaluates member countries' level of public trust in government institutions based on a poll of 1,000 people in each country by asking if they have confidence in their central government.

The poll results show that the level of public trust in Korean government institutions was lower than European countries. In the 2018 survey, Korea ranked 25th by moving up seven ranks from the previous year, but the people who answered that they had trust in the government accounted only for 36%. In other words, more than six out of 10 Koreans still do not trust the government. Korea has been hovering between 25th and 32nd in the ranking since 2013, with only 23-36% of Koreans saying they trust the government. In Switzerland, on the other hand, the number of people who answered they had trust in the government accounted for 82% of the respondents. Luxembourg, Norway and the Netherlands also ranked tops in public trust in their government.

Economic achievements are most important for the government

Ranking of the Confidence in National Government of OECD Countries

Country \ Year	2013	2015	2017	2018
Switzerland	1st	1st	1st	1st
Luxembourg	2nd	4th	2nd	2nd
Portugal	29th	36th	23rd	13th
Korea	**29th**	**26th**	**32nd**	**25th**
Italy	24th	31st	32nd	33rd
Number of countries measured	34	40	35	34

Source: World Gallup Poll, OECD and KDI (Lim, Wonhyuk, Shun) 2018

to earn trust from the people. It is proved by the fact that income levels are in direct proportion to government confidence index. The government can build trust only when it is recognized in the efficiency of administrative services, openness of public data, response to disasters and integrity, on top of economic development.

In this regard, the Korean government lacks many things. Some examples are the low-growth rate, frequent safety accidents and administrative practices that bring inconvenience to the people, among many other things, although there has been some improvement. The government should spend its budget on public service instead of politically motivated policies. Only then the government can build the trust that it has lost.

POOR CORRUPTION PERCEPTION INDEX IS ANOTHER CAUSE OF PUBLIC DISTRUST IN GOVERNMENT

The government's inability to solve the people's distrust problem has a lot to do with the nation's transparency. Korean's corruption perception index is so poor that it barely avoided a failing grade, just like the people's trust in government. As of 2017, Korea ranked

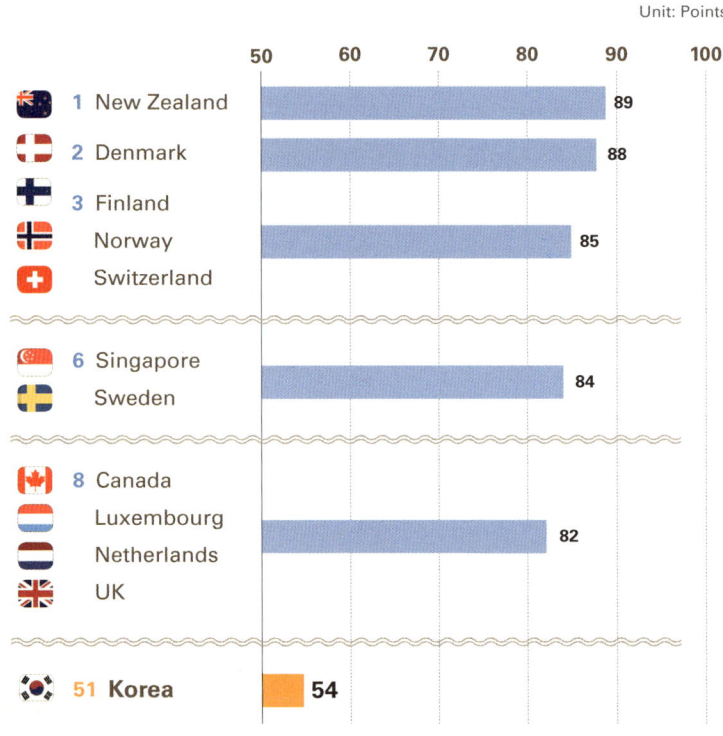

*As of 2017, 180 Countries

Source: Transparency International

Corruption Perception Index in Korea by Year

Source: Transparency International

51st out of 180 countries with a score of 54 out of 100 points in the Corruption Perceptions Index (CPI) released by the Korean branch of the Transparency International (TI) that is headquartered in Berlin, Germany. Among OECD member countries alone, Korea ranked 29th out of 35 countries, which put Korea at the bottom.

It was in 2016 that Korea ranked lowest since the corruption index started in 1995 because that's the year when the presidential impeachment was triggered by major political scandals. That year, Korea's ranking dropped to 52nd with 53 points. Korea has been moving up the ranking little by little lately but considering how Korea has been hovering between 20th and 40th for 20 years, Koreans need to try harder to build a more transparent society.

The world's least corrupt nation turned out to be New Zealand with 89 points, followed by Denmark with 88. Finland, Norway and

Switzerland also fared well on the ranking with 85 points. Among Asian countries, Singapore scored 84 points and Japan, 73 points. Korea needs to learn and benchmark how and with what system these countries can maintain a high level of transparency. Some of the wide variety of measures Korea can take include the establishment of an independent anti-corruption agency, protection of whistleblowers and expansion of anti-corruption training.

THE NUMBER OF BILLS PENDING AT THE NATIONAL ASSEMBLY IS PUSHING 10,000

The National Assembly's low productivity is another problem. Lawmakers from ruling and opposition parties propose numerous bills to maintain voter support whenever there are issues, but they are not so enthusiastic about passing those bills. Most of the proposed bills were also prepared in such a rush that their original objectives often got sidetracked during the consultation process. There are also numerous bills that have been stuck in a corner without having so much as a chance to be brought to the table.

The National Assembly failed to pass more than 10,000 bills before the end of 2018. Among them are many bills that have direct impact on people's livelihoods. A look at the data from the first half year of the 20th National Assembly alone reveals just how unproductive Korean lawmakers have been. In particular, the Public Administration and Security Committee had the largest

Overview of the Bills Processed by the National Assembly by Year

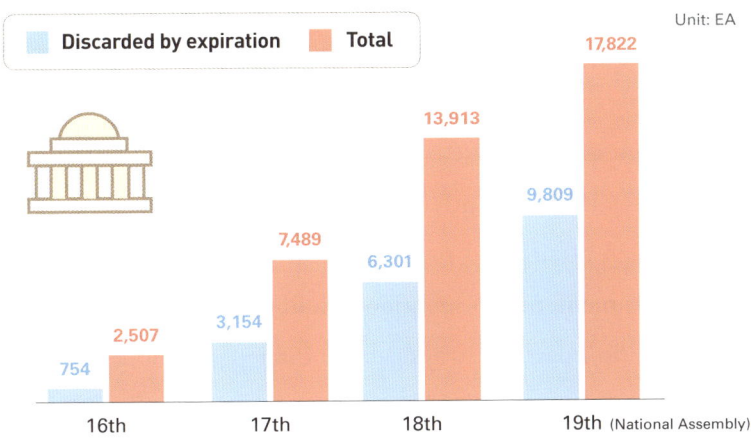

Source: National Assembly Bill Information System

number of pending bills with 1,564. Of the 1,890 bills proposed by the 20th National Assembly, the Committee processed only 326 of them, recording a mere 17.2% processing rate. The Legislation and Judiciary Committee received 1,348 bills and handled only 214 of them, leaving 1,144 bills pending.

According to the National Assembly's Bill Information System, a total of 13,303 bills were submitted during the first two years of the 20th National Assembly, of which 3,564 were processed, recording only a 27% processing rate. The 19th National Assembly had a processing rate of 32%. Korean lawmakers' poor performance is such a serious problem that even the National Assembly speaker himself lamented, "I am so ashamed of it," referring to the performance of lawmakers in the first half year of the 20th National Assembly.

INTENSE CONFLICT BETWEEN RULING AND OPPOSITION PARTIES INCAPACITATES THE NATIONAL ASSEMBLY

One of the reasons the National Assembly became so incompetent is the intense conflict between the ruling and opposition parties. They are constantly locking horns over virtually every issue from foreign affairs and national security to the economy, society, and environment, not to mention a political agenda. Both the ruling and opposition parties always call for inter-party cooperation, but in reality, they fight over every issue, all because they are being driven by politically motivated decisions instead of thinking from the people's perspectives and following great causes.

When holding confirmation hearings for Cabinet ministers nominated by the president, the lawmakers from the opposition parties use the hearings as an opportunity to criticize political rivals and expose their corruption instead of trying to evaluate the nominees' ability to perform their duties. The president also pushes forward with the appointment of nominees ignoring rational reasons to disqualify them. If the opposition party raises objections, lawmakers from the ruling party make a counterattack to defend the President. With a situation like this, there is no hope for cooperation between the ruling and opposition parties.

The presidential office, the government institutions, and the ruling party need to consult with the opposition parties before making decisions on critical items such as the North Korea issue. But that

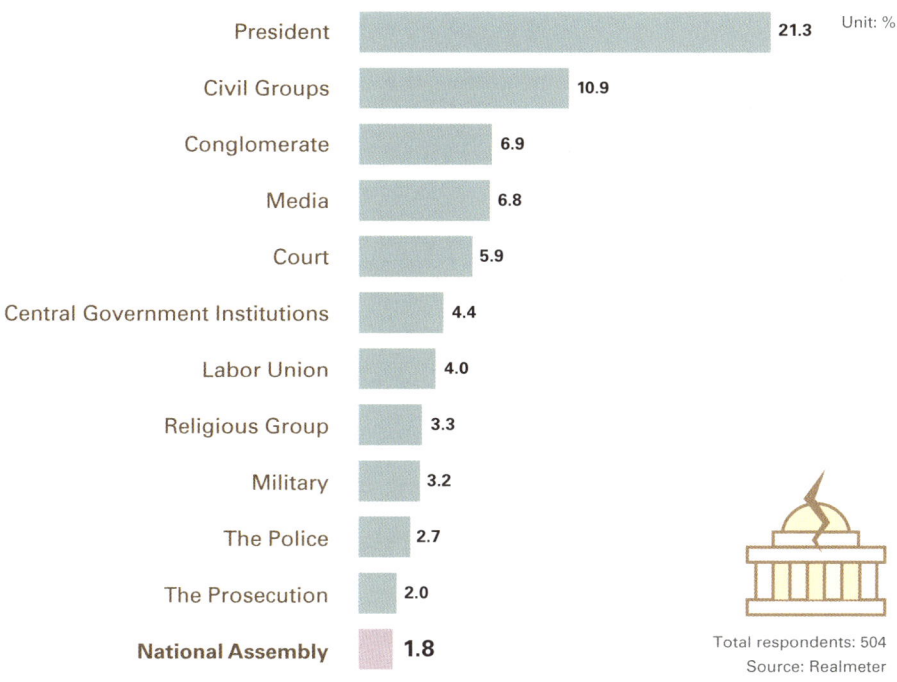

The Level of Public Trust in Government Institutions 2018

Unit: %

Institution	%
President	21.3
Civil Groups	10.9
Conglomerate	6.9
Media	6.8
Court	5.9
Central Government Institutions	4.4
Labor Union	4.0
Religious Group	3.3
Military	3.2
The Police	2.7
The Prosecution	2.0
National Assembly	**1.8**

Total respondents: 504
Source: Realmeter

is not what happens in reality. A trilateral consultative body that includes the presidential office, the ruling party and the opposition parties has been set up to discuss pending issues together, but it is not enough to resolve the conflict problem because both ruling and opposition parties are not making sincere efforts to work together. Once a decision is made on a policy, the ruling party pushes forward with it regardless of the objections from the opposition parties, consequently antagonizing the opposition parties and making them revolt. The ruling and opposition parties should make small concessions to reach an agreement on issues, but concession is hard to find in Korean politicians. The bitter conflict between the ruling and opposition parties is incapacitating the National Assembly, and the people have to pay the cost.

PUBLIC DISTRUST IN POLITICS IS AT A SERIOUS LEVEL

In a 2015 survey of 2,000 adult men and women across the country by the Presidential Committee for National Cohesion (PCNC), some 51.8% of the respondents cited "political conflict between the ruling and opposition parties" as the most aggravating conflict in our society. Many respondents also cited dishonest, incompetent politicians, law-bending politicians, and politicians who incite regionalism as the obstacles to national unity.

A survey of 1,050 adult men and women conducted by the Korea Press Foundation in 2018 showed similar results. In survey results by social sector, the level of public confidence in politicians and politics was the lowest at 6.9%. This percentage was lower than the average level of public confidence in society as a whole which was rated at 32.2%.

It mirrors the results of a poll conducted by Metrics with 1,000 men and women at the request of Maeil Business News (MBN) regarding the proportional representation voting system. According to the poll results, seven out of 10 respondents said they were against

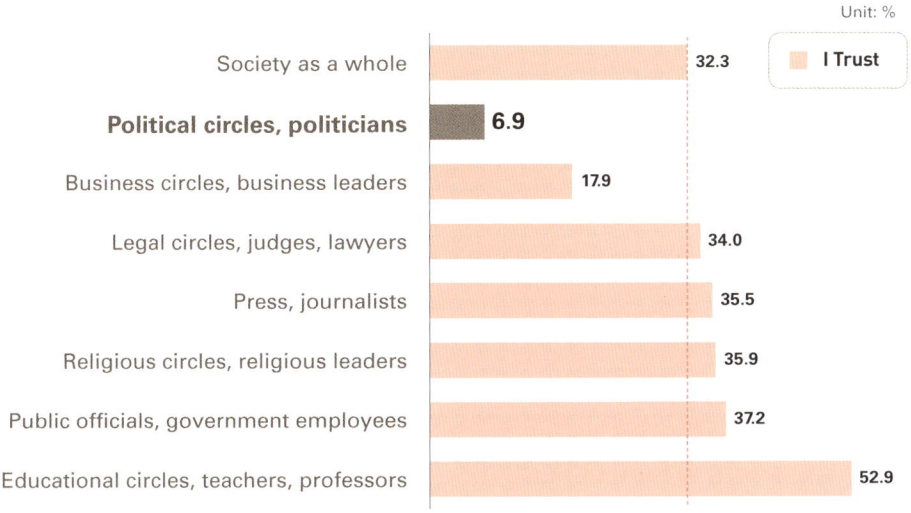

increasing the number of lawmakers. These poll results speak volumes about how high the level of public distrust in politics really is.

Korean politicians must know the reason. There are lawmakers who constantly use gutter talk like lowlifes, and there are lawmakers who abuse their power and authority until they become the subject of political scandals. More than a few politicians have criminal records, and a fair number have built wealth by speculating on real estate.

If the moral standard falls below that of the average person, the least they can do is be good at the job to make up for it, but they aren't. Rather than racking their brains to present visions and policies that will sustain us for 10 years or even 100 years, they come up with rashly hatched legislative measures only to please their supporters, and they have no problem changing their claims whenever necessary. Few politicians are willing to sacrifice themselves for social integration, because they are committed to smearing their rivals to gain a politically advantageous position. Then there are the many policies that keep changing each time a new administration is established. Korean politics can never regain public trust unless they are willing to push forward with a complete overhaul.

LOW FISCAL SELF-RELIANCE RATIO OF LOCAL GOVERNMENTS RESULTS IN HIGH DEPENDENCE ON THE CENTRAL GOVERNMENT

In Korea, all power and resources are concentrated in the central government. On the surface, everybody seems to be calling for decentralization and autonomy of municipalities, but in reality, the central government is monopolizing any influence on the nation and society as a whole. Except for Seoul, the metropolitan area and some metropolitan cities, most municipal governments have a low self-reliance ratio.

According to the 2017 local governments' finance information that was released by the Ministry of Public Administration and Security on the Local Finance Integration Open System website(lofin.mois.go.kr), Korea's national average fiscal self-reliance ratio stood at 55.23%, down 0.59% from the previous year. The fiscal

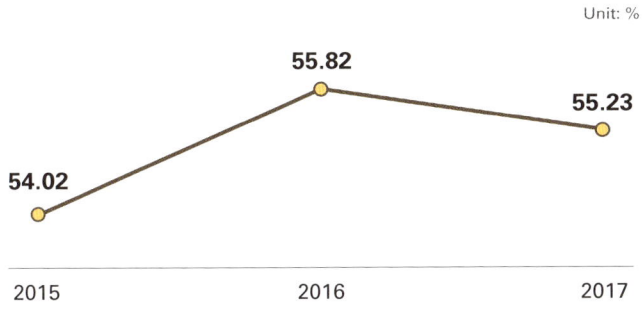

Trend of the Local Governments' Fiscal Self-Reliance Ratios

Source: Ministry of Public Administration and Security

self-reliance ratio refers to an index that shows the ability of a local government to raise the money they need to run the government.

The fiscal self-reliance ratio was high in the capital areas including Seoul (86.39%), Sejong (73.58%), Gyeonggi (70.6%), and Incheon (66.83%), while the ratio was in the low 30% range in North and South Jeolla Providences, North Gyeongsang Province and Gangwon Province. The data shows that the fiscal self-reliance ratio is poor in places marked by a low density of companies and population, thereby have a poor ability to create value-added products. Debt owed by local governments was on the decline, but the financial dependence on the central government in terms of shared tax and subsidy was increasing. Local governments are relying on the support of the central government because, even though their tax revenues from local taxes and others are on the rise, the amount is not sufficient.

THE BUREAUCRATIC COMPLACENCY IN GOVERNMENT EMPLOYEES HINDERS REFORM AND INNOVATIVE ADMINISTRATION

Civil servants enjoy relatively good job security compared to employees of private companies. They can keep their job until retirement, and they receive a generous amount of pension even after retirement, unless they make critical mistakes and lose their job. That is the reason excellent human resources flock to take civil service examinations. However, once they become government employees, they do not utilize their abilities to the fullest. It is because they don't get the recognition even if they demonstrate good job performance, and if they make a mistake while working devotedly, they could face severe consequences such as being left out in this round of promotions. That is the reason government employees easily fall into the trap of developing an apathetic mentality.

But they are not the only ones to be blamed for this reality. Once they pass the extremely competitive civil service exam, they start their career with pride, but the reality they face as a newly hired civil servant often undermines their pride and self-esteem, and even prevents them from being motivated to work with creativity. While they are a low-ranking civil servant, they must write reports, being careful not to displease their superiors, and even when they move up the ladder to become high-ranking officials, they are exposed to others who are in the position to reprimand them, the most typical example of which is politicians. Lawmakers constantly criticize and reprimand government officials. Government officials also have to read the minds of the politicians from the opposition parties and those who work in the presidential office, and they have to be on a constant look out for the movements of citizen organizations.

However, just doing as they are told to by their superiors is not the answer to their problem, because they have to consider the possibility of being accused of being a part of the so-called "deep-rooted evils" once the administration is changed. That is the reason behind the "Byun Yang-ho Syndrome," which refers to the government officials who try to avoid getting involved in any issue that could backfire later on. People claim that government officials and civil servants should be allowed to raise objections or refuse to follow orders from

The Number of Government Employees Sued for Having Abused Authority & Obstruction of Exercise of a Right

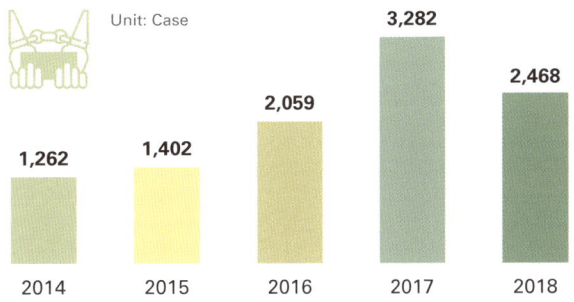

Unit: Case

2014	2015	2016	2017	2018
1,262	1,402	2,059	3,282	2,468

*As of the First Half Year for case of 2018

Source: Supreme Public Prosecutor's Office

superiors if the orders have something to do with illegal activities, but it is not easy for government employees to refuse demands from their direct superiors.

SLOW PROCESSING OF CIVIL AFFAIRS, ANOTHER SIDE OF THE BUREAUCRATIC COMPLACENCY

The apathetic mentality of government employees is most clearly seen in the way civil affairs are handled and processed. One can often see government employees refusing to grant permission for no reason or abandoning civil complaint files in drawers. There are also various types of damage caused by government employees who take forever to process civil affairs such as citizens' complaints and petitions.

People in business often have their plans for the construction of a factory or warehouse go astray due to the corrupt government employees working in municipalities. In a worst scenario, their projects and plans could even become scrapped all together. There are more than a few businessmen who have suffered hardships because of the government employees intentionally harassing them by taking forever to grant permission or licenses. Some even kill themselves after they are pushed to a crisis or forced to file for bankruptcy because of the government employees who keep procrastinating to take care of civil affairs.

There are many reasons civil servants harass people using civil affairs as their weapons. There are government employees who

Overview of the Inprocessing of Civil Petitions for Grievance

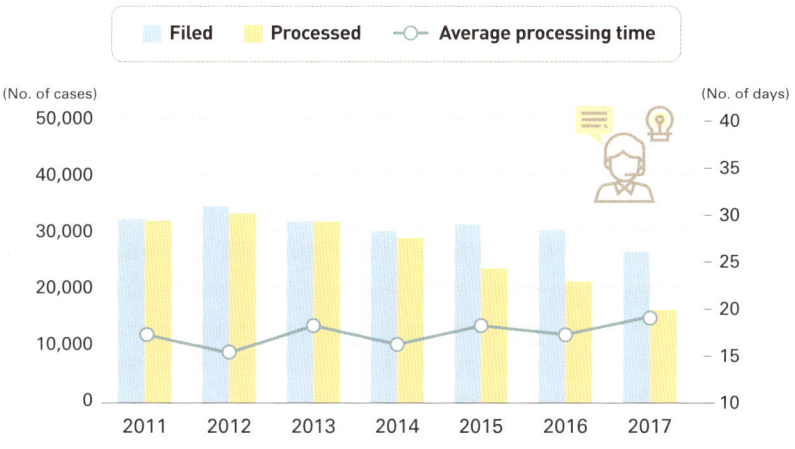

Source: Anti-Corruption and Civil Rights Commission (National Rights White Paper)

intentionally take time to process civil affairs with an anticipation for bribes, but there are also many cases in which passive government employees try to avoid getting involved in anything that could put them in hot water later due to complicated interests. If a permit is granted, they could face complaints from other residents, and if they are afraid of having to take responsibility later, they give all kinds of excuses to delay the process. They delay until the petitioners are so tired of waiting that they give up on their own. It is because of these behaviors that people think civil servants have developed an apathetic mentality.

To improve this, the government needs to create an environment where they can work with a sense of calling and mission. They have to be compensated for their performance, and they should not be asked to take responsibility for the work that they had to do. Only then can they break free from the apathetic attitude and the habitual delay in processing civil affairs.

LACK OF COORDINATION BETWEEN GOVERNMENT INSTITUTIONS UNDERMINES THE EFFICIENCY OF THE NATIONAL ADMINISTRATION

Close cooperation among government institutions is essential to enhance the efficiency of the national administration. Many policies are designed to improve performance only when various government institutions work together. Issues that need to consider multiple factors together --- such as environmental and industrial policies as well as the approval of new high-tech technologies --- must go through the process where government institutions work together to coordinate their efforts. Otherwise, it is likely to create inefficiencies such as overlapping regulations and over-support. In this regard, the Korean government has a lot of room for improvement, because there are high walls that keep government institutions separated from each other compared to advanced countries.

Government officials agree that coordination in the government is necessary and they are putting together various measures. One of the measures is the establishment of the Government Statistical Service (GSS) to ensure smooth cooperation among government agencies

Examples of Poor Coordination in Government

Competing Subjects	Competing Cause	Competing Pattern and Behaviors	

Fair Trade Commission vs. **Ministry of Land, Infrastructure and Transport**	⟨Organizational psychological factors⟩
	° selfishness of each ministry
	° the tendency to maximize the interests of the ministries
	
	⟨Institutional factors⟩
	° overlapping jurisdiction
	  - execution of transversal/substantial work of consumer policy
	
	⟨Environmental factors⟩
	° increasing complexity and importance of consumer issues
	  - uncertainty of the responsible subject
	  - Increased interest and involvement in consumer policy
	° scarce resources
	  - Conflict in securing resources
		⟨a competition for leadership in a particular field⟩
		° a competition for leadership in a particular field
		° Competing in Existing Territories
		° competition over new territory
		
		⟨Competition for policies⟩
		° competition for policy capacity building
		  - supporting law, resources, budgets, manpower, efforts to secure organization and external cause
		° Competition to mass-produce similar policies
		  - an excess of policy
			⟨Competition behavior⟩
			° a jurisdictional claim
			° a break in communication and cooperation
			° Avoid disclosure (sharing) data
			° avoidance of policy coordination
			° Establishment and execution of individual policies/businesses

Source: Korea Consumer Agency, Issue 49, Vol. 1

for the purpose of developing national statistics. But the GSS did not produce any visible results. GSS was staffed with manager-level heads of different government institutions, but it became so crippled that they could not even hold meetings properly. Members of the GSS claimed they were too busy to attend meetings, but that is not the real reason: They are reluctant to disclose the data that they have, and they are also worried that any leaked information would backfire and they will be held responsible for it. This is largely because they don't trust each other. Because they do not trust each other, each government institution became selfish, and they built higher walls to shield themselves from other government institutions. Unless the walls that keep them separated from each other are removed, it will be difficult to implement flexible and timely policies.

INCONSISTENT POLICES THAT LEAVE THE PEOPLE IN CONFUSION

Inconsistent administration is another reason the public trust in the Korean government is not improving. Education is the area where inconsistent administration is the most noticeable. One good example is the administration regarding college admission. Whenever there is a change in the government or the education minister, the ratio of students admitted to college through the regular college admission and the nonscheduled college admission is changed. The sub-categories for the evaluation of students applying for the nonscheduled college admission change so frequently that they only confuse parents and students. The result is the ever-expanding shadow education businesses such as private after-school academies and consulting services. According to the 2017 Private Education Expenditure Survey jointly conducted by the Ministry of Education and Statistics Korea with 40,000 parents from 1,484 schools nationwide, the total amount of private education expenditure amounted to KRW18.6 trillion and the average monthly private education expenditure per student was KRW271,000.

The same is true of the health and welfare administration when it comes to the lack of consistency. The promotion of people's health

Trend of Monthly Shadow Education Expenditure per Person

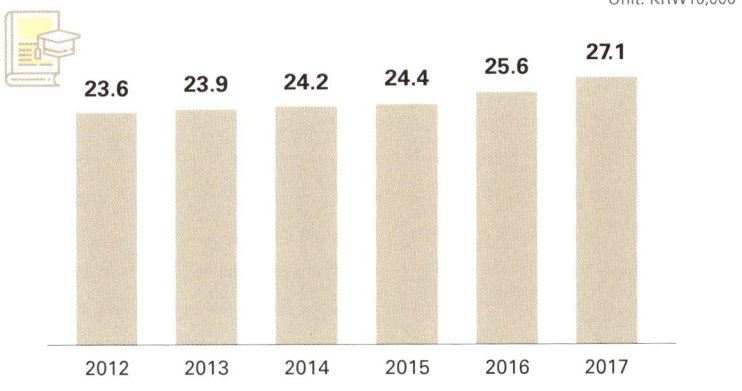

Unit: KRW10,000

23.6 — 2012
23.9 — 2013
24.2 — 2014
24.4 — 2015
25.6 — 2016
27.1 — 2017

Source: Ministry of Education, Statistics Korea

remains the same as the ultimate goal of the health and welfare administration, but the details of related policies are subject to constant changes depending on the ruling power group. This is the reason the budget allocated for the health and welfare administration is constantly changing. There is a difference in degree, but inconsistent administration and policies can be found in almost all areas including industry, energy and the environment. It is one of the maladies that must be fixed in order to improve public trust in the government and the transparency of policies.

SHORTAGE OF RAW MATERIALS AND INSUFFICIENT FOREIGN SUPPLIERS

Korea's rapid economic development and people's higher standard of living resulted in the rapidly increasing consumption of electricity and energy such as oil and coal. As petroleum products are widely used in various fields, Korea's oil consumption increased to rank eighth in the world, and Korea's consumption of coal for the generation of electricity is second only to Australia among OECD countries. Rapid industrial development also means increased consumption of electricity. Korea's per capita electricity consumption ranks seventh in the world and its total energy consumption, fifth.

However, the rate of dependence on raw material imports is more than 96%, because Korea has to import most resources. It is unavoidable because Korea has a shortage of natural resources, but the raw materials can become an Achilles' heel for the Korean economy. Nevertheless, there are not enough efforts to reduce the dependence on raw material imports. The only solution is overseas resource development, but investments for this solution have been decreasing every year. Consequently, the Korean economy takes a serious blow if the international raw material prices fluctuates even just a little.

KOREA IS THE WORLD'S 8TH LARGEST PETROLEUM CONSUMER

Petroleum is the most used energy source in Korea, because the rapid economic development caused a surge in the use of electricity and oil products. Korea was the world's eighth largest energy consumer in 2015, according to estimates from the BP Statistical Review of World Energy (BP Stats Review). The U.S. topped the list with an average daily consumption of 19.39 million barrels, accounting for 20.4% of global consumption, followed by China with 1,1968 million barrels. In other words, the two superpowers are using one-third of the global oil consumption. The data also showed that India and Japan each use 4.15 million barrels, while Saudi Arabia uses 3.895 million barrels, Brazil uses 3.157 million barrels and Russia uses 3.113 million barrels. Following these countries were Korea with 2,575,000 barrels, Germany with 2,338,000 barrels and Canada with 2,322,000 barrels.

Korea ranks higher when compared in terms of the annual oil consumption per person. Singapore topped the ranking with 86.15 barrels per person, followed by Saudi Arabia with 51.22 barrels, Canada with 24.14 barrels and the United States with 22.03 barrels. Korea ranks fifth with 19.13 barrels per person.

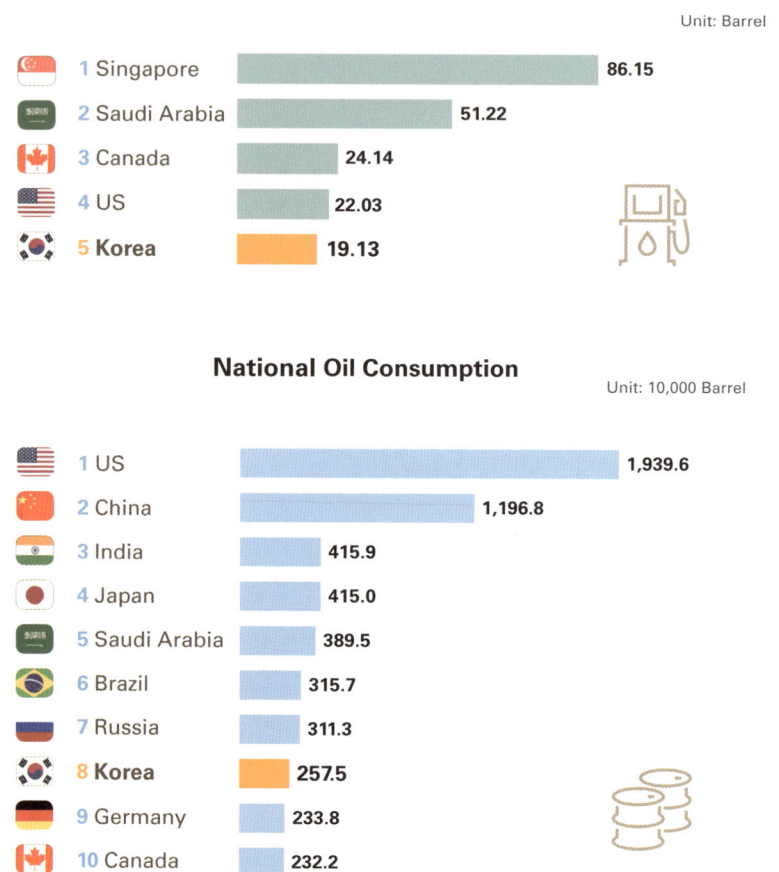

Advanced countries are cutting back on oil consumption by increasing the share of renewable energy, but the oil consumption in emerging economies such as China, India and Southeast Asia are on the rise. Experts predict that, unless the paradigm of energy use is completely changed, oil consumption will continue to grow.

Worldwide demand for oil is expected to keep rising over the next 20 to 25 years according to the World Energy Outlook published by the International Energy Agency (IEA) and the World Oil Outlook published by OECD as well. This is also the reason Korea should not be negligent in developing oil resources.

KOREA IS THE SECOND LARGEST COAL CONSUMER AMONG OECD COUNTRIES

Coal is the most used fossil fuel source in Korea. According to Statistics Korea and the energy industry, Korea's per capita coal consumption stood at 1.6 TOE as of 2016, ranking second among OECD countries after the world's largest coal producer Australia, which recorded 1.8 TOE. The figure is up 45.5% from a decade ago. TOE stands for "tonne of oil equivalent", and it is a unit of energy representing the amount of energy released by burning one tonne of crude oil.

None of the major OECD countries recorded an increase in per capita coal consumption. The reason for the increase in coal consumption in Korea is found in sharply increasing electricity production. Korea used a total of 77.61 million tons of bituminous coal to generate electricity in 2016, which accounts for 65% of total energy consumption. Korea is using coal to generate electricity despite the fact it is causing environmental problems such as fine dust because it is cheap. Coal power generates about 40% of Korea's

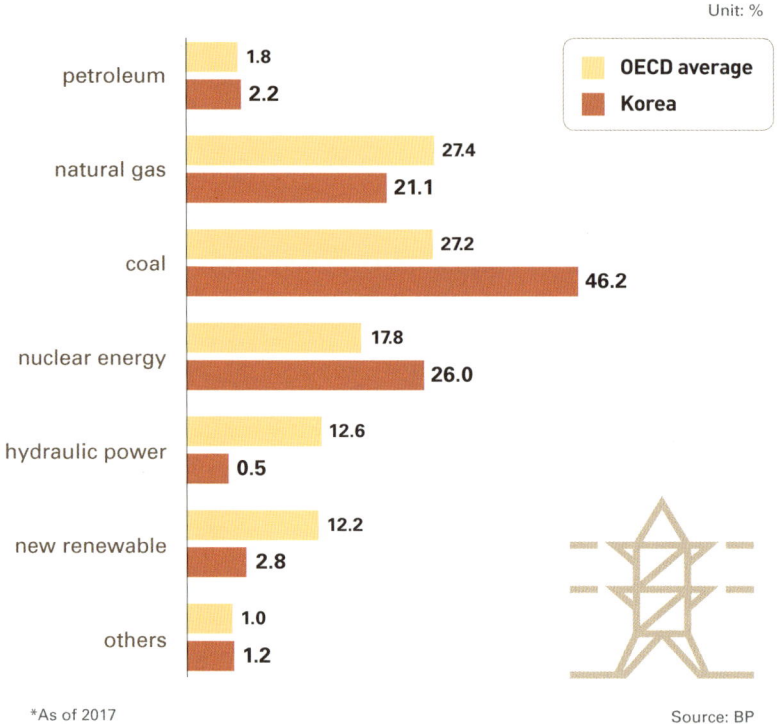

total electricity as of 2017, according to BP's 2018 World Energy Statistics Report. It is a very high number compared to the OECD average of 27.2%.

PER CAPITA ELECTRICITY CONSUMPTION THAT IS HIGH RELATIVE TO THE POPULATION AND THE SIZE OF THE ECONOMY

The consumption of coal to generate power is not decreasing rapidly in Korea even though it is the main cause of extreme air pollution, because Korea is the world's seventh largest electricity consumer. Korea is using a lot of electricity relative to its population and the size of the economy. According to the European energy consulting firm Enerdata, Korea's electricity consumption totaled 534 TWh in 2017, up 2.3% from a year earlier. China topped the ranking with 5,683 TWh, followed by the United States with 3,808 TWh, India with 1,156 TWh, Japan with 1,091 TWh, Russia with 889 TWh, and Canada with 572 TWh.

Korea's ranking in electricity consumption has been going up by one notch each year from ninth in 2015. At this pace, Korea is expected to overtake Canada and narrow the gap with Russia before long. Korea's electricity consumption increase rate has been averaging 4.3% since 2000, making Korea the second largest consumer among OECD members after Turkey whose rate is 5.5%.

Of course, Korea's increase rate is not very high relative to countries around the world. During the same period, China recorded a 9.9% increase rate of electricity consumption, and the UAE's rate was 7.0% and India, 6.8%. However, the increase rate of electricity consumption in most advanced countries, including the United States, Japan and Germany, is less than 1%. Korea's high electricity

Trend of Energy Consumption in Korea

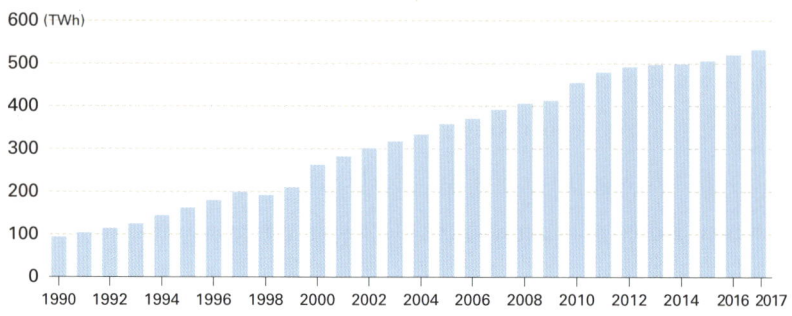

Source: Enerdata

consumption can be explained by its strong manufacturing industries such as automobiles and steel and petrochemicals and semiconductors.

KOREA IS THE WORLD'S FIFTH LARGEST ENERGY CONSUMER

Korea is using oil, coal, and electricity relatively more than countries of similar economic size. As a result, Korea is among the top group in the total energy consumption ranking. According to Statistics Korea and the energy industry, Korea's per capita energy consumption stood at 5.6 TOE as of 2016, making Korea rank fifth among OECD countries. The figure is higher than Japan (3.5 TOE), Germany (3.9 TOE) and France (3.6 TOE), whose economies are bigger than Korea. Only a few countries were using energy more than Korea, including Norway (9.2 TOE), Canada (9.1 TOE), the

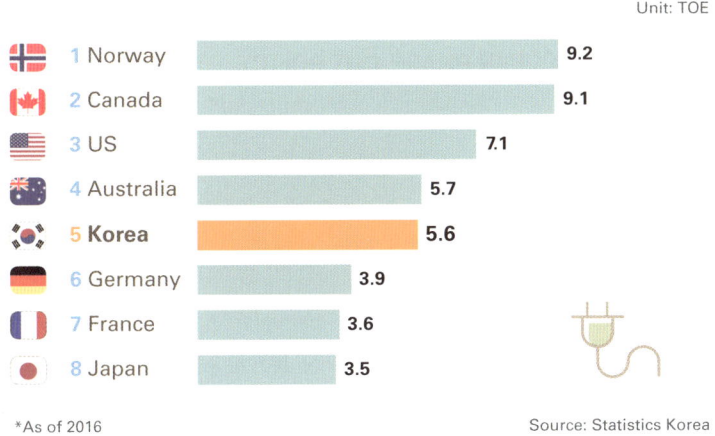

Per Capital Energy Consumption in OECD Countries

Unit: TOE

	Country	TOE
1	Norway	9.2
2	Canada	9.1
3	US	7.1
4	Australia	5.7
5	**Korea**	5.6
6	Germany	3.9
7	France	3.6
8	Japan	3.5

*As of 2016
Source: Statistics Korea

U.S. (7.1 TOE) and Australia (5.7 TOE).

Another reason that explains Korea's high energy consumption rate is that electricity costs are cheaper here than in other countries. Koreans have less incentive to save energy because electricity is cheap. There is a need to raise electricity rates, but it is not easy to. That is because raising electricity rates could reduce the competitiveness of the industry and also could result in a severe public outcry. In order to reduce energy overspending, electricity costs have to be adjusted to a realistic level. In addition, Korea needs to build a system to use energy more efficiently.

THE COLLAPSE OF THE NUCLEAR PLANT INDUSTRY'S ECOSYSTEM AND SURGING ELECTRICITY PRICES, THE DILEMMA OF THE NUCLEAR PHASE-OUT POLICY

Nuclear power is a dangerous source of energy, but it is an ideal energy source for countries like Korea that have a shortage of natural resources but a robust manufacturing industry. Nuclear power plants accounted for 26.0% of Korea's electricity generation in 2017 according to the BP Statistical Review of World Energy 2019. That means nuclear power is one of the two biggest power sources along with coal, which accounts for 46.2%. Korea's nuclear power generation recorded 148.4 TWh, ranking fourth in the world after the United States, China and Russia. In terms of the percentage of nuclear power generation to the population, Korean ranked second only following Ukraine, the data showed.

Nuclear power plants are highly efficient, but they have deadly risks as shown by the Fukushima nuclear accident in Japan. That's the reason it is not easy to make a decision on whether to expand or reduce them. One thing is clear: If the government implements the nuclear phase-out policy too fast, it would deal a significant blow to people's livelihood and the Korean economy due to the soaring electricity prices and the collapse of the nuclear plant industry's ecosystem.

According to the "Analysis of the Power Generation Cost Resulting from the Government's Nuclear Phase-Out Policy"

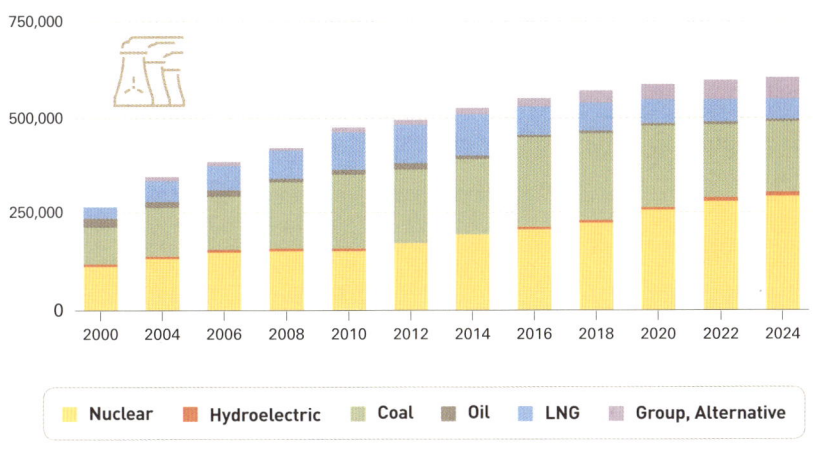

Current Power Generation by Energy and Forecast

Unit: GWh

Source: Korea Electric Power Corp., Ministry of Trade, Industry and Energy

released by the Korea Hydro and Nuclear Power - Central Research Institute, the unit price of electricity is expected to increase to KRW57.41 per kilowatt-hour by 2030 if the government expands the share of solar and wind power facilities. Since the current unit price of electricity for households is around KRW100 per kilowatt-hour, it means the price will increase by 50%. The cost of expanding solar and wind power facilities was also estimated to push KRW174.58. For this reason, almost all countries are being cautious about adopting a nuclear phase-out policy.

Nuclear power plants are highly efficient, but they have deadly risks as shown by the Fukushima nuclear accident in Japan. That's the reason it is not easy to make decision on whether to expand or reduce them. One thing is clear: If the government implements the nuclear phase-out policy too fast, it would deal a significant blow to people's livelihood and the Korean economy due to the soaring electricity prices and the collapse of the nuclear plant industry's ecosystem.

According to the "Analysis on the Power Generation Cost Resulting from the Government's Nuclear Phase-Out Policy" released by the Korea Hydro and Nuclear Power - Central Research Institute, the unit price of electricity is expected to increase to KRW57.41 per kilowatt-hour by 2030 if the government expands the share of solar and wind power facilities. Since the current unit price of electricity for households is around KRW100 per kilowatt-hour, it means the price will increase by 50%. The cost of expanding solar and wind power facilities was also estimated to push KRW174.58. For this reason, almost all countries are being cautious about adopting nuclear phase-out policy.

RENEWABLE ENERGY HAS A LONG WAY TO GO

Increasing the share of renewable energy is the right direction to take in order to avoid the danger of nuclear power plants and reduce air pollution caused by coal fired power plants.

However, renewable energy still has a low return on investment. That is the reason the renewable electricity generation cannot increase quickly even if the government pushes forward with the

Renewable Electricity Generation and Percentage in 2030

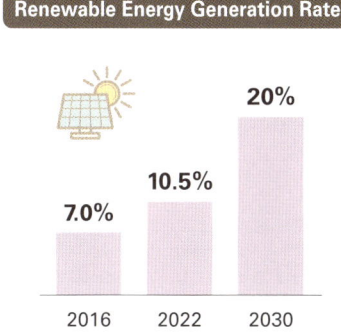

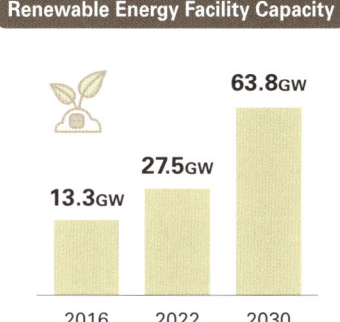

Source: Ministry of Trade, Industry and Energy

nuclear phase-out policy. In Korea, it is not easy to increase renewable energy generation facilities because Korea does not have the territory and national environment that are suitable to generate power using the su or wind.

In the case of solar energy, Korea has a disadvantage in terms of location compared to other countries because Korea has a small land area and not enough sunlight. Power generation facilities are concentrated in hills and other areas near the energy consumers' residences, because economic feasibility can be ensured only when they are close to where there is electricity demand. This situation entails serious aspects: There are constant complaints from the locals about electromagnetic waves and the facilities damaging the aesthetics of the village landscape. There is also a higher risk of landslides or flooding resulting from the destroyed forests. In fact, a solar power plant installed in an area of Cheongdo County, North Gyeongsang Province had a landslide incident in 2018.

Of course, the share of renewable energy will gradually increase when its production costs drop. According to the "New Energy Outlook" published by Bloomberg New Energy Finance, renewable energy and gas will account for 72% of Korea's electricity production by 2050 by replacing nuclear power plants and coal fired power plants, respectively. The government will also make policy-level efforts to increase the share of renewable energy. Even so, there is a very long way to go until renewable energy can replace existing energy sources.

RESOURCE POOR KOREA HAS A STRUCTURE VULNERABLE TO RESOURCE SHOCK

Being a country that imports most of its resources, Korea is vulnerable to fluctuations of raw material prices in the international market. There are many reports that support this reality.

Hyundai Research Institute analyzed the correlation between rising international raw material prices and inflation in the Korean economy and released the results in a report. The report showed that rising international raw material prices served as a factor in employment costs and interest rate hikes, eventually causing inflation.

Similarly, Korea International Trade Association found while researching the business environment of exporting companies

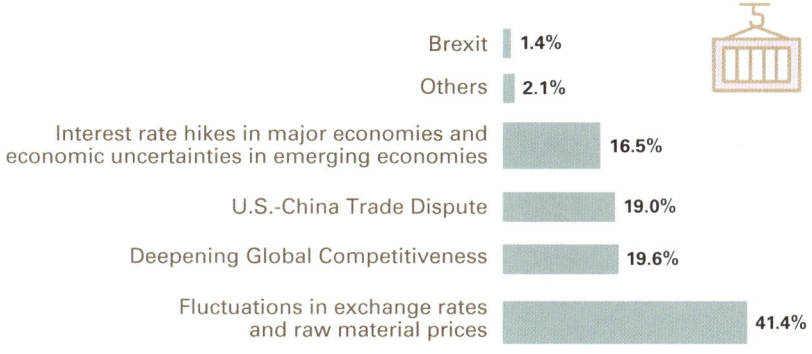

Issues That Will Have the Greatest Impact on The Export Environment in 2019

Source: Korea International Trade Association

in 2019 that "exchange rates and fluctuating raw material prices" was the factor that would have the biggest impact on the business environment.

In the report of the research results, the Korea International Trade Association estimated that the impact of fluctuations in exchange rates and raw material prices on the management environment will be 41.4%, which is more than double the 19.6% impact rate of "the intensifying competition in the global market," which was the factor that will have the second biggest impact on the business environment

ENERGY SELF-RELIANCE NEEDS TO BE IMPROVED BUT RESOURCE DEVELOPMENT HAS A LONG WAY TO GO

In order to overcome the crisis resulting from raw material shock on a structural level and increase the level of energy self-reliance, a stable source of supplies must be secured through overseas resource development. But the Korean government has been consistently implementing negative policies ever since Korea suffered huge losses in overseas resource development projects during the Lee Myung-bak administration. Investments in overseas resource development fell sharply to $2.78 billion in 2016 from $8.77 billion in 2012, according to the Ministry of Trade, Industry and Energy. This is because the budget for the development has been cut by billions of won each year. This reality makes a big contrast with other countries.

According to a report titled "Comparison of Overseas Resources Development Between Korea, China and Japan" which was released by the Federation of Korean Industries (FKI), Korea's investment

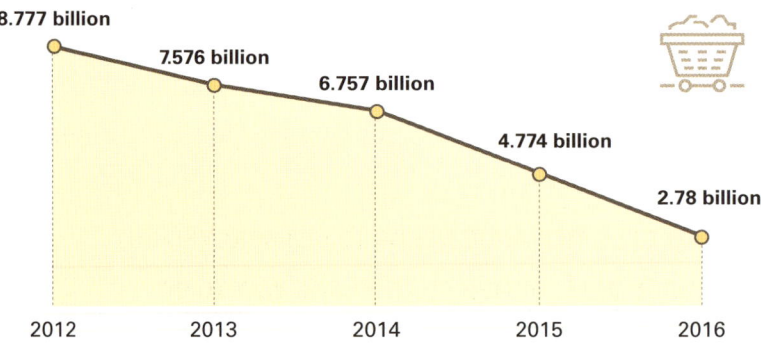

Status of Investment in Overseas Resource Development Projects

Source: Ministry of Trade, Industry and Energy

in overseas resource development is significantly smaller than that of Japan and China. Korea's budget for resource development was KRW95.8 billion in 2016, which was just a sixth of that of Japan. According to the report, there were many years when the amount of investment the Korean government spent for overseas resources development was less than one-tenth that of China and Japan.

It is true that Korea suffered huge losses in overseas resource development because of the misjudgment of state-run companies, but that doesn't mean the Korean government should give up on the development all together. Resources development is necessary to prepare Korean industry for the possible resources crisis, but it is also necessary to build stronger energy security capabilities. It is something Korea needs to take seriously to secure a stable source of supplies as well. Korea needs to establish an environment where private companies can join in overseas resource development if the state-run companies prove to have been inefficient.

PART 4

FOR YET ANOTHER MIRACLE

ECONOMIC FREEDOM SHOULD BE EXPANDED TO MAXIMIZE CREATIVITY

The European Chamber of Commerce in Korea (ECCK) had once declared that "Korea is a 'Galapagos regulation' country." ECCK even went on to publish a white paper that included 123 regulations, similar examples of which are hard to find anywhere in the world, and its suggestions for improvement. Over the past three decades, Korean companies have been steadily relocating their factories to foreign countries, and the country's economic growth rate has been falling from an annual average of 7% in the late 1990s to around 2% now. There may be many reasons, but various regulatory barriers that constrain corporate activities could very well be the first to take the blame for it.

ECONOMIC FREEDOM MUST BE REVIVED AGAIN IN KOREA

The freedom of the individual becomes increasingly important as the world enters the era of the Fourth Industrial Revolution, which

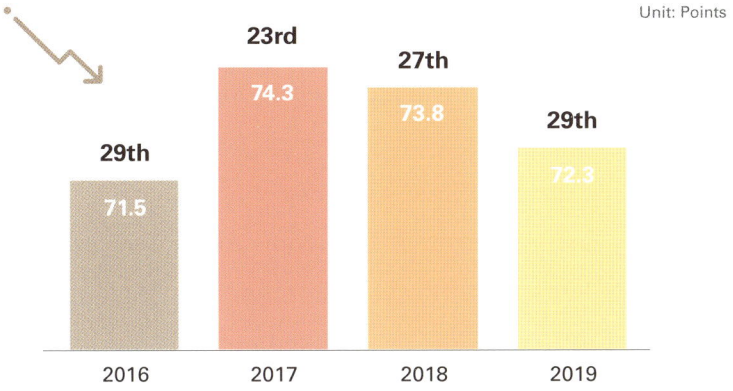

Korea's Falling Ranking in the Economic Freedom Index

is driven by creativity. Therefore, the school classrooms have to be filled with freedom so that every student can give full rein to their imagination. Everyone should be able to produce and consume goods and services while controlling their own labor and wealth as they please. This economic freedom is the most basic right in a free and democratic society. However, it is worrisome that Korea's economic freedom is gradually going backward.

In the "2019 Economic Freedom Index" released by the US-based Heritage Foundation, Korea ranked 23rd in 2017 in its economic freedom, but it has been downgraded to 27th in 2018 and to 29th in 2019. The Heritage Foundation has been publishing the Economic Freedom Index since 1995 to measure the level of economic freedom for individuals and companies participating in the production, distribution, consumption and labor force of over 180 countries based on a wide range of criteria including government interference, open markets, rule of law, protection of property rights, corporate freedom, and labor freedom.

Regarding the overall score decrease, the foundation commented it was "because of sharply lower scores for judicial effectiveness and the tax burden and declines in monetary freedom and labor freedom." The foundation also pointed out that the government's increasing intervention undermined economic freedom because it increased corporate taxes and marginal income tax rates and raised the minimum wage.

Korea has been receiving exceptionally low scores in the labor freedom category. In 2018, Korea ranked 97th among the countries reviewed with 58.7 points. Korea's labor freedom is on about the same level as Djibouti, Lesotho, Jordan and Syria. The labor freedom score went down further to 57.4 in 2019. It is another indicator that shows how urgent labor market reform is.

ESTONIA'S "DIGITAL REVOLUTION" CALLS FOR ATTENTION

In Estonia, a small northern European country with a population of 1.3 million, 99% of the public services are digitalized and available online, except for marriage, divorce and real estate transactions. In Estonia, a mother does not have to go to government offices to

Digital Powerhouse Estonia in Numbers

0	•	Corporate tax rate (taxable when dividend), Inheritance tax rate, Gift tax rate
3 minutes	•	Time it takes to make tax payment online
3 hours	•	Time it takes to establish a company
45,000	•	Number of e-Residency applicants

Kersti Kaljulaid
President of Estonia

Source: 2018 World Knowledge Forum

register the birth of her child. A digital ID is issued for the baby even before the baby's name is decided, and medical staff measures and records the baby's blood pressure and pulse and all other vital data. If a patient allows doctors to access their personal information, doctors can check the patient's medical history and progress of treatment, and patients can also access their own medical history and treatment process.

Estonia, a country that gained independence from the former Soviet Union in 1991, introduced the world's first Blockchain-era identification card program called e-Residence in late 2014. Anyone in the world can apply for this transnational digital identity, which also enables entrepreneurs to start a trusted location-independent

EU company online without having to visit Estonia. There is no tax on corporations and entrepreneurs are required to pay tax only when the company earns profits and distributes them to shareholders. This is how 10,000 startups are established every year in Estonia. One of the most successful startups born in this country in August 2013 is the ride-sharing platform, "Taxify," which is already making forays into markets beyond Europe to Africa and the Middle East.

Estonia has moved its national system and private ecosystem into a Blockchain world, and the country became the first in the world to introduce electronic voting in general elections. These changes built upon the trust between the government and the people are a national innovation model that the world should pay attention to in the era of the Fourth Industrial Revolution. Estonia's President Kersti Kaljulaid had visited Maekyung Media Center during her visit to Korea for the PyeongChang Winter Olympics in February 2018. She visited Korea again to attend the World Knowledge Forum as a keynote speaker in October that year. In her speech, she asked people to "look at Estonia as a service like an app store rather than as a country."

TWENTY YEARS OF REGULATION REFORM IN KOREA, BUT THERE ARE MORE REGULATIONS NOW THAN BEFORE

Korea started to work on the regulatory rigidity problem on a pan-government level in late 1997 when the country was hit by a foreign exchange crisis. When the International Monetary Fund

(IMF) supported Korea with funds during the crisis, it recommended "improving the uncertain regulatory environment," and the Regulatory Reform Committee was created under the direct control of the president in 1998. Even though Korea was forced to make these moves to reform regulations, the Kim Dae-jung administration was so committed to the reform that government institutions were mandated to "cut down the number of regulations." It was during this process that the trucking business regulation was changed from a license system to a registration system and eliminated barriers for people to enter the business. As a result, the number of truck drivers doubled from 96,000 in 1998 to 179,000 in 2003. This is an example

Increased Regulations Despite The Presidents' Words

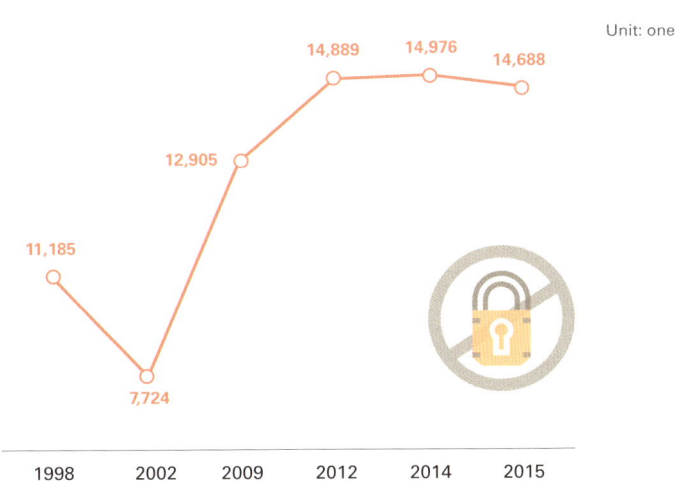

Source: Regulatory Information Portal

of how deregulation affects job creation.

The following Roh Moo-hyun, Lee Myung-bak and Park Geun-hye administrations continued the deregulation policy without exception. In 2003, the Roh Moo-hyun administration introduced a new "regulatory total amount system," and Lee Myung-bak administration declared "we will root out the regulatory poles" before pushing forward with the license and permission process overhaul in addition to deregulation. The Park Geun-hye administration declared "we will pull out the splinter from under the nails" and introduced various measures including setting the goal of reducing the number of regulations. However, the number of regulations only kept growing. The number of regulations increased from 7,724 in 2002 to 14,889 in 2012 during the Roh Moo-hyun and the Lee Myung-bak administrations, and the government stopped collecting data in 2015 when the number recorded 14,688 during the Park Geun-hye administration.

President Moon Jae-in also advocated deregulation reform and claimed, "we must take down the red flag," but the initiative is blocked by barriers in the sharing economy, telemedicine, drone, and self-driving car industries. The power groups with vested interests are fiercely resisting the introduction of new technologies and services, and the National Assembly is constantly introducing bills with new regulations.

KOREA NEEDS TO SPEED UP WITH THE TRAFFIC REVOLUTION LED BY RIDESHARING AND SELF-DRIVING VEHICLES

The world is experiencing a traffic revolution following the emergence of car sharing services and self-driving cars. Vehicle-sharing services are becoming an integral part of everyday life in major cities in the U.S., Europe and Southeast Asia. Uber, the leading US-based ridesharing service provider, is serving an average of 13 million riders a day in 65 countries around the world. Slated to go public soon, Uber's corporate value is estimated to be US$120 billion at the end of 2018, which is six times that of Hyundai Motor. GRAB--- a ridesharing service provider that is dominating markets in eight Southeast Asian countries--- also saw its corporate value increase to $11 billion in seven years. Among major Asian countries, Korea and Japan do not allow Uber's ridesharing service to protect the domestic taxi industry. Kakao tried to launch a carpooling service, which was a lower level service than the ridesharing service, in 2018, but the plan was foiled due to the resistance from taxi drivers who were so against it that a few even protested by setting themselves on fire.

Meanwhile, self-driving cars built on artificial intelligence (AI) technology is another new reality. A Google-affiliated company, Waymo, launched the world's first self-driving taxi service in Phoenix, Arizona, in December 2018. Passengers who use the Uber app for a ride have the choice between a regular vehicle and a self-

Number of Self-driving Cars in The U.S. and Korea

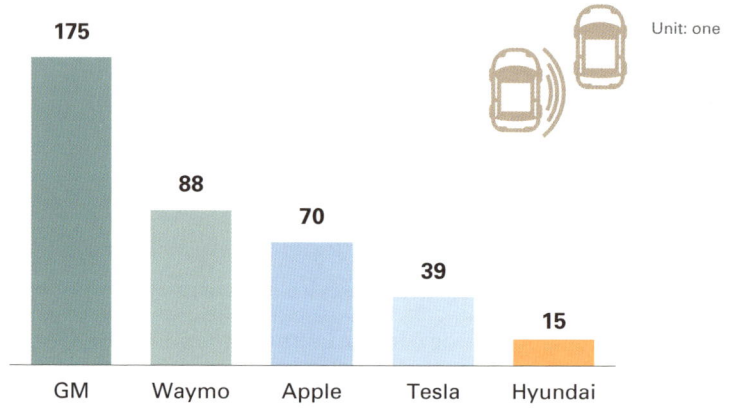

Unit: one

- GM: 175
- Waymo: 88
- Apple: 70
- Tesla: 39
- Hyundai: 15

* As of the end of 2018 / *U.S. is based on California data, Hyundai Motor data is based on the report by Ministry of Land, Infrastructure and Transport

Source: DMV, Ministry of Land, Infrastructure and Transport

driving one. In Korea, however, it is difficult to launch a self-driving car business due to various regulations such as the Road Traffic Act and the Automobile Management Act. As a result, Korean self-driving car startups are trying their luck in the US market.

Even though Korea is the world's seventh-largest automobile producer, it is lagging behind the fast-paced traffic revolution that is spearheaded by car sharing and self-driving car markets. In the meantime, car-sharing providers and self-driving car makers in the United States, Europe and Southeast Asia will accumulate a lot of data, and that mountain of data will contribute to the creation of another set of values and jobs.

DEREGULATING TELEMEDICINE AND DRUG DELIVERY CAN SOLVE THE INCONVENIENCE PROBLEMS EXPERIENCED BY EIGHT MILLION PEOPLE

In the medical sector, information and communication technology is also creating a revolution. In the United States, Japan, China and Southeast Asia, doctors and patients are enjoying the convenience of telemedicine services that are available to smartphone and computer users. In the U.S., one out of every six treatments is done remotely, and in China, the number of telemedicine users passed the 100 million mark.

In Korea, however, it has remained at the repeated pilot project stage for 19 years since 2000.

According to the Ministry of Health and Welfare, telemedicine can benefit 8.36 million people including those with chronic diseases such as high blood pressure and diabetes, not to mention those with disabilities who have limited mobility. More than 75% of patients who participated in telemedicine pilot projects also expressed satisfaction. Nevertheless, the medical communities have been opposing telemedicine services, citing possible loss of business for small neighborhood hospitals and the risk of misdiagnosis.

The same is true of visiting medical services and drug delivery. In the U.S., 20 to 30 venture firms specializing in visiting medical care services have been in business since 2014. In Japan, more than 700,000 people are using a 24-hour house-call medical service

Patient Satisfaction in the Telemedicine Pilot Projects

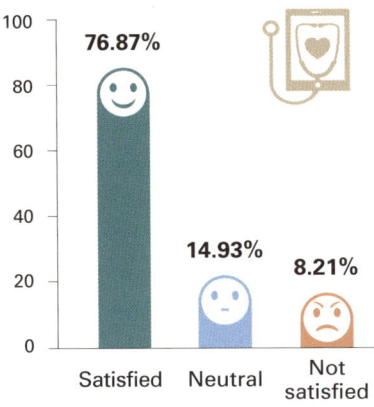

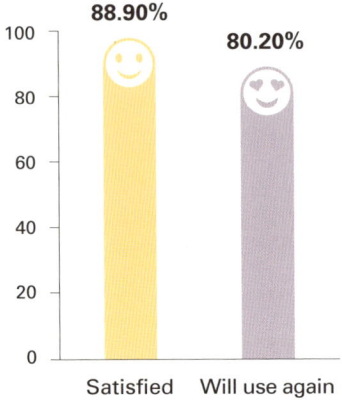

* Ministry of Health and Welfare Telemedicine Survey of 845 patients in the first pilot project (Sept. 2014-Mar. 2015)

* The second telemedicine pilot project (Mar. 2015 - Jan. 2016)

Source: Ministry of Health and Welfare

providing system, while elderly people in the isolated island regions receive drugs delivered by drones. Although the number of elderly people is growing rapidly in Korea, drug delivery is still illegal, and the physician house-call service has been allowed on a very conditional basis since 2019.

In the U.S., Apple Watch 4, which was released in 2018, received approval from the U.S. Food and Drug Administration (FDA) for medical devices and installed heart rate monitor on the smartphone for the first time. This makes a big contrast to what's going on in Korea, where the smartphone with a built-in heart rate monitor was developed three years ago but could not be released to the market due to strict regulations on medical devices and telemedicine. It is unfortunate that Korea is losing a big opportunity due to resistance from groups with vested interests, and that millions of consumers are suffering from inconvenience as a result, even though Korea has an excellent information and communication technology that can be more competitive than any other country in telemedicine.

ICO IS A HOT TREND IN OVERSEAS, BUT IS COMPLETELY BANNED IN KOREA AND CHINA

In response to the growing popularity of the blockchain technology-based virtual currencies, a new method of funding called "Initial Coin Offering (ICO)" was introduced around 2015. ICO is very different from IPO (Initial Public Offering), which is about raising funds through stock market.

While IPO is about issuing stocks by companies that meet certain requirements such as sales and operating profit, ICO is about issuing virtual currencies by any company without the need of qualification. An IPO investor, as a shareholder, is entitled to receive an annual dividend with a stake in the entity, but an ICO investor has nothing to do with the dividend and voting rights of that entity. The reason and the process of price increase of virtual currencies issued by ICO is also not clear. Despite such concerns, most countries, including the U.S. and Britain, allow ICOs, but Korea and China ban ICOs out of concern that they can be used for financial fraud.

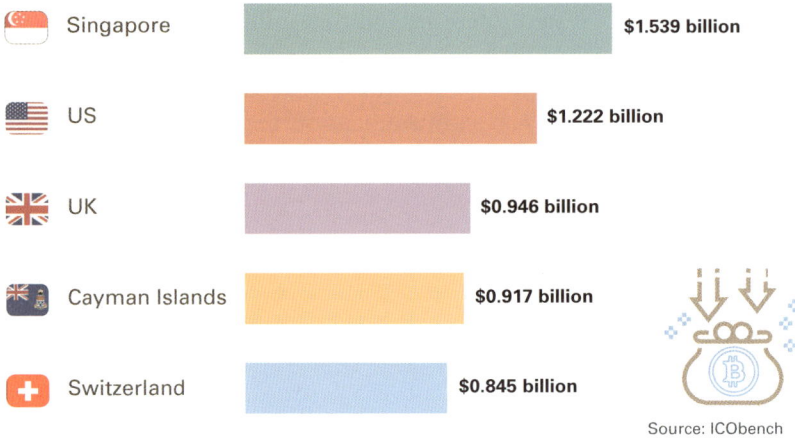

Source: ICObench

The U.S. Internal Revenue Service (IRS) is collecting income tax, corporate tax and transfer income tax on virtual currencies under the 2014 guideline that says, "virtual currencies are considered a capital asset," and leaves the investment responsibility to involved parties while acknowledging that there are funds in the market that favor high risk-high return investment. In comparison, the Korean government banned ICO in September 2017 out of concern that virtual currencies could be used for fraud. In 2018, the Korean government announced its plan to shut down the virtual currency exchange market, claiming that it was "like a speculative gamble."

The plan to close the virtual currency exchange market has been withdrawn after it was met by strong resistance, but the ICO is still banned. According to the ICO rating platform and a blockchain community, ICObench, funds raised by ICOs worldwide amounted to about $11.6 billion in 2018. Singapore raised the largest amount of funds at $1.5 billion, followed by the United States, the British Cayman Islands and Switzerland. Within the market, investors are cautious after witnessing 1,505 out of a total 2,517 ICOs attempted in 2018 failed to raise funds due to a sharp drop in the prices of virtual currencies such as Bitcoin and Ethereum, but in Korea and China, they are "banned from the very foundational level" by regulations.

KOREA IS MISSING THE POTENTIAL OF BIG DATA, THE OIL OF FUTURE INDUSTRIES

All kinds of data generated in everyday life, including shopping, travel and medical treatment, are called "oil for future industries." As the amount of data that can be processed with artificial intelligence increases, the range of data usage is becoming infinite. For example, internet banks might be able to evaluate customer credit more accurately by using their shopping information collected from eBay and Amazon and the accumulated medical information of countless patients might also contribute to the development of new drugs.

The world's big data market is growing fast, but in Korea, it has been stalled due to ambiguous laws and regulations. In 2018, Korea ranked 31st out of 63 countries on the list of "Use of big

Big Data Spread Scores in Major Countries

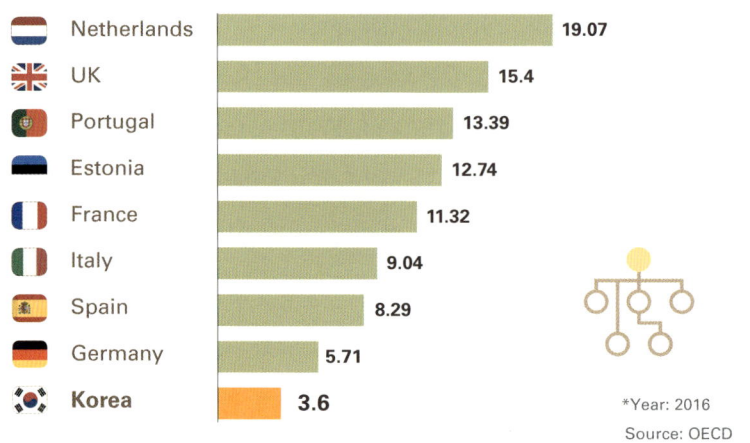

Unit: %

Netherlands	19.07
UK	15.4
Portugal	13.39
Estonia	12.74
France	11.32
Italy	9.04
Spain	8.29
Germany	5.71
Korea	3.6

*Year: 2016
Source: OECD

Hyper-scale Data Centers Worldwide and Percentage by Country

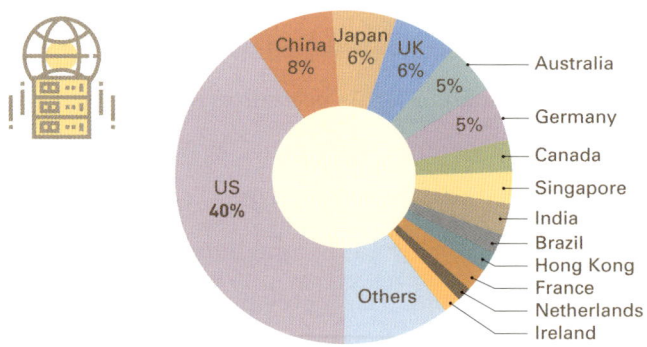

- US 40%
- China 8%
- Japan 6%
- UK 6%
- Australia 5%
- Germany 5%
- Canada
- Singapore
- India
- Brazil
- Hong Kong
- France
- Netherlands
- Ireland
- Others

Source: Synergy Research Group

data and analytics" by the IMD, a business education school located in Switzerland, lagging behind not only China (12th) but also Indonesia (29th). In the OECD's 2017 Digital Economy Outlook, Korea received 3.6 points in the big data spread analysis, which was the lowest among the major countries.

The key to utilizing big data is "de-identified information." Referring to information that has been processed so that the identification of a particular individual cannot be established, the de-identified information is relatively free to use in the U.S., the European Union (EU), and Japan. In the case of the EU and Japan, the de-identified information is grouped into anonymous data and pseudonymous data, with the anonymous data free to use while use of the pseudonymous data is allowed under certain conditions.

In Korea, however, names, resident registration numbers and even videos and other information that can be easily identifiable by linking with other information are protected as vaguely defined private information under the Personal Information Protection Act. Then in November 2017, some civic groups accused a few major companies of having violated this act and filed complaints with the Public Prosecutors' Office. Since then, the use of big data has been frozen.

Major countries around the world are building hyper-scale data centers, but not a single one is built in Korea because it is impossible to utilize big data here. As of the end of 2018, there are 430 hyper-scale data centers worldwide that have the optimal conditions to use big data, 40% of which is in the U.S., 8% in China, 6% in Japan and 5%

in Australia and Germany, respectively.

50 YEARS OF RESTRICTION IN THE CAPITAL REGION WEAKENS THE URBAN COMPETITIVENESS

It is an era in which urban competitiveness means national competitiveness, Korea is the only OECD member that restricts the development of the capital region with law and regulations on account of balanced national development. These regulations that restrict the development of the capital region started in 1964 to curb the overcrowded population of large cities, but they still remain the same today. Construction of factories and universities have been restricted in Seoul, Incheon and Gyeonggi Province since 1982 when the Seoul Metropolitan Area Readjustment Planning Act was enacted, and restrictions on the construction of new factories or expansion of them have been tightened since the Total Industrial Site Volume Control System in the Capital Region was introduced in 1994.

The British company GlaxoSmithKline tried to build a new vaccine plant in Hwaseong, Gyeonggi Province in 2006 but had to move it to Singapore after their plan was foiled by regulations such as the Total Industrial Site Volume Control System in the Capital Region. There are growing number of people at Pangyo Techno Valley in Gyeonggi Province who are calling for the need to bring universities to the region because that's where venture companies are flocking to. Silicon Valley in the U.S. is exchanging knowledge and information with Stanford University and UC Berkeley that are nearby and so is the Chinese technology hub, Zhongguancun, with the nearby Tsinghua University, but a Korean version of Silicon Valley Pangyo is not able to attract universities to the city because of the regulations that restrict development in the capital region.

Being home to about 48% of registered factories, the capital region is where the fate of Korean manufacturing industries is at stake. However, many companies are forced to move their factories to foreign countries or lose the right time to make investments in the region all because of the regulations that restrict development in the capital region. In its 2016 data, the Korea Economic Research Institute analyzed that if the government allows the expansion, construction, and relocation of factories in the industrial complex in Gyeonggi Province, 417 companies would invest KRW67 trillion that they have been reserving and create 140,000 new jobs in the region. There have been several attempts to loosen the regulations in the capital region to foster high-tech industries or revitalize the economy, but they have all failed to overcome the resistance from people who are calling for balanced regional development.

THE CAUSE OF THE DECLINING QUALITY OF BUSINESSES SUITABLE FOR ENTERPRISES TO SUBSIST AND REVERSE DISCRIMINATION AGAINST DOMESTIC COMPANIES

Kimchi, dumplings, fermented soybeans, and dried laver are some of the important traditional Korean food items in the globalization of Korean cuisine. However, CJ Cheil Jedang's Bibigo Kimchi and Daesang's Jongajip Kimchi are subject to strict restrictions in research, development, and facility investment, because kimchi has been designated as a "suitable item for small and medium-sized enterprises (SMEs)." While large Korean corporations such as CJ and Daesang are restricted in spending money and efforts for kimchi-related products, 270,000 tons of Chinese-made kimchi was imported to Korea in 2017 and grabbed 30% share of kimchi distributed in Korea.

In the beginning, the businesses designated as being "suitable for SMEs" by the National Commission for Corporate Partnership were under the self-imposed control of companies, but after the "Special Act to Designate the List of Business Categories Suitable for Only Micro-Enterprises to Subsist" went into effect, large corporations are punishable by law if they violate this regulation. If a large corporation starts or expands a business designated as being suitable for micro-enterprises to subsist, the company is punished by two years or less in prison or up to KRW150 million of penalty.

The government designated a list of business categories suitable

Businesses Suitable for SMEs and Micro-Enterprises to Subsist

Category	Businesses Suitable for SMEs	Business Categories Suitable for Micro-Enterprises to Subsist
Subject	Commission for Corporate Partnership	Ministry of Small and Medium Venture Business
Target	a total of 73 items	Applications among SMEs
Processing	Agreement on Self-recommendation	In case of violation, the implementation fee (5% of sales amount)
Period	3+3 years, total 6 years	5 years

for micro-enterprises to subsist following after a list of suitable businesses for SMEs in the name of protecting small business owners, but the government's move has been continuously criticized for not really being helpful to small business owners, and also for having contributed to the declining quality of Korean products while helping foreign companies make more money in Korea instead.

Some of the best examples are kimchi, tofu and makgeolli. There was a time when the government's policy intended to promote rice consumption resulted in a significant increase in the production and exports of makgeolli, but the makgeolli market quickly cooled down after it was designated as a business item suitable for SMEs in 2011 at the demand of small-scale brewers. Exports of makgeolli fell 64% in two years from KRW59 billion in 2011. The startled government excluded makgeolli from the list of businesses suitable for SMEs in 2015, but the damage was already done because large companies had already discarded production facilities and lost interest as well by then.

The tofu market also grew rapidly after it dropped from the list of business items suitable for SMEs in 2006, but when it was designated as the business suitable for SMEs again in the mid-2011, it resulted in the sharp decrease of the price of its main ingredient, soybean, by more than 40%. It was because while large companies used only domestically grown soybeans, most SMEs were using cheaper Chinese soybean imports.

In some cases, regulations designed to protect Korean SMEs turned out to have helped foreign companies to make more money in the Korean market. For example, after the LED industry was designated as a business suitable for SMEs in 2011, the market share of foreign companies, including Osram and Philips, jumped to more than 10% in 2013 from 4.5% in 2011.

COMPANIES LEAVING FOR OVERSEAS IN SEARCH FOR FREEDOM IN BUSINESS ACTIVITIES

More and more companies are investing in foreign countries to avoid the regulatory barriers they are subjected to in Korea. If these companies are making forays into global markets to expand their business territories, it is a welcoming development, but they are in fact moving their businesses to foreign countries because they cannot do businesses in Korea due to regulatory barriers. Investment conditions and business environments for companies must be changed from the fundamental level.

In 2018, Korean manufacturers invested $16.3 billion to establish or expand their factories in overseas, and this was the largest amount since 1980 when the earliest statistics were available. The amount was twice that of 2017. Korean companies' investment in overseas has increased, but their investment in Korea has decreased. Facility investment in the country's manufacturing sector dropped by 2.5% in 2018, while the investment in non-manufacturing sector dropped by 6.7% as well.

The total amount of overseas investment in the financial, service and manufacturing industries stood at $49.7 billion in 2018. During

Overseas Direct Investment Amount by Domestic Companies

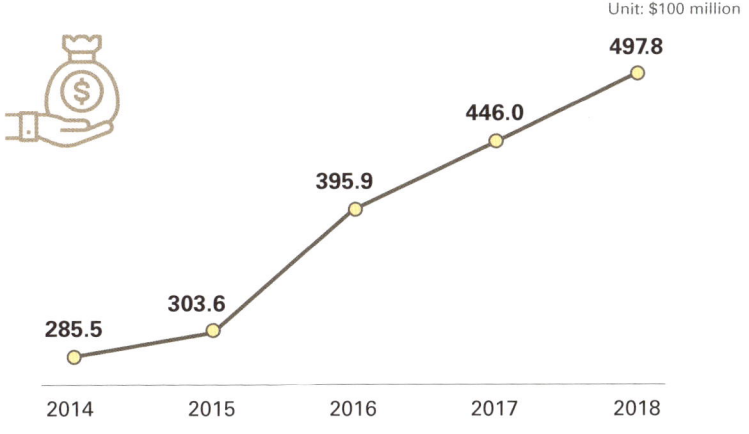

Source: Export-Import Bank of Korea

the period, the amount invested by foreign companies in Korea was $16.4 billion based on the amount of arrival, which indicates a net outflow of $33.3 billion. Small and medium-sized enterprises, which account for 87% of jobs, also invested $4.3 billion directly overseas during the first half of 2018, marking the highest amount since 1980 when the statistics were compiled for the first time. Compared with the first half of 2014, overseas investment by small and medium-sized companies has more than tripled in five years.

Naver and Kakao also started to increase their overseas investments in earnest in 2018. This is because there were double and triple regulations on vehicle sharing, telemedicine, fintech and big data businesses in Korea, which was sarcastically dubbed as "a country of digital seclusion." The U.S., Japan and China are striving to attract companies to their countries by lowering taxes and lifting regulations, but unfortunately, Korea is forcing even future growth industries out to foreign countries.

REGULATION SANDBOX AND FREE-ZONE SHOULD BECOME THE CATALYST FOR INNOVATION AND GROWTH

In the past when the pace of technological development was slow, the government could expect to develop the industry with positive regulations that approve new businesses as exceptions after comprehensively banning issues that could infringe upon the basic rights of the people. However, in today's era of complex, diversified

Five "Regulatory Sandbox" Laws to go into Effect in 2019

Regulations	Main Contents	Enforcement time	Government Agency
Special Act on Special Regulations for Free Regions	Designated free zones in non-metropolitan areas	April	Small Venture Business Department
Administrative Regulation Framework Act	Stipulate the principle of permission first, regulation next, overhaul regulations on new industry areas, establish and enforce basic plan once every three years	July	Ministry of Strategy and Finance
Special Act on Information and Communications Convergence	Introduction of negative regulation principle, improvement of provisional permission system, introduction of prompt confirmation system, Establishment of batch processing system	January	Ministry of Science, Technology and Information
Special Act on Financial Innovation Support	Establishment of Innovation and Financial Review Board to designate innovative financial services	April	Financial Services Commission
Industrial Convergence Promotion Act	Swift verification of regulations, special regulatory exemption system, introduction of a temporary permit system, expansion of the ombudsman function to promote industry convergence	January	Ministry of Trade, Industry and Energy

and rapidly changing technologies, it is hard to spearhead changes unless the government implements negative regulatory methods that allow all the rest with minimal restrictions.

Fortunately, Korea is slated to enforce the "regulatory sandbox law" and "regulatory free-zone law" beginning from 2019. Regulatory sandbox refers to a scheme to remove or postpone existing regulations to help companies provide new products or services in the new technology or industry fields. It is called a regulatory sandbox, because it is about creating a free and unrestricted environment comparable to a sandbox where children can play free and unrestricted. When a company requests the application of regulatory sandbox, the government can grant the company with "temporary approval" or recognize it as a pilot project after going through a screening process under the principle of "allow first, regulate later." It also includes the "rapid verification of regulations" system, which is about verifying regulations within 30 days and if it takes more than 30 days, it is considered that the project is subject to no regulations, and the "regulatory exception for empirical evidence," which is about approving testing and verification when regulations are ambiguous.

The Regulation Free Zone law stipulates the designation of "regulatory free zones" and provides special exceptions in order to foster regional strategic industries. It has been implemented since 2015 under the goal of fostering 27 strategic industries in 14 metropolitan cities and provinces, excluding the capital city. The Democratic Party of Korea initially opposed the regulation free zone law, claiming that it could "eliminate environmental and safety regulations and give preferential treatment to conglomerates," but the party passed the bill only after it became the ruling party. The ruling and opposition parties should work together when it comes to the initiative designed to make companies invest as much as they want and exercise their competitiveness.

DEMOGRAPHIC CLIFF, SEARCH FOR A NEW GROWTH ENGINE FOR THE ERA OF 100 YEARS OF LIFE EXPECTANCY

The world's population exceeded 6 billion in 1999 and just 12 years later, it surpassed 7 billion in 2011. Even now, four children are born each second in the global community, and the world's population is steadily expanding until it is estimated to push 7.7 billion by 2019. But Korea is facing a completely opposite concern: Korea is faced with the world's lowest birthrate and fast aging population. Korea's productive age population has started to decline after it peaked in 2016, and the total population is expected to decline beginning from 2029. Declining population entails numerous social and economic consequences.

DISAPPEARING DEMOGRAPHIC DIVIDEND EFFECT, SHIFT TO THE ERA OF DEMOGRAPHIC ONUS

Korea's productive age population (ages 15 to 64) declined for the first time in a general survey of population and housing in 2017. It

Population Reaching Retirement Age Beginning From 2019

Unit: person

- 2019 (1959): 849,000
- 2020 (1960): 920,000
- 2021 (1961): 912,000
- 2022 (1962): 879,000
- 2023 (1963): 792,000
- 2024 (1964): 832,000

*birth year in parenthesis

Source: Statistics Korea

2017 Demographic Structure by Age Group

Unit: person

- Elderly population (age 65 and over): 7.07 million (13.7%)
- Child population (age 0-14): 6.72 million (13.1%)
- Productive age population (age 15-64): 37.57 million (73.2%)

*ratio in parenthesis

Source: Statistics Korea

means that the number of people who can work is declining. Korea's population has increased sharply from 28 million to 51.7 million since the beginning of its economic development. As a result, Korea enjoyed the so-called "demographic dividend effect" or "demographic bonus effect," which refers to the natural promotion of economic growth as the result of population increase.

But now, there are more people who are retiring than the people who start new economic activities. The number of people who reach the retirement age of 60 in Korea is about to surpass 800,000 a year for the first time in 2019. An annual average of 880,000 baby boomers will reach retirement age until 2034. Even considering the fact that a considerable number of people retire before reaching the retirement age through voluntary resignation, more than 500,000 people are expected to leave their workplaces every year. In comparison, the number of people who reach the age of 15 and become a part of the productive age population has already dropped to the 400,000 level in 2017 and continues to drop.

Korea's productive age population stood at 36.2 million in 2017, down 110,000 from 2016. The future is even more worrisome as Korea entered the era of demographic onus, where the population decline results in declining economy. The year 1971 was the year when Korea had the highest birthrate. When the 1.02 million children born in 1971, the year of "golden boar", entered elementary school, their classrooms were overcrowded to the point where schools had to offer morning classes and afternoon classes. Korea's future is facing a bigger challenge because in 2018, the number of newborns stood at only 326,900 and the number is expected to drop even further in the coming years.

GOVERNMENT SPENDS W126 MILLION TO FIX THE LOW BIRTH RATE PROBLEM AND SHIFTS PARADIGM TO THE "QUALITY OF LIFE"

The Presidential Committee on Ageing Society and Population Policy announced in December 2018 that it will shift the paradigm of its low birthrate policy from "supporting when giving birth to a child" to "the direction of improving the quality of life." That means the government is planning to move its focus from giving direct incentive to couples who have children to creating environment for couples to have children. The government spent KRW126 trillion to tackle the low birthrate problem since 2006, but the birthrate has been steadily declining. The total fertility rate, which refers to the number of children a woman is expected to have in her lifetime, fell below 1.0 in 2018. It is far below the 2.1 rate needed to maintain the current population, and it is also the lowest among the OECD countries because it is far lower than the OECD average of 1.68.

When the existing measures to remedy the low birthrate problem were found to be ineffective, the government changed its main objectives of policies to "improve the quality of life," "implement gender equality" and "prepare for changes in the population structure." That means the government is accepting the reality that, while the number of marriages falling by more than 20% compared to 10 years ago, having children is no longer a natural course in life but a hard decision made after much consideration. And it is also a

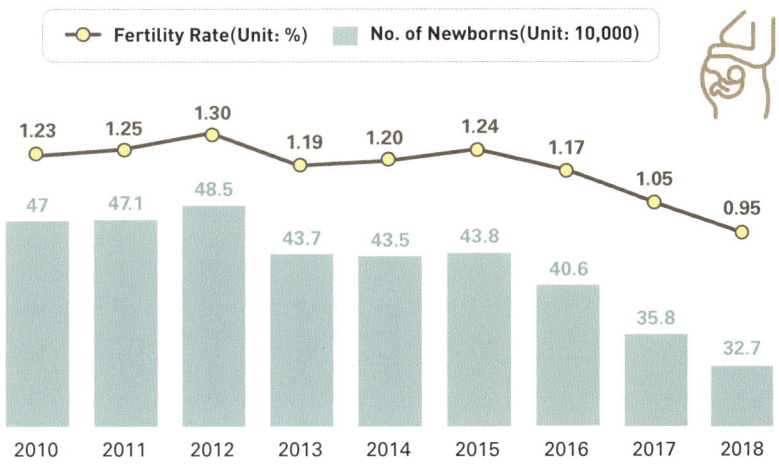

Declining Birth Rate and Number of Newborns

Source: Statistics Korea

policy change that reflects the fact that even when a child is born, the child does not grow on its own, and that the family, society and the nation must join to raise and care for the children together.

However, Korea's birth rate is falling so fast that people are worrying that it could lead to a national disaster at any time, but the "improving the quality of life" is so vague that people don't really feel any difference. It takes a lot of time and effort to motivate people to get married by increasing youth employment and income levels, and so is true to increase public childcare facilities to change people's awareness of childbirth and childcare. These discrepancies are the reason some people claim the government policy intended to fix the low birthrate should be converted back into a population policy. They say that instead of just focusing on increasing the birth rate alone, the government should also proactively bring in young and talented human resources from around the world.

JAPAN BECOMES A SOCIETY OPEN TO FOREIGNERS DUE TO THE LABOR SHORTAGE

Japan's productive age population dropped by 11 million over two decades after it peaked at 87 million in 1995. When faced with a serious labor shortage, the Japanese government received foreign students and unskilled workers to help plug the labor gap. The number of foreigners working in Japan increased from 480,000 in 2008 to 1.27 million in 2017, and 7% of part-time employees working at three major Japanese convenience stores including 7-Eleven were filled with foreign workers.

When more than 300 small and medium-sized companies were forced to close business due to a shortage of workers in 2018, the Japanese government changed its immigration control law to accept more foreign workers beginning from April 2019. The Japanese government introduced "type 1 specified skills" visa that allow workers who have simple skills and employed at fourteen industries including nursing, agriculture and construction to stay for up to five years in Japan. The Japanese government also introduced "type 2 specified skills" visa that grants permanent residency to skilled workers and their families.

Number of Foreign Workers in Japan

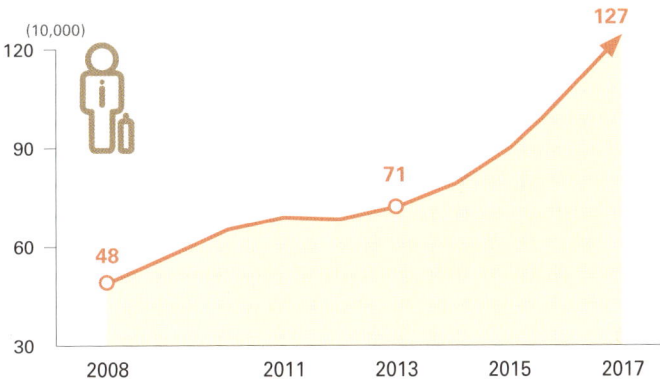

Source: Ministry of Health, Labor and Welfare

The Japanese government plans to accept 340,000 more foreign workers with a similar revision of law, but there is a significantly growing animosity within the Japanese society toward foreign workers. That is the reason the Japanese government is stressing that "it is only a measure to address the labor shortage problem, not a policy to accept immigrants." If the international standard, which categorizes foreigners staying for more than a year on a tourist visa as immigrants, then Japan is already turning into an immigrant powerhouse. According to an OECD data, Japan had 420,000 inbound foreigners in 2016, which was the fourth largest number after Germany, the United States and Britain. A country is destined to become more open to foreigners, whether they like it or not, if it fails to effectively respond to the sharp population decline problem.

IMPROVED GENDER EQUALITY CAN ADD W173 TRILLION TO GDP

There are two possible solutions to overcome the economic shock caused by the shrinking population: increase the labor productivity or increase the employment rate. Lately, the rate of women's participation in economic activities has been increasing rapidly in Korea, but still the rate is so much lower than that of European countries that Korea is being criticized for "wasting female talent."

The economic participation rate of Korean women was 58.4% in 2016, which was lower than the OECD average of 63.6%. Korea ranked 15th among the 19 OECD countries where the statistics were available for comparison, and among these countries, only a handful of countries --- Chile, Italy, Mexico and Turkey--- ranked lower than Korea. However, it is true that Korea's female economic participation rate is increasing rapidly. During the 15-year period until 2016, Korea's female economic participation rate went up by 8.5%, which exceeded the OECD average of 6.6% during the same period.

The proactive participation of women in economic activities has many positive effects, because the increase in labor supply translates into the promotion of economic growth and improvement in the income inequality problem. The International Labor Organization (ILO) analyzed that if the gap between men's and women's economic participation rates is reduced by 25% by 2025, the world's GDP will increase by 3.9%. The McKinsey Global Institute (MGI) also said in

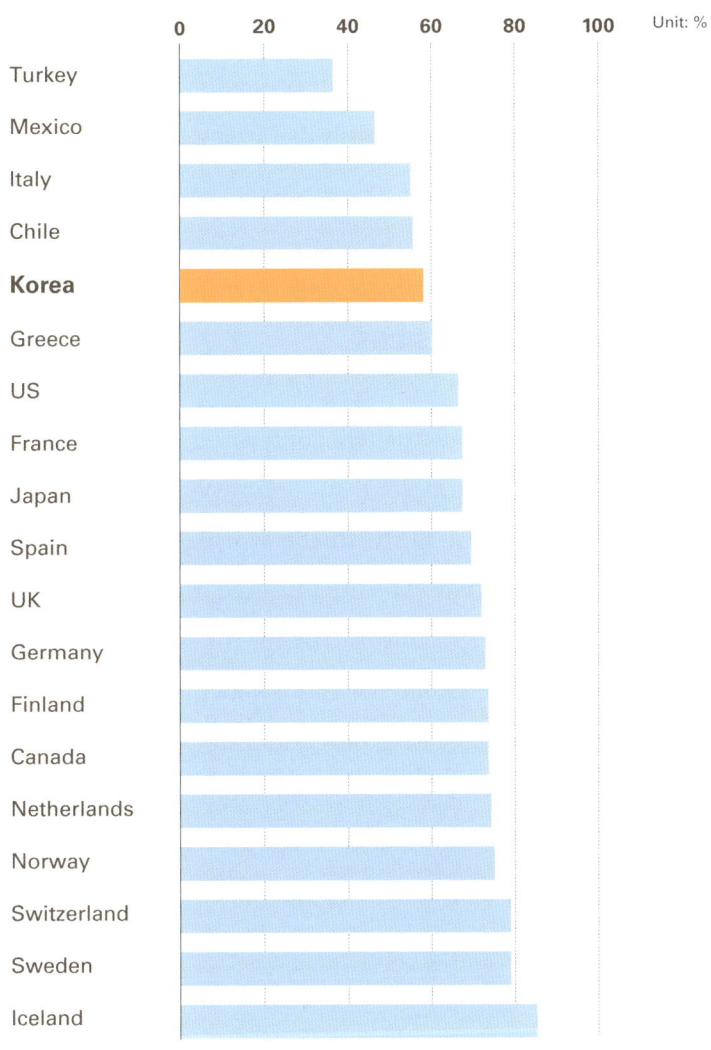

The Economic Participation Rate of Korean Women

*As of 2016

Source: OECD

a report titled "The Power of Equality: Improving Gender Equality in Asia-Pacific 2018) that if Korea drastically improves gender inequality, it could increase GDP by up to US$160 billion by 2025. In the report, MGI pointed out that trying to grow economy without fully utilizing women's potentials is like trying to fight with one hand tied behind back.

INCREASING FEMALE EXECUTIVES CAN HELP COMPANIES MAKE MORE RATIONAL DECISIONS

Korea received two extremely contrasting results in the level of gender equality survey in 2018: In one survey, Korea ranked 10th, and in another survey, 115th in the world. The United Nations Development Program (UNDP) ranked Korea 10th in gender equality, the highest in the world except for some Nordic countries such as Switzerland, Denmark and Sweden. Korea received good scores in the survey because Korea had a low pregnancy and death-related death rate and a low teen pregnancy rate. In comparison, the World Economic Forum ranked Korea 115th in its 2018 report on gender equality. Korea ranked lower than Rwanda, Namibia and Uganda in Africa.

The World Economic Forum gave the worst assessment scores to Korea mainly because it evaluates gender gap in terms of wages, economic activity participation rates, the ratio of senior managers and tertiary education rates. For example, even though the wage level of women is very low in Rwanda, their wage gap between men and women is small, while in Korea, the wage gap between men and women is significant, even though the wage level of women is much higher than Rwanda.

The "glass ceiling" that symbolizes discrimination against women is found throughout the Korean society, and this is a fact verified by many statistics. Korea ranked 29th in the London-based Economist magazine's 2018 evaluation of gender equality in the workplace, trailing Turkey and Japan. The ratio of women among corporate

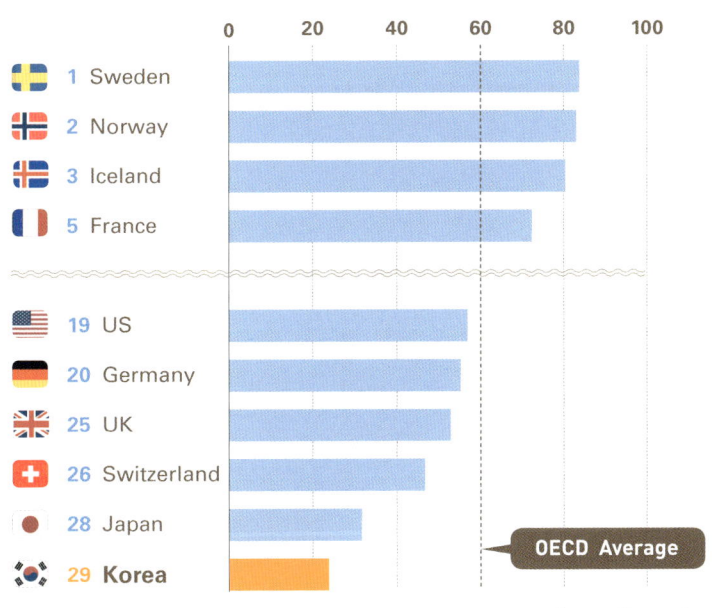

management executives in Korea was 10.5%, which was far below the OECD average of 31.8% and played a significant role in Korea's low score that put the country at the bottom in the ranking. Global companies put together boards with members from diverse backgrounds in terms of gender, race, and nationality to ensure rational and transparent decisions, but in Korean companies, only 2.1% of board members are women. The Shinzo Abe administration is advocating the so-called "Womenomics" and striving to increase the ratio of female executives at listed companies from the current 3.3% to more than 10% by 2020, and Korea is not in a position to just sit and do nothing about the issue.

THE WORST WAGE GAP AMONG OECD COUNTRIES AND THE NEED TO PREVENT CAREER INTERRUPTION OF WOMEN

The "Me Too Movement," a movement against workplace sexual harassment and sexual assault, began in the U.S. in 2017 and spread throughout the world. Shortly after, the "Pay Me Too Movement", a movement against the wage gap between men and women, also spread to Britain and France as well as Wall Street in the U.S.

According to data compiled by the OECD on the wage gap between men and women as of 2016, women in the U.S. receive an average of 18.1% less than male workers, while women in Britain receive 16.8% less than men. Women in the U.S. and Britain were furious at the wage gap, which was larger than the OECD average

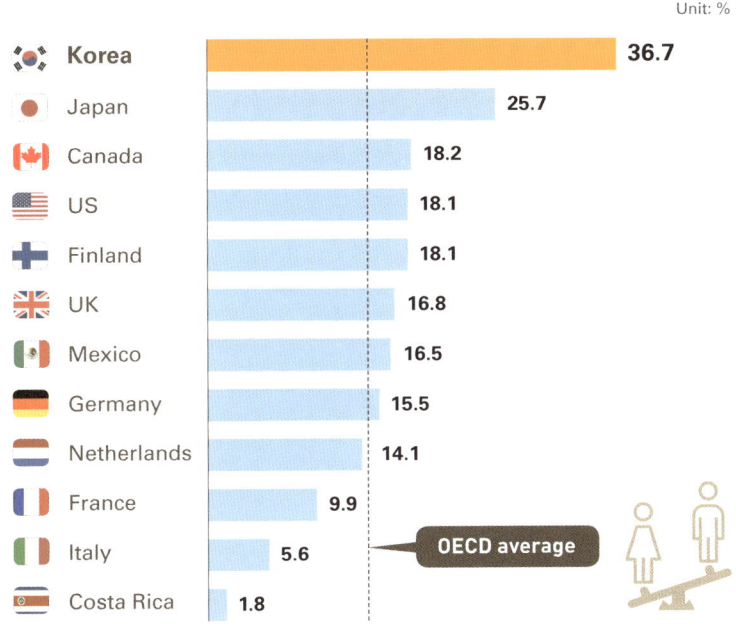

Wage Gap of OECD Member Countries

of 14.1%. In Korea, women receive a whopping 36.7% less than their male counterparts. Korea tops in the ranking and the ranking has never changed since 2000, when the OECD began releasing data on the wage gap between men and women.

According to data analyzed by Statistics Korea in 2017, the median monthly income was KRW3.37 million for men, and KRW2.13 million for women, which is 63% of the men's income. While 39% of employed men had a job that paid less than KRW2.5 million a month, more than half of the career women, or 71% of them, were working at the same level low-wage jobs. Considering the fact that women's college entrance rate has been higher than men's since 2009, one can see that such a wage gap is not caused by educational level.

There may be many reasons for the wage gap between men and women, but some of the major reasons include the fact women are more likely to have career interruptions and they are less likely to get promoted to higher positions. This is supported by the fact that women's average income is the highest in their 30s, while men's average income is the highest in their 40s, and the gap in average monthly income between men and women increased to KRW2 million a month when they reach their 50s. In order to narrow the wage gap between men and women, the government should continue to improve the childbirth and child raising environment for women so that they become less likely to have career interruptions.

THE NEED TO ADD MORE JOBS AND RAISE RETIREMENT AGE FOR THE ELDERLY IN THE AGE OF 100 YEAR LIFE EXPECTANCY

There are many debates over the standards for the age group defined as the elderly. After winning the war in 1889, German Chancellor Bismarck had soldiers aged 65 or older to retire and paid pensions instead to give jobs to younger soldiers. With the introduction of this social welfare system, 65 years old became the standard for senior citizens at a time when the average life expectancy

Retirement Policies by Country

Country	Main Point	Enforcement Year
Korea	**2016-2017, legislate for mandatory retirement age of 60**	**2013**
Spain	From 65 to 67 years old	2013
Italy	Men from 65 to 66, women from 60 to 62 years old	2012
UK	Abolishing the current provision regarding the mandatory retirement age of 65	2011
Japan	From 60 to 65 years old	2013
Germany	From 65 to 67 years old	2012
US	Abolishing the provision regarding mandatory retirement age itself	1986
France	From 60 to 62 years old	2013

of Germans was 49. The U.N. has been classified those aged 65 or older as elderly since 1956 when measuring the level of population aging in advanced countries. Korea also has preferential clauses on the Welfare Law for the Elderly for citizens aged 65 or older, and those who are aged 65 or older are eligible to receive the basic pension.

In 2015, the U.N. challenged this long-standing age classification standards when it defined a new criterion that divides human age into five groups, and classified people up to 65 years old as "young people." Korea's Supreme Court also raised the maximum age of people to physically engage in work to 65 from 60 in 2019.

Korea also raised the official retirement age from 55 to 60 in 2016, but this decision is already being criticized for having failed to properly reflect the average life expectancy or health condition. The U.S. and Britain have abolished the retirement age system altogether, while Japan mandated retirement at age 60 in 1998, but raised the age to 65 in 2013 and is now talks are underway to raise it again to 70. The plan is aimed at easing the labor shortage problem while cutting down the social security costs, including pensions.

The average life expectancy in Korea is 82 years, not much different from 84 in Japan, but the official retirement age is 60 in Korea. The age qualified to receive national pension will be delayed to 65 by 2033. This means that Koreans will have no income or pension for five years following retirement. The government is looking into a plan to raise the official retirement age to 65 as a solution to this gap in income, but there are growing criticism about the uniformed aged-based definition of the individual's ability to work. The critics argue that the official retirement age system should be abolished altogether and that the freedom to work and sign contract should be left to individual decision.

SMART HEALTHCARE SHOULD BE ALLOWED TO TAKE A LEAP OF GROWTH

In 2018, Korea entered an aged society where the people aged 65 and older accounts for 14.3% of the population, and by 2026, the country will enter a super-aged society where than 20% of the population will be aged 65 or older. The proportion of income and

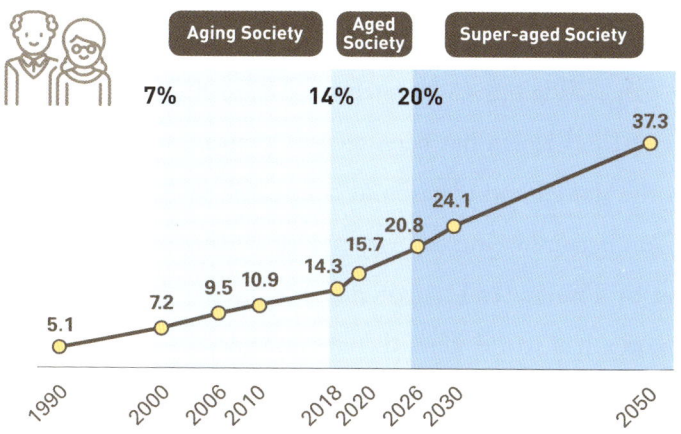

*Figures are estimate from 2010   Source: Statistics Korea

assets of people aged 65 and older is also growing. In Japan, people aged 60 or older own 70% of the total assets, and the national economy is powered largely by the elderly population and how they spend money. This is an era when everything from roads to public transportation and public facilities needs to be changed to "elderly-friendly infrastructure."

In 2010, Samsung Chairman Lee Kun-hee predicted that "most Samsung businesses and products will disappear within 10 years" and selected top five new businesses for the future, including medical devices, bio and pharmaceutical products along with solar cells, automotive batteries and LEDs. It is hardly a preemptive response considering how traditional IT companies such as GE and Philips have already shifted their focus to healthcare.

Despite being a global IT powerhouse, Korea has been recording trade deficit in the medical device sector. In the case of the majority of high value-added products such as MRI and CT, Korea is relying on imports, and Korea has been recording strong performance lately only in the dental and ultrasound diagnostic devices areas. Medical devices are becoming increasingly precise as they are combined with Internet of Things (IoT), artificial intelligence (AI) and big data. Since Korea has world-class display and mobile technologies, it is expected to make a leap forward in the medical device sector as well, but there is the regulatory barriers problem.

Korea has been only carrying out pilot projects for telemedicine since 2000, but China had already allowed the telemedicine services in 2016. Then in 2018, Alibaba introduced Chunyu Doctor, the largest telemedicine platform in China where doctors can remotely diagnose patients and delivers drugs, while Tencent developed an AI-based doctor, Dibai, who can provide medical services to patients by using the medical records of over 300 million patients. Japan's 2015 budget for the development of nursing robots amounted to 162.8 billion yen (approximately KRW1.6 trillion), while Korea's total budget for the robot sector was KRW130 billion. The government should make deregulate and make bold investment in the healthcare industry in preparation for the aging society.

BIO MARKET WHICH IS THREE TIMES OF SEMICONDUCTOR MARKET SHOULD BE THE SPRINGBOARD FOR GROWTH

Korea's exports of new drug technology reached about KRW5.3 trillion in 2018, which marks 3.7 times of increase from the previous year. Expectations are high for the bio industry after SK Chemicals developed Korea's first anti-cancer drug "Sunflower" in 1993 and Hanmi Pharmaceutical and Yuhan Corp. succeeded in exporting their bio technologies beginning from 2015, but there is still a long way to go for the Korean bio industry.

The global pharmaceutical market is three times larger than the semiconductor market at KRW2,080 trillion in 2018. With the advent of the age of 100-year life expectancy the convergence of genetic analysis and treatment technologies with information and communication technologies, the potential of the bio industry is growing bigger. The OECD even predicts that the world will enter

Bio Competitiveness Ranking of Korea

Country	2009	2013	2018
US	1st	1st	1st
Japan	13th	18th	11th
UAE		40th	24th
Korea	15th	24th	26th
China		26th	27th

Source: Scientific American

the era of bio-economic in 2030.

If Korea can grab 5% share of the global bio market, the share of the bio industry will surpass the share of semiconductors in Korean economy, but in reality, Korea is headed the opposite direction. The U.S. scientific journal Scientific American ranked Korea's competitiveness in the bio industry at 15th out of 54 countries in 2009, but Korea kept going down the ranking until it ranked 26th in 2018. Supported by negative regulations, the U.S., Singapore and Denmark remain at the top three places, but Korea has been held back in the industry due to the regulatory barriers that make it take a long time to commercialize new drugs and new technologies.

A similar assessment was made in the 2017 Bio Pharmaceutical Competitiveness & Investment Survey, which was released by U.S. bio consulting firm Pugatch Consilium. Korea was considered to belong to the leading group among emerging economies along with Singapore, Israel and Taiwan in 2016, but in 2017, it was classified as a "chaser group" along with Chile, Mexico and Malaysia. Domestic drug production went up by 64% over the 10-year period to KRW18.8 trillion in 2016, but the share of new drugs in Korea went down from 1.1% to 0.9%. A system should be in place to facilitate the development of new drugs, which usually requires 10-15 years and more than KRW1 trillion of investment.

THE NEED FOR TAXATION AND REGULATION SYSTEMS THAT RESPECT ENTREPRENEURSHIP

As CEOs who founded and started their businesses when the Korean economy was taking off enter retirement age, passing down their family businesses or management to next generation is becoming a major concern for them. It is no exaggeration to say that most parents instinctively have the desire to hand over their hard-earned wealth to their children. According to a survey of 500 small and medium companies, 60 percent of the respondents are planning for family business succession, and 96% of them are planning to pass their businesses on to their children. The Korean government is making it difficult to pass on businesses family members due to the world's highest inheritance tax rates, and Korea is facing numerous negative problems as a result.

COMPANIES WITH OVER 200 YEARS ABOUND IN JAPAN AND GERMANY, BUT NONE IN KOREA

The world's oldest company is Kongo Gumi, a Japanese construction company which has been operating for over 1,400 years since it was founded by Yoo Jung-gwang from the Baekje Dynasty in 578 at the request of Prince Shotoku to build a temple to worship the four heavenly kings, known as the Shitenno, and take the responsibility of maintaining and repairing the structure. Japan is famous for having many companies with long history. There are 22,219 companies in Japan that are more than 100 years old. There are 3,313 companies that are more than 200 years old, and 39 companies that have been operating for more than 500 years. Germany is famous for having many old companies in Europe, and there are 1,563 companies that are more than 200 years old. The numbers speak volumes about the overwhelmingly large number of companies with long history in Japan.

Critics say that long-lived Japanese companies are an outdated model of business whose ownership and management are not separated, but their ability to maintain business while maintaining consistent business values should never be taken lightly. Various factors are cited to explain the reason Japan has so many long-lived companies, a few examples of which include their craftsmanship and social class system. Another noteworthy factor is their unique system of using adopted children or sons-in-law to pass on their family

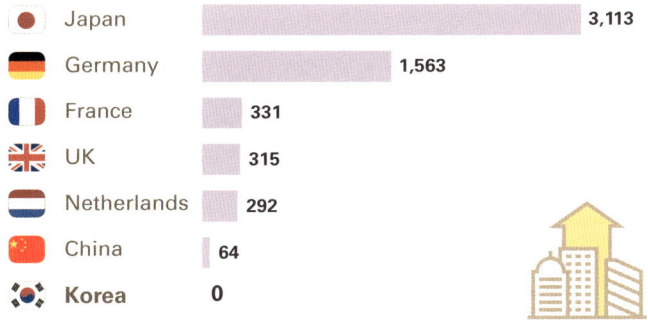

Distribution of Over 200-Year Old Companies

Source: Bank of Korea 2011 Report on the Overview of Corporation Succession in Japan and Its Significance

businesses for generations.

Unfortunately, few companies in Korea are more than 100 years old. According to a survey on the year of the establishment of 20,000 companies subject to external audits, only six of them --- Doosan, Donghwa Pharmaceutical, Mongo Food, Gwangjang, Shihan Bank and Woori Bank --- were founded over 100 years ago. It could be due to the tumultuous history marked by the transition from the agriculture-based Joseon Dynasty to the Japanese colonization and the Korean War, but in the case of China, there are 64 companies that are more than 200 years old even though China went through a similar tumultuous history including the communist revolution. Korea has succeeded in industrialization, and now is the time to pay attention to reviving the history and tradition of Korean companies.

THE WORLD'S HIGHEST 65% INHERITANCE TAX GOES AGAINST THE GLOBAL TREND OF THE WORLD

In Korea, the record of highest inheritance tax payment was broken in 2018 when the LG Group Chairman Koo Bon-moo passed away and his surviving families reported inheritance taxes that exceeded KRW920 billion. Korea's inheritance tax rate is up to 50%, but the rate can go up to 65% because of the premium charge of the largest shareholder's stock. That makes Korea a country with the world's highest inheritance tax rate.

Among OECD members, 22 countries impose inheritance taxes, with the highest rate of inheritance taxes averaging 26.3%. The number speaks volumes about how high Korea's inheritance tax rate really is. Major countries around the world have recently abolished inheritance taxes altogether. China, Hong Kong and Singapore originally had no inheritance tax, and Canada and Australia abolished the inheritance tax in the 1970s. Israel and New Zealand also eliminated inheritance taxes in 1981 and 1992 respectively. In the 2000s, Portugal, Slovakia, Sweden, Mexico, Austria, the Czech Republic and Norway abolished inheritance taxes. Among them, Australia, Canada and Sweden eliminated inheritance taxes and replaced them with capital gains taxes, which means they are not required to pay tax when they take over the companies, and they are required to pay tax only when they sell the company for capital gains.

The reason many countries abolished inheritance taxes is

Countries Without the Inheritance Tax

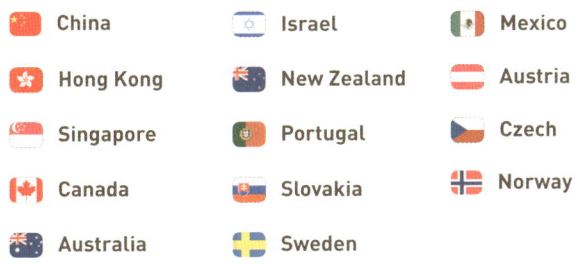

The Highest Inheritance Rate by Country

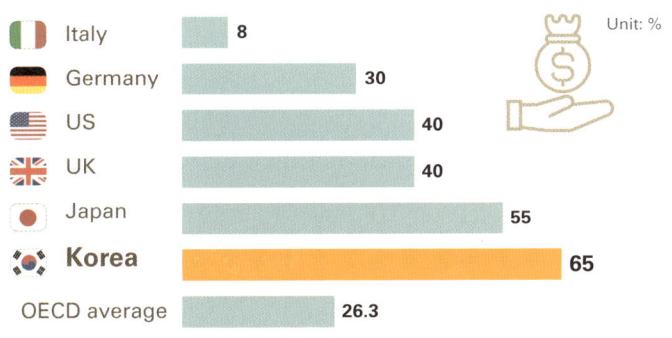

*Maximum nominal tax rate, stock premium included in the case of Korea, the maximum tax rate applied to inheritance to children in the case of Germany

because they believed that stable business management was good for employees and business partners. And they also realize that if concerns regarding family business succession make people become less focused on their business activities and even tempt them to commit illegal activities, that was a loss to the national economy.

Korea's inheritance tax rate started at up to 90% in the 1950s, but it was reflecting the reality of the time when, without the means to track down income tax evasion, the government was trying to collect the tax all at once as an inheritance tax. In the 1960s, the maximum inheritance tax rate went down to 30%, but it has been increasing steadily since 1996 until it reached the current rate. The tax rate increase might be reflecting the growing resistance to the concentration of economic power and anti-business sentiment.

PUNITIVE DOUBLE TAXATION ON INHERITANCE TAX RATE THAT IS HIGHER THAN INCOME TAX RATE

Inheritance has long been subjected to controversy over double taxation, because people claim that they are required to pay tax when they hand over the property and assets for which they have paid income tax already. This is why most countries raise their income tax rates while lowering inheritance tax rates. In fact, the highest income tax rate of OECD member states is 35.9% on average, but the highest tax rate of inheritance tax is lower than that at 26.6% on average.

Korea is an exceptional country that maintains the world's highest inheritance tax rate and also raises its income tax rate. Korea ranks second in the highest inheritance tax rate and 14th in the highest income tax among 34 OECD countries. Only six of the OECD members -- the United States, Japan, Spain, Denmark and

The Highest Inheritance·Income Tax Rate by OECD Country

Unit: %

Rank	Country	Inheritance Tax Rate	Income Tax Rate	Sum
1	Japan	55	45	100
2	Korea	50(65)	42	92(107)
3	France	45	45	90
6	US	40	37	77
7	Germany	30	45	75
	OECD average	26.6	35.9	62.5

Source: Korea Economic Research Institute

Switzerland -- have higher inheritance tax rates than income tax rates like Korea.

Korea also ranks first among the OECD country in the combined number of the highest income and inheritance tax rates. Korea has maximum inheritance and income tax rates of 50% and 42% respectively, and the combined number of these two rates is 92. Japan has a higher combined number because their maximum inheritance and income tax rates are 55% and 45% respectively, and the combine number is 100, In Korea, however, 30% premium charge is added to the inheritance tax when the largest shareholder takes over the management rights of a company. The inheritance tax premium system was introduced in 1993 because shares held by the largest shareholder have a management premium in addition to the assets and profit value of the company. If the largest shareholder's stake is less than 50% in a large company, 20% will be added as a premium charge, and 30% of premium charge will be added if the largest shareholder has more than 50% stake in the company. If this premium charge of the largest shareholder's stock is accounted for, the Korean inheritance tax rate will rise to 65%, and if this number is combined with the highest income tax rate, the combined number is 107, which is higher than that of Japan.

PETER PAN SYNDROME CAUSED BY INHERITANCE TAX AND WEAKENING COMPETITIVENESS

Nongwoo Bio was a Korean company that boasted Korea's number one seed breeding technology. When the founder died in 2013, however, the management of the company was transferred to another company, because the founder's surviving family members were forced to sell off their holdings in order to pay KRW120 billion in inheritance tax. Founded in 1967, the company had survived and protected Korea's seed technology even when numerous Korean seed companies were sold to foreign capital during the Asian financial crisis. But the company could not overcome the barrier of inheritance tax and had to hand over management right to other company.

Most companies would find it hard to protect their management rights if the sons and grandchildren of their founders have to pay 65% of inheritance tax. It is hard to stimulate entrepreneurship if company owners cannot give their companies to their children no matter

Difficulties in The Succession of Midsize Businesses

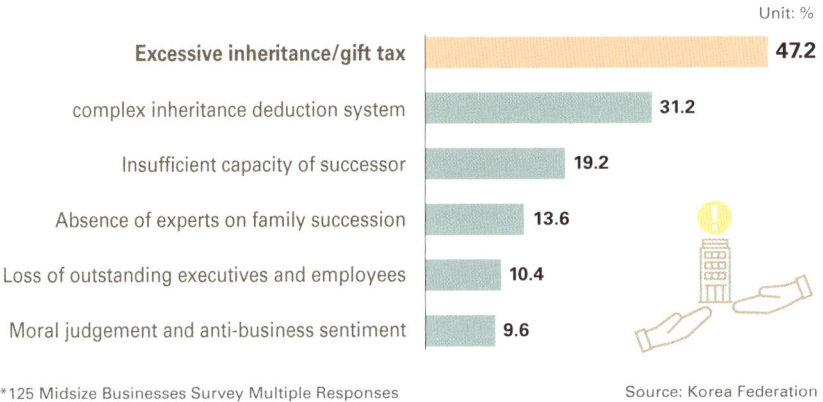

Unit: %

Category	%
Excessive inheritance/gift tax	47.2
complex inheritance deduction system	31.2
Insufficient capacity of successor	19.2
Absence of experts on family succession	13.6
Loss of outstanding executives and employees	10.4
Moral judgement and anti-business sentiment	9.6

*125 Midsize Businesses Survey Multiple Responses

Source: Korea Federation

how hard they'd worked to build a successful company. Small and medium-sized companies and venture firms may fall into the early stage of "Peter Pan Syndrome," in which they are discouraged and stop trying to grow their companies. In addition to weak morale, they might even be tempted to try various expedient or illegal methods, such as controlling shareholder-related transactions to cough up the money to pay the inheritance tax. If the company management is more concerned about finding ways to succeed management than business activities, it is highly likely that its corporate competitiveness will weaken as well. Some might even attempt to move the business to overseas to avoid inheritance tax bombs. This means that excessively high inheritance tax rates could be a move to incur a great loss by pursuing a small profit, and eventually result in the outflow of national wealth.

According to a 2017 survey of 125 mid-sized companies by the Federation of Middle Market Enterprise of Korea (FOMEK), 47.2% of the companies cited "excessive inheritance and gift taxes" as the biggest stumbling block to corporate succession, while 31.2% cited "complex inheritance and deduction systems." Inheritance and gift taxes account for less than 1% of the nation's tax revenue, but the involved taxpayers are heavily burdened by them and they are the sauce of all kinds of negative side effects.

FAMILY SUCCESSION DEDUCTION SHOULD BE PROMOTED LIKE JAPAN AND GERMANY.

Japan has a maximum inheritance tax rate of 55%, which is higher than that of Korea, but it becomes a different story if various tax breaks are applied to the inheritance of small and medium-sized enterprises. The Japanese government introduced a new business succession system in April 2018 when a growing number of small and medium-sized companies were forced to shut down business because they could not find a successor. The Japanese government introduced a clause that allowed companies to defer payment of inheritance and gift taxes for five years, in addition to the expansion of conditions for tax reduction so that the deferred tax can be exempt if the businesses are handed down to their grandchildren's generation. The Japanese government also expanded the conditions for tax waiver

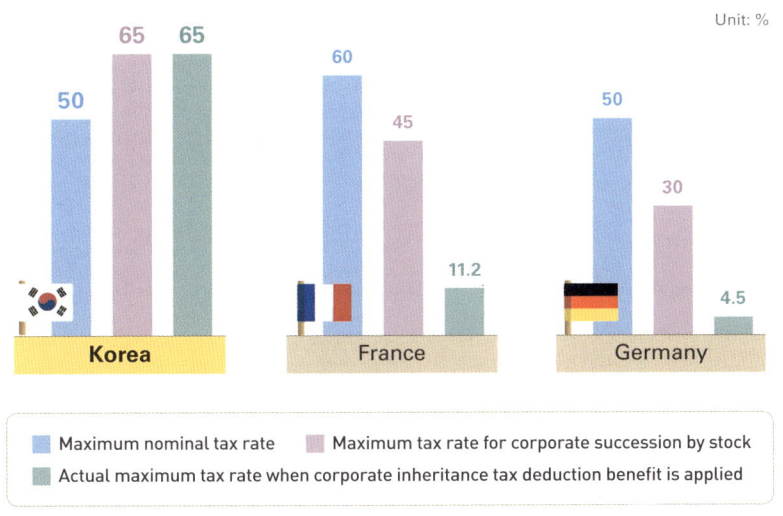

and exemption, which used to be limited to two-thirds of inheritance and gift stocks, to include the entire inheritance and gift stocks. It also abolished or eased the condition that employment should be maintained at 80% for five years after inheritance and transfer.

Germany also has a maximum tax rate of 50% for inheritance tax, but the maximum tax rate will be lowered to 30% when the family business is handed over to direct family members such as sons and grandchildren. If the deduction for family business inheritance is applied to this, the maximum tax rate is only 4.5%. In France, the maximum inheritance tax rate will be lowered to 4.5% from 60% when the direct family member succeeds the family business, and if the deduction benefit is applied, the actual inheritance tax rate will be only 11.25%. In Britain, Switzerland and France, inheritance taxes are exempt if their spouses succeed in the family business.

Korea also has a tax deduction system for family business succession, but the conditions are too tricky. To qualify for this deduction, the average sales should be less than KRW300 billion for the three years leading up to the inheritance, and that the average number of workers in the two years before inheritance should remain at least 80% for 10 years. The benefits are not so great either. Only about KRW20 billion of the total shares will be deducted and the remaining shares will be subject to a 50% tax rate. That is why fewer than 70 companies use the family inheritance deduction system every year. Inheritance deductions and deferment of payments should be greatly expanded so that penny-pinching small and medium sized companies can focus more on technology development and investment.

VARIOUS MEANS OF SUCCESSION TO LONG-LIVED ENTERPRISES OVER 100 YEARS ABROAD

Unlike in Korea, the management of the global long-lived companies such as Ford, BMW, and Heineken have been under the control of the founders' family members for more than 100 years by using various managerial succession measures. Ford Motor Co. of the U.S. established a process for managerial succession through the creation of dual-class common stock and public utility foundation in 1935. Although the Ford family owned 7% of the shares, it could exercise 40% of the voting rights because of the dual-class stock system.

Wallenberg Group, which accounts for 30% of Sweden's GDP, has also been inheriting management control for five generations for more than 160 years. The Wallenberg family was guaranteed by the government a "golden share" and a "dual-class common stock" which gave them the right to veto key management issues in exchange for promising employment stability at the 1938 Saltsjöbaden Agreement between labor, management and government. The Wallenberg family can inherit only 5.3% of the holdings through the public utility foundation, but the family has 21.5% voting rights thanks to the dual-class common stock.

Germany's BMW reduced the burden of inheritance and gift taxes by setting up a BMW equity management company as a limited partnership and giving its shares the owners' children over six years by using laws that allow for various types of companies. The German company Henkel maintains stable managerial control through a 1985 contract in which family shareholders jointly exercise voting rights, or a family equity pooling agreement. The Dutch company Heineken succeeded its management control through a multi-layered holding company structure. A multilayered holding company structure is about establishing a share management company for the holding company, and another share management company in charge of managing shares of the share management company. The owner's family members can inherit the shares of the last stage share management company. Renault of France and Nissan of Japan are consolidating their management rights through mutual investments.

Many countries around the world are abolishing inheritance tax, but even if they keep inheritance tax, they are using various systems that are not found in Korea to allow the inheritance of management rights.

FEARING TO LOSE ALL THE UNICORNS TO THE U.S. CHINA INTRODUCES DUAL VOTING RIGHT SYSTEM

China's largest e-commerce company Alibaba was listed on the New York Stock Exchange in 2014, instead of listing on the Shanghai and Shenzhen Stock Exchange. Alibaba Chairman Jack Ma cited the "dual voting right" as the selling point for him to choose New York Stock Exchange. Since then, one after another Chinese company including Baidu, Jingdong.com, and Weibo went public by listing in the U.S. stock market to take advantage of the dual voting right system. When these companies' stock prices surged, there were voices in China that criticized them for having leaked China's national wealth to the U.S. The Chinese government eventually changed the 2018 law to allow dual voting right to technology companies. It was a desperate move to keep promising tech companies in the Chinese stock market.

Prior to China, the Hong Kong Stock Exchange and the Singapore Exchange also revised the listing rules to adopt the dual voting right system. The dual voting right system played a significant role in the successful listing of Xiaomi --- the biggest IPO news of the year --- on the Hong Kong Stock Exchange in 2018.

The dual voting right has been recognized in the U.S. for many years, and in 1994, the New York Stock Exchange allowed the listing of the dual-class shares. In response to the growing complaint among companies over the increasing number of hostile takeover of firms (M&A) by private equity funds, the New York Stock Exchange broke the principle of one vote per share to strengthen the control of major shareholders. Google (Alphabet) is a good example of dual-class shares. Google issues shares in three classes: Class-A, Class-B, and Class-C. Class A is shares held by regular investors with regular voting rights, Class B is shares held by the founders and has 10 times the voting power compared to Class A, and Class C is shares normally held by employees and have no voting power. Google founders Larry Page and Sergey Brin have secured 50% of the Alphabet voting rights with their Class B shares. Facebook and LinkedIn are also using dual-class share system, and Japan, Britain, France and Singapore have introduced the system, but in Korea, there is continuing debate whether or not to introduce it by early 2019.

THE KOREAN VERSION OF ELLIOTT IS ALLOWED GROWING THREAT ON MANAGERIAL CONTROL

The American hedge fund, Elliott Associates, objected to the merger of Samsung C&T and Cheil Industries in 2015, and it also demanded a governance overhaul of Hyundai Motor Group in 2018. This kind of management pressure supported by the shareholder activism has been considered as to found only in foreign financial companies but not anymore.

The National Pension Service (NPS) decided to introduce the stewardship code in 2018 and exercise its shareholder rights to listed companies. The stewardship code refers to a set of action principles aimed at influencing institutional investors who manage other people's money to be active and engage in corporate governance in the interests of their clients. the NPS has stakes of 5% or more in 278 companies. The NPS pension operating committee decided to exercise "the limited-level shareholder right to intervene in the management" of Hajin KAL, whose parent company is Hanjin Group, for the first time in 2019.

In addition, the government removed restrictions that had limited the exercise of shareholder rights by dividing domestic private equity funds into management-participating PEFs and professional investment-type hedge funds in 2018 and allowed these fund managers to exercise their shareholder rights at will. Up until then, management-participating private equity funds have been allowed to participate in corporate management only after acquiring more than 10% of shares, and in the case of the professional-investment hedge funds, it was allowed to exercise voting rights only for stakes less than 10%. But these restrictions were removed. It paved the way for the Korean version of Elliott Associates.

As for the active exercise of shareholder rights by national pension or private equity funds, there is a positive assessment that it encourages transparent management of companies or shareholder-oriented management. In contrast, there are concerns that long-term competitiveness of companies will be weakened and management uncertainty will only increase if activist funds make exit after making short-term capital gains. Critics say the national pension fund will fall into "the pension socialism trap" if it only keeps satisfying the government's intentions.

KOREAN COMPANIES NEED PROTECTION ON MANAGEMENT RIGHTS

In 2003, Sovereign Asset Management attempted to take over the management rights of SK Group. Sovereign secured a 15% stake in SK Group and fought with SK Group in a two-year long ownership battle, during which process SK Group is estimated to have spent KRW900 billion to defend its managerial rights. Companies need to focus in investing in large-scale research and development in order to achieve innovation and growth, but if they get caught up in a battle with speculative funds and become distracted like in this case, it is a cause of grave concerns.

Advanced countries such as the United States, Japan, the United Kingdom, and France are appropriately operating four systems to ensure stable corporate management rights, and these systems include: poison pill, dual-class share, supermajority voting rule, and gold share. France and Japan allow all four systems, while the United States allows three except for the golden share, and the UK allows dual-class share and golden share systems. However, Korea allows only one system: supermajority voting rule. The supermajority voting rule is about amending a company's corporate charter to require a large majority of shareholders to approve important changes such as resignation of board member. Poison Pill is a tactic to discourage attempts of a hostile takeover by an acquirer by allowing existing shareholders the right to purchase additional shares at a discount, but this is not allowed in Korea.

The managerial right defense mechanism set aside, regulations on the holding company is another problem. If the Korea's Fair Trade regulations are applied, such global companies as Berkshire Hathaway run by Warren Buffet, the Wallenberg family in Sweden, and the luxury brand Louis Vuitton will all be accused of illegal business practices. For example, the Wallenberg family is violating Korea's Fair Trade Act that stipulates that "a general holding company cannot have a financial subsidiary," because the Swedish family owns a financial subsidiary called Investor AB. So is Berkshire

Management Right Defending Systems of the World's Major Economies

Category	US	Japan	UK	France	Korea
Poison Pill	O	O	X	O	X
Dual-class Share	O	O	O	O	X
Supermajority Voting Rule	O	O	X	O	O
Golden Share	X	O	O	O	X

Hathaway violating Korea's Fair Trade Act because the company is a financial holding company and has a variety of general subsidiaries. LVMH Group, a holding company that owns Louis Vuitton, once owned a 25% stake in a non-affiliated company, which is also illegal in Korea. Korea needs to overhaul all these old regulations on holding companies.

CORPORATE TAX IS ALSO GOING BACKWARD, SAMSUNG ELECTRONICS PAYS TAX TWICE OF APPLE

Korea's corporate tax rate policy is also moving backwards from the global trend. Samsung Electronics makes most of its sales in foreign countries, but it pays more than 80% of its corporate taxes and utility bills in Korea. As of the first half of 2018, Samsung Electronics earned KRW31.58 trillion and paid KRW8.85 trillion in corporate taxes. In comparison, Samsung's rival Apple paid only KRW4.57 trillion in corporate taxes, which is just half of Samsung

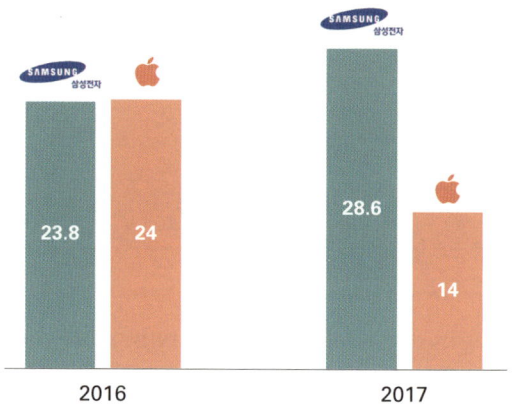

The Ratio of Corporate Tax Burden

Unit: %

*The ratio of corporate tax burden = Corporate Tax divided by Earnings Before Taxes (EBT)
Source: Korea Economic Research Institute

Electronics, even though it earned KRW32.78 trillion.

Since President Donald Trump took office, the U.S. followed through with his campaign promise to cut tax by slashing its corporate tax rate from 35% to 21%, which is less than the OECD average of 22%. The Abe administration of Japan also cut tax three times and lowered the maximum corporate tax rate from 30% to 23.4%. On the contrary, Korea kept raising its corporate tax rate from 22% to 25% in 2017, a reversal in tax rate even with the U.S. companies. There are raising concerns that President Trump's tax cut will widen the budget deficit, but it proved to have the good function of making corporate investment return to the U.S.

Ireland is the most dramatic example of the effects of business-friendly policies such as corporate tax cuts. Ireland had applied for a bailout from the International Monetary Fund (IMF) in 2010 due to a financial crisis, but graduated from the bailout in 2013. In the process, Ireland maintained its corporate tax rate at a low 12.5%, which is far lower than France's 33.3%, Germany's 30.0%, Italy's 24.0% and Britain's 19.0%, despite concerns over tax revenue shortages. As a result, the small country with a population of 4.5 million was able to attract more than 1,300 global companies. Google, Apple, Facebook, Twitter, Microsoft and Pfizer are just a few companies that have teir European headquarters in Ireland and offering jobs.

LABOR MARKET REFORM IS THE ANSWER TO THE POLARIZATION AND LOW PRODUCTIVITY PROBLEMS

There are two reasons that never fail to be mentioned when talking about the reasons for Korea's falling competitiveness: extreme labor-management conflicts and low labor productivity. There are many companies that are hesitant to invest in Korea due to labor disputes and end up moving their factories abroad. Korea ranked 15th in the 2018 national competitiveness index released by World Economic Forum (WEF), but in the labor market competitiveness, Korea fell to 48th. Korea ranks 114th and 124th in the cost of layoffs and labor-management cooperation, respectively, which put Korea among the lowest in the world. Everyone knows there are many tasks to be reformed in the labor market, but there has been little progress in reforms.

A NEED TO OVERHAUL THE WAGE STRUCTURE THAT PAYS 50% MORE TO WORKERS AT LARGE COMPANIES

If the most urgent task Korea had faced with in the 1960s was absolute poverty, the task Korea is faced with today is relative poverty. In a report titled "Double Structure in the Korean Labor Market" in 2018, the Bank of Korea analyzed that the wage gap between large companies (with more than 300 employees) and small and medium-sized businesses was 1.1 times in 1980, but it increased to 1.7 times in 2014. The Korea Economic Research Institute also pointed out that the average wage of full time employees at small and medium-sized companies in 2017 was only 56% of those at large companies.

According to an OECD report, the wages of the top 10% of Korean workers are 4.3 times that of the bottom 10%. Korea's wage gap is significantly higher than Japan's 2.85 times and Italy's 2.25 times. The wage gap is the second largest among OECD members after the United States. According to the report by the Economic, Social and Labor Committee, when the average wage for Korean conglomerates (with more than 500 employees) is considered to be 100, the average wage of companies with five to nine employees and companies with one to four employees is only 48.3 and 32.6 respectively. The U.S. stood at 64.8 and 78.8, and Japan at 72.6 and 65.1, all of which show far narrower wage gap than that of Korea.

The role of labor unions is often cited as one of the reasons for the widening wage gap between large and small-to-medium

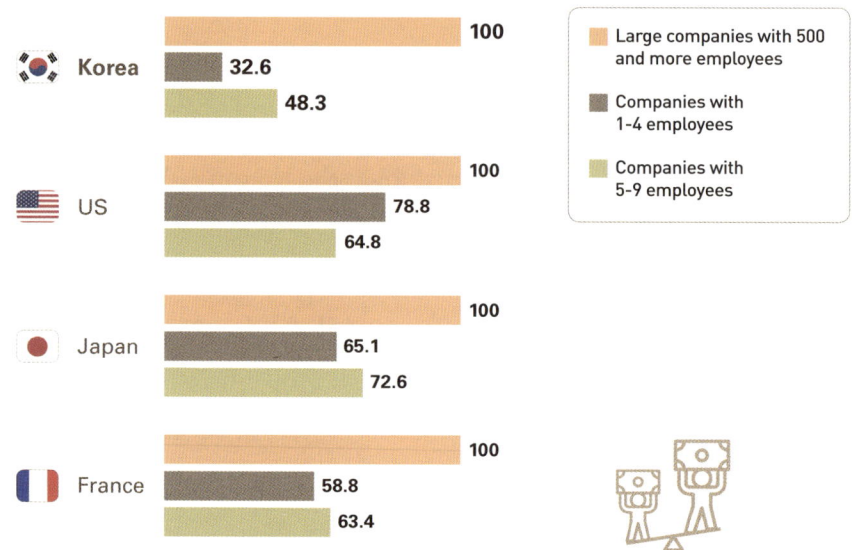

*Korea is based on 2017 data, the U.S. and France, 2015, and Japan, 2016.

Source: Report by Roh Min-sun, a researcher at the Korea Small Business Institute (KOSBI), prepared for the policy debate meeting at the Economic, Social and Labor Committee

companies and between regular and non-regular workers. Of the 19.56 million workers who are qualified to join a labor union in Korea, 10.7% joined the union as of the end of 2017, far lower than Finland's 64.6%, Britain's 23.7%, Japan's 17.3% and Germany's 17.0%, and even those who join a union are mostly concentrated in large companies and public institutions. The union membership rate among companies with 300 employees or more is 57%, but in companies with 100-299 employees, the number stands at 15%, and it is only 3.5% among companies with 30 to 99 employees. These numbers indicate that labor union activities for wage increase and job security are mostly taking place centering on large companies and public institutions.

CONCESSION OF THE REGULAR WORKERS FOR LIFETIME JOB SECURITY IS THE KEY TO SOLVE THE POLARIZATION PROBLEM

Korea has lower per capita income than the United States, Japan and France. The average monthly income of workers also stands at $3,300 as of 2017, which is 78-94% of the American employees whose average monthly income stands at $4,200, Japan at $3,500, and France at $3,800. However, employees at large Korean companies earn more in average than their counterparts in the U.S., Japan and France.

According to data released by the Korea Small Business Institute at the Economic, Social and Labor Committee's 2018 policy debate on "Solution to the Polarization and Creation of Jobs," those who are employed at Korea's large companies with more than 500 employees received an average of US$6,097 per month. The figure was higher than that of France ($5,238) and the U.S. ($4,736). The figures were based on the purchasing power parity (PPP) reflecting prices, and it is found that Korean employees were getting paid about 1.5 times more than their counterparts in Japanese large corporation were.

These high levels of wages have direct impact on industrial

Comparison of Average Wage of Large Companies by Country

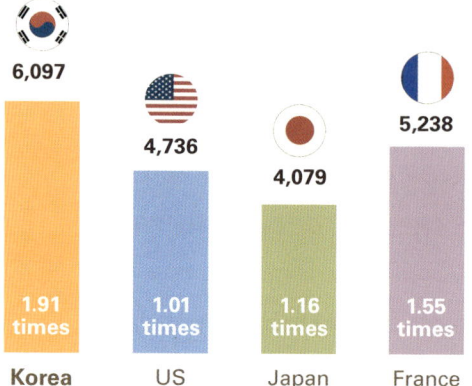

*Based on the purchasing power parity (PPP) as of 2017 in Korea, 2015 in the U.S. and France, and 2016 in Japan
*The number within the bar is ratio to per capital GDP

Source: Report by Roh Min-sun, a researcher at the Korea Small Business Institute (KOSBI), prepared for the policy debate meeting at the Economic, Social and Labor Committee

competitiveness. Japan's automaker Toyota had suffered a KRW5 trillion loss of business in the wake of a massive recall incident that coincided with the 2008 global financial crisis, and its president was grilled at the U.S. congressional hearing. The atmosphere at the time gave an impression that Hyundai and Kia would overtake Toyota at any moment, but the market mood was moving in a completely different direction. Toyota bounce back up like a roly-poly after the union of Toyota, which has maintained its strike-free tradition since the 1960s, gave its support for the revival of the company and also declared a four-year freeze in wages.

In comparison, Hyundai Motor's labor union cared only about

the interest of workers and staged one after another strike, causing production disruptions amounting to KRW7 trillion for five years until 2018. The average wage of five Korean carmakers is KRW90.72 million as of 2017, which is far more than Toyota's average of KRW78. The share of labor costs in sales is also more than double the share of Toyota. Due to this wage structure, the share for suppliers is decreasing and the competitiveness of the auto industry is falling. Concession from regular workers at large companies who are paid excessively high wages for productivity is essential for the co-prosperity of large and small companies.

THE RIGHT TO UNIONIZE AND THE EMPLOYERS' RIGHTS TO DEFEND THEMSELVES SHOULD HAVE BALANCE

The issue of ratifying some of the key conventions of the International Labor Organization (ILO) is a task that Korea has been agonizing over for about 30 years. Korea joined the ILO in 1991, but Korea has yet to ratify four key conventions including the freedom of association and the abolition of forced labor. Citing the fact that 143 of the ILO members ratified all eight key conventions, the labor community has been pressing the government that it should "ratify the conventions for the sake of guaranteeing the right to organize labor unions." If the ILO's key conventions are ratified, that means Korean government has to allow dismissed workers to join labor union, pay wages to former union members, establishment of unions of persons in special types of employment, and substitute military service system, as well as the expansion of the right of collective organization for teachers and government employees. But countries have different situations with regards to these issues. That is the reason the U.S. has yet to ratify six conventions and Japan, two key conventions.

If the right to organize labor union is expanded, it is important to increase the employers' rights to defend themselves have to be expanded to ensure labor-management balance. In Korea, negotiations over wage increase and strikes are taking place as if they are annual events, but this is a situation that can be found in few countries in the world. According to the Korea Labor Institute's "2018 Overseas Labor Statistics," Korea sustained 2.34 million days of labor loss due to the labor strikes in 2016. Labor loss is calculated by multiplying the number of strikers and the length of the strike. In the case of Japan, it was only 3,000 days in 2016. It means Korea's loss of labor as the result of strike was 670 times that of Japan. In most countries including the U.S. and Japan, companies are allowed to use substitute workers when the union goes on a strike, but Korean companies are helpless because Korea's labor law is prohibiting the use of substitute workers. It is said that the only country other than Korea that bans the use of substitute workers by law is Malawi in Africa.

The world is expanding the wage negotiation cycle. The US-based General Motors has changed its collective bargaining cycle from one year to four years, and majority of Japanese and German carmakers are also having wage negotiations once every two years, or 3-4 years. In Korea, however, it is mandated by law to hold collective negotiations once every two years. Korea can reduce the cost of labor-management conflicts only when this cycle is expanded.

EMPLOYMENT AND DISTRIBUTION SHOCK CAUSED BY THE 30% MINIMUM WAGE HIKE

Under the banner of income-led growth, the Korean government raised the minimum wage by 16.4% in 2018 and again by 10.9% in 2019. Naturally, the minimum wage dealt a big blow to the labor

Korea Ranks Fourth in the Minimum Wage to GNI Among OECD Countries

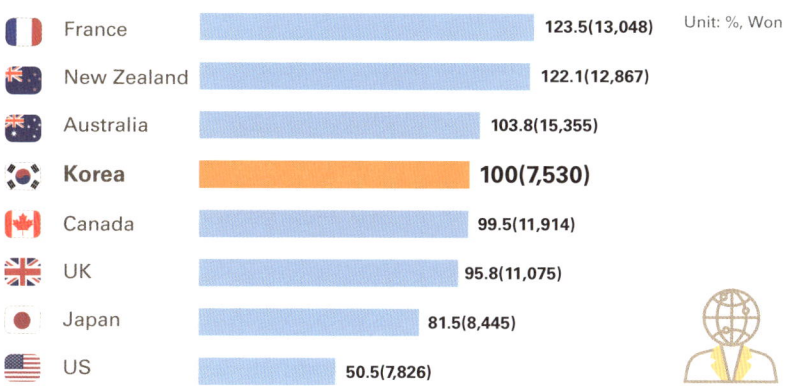

		Unit: %, Won
France	123.5(13,048)	
New Zealand	122.1(12,867)	
Australia	103.8(15,355)	
Korea	**100(7,530)**	
Canada	99.5(11,914)	
UK	95.8(11,075)	
Japan	81.5(8,445)	
US	50.5(7,826)	

*Comparison based on the assumption that Korea's minimum wage to GNI is 100
* The number within parenthesis is the amount of each country's minimum wage converted to won, as of 2018

Source: Minimum Wage Commission

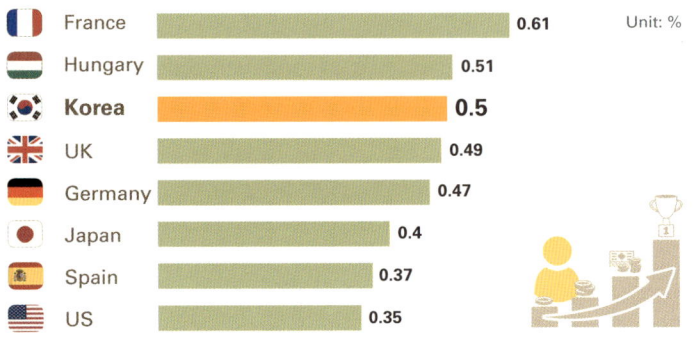

Korea Has a Relatively High Minimum Wage Relative to Median Wage

France	0.61	Unit: %
Hungary	0.51	
Korea	0.5	
UK	0.49	
Germany	0.47	
Japan	0.4	
Spain	0.37	
US	0.35	

Source: OECD

market because it increased by 30% in just two years while the economic growth rate remained below 3%. Micro-enterprise owners and small business owners who failed to increase their sales and operating profits to accommodate the wage increase had to cut down the number of employees because they could not afford to pay higher wages. Consequently, the number of unemployed increased by more than 200,000 in January 2019 from a year ago, which is the highest unemployment rate in 19 years. It simply is an unemployment crisis.

It was also pointed out at the 2019 joint academic conference on economics that, according to a study, some 210,000 jobs were lost because of the minimum wage increase. With majority of the jobs for part-timers, low-income workers and non-regular workers gone, the income distribution reached its worst level since 2017 because while the monthly income of the top 20% of the income bracket has

Differential Application of Minimum Wage by Country

Country	Region	Job	Age
Korea	X	X	X
Germany	X	X	X
UK	X	X	O
France	X	X	O
Australia	X	O	O
US	O	X	O
Japan	O	O	X
Canada	O	O	O

Source: Minimum Wage Commission

increased, the bottom 20% has declined.

The truth is, even though politicians and labor communities brought the minimum wage issue into a presidential election issue, the minimum wage in Korea was not low in the first place. In a report by the Minimum Wage Commission, Korea's minimum wage to GNI in 2018 was the fourth-highest among OECD members after France, New Zealand and Australia. Even when compared with the median wage of workers, the minimum wage in Korea was 50%, which was significantly higher than that of Britain, Germany and Japan.

The percentage of workers subject to the minimum wage among all workers also made a sharp increase from 17.4% in 2017 to 25% in 2019. The minimum wage can be effective only when it is increased by comprehensively reflecting various factors such as the economic growth rate, prices and the employers' ability to pay. If the political and labor communities recklessly raise minimum wage out of commitment only to cause numerous low-income workers end up losing jobs, it would be better off without any policy on the minimum wage at all.

PRODUCTIVITY HAS TO IMPROVE TO ENSURE SHORTER WORK HOURS AND "LIFE WITH EVENINGS"

Korea is one of the countries where employees work the longest hours in the world. The average working hours per year in Korea was 2,024 in 2017, which was the third longest working hours among OECD comparison countries after Mexico and Costa Rica. The number indicates that, considering how the OECD average was 1,759 hours, Korean employees are working about one month longer a year than their counterparts in other countries. Under this circumstance, Koreans started to use such slogans as "Let's find a life with evenings by reducing work hours" or "Let's find the work-life balance."

The government decided to reduce Korea's statutory maximum working hours by 16 hours from 68 hours per week to 52 hours, and this new law will take effect on July 2018 for businesses with 300 or more employees; January 2020 for businesses with 50 to 299 employees; and July 2021 for businesses with 5 to 49 employees. However, it is worrisome that the working hours are cut down too much all at once. It makes difficult for companies to produce and

Korea's Declining Working Hours Per Year

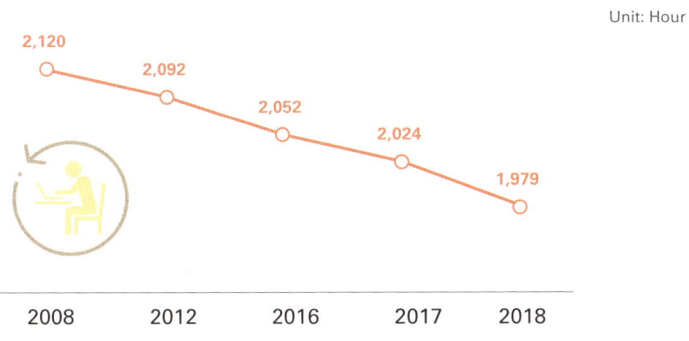

Source: Ministry of Employment and Labor

Working Hours and Productivity of OECD Countries

deliver orders on time, and for consumers, it is difficult to get repair services at night hours or weekends even if their boiler is broken down in the middle of winter. It will be also difficult for Korea to claim to be the best in fast warranty services.

Korea's labor productivity ranks near the bottom among the OECD member countries, and it is a problem that needs to be resolved as soon as possible. Korea's gross domestic product per hour worked stands at $34.30 as of 2016 based on purchasing power parity (PPP), which is 66% of the OECD average that stands at $52.0. Compared with Germany, Korean workers work four months more a year than German workers, but their annual wages are only 70% of that of Germany. That means the actual wage per hour is less than half that of Germany. If working hours are shortened under this condition, low-income workers have to look for second jobs in order to compensate for reduced wage. Unless productivity is increased, Korean workers might face with a "life with no time to eat dinner" instead of welcoming a "life with evenings."

TEMPORARY AGENCY WORKERS SHOULD BE ALLOWED IN MANUFACTURING INDUSTRY FOR INCREASED LABOR FLEXIBILITY

Korea is going a different direction from major countries such as the United States, Britain and Germany in terms of temporary agency workers as well. The U.S. and Britain have no regulations with regards to temporary agency workers, while Germany and Japan have drastically loosened restrictions on temporary agency workers in order to expand employment. Initially, Germany strictly limited the temporary placements of workers, but it greatly loosened the regulation on the scope of its application beginning from the late 1990s and even removed the restriction on how long temporary agency workers could work in 2003 with "Hartz Reform." Currently, temporary agency workers are allowed in all industries except the

A Comparison of Labor-Management Relations among Global Automakers

Category	Japan (Toyota)	Germany (Volkswagen)	US (GM)	Korea (Hyundai)
Wage system	Job/Performance	Job function	Job/Performance	Seniority
Temp Agency Workers	Allowed	Allowed	Allowed	Not allowed
Substitute Workers During Strike	Allowed	Allowed	Allowed	Not allowed
Turnover	Possible	Possible	Possible	Prior agreement with the union
Wage & Collective Bargaining Cycle	1 Yr.	1 Yr.	4 Yr.	1 Yr.

Source: Korea Automobile Manufacturers Association

construction industry, and in the case of BMW's Leipzig plant, temporary agency workers account for a whopping 57% of all employees.

Japan also revised the law regarding temporary placements of workers in 1999 and shifted to negative regulations that allow temporary agency workers in all industries except for a few special industries such as construction, port transportation and medical services. In 2004, Japan lifted ban on the manufacturing industry as well, which resulted in creating 1.37 million jobs in a span of five years. In Japan, in-house subcontracting is also allowed and used as an important production method in shipbuilding, automobiles, chemicals and steel industries. The ILO also recommended "allow in principle, but don't abuse" approach with regards to temporary placements of workers in Convention C181, 1997, citing that it "helps to improve flexibility in the functioning of labor markets and to relieve unemployment problem."

Korea used to strictly ban the temporary placements of workers, but the act on the temporary agency workers was passed in 1998 to allow temporary agency workers in 32 industries including cleaning and security, but not yet in manufacturing industries. Korea is the only country among major competitors that doesn't allow temporary agency workers in manufacturing industries. In Korea, the standards between legal and illegal temporary placements of workers are ambiguous, and there are constant legal disputes over the issue. Attempts to expand the range of temporary placements of workers to keep pace with international trend have been always blocked by the National Assembly. The bill intended to allow temporary agency workers in some fundamental industries such as molds, casting and welding and high-paying jobs is also opposed by labor unions that claim it would make "the poor get poorer and the rich get richer."

KOREA RANKS FIRST IN THE WORLD IN THE UTILIZATION RATE OF ROBOTS

Korea is the country that uses industrial robots the most actively. According to data from the International Federation of Robotics (IFR), the Korean manufacturing industry ranked No. 1 in the world for two years straight in a comparison of "robot density" in 2017. The number of industrial robots stood at 710 per 10,000 employees, far higher than 658 in Singapore, 322 in Germany and 308 in Japan. Compared to the world average of 85 robots, the number is more than eight times higher.

Robots can easily handle substances that are harmful to humans in dangerous environments. Robots can work 24 hours a day without making mistakes due to overwork, and once you install them, they cost less than humans. Along with technological development, it is natural that the number of industrial robots increases at manufacturing fields. Automated factories is also cited as a major alternative in the process of bringing back companies that have fled

Korea Ranks No.1 in the World in Robot Density

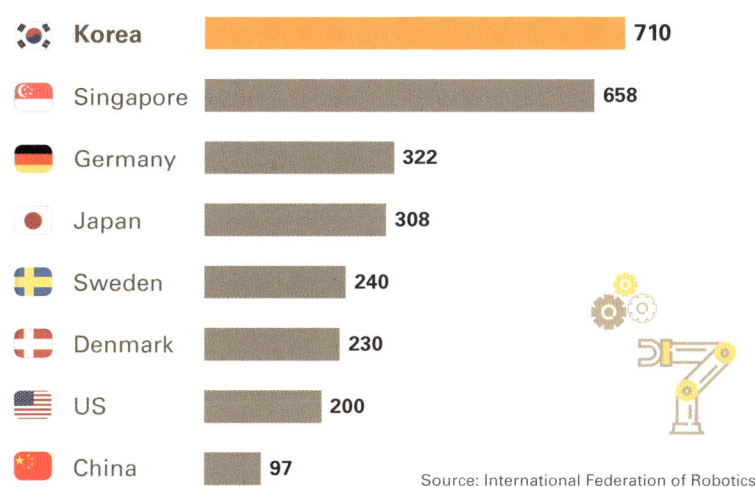

Source: International Federation of Robotics

to foreign countries to avoid militant labor unions or high wages.

The robot industry is not only a future growth industry in itself, but it is also cited as a variable that greatly affects the competitiveness of the manufacturing sector or the labor market structure. Japan's Fanuc, Germany's Kuka and Switzerland's ABB rank first to third in the global robot industry in terms of sales in 2017. Hyundai Robotics of Hyundai Heavy Industries Co. ranks sixth in the world, but it has a market share of only 3%, falling significantly behind the world's top five companies whose market shares are two digits.

Robots can make people lose jobs in certain areas, but they also create new jobs that require the involvement of human workers as well. China's Midea Group acquired Germany's Kuka in 2016, and in 2017, China overtook Japan and became the world's largest producer of industrial robots. Korea, a country that ranks first in robot density, should also step up efforts to secure technologies to produce and utilize robots in order to strengthen national competitiveness.

THE NEED TO MOVE BEYOND THE SENIORITY-BASED WAGE SYSTEM TO INCREASE PRODUCTIVITY

The wage gap between new hires and senior employees in Korea is among the highest in the world. According to the Korea Economic Research Institute (KERI), wages for those who have been employed for more than 30 years amounted to 3.11 times that of those who have been employed for less than a year. The wage gap is much larger

Wage Gap Between Korea and Japan Based on the Length of Employment

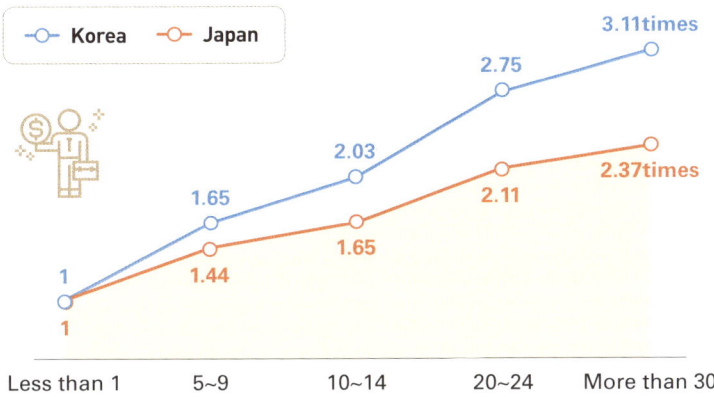

*Based on ratio relative to the wages for less than one year of employment, as of 2017
Source: Korea Economic Research Institute

than Japan's 2.37 times. This indicates that Korea's wage system places great importance on seniority, and this method of paying wage is blamed to be the key factor that slows down labor productivity. A structure where wages increase according to the number of years of employment regardless of job difficulty or performance is contributing to the wide-spreading complacency and decreasing organizational dynamism. It also makes companies reluctant to hire regular full-time workers, thereby making improved productivity all the more unlikely to happen.

Starting in 2016 when it became mandated to retire at age 60, talks were underway in Korea to change the system to pay wages based on job function and performance, because if the wage system remained unchanged after the mandatory retirement age was expanded, companies would have to face with significant increase of wage burden. As a result, the number of businesses applying the seniority-based wage system in Korea fell from 76% in 2010 to 60% in 2017, while the wage gap between workers with less than one year of service and over 30 years of service was also reduced by 3.11 times in 2017 from 3.48 times in 2007. The number of businesses that accepted the wage peak system --- in which there is no wage increase once an employee reaches a certain age --- also rose from 9% in 2009 to 40% in 2018.

Still, Korea still has a high percentage of companies whose wages are based on seniority. It is estimated that the percentage of workers over the ages of 50 will go up to 49.4% by 2023. If the employees aged 50 and over account for more than half of the entire employees under a circumstance where companies can hire three new employees for the same wage to pay one employee in their 50s, it could further decrease Korea's economic productivity.

SCIENCE AND TALENT SHOULD BE TREASURED TO BECOME THE LEADER IN THE FOURTH INDUSTRIAL REVOLUTION

With the coming of the era of the Fourth Industrial Revolution, there is a growing need of creative professionals who will lead key areas of competition, such as artificial intelligence (AI). There is also a fierce competition for talent at the national level as well. Since 2006,

Artificial Intelligence Patent Applications by Country

Unit: %

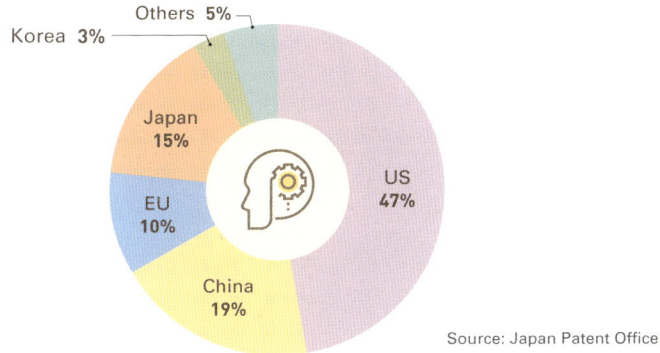

- Others 5%
- Korea 3%
- Japan 15%
- EU 10%
- China 19%
- US 47%

Source: Japan Patent Office

Shortage of AI Specialists in Korea

Unit: Persons

Country	Persons
US	12,027
UK	2,130
Germany	902
China	619
Japan	321
Korea	**180**

Source: Tencent Research Institute, 2017 Global AI Specialists White Paper

China has been pushing forward with the "111 Project" with the goal of developing around 100 world leading research discipline bases in Chinese universities with 1,000 top talents from the world's top 100 universities to work with Chinese researchers. China also announced

Comparison of Artificial Intelligent Technology by Country

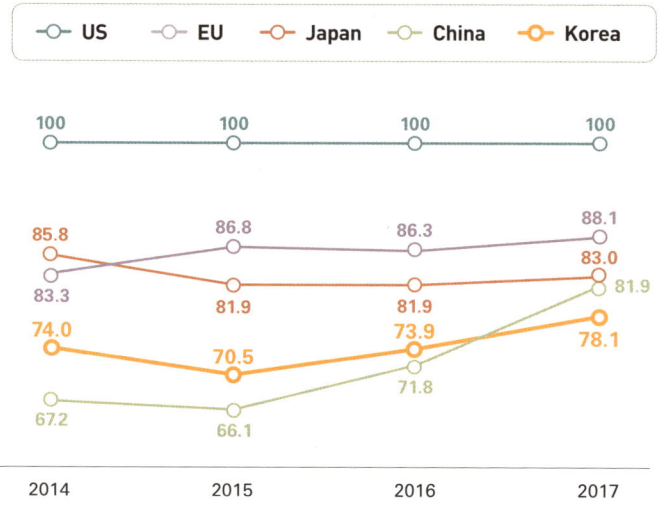

* Technology level of each country when the AI technology of the US is scaled to be 100
Source: Information and Communications Technology Promotion (IITP)

the "AI Talent Cultivation Plan" in 2018, under which China will nurture more than 5,000 students and 500 teachers in AI from top universities within five years. Singapore launched the "AI Singapore" project in 2017, and Japanese Prime Minister Shinzo Abe also announced a government-led initiative to nurture 30,000 to 40,000 AI talent.

Korea is lagging behind in this trend. According to a report by the Institute for Information and Communications Technology Promotion (IITP), if the AI technology of the United States is assumed to be 100, Korea's AI technology is only 78.1. That means Korea is behind Europe whose average score is 88.1 and Japan whose score is 83.0. Korea was outpaced by China in 2017 when China scored 81.9. If Korea cannot secure human resources and data, Korea cannot be in the leading group in AI technologies, and without AI technology, it is impossible to realize innovative growth in the Fourth Industrial Revolution era.

During his visit to Pyongyang as a part of the economic mission for the inter-Korean summit, Samsung Electronics vice chairman Lee Jae-yong expressed that he was deeply impressed at how highly the North regarded science and top talent. But in South Korea, scientists are often excluded from important decision-making processes. For example, in the process of public debate on whether to continue the construction of the Shin-Kori 5 and 6 reactors, scientists were excluded, and the decision was made by those who were not from the science communities. Scientists have been even called the "nuclear mafia" and have been treated as if they were "deep-rooted evils" of the society.

Korea did not produce any Nobel Prize winner in the science category since it was established in 1901. Japan has produced 23 winners in science and China has also produced a Nobel Prize winner in Physiology or Medicine in 2015. The future cannot be bright for a society that is swayed by the claims of environmental and civic groups instead of highly regarding the voices of scientists.

A NEED OF LEADERSHIP AND COMMUNICATION FOR A GRAND COMPROMISE BETWEEN LABOR, MANAGEMENT AND THE GOVERNMENT

In Korea, where labor-management relations have been a drag on national competitiveness, "grand social compromise" has been cited as a national task for more than 25 years. The 1982 The Wassenaar Arrangement of the Netherlands and the 2002 Hartz reforms of Germany, through which these two countries were able to find the driving force to break free from the low-growth, high unemployment crises by successfully realizing grand consensus between the labor, management and the government, were considered models to emulate for Korea.

In Korea, labor movements have spread like wildfire following the June 1987 democratic uprising, consequently making the need for dialogue between labor and management more important than ever. In 1990, Korean Confederation of Trade Unions and the Korea Employer's Federation set up the National Economic and Social Council and attempted a dialogue between labor, management, and government for the first time in 1993, and in 1996, the Presidential Labor-Management Committee was established, but no visual results were produced.

The "Social Agreement to Overcome the Economic Crisis" signed by the Labor-Management-Government Committee in February 1998 in the aftermath of the foreign exchange crisis in late 1997 is

Labor Reforms of Major Countries

Country	Reform Method	Reform Effect	Result
England	Led by the government (Prime minister Margaret Thatcher's Labor Reform)	· Restrictions on the immunity of union leaders · Mandate secret voting when deciding to strike · Revision of social security system, including introduction of work-seeker's allowance	Success
Germany	Grand Compromise Between Labor, Management, Government (2002 Hartz Reforms)	· Flexible labor market · Diversifying employment types · Promote startups · Reduced welfare for the unemployed	Success
Netherlands	Grand Compromise Between Labor, Management, Government (1982 Wassenaar Arrangement)	· Labor union: wage increase control · Management: shorter working hours · Government: financial/tax support	Success
Spain	Led by the Congress	· Mitigate overprotection of regular workers · Mitigate transition of temporary workers to full-time status (Understanding the deep-sea effect of dual labor market)	Failure
Italy	Led by the government	· Reducing lifetime employment · Mitigate layoff procedures for flexible labor market · Reform of unemployment benefits to enhance stability (the gap in unemployment between academic backgrounds due to lack of job training systems)	Failure

Source: Korea Automobile Manufacturers Association

the most noteworthy achievement. The agreement --- which included wage freeze, wage cuts, and employment flexibility --- was rejected at a meeting of representatives of the Korean Confederation of Trade Unions, and the Korean Confederation of Trade Unions has not been returning to the Labor-Management-Government Committee since then. The Labor-Management-Government Committee was changed to the Economic and Social Development and Labor Affairs Committee in 2007 and again to the Economic and Social Development Commission in 2018, producing 84 agreements during the process. However, the contents of these agreements are so abstract and not legally binding that they are mocked as NATO: No Action Talk Only Committee.

The "Gwangju-type job negotiations" that concluded in early 2019 presented a win-win model for labor and management and paved the way for the first construction of a finished car manufacturing plant in Korea in 23 years. The government should continue to make efforts to achieve such tangible results through a grand compromise between labor, management and the government, but when that is impossible, labor reform, in which the government suggests directions decisively, should be considered as an alternative.

KOREA HAS TO FOSTER HALLYU CONTENT, TOURISM, FINANCE, AND SERVICE INDUSTRIES

The Korean economy has grown while tapping the export market with products from manufacturing industries such as semiconductors, shipbuilding and automobiles. It was a way to overcome the limit of small domestic market, but export-driven economic growth has made the Korean economy heavily dependent on foreign countries and become vulnerable to global market conditions. As production facilities for semiconductors and automobiles have been automated, "growth without employment" has also emerged as a concern. Korean manufacturing accounted for 14% of the job market in 1970, but it went up to 28% in 1989 and then started to decline to the 17% level again. That is the reason Korea needs to turn its attention to service industries where job creating effect is twice that of the manufacturing sector.

70% OF EMPLOYMENT IN THE SERVICE INDUSTRY, NOW IS THE TIME TO IMPROVE ADDED VALUES

The service industry accounted for 70% of jobs available in Korea, up from 50% in 1992. The figure is not much different from the OECD average of 74%. In comparison, the share of value-added production in the service industry went down from 55% in 2008 to 53% in 2017. In the World Bank comparison data, Korea's share of added value in the service industry lags far behind 77% in the United States and 69% in Japan, and it is lower than the global average of 65%.

Korea's per-employee value-added output in the service sector stood at $51,700 in 2015, less than the OECD average of $68,000, and it placed Korea at the bottom of the list among 31 member countries. It is because many people who were laid off while working in the service industry during the restructuring process found jobs in low productivity sectors such as the wholesale & retail, food and lodging industries, and also because R&D investment to innovate in productivity has been sluggish in the service industry as well.

According to a report released by the Korea Institute for Industrial Economics and Trade in 2019, R&D investment by Korean service companies was $4.5 billion in 2013, which was significantly lower than the US whose investment stood at $89.9, France at $16.1 billion, Japan at $11.6 billion and Germany $8.3 billion of Germany. The ratio of R&D investment in service industries was 8% of the

R&D Investment in Service Industries in OECE Countries

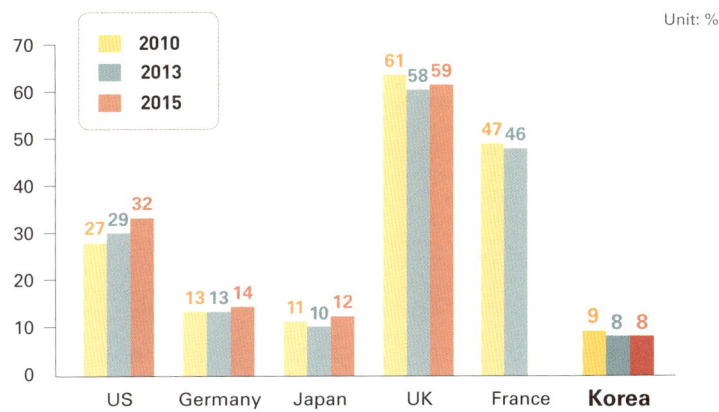

Source: Korea Institute for Industrial Economics and Trade 2019 Report on the "Overview of Investment by Korea's Service Industries and Policy Task"

Service Sector Value Added to GDP

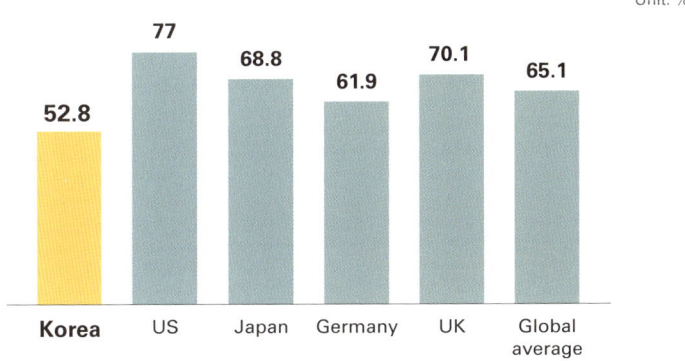

* As of 2017 for Korea, and 2016 for the rest

Source: World Bank

FOR YET ANOTHER MIRACLE

total R&D investment in 2015, which was also significantly less than that of the UK at 59% and the US at 32%. Korea's R&D in the service industry is almost a wasteland level even compared with two manufacturing powerhouses of Germany and Japan whose investment stood at 14% and 12% respectively.

The " Basic Law on Service Industry Development " which includes plans to support R&D in the service industry and easing regulations has been stuck at the National Assembly for more than seven years since 2012. It is a pity that the service industry, including medical, financial and tourism, has failed to develop it into a high value-added industry due to opposition from the group with vested interests, despite its huge growth potential.

A NEED TO DEVELOP CONTENT INDUSTRY FILLED WITH FUN AND TALENT BY USING HALLYU AS THE FOUNDATION

Walt Disney acquired 21st Century Fox's movie studio and content assets and liabilities for $71.3 billion in 2018. The huge merger and acquisition, which amounted to KRW80 trillion, was a reminder of the value of content industry. Netflix's explosive growth, which started as a video rental company in 1997, is also symbolically showing us the importance of content industry. The company, which grew into the world's largest on-demand video service provider, spent about KRW9 trillion, or 85% of its new investment funds, in 2018 to produce original content products such as movies, dramas and shows.

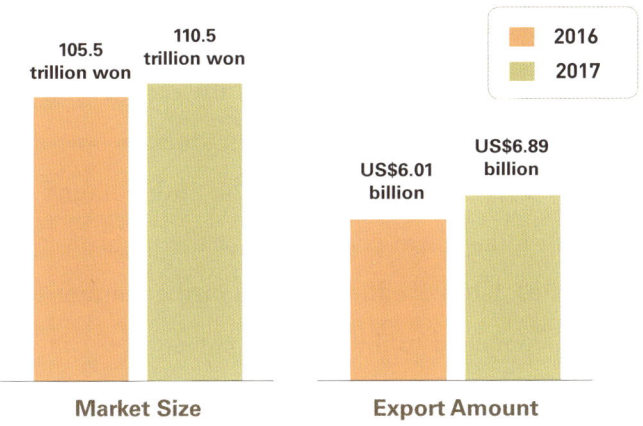

Supported by this endeavor, Netflix secured 130 million subscribers and its market value is estimated to be $153 billion as of the early 2019.

Supported by the hallyu boom, Korea is also finding a good opportunity to develop its content industry. Korea should make the most out of Korean's innate penchant for entertainment and talents to capture the eyes and ears of people around the world with various content products such as beauty, games, mukbang and animations, not to mention K-pop drama films. Korea Creative Content Agency is estimating the size of the Korean content market in 2017 to be KRW110 trillion, which is five times larger than the pharmaceutical market and is half the size of the food and restaurant market. Exports of content products also exceeded KRW7 trillion, which is equivalent to the export of 200,000 mid-sized cars.

The growth rate of content product exporting industry reached 27% in the first half of 2018, consequently contributing to revitalize the Korean economy, which has been stuck in low growth. The cultural sector also has excellent job inducement effect. The "employment inducement coefficient," or the number of jobs created when investing KRW1 billion, is 12.0 in the cultural sector, which is very high compared to 4.9 in semiconductors, 6.1 in shipbuilding and 7.7 in automobiles. Within the service industry, the employment inducement effect in the cultural sector is greater than that of 6.9 in finance or 8.1 in telecommunications.

GAME IS THE LEADER IN CONTENT EXPORTS, BUT IT'S STRONGLY REGULATED IN KOREA

When Kim Jung-joo, the founder of Korea's leading game company Nexon, tried to sell his share (47.98%) in early 2019, the news sent shock wave to the Korean online game market. His move grabbed further attention when Tencent, China's largest game company that is also involved in messenger, electronic payment, and broadcasting services, joined the race to buy the share. In 2006, Nexon had filed a lawsuit with a Chinese court, claiming that Nexon suffered "damage by Tencent's online game plagiarism," and now ten years later, people cried out, "a copycat is trying to hunt down a tiger."

He tried to sell Nexon despite concerns that his move will result in fast decline of the Korean game industry that which had posted a trade surplus of KRW6 trillion in 2017, largely because of all kinds of regulations and negative images of the game industry. A few examples of the "Galapagos regulations" that are found only in Korea include the so-called "Cinderella Law" that mandated the shutdown of online games for children at midnight and the restriction on online game payment.

Games account for only 12% of sales in the Korean content industry, but games accounted for 62% of the content industry's exports in the first half of 2018. Games have been exploring overseas markets and contributing to the revival of the Korean content industry more than any other sector, but the game industry has been constantly criticized for promoting addition and violence.

Since the World Health Organization made the announcement about classifying game addiction as a disease starting in 2018, the Ministry of Health and Welfare and the Ministry of Culture, Sports and Tourism are showing two contrasting approach towards the issue. While the Ministry of Health and Welfare is classifying game addiction as a disease and trying to focus on the prevention and treatment, the Ministry of Culture, Sports and Tourism is trying to focus on promoting Korea's game industry that is fourth largest in the world. Rather than jumping to conclusions on either side, the government should scientifically analyze causality and then try to make a social consensus on the issue.

SHRINKING FINANCIAL SYSTEM CANNOT BUILD A STRONG ECONOMY

The Korean government announced an ambitious blueprint in 2003 about becoming a Northeast Asian financial hub on par with Hong Kong and Singapore. Following this "Northeast Financial Hub" vision of the Rho Moo-hyun administration, the Lee Myung-bak administration presented the vision of "Mega Bank" and the Park Geun-hye administration presented the vision of "Creative Economy," but the Korea's financial industry has been only moving backwards. Instead of attracting foreign financial firms to flock to Korea, Korea lost eight foreign financial firms including the UK-based Barclays, which either withdrew from Korea or scaled back their businesses, in the four-year period until 2018. This is due to regulations that allows the government to interfere every business activity including the product development, business patterns, and fund fees.

In the Global Financial Centers Index published by the British consulting group Z/YEN, Seoul ranked sixth in 2015 but plummeted to 33rd in 2018. While New York, London, Hong Kong, Singapore, Shanghai, China, and Tokyo are ranked first to sixth, Seoul ranks only 11th even in Asia alone, and is falling behind Shenzhen and Guangzhou. The advancing IT technology is Global financial markets are changing rapidly while converging with IT industry, but Korea's financial industry is not able to take the lead in such changes

Changing Rankings of Asian Cities in the Global Financial Centers Index

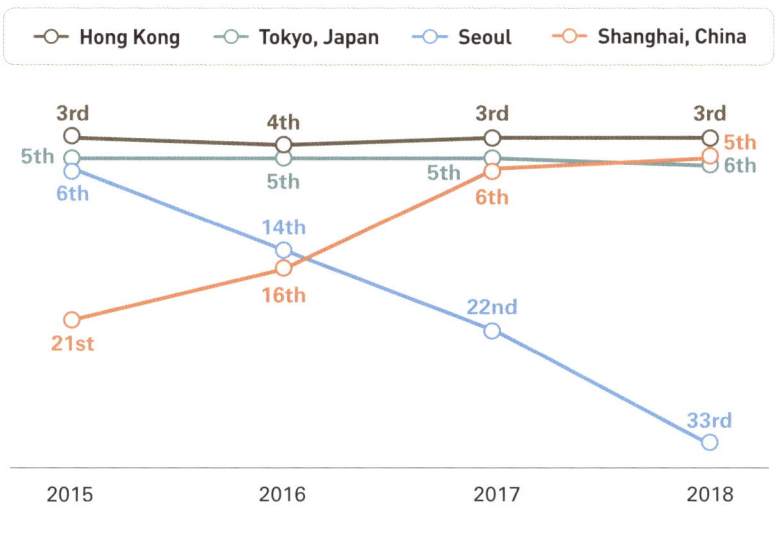

*Based on the September release each year
Source: UK consulting group Z/Yen

as fintech, artificial intelligence and big data due to the high levels of regulation.

The Banker, a UK-based monthly international financial affairs publication, published the "World's 50 biggest banks" in 2018, but none of the Korean financial companies made it to the list. KB Financial Group ranked 471st on the 2018 Fortune Global 500 and became the only Korean financial company to make it to the list. The share of financial sector in GDP also fell to 4.96% in 2017 from 5.50% in 2012, and the number of people employed in the financial sector also declined to 790,000 in 2017 from 870,000 in 2013. That means

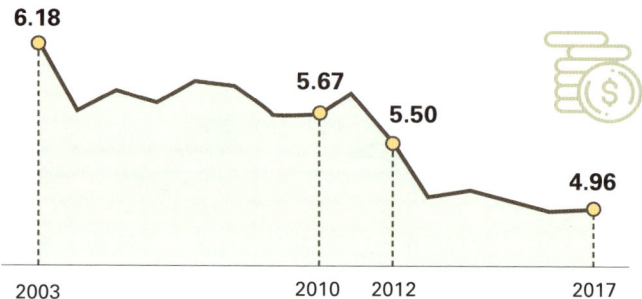

80,000 jobs have disappeared from the financial industry in four years.

Stressing the importance of financial education, the former U.S. Federal Reserve Chairman Alan Greenspan said, "illiteracy makes life uncomfortable, but financial illiteracy makes it impossible to survive." The U.S., Canada and the U.K. require financial education at elementary, middle and high schools, but Korea is unenthusiastic about financial education.

A NEED TO ATTRACT FOREIGN TOURISTS TO VITALIZE DOMESTIC MARKET

Korea and Japan have been making a stark contrast in the field of tourism during the past ten years. Incheon International Airport is booming with travelers leaving for foreign countries every holiday. Korea has been recording a travel account deficit since 2001. The number of outbound Koreans was 28.69 million in 2018, which is nearly double the 15.34 million inbound foreigners. Foreigners spent KRW14 trillion in Korea in 2017, but Koreans spent KRW32 trillion abroad in the same year.

On the contrary, Japan has been in the black since 2014. In 2015, the number of foreign tourists to Japan surpassed the number of outbound Japanese for the first time in 45 years. Japan has been aiming at turning Japan into a "tourism-based country" since 2013, envisioning that Japan could "fill the gap of consumption left by one less permanent resident with the spending of eight tourists." Prime Minister Shinzo Abe supported the promotion of tourism by easing visa requirements and expanding duty-free shops while presiding over frequent meetings for the promotion of tourism strategies. In 2017, Japan recorded KRW38 trillion in travel account surplus, and now, tourism is considered the second-largest export industry after automobiles in Japan.

In Korea, the National Tourism Strategy Conference was originally intended to be under the Presidential office but was downgraded to be a conference under the Prime Minister's office, and the policy of globalization of Korean food seems to have been pushed aside since the administration has changed. There is little sign that the government has been attracting more foreign tourists either. In the Mastercard's 2018 Global Destination Cities Index, Seoul ranked 10th in list of cities frequented by foreigners, but it did not make it to the list of top 10 cities by dollars spent. In the case of Dubai, some

Number of Foreign Tourists Visiting Korea and Japan

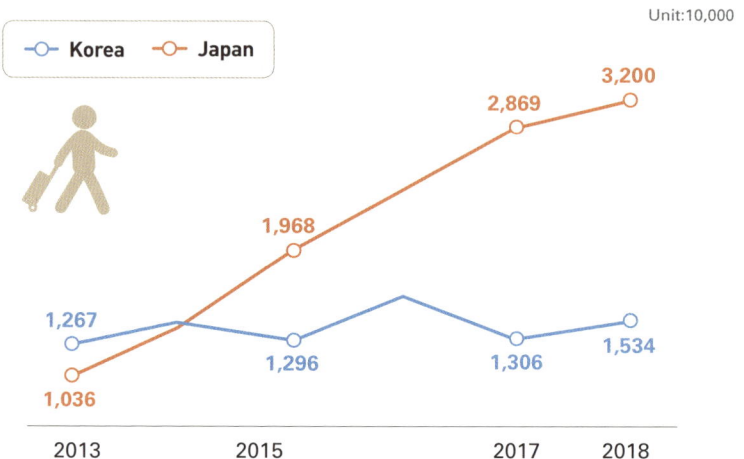

Unit:10,000

- Korea
- Japan

Year	Korea	Japan
2013	1,267	1,036
2015	1,296	1,968
2017	1,306	2,869
2018	1,534	3,200

Source: Tourism Organization, Japan National Tourism Organization

The Global Top 10 Destination Cities

Rank	Cities	No. of international visitors	Average length of stay	Average spend per day
1	Bangkok	25M	4.7 nights	$173
2	London	19.83M	5.8 nights	$153
3	Paris	17.44M	2.5 nights	$301
4	Dubai	15.79M	3.5 nights	$537
5	Singapore	13.91M	4.3 nights	$286
6	New York	13.13M	8.3 nights	$147
7	Kuala Lumpur	12.258M	5.5 nights	$124
8	Tokyo	11.93M	6.5 nights	$154
9	Istanbul	10.7M	5.8 nights	$108
10	Seoul	9.54M	4.2 nights	$181

Source: Mastercard

15.59 million foreigners visited the city in 2017 and spent an average of $537 per day. But in the case of Seoul, 9.54 million tourists visited Seoul and spent only $181 per day on average. The government needs to develop tourism products so that more foreign travelers visit Korea, stay more, and spend more during their visit to Korea.

KOREA'S POTENTIAL FOR MEDICAL TOURISM SHOULD HAVE THE SUPPORT IN THE FORM OF OPEN INVESTMENT HOSPITALS

Being a country with excellent medical technology, Korea has great potential as a "medical tourism destination" by taking advantage of the hallyu fever. The US-based auditor PricewaterhouseCoopers (PwC) forecasts that the global medical tourism market will nearly double in the five-year period from $68.1 billion in 2016 to $124 billion in 2021. While overseas travel has become cheaper due to the widely available low-cost airlines, the increasing income of Chinese people is emerging as a variable. China's population is aging rapidly, and it is difficult to keep up with their consequential increase of medical needs. Therefore, it is natural for Chinese to seek medical services in foreign countries.

Realizing this situation, countries around the world are revamping their medical systems to attract more foreign patients by loosening regulations on visa, improving interpretation services, and improving medical dispute settlement procedures. Korea also allowed medical providers to attract foreign patients in 2009, and it resulted in a sharp

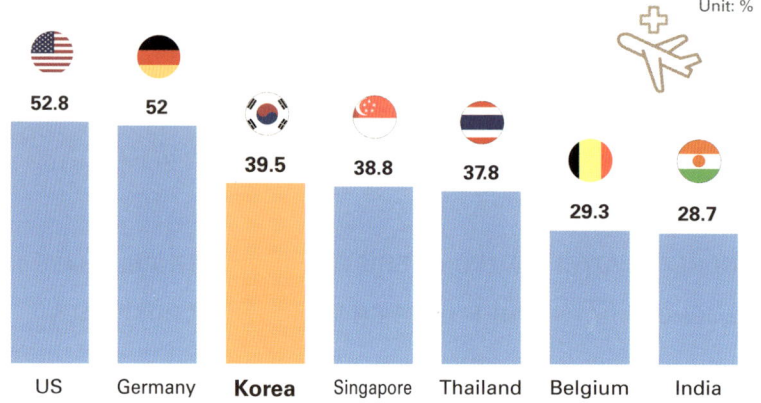

Preference of Korea as the Medical Tourism Destination by Country

Source: 2017 Korea Medical & Wellness Tourism Overseas Awareness Survey by the Korea Tourism Organization

increase of foreign patients visiting Korea from 120,000 in 2011 to 360,000 in 2011. Nevertheless, Korea is not making the most out of its potential because Korea is outnumbered by Thailand that attracted 3.3 million medical tourists in 2017, and even by Turkey (700,000) and India (500,000) in the same year.

According to the 2017 Korea Medical & Wellness Tourism Overseas Awareness Survey released by the Korea Tourism Organization, foreigners picked Korea as the third country they preferred to visit for medical tourism after the U.S. and Germany. Korea's potential as the destination for medical tourism has increased proportionally to excellent medical staff and the state-of-the-art medical equipment in addition to the hallyu fever. Patients who go on medical tours usually visit health check-up centers the most, but in the case of Korea, they are visiting plastic surgery or dermatology specialists more than check-up centers. It is signifying that the medical tourism is also affected by the hallyu. Jeju Island has five cities with a population of more than 10 million that can be reached within two hours by plane. The island has an optimal environment as a medical tourist destination because of its excellent scenery and visa-free entry policy. Although Greenland International Medical Center was approved and constructed in 2017 as the first for-profit hospital to attract Chinese medical tourists, the permission was canceled after the hospital was stuck in the trap of being a "for-profit hospital" for years to everybody's great regret.

DISTRIBUTION IS ANOTHER EXPORT INDUSTRY: CONVENIENCE STORES AND MARTS ARE BEING EXPORTED

Distribution outlets such as department stores, discount stores and convenience stores are also showing their potential as export industries. The move is aimed at bringing successful distribution business models from Korea to foreign countries to receive royalties and serve as bridgeheads for introducing Korean culture and products to foreign markets at the same time.

Lotte Department Store entered Vietnam's economic capital Ho Chi Minh in 2014 and operated two "Diamond Plazas," while building its corporate image as a top-notch department store and maintaining the top selling department store in Vietnam. The plazas are becoming a space where young people enjoy meeting their friends, while being a symbol of the upper class of the country. Lotte Mart entered Vietnamese and Indonesian markets in 2008 and have been selling some 1,300 of its own brand products in Vietnam alone. Lotte is also pushing forward with a large-scale complex development in Ho Chi Minh and Hanoi, respectively, which will house department stores, shopping malls, theaters, hotels and offices all within the complex.

GS Retail is another Korean company that made inroads into Vietnam with its convenience store GS25 in 2018 and since then increased the number of stores to 18, while BGF opened CU convenience store franchise in Mongolia. BGF, a "family mart" that had been paying royalties to Japan for 22 years, exported its know-how in managing convenience stores six years after it changed its name to its indigenous brand CU and is receiving part of the sales as royalties.

Since department stores, discount stores and other retail outlets are sensitive to cultural and political environments and also subject to territorial sentiment, it is not easy for these businesses to make foray into overseas markets. This is the reason Lotte Department Store and E-Mart made inroads into Chinese market in the mid-1990s but struggled due to poor business performance. If Korean companies gradually expand the export of distribution stores using these experiences of failure as good lessons, their activities will be a big boost to Korean manufacturing exports as well.

TARGETING BEYOND THE AMAZON EFFECT TO THE GUANGGUN JIE EFFECT

Online shopping is growing at a fast pace across borders as well as in the domestic market. Korea's online retail sales accounted for 18.2% of its total retail sales at KRW80 trillion in 2017, but it went up to KRW112 trillion in 2018.

"Amazon effect," which refers to the impact of online sales on employment and prices, is a challenge while at the same time an opportunity for Korea. The Bank of Korea said in a report titled "The Effects and Implications of the Growing Online Transactions" released in late 2018 that 16,000 jobs in wholesale and retail sectors have disappeared every year over the past four years. The high-level price transparency of online transactions also resulted in bringing down the inflation rate by an annual average of 0.2%. The analysis of this report did not take into account the increased number of jobs in IT and logistics sectors, but we need to pay attention to the opportunities that are being created as the result of increasing online shopping.

Korea, a country that has a large share of online transactions along with China and Britain, had posted a trade deficit in the online shopping market until 2015, but it started posting a trade surplus since 2016. In 2018, online direct sales to overseas amounted to KRW3.57 trillion, which was about KRW650 billion more than Korean consumers' direct purchases from abroad. Majority of the

Direct Online Purchases and Sales

Source: Statistics Korea

consumers were from China, Japan and Southeast Asia who ordered Korean cosmetic and fashion products directly from Korea, indicating that Korea should make the most out of the hallyu trend in those countries.

The " Guanggun Jie," an online big discount event held by China's Alibaba on Nov. 11 every year since 2009, has also been a big opportunity for Korean companies. The daily sales of the Guanggun Jie event was about KRW35 trillion in 2018, about 10 times larger than that of Black Friday in the U.S. In the online discount event participated by 75 countries with over 19,000 brands, Korea was the third largest selling country after Japan and the United States, excluding China.

KOREA SHOULD LEAD THE EDUTECH EDUCATION REVOLUTION FOR CREATIVE TALENT

Education is facing a revolutionary change with the introduction of such cutting-edge technologies as artificial intelligence (AI), virtual reality (VR) and augmented reality (AR). Around the year of 2005, eLearning that combines education with the internet was the focus of attention, but today, it evolved into the "Edutech" that combines education and technology as the world is welcoming the Fourth Industrial Revolution.

In Korea, all schools were allowed to choose and use digital textbooks in 2018, which was an important step forward for Edutech. Digital textbooks are not just about digitalizing existing textbooks: It is about including videos, 360-degree camera, and augmented reality to allow a new level of education. Software coding has also been added as a required subject in middle schools since 2018, and it will become a required subject in elementary schools beginning from 2019 as well. Although it was planned to expand its wireless internet infrastructure in all elementary, middle and high schools by 2021 to use digital textbooks, Korea is considered to be slower than other advanced countries such as the US and the UK in the introduction of Edutech.

The US-based Global Industry Analysts, Inc. (GIA) predicts that the size of the global Edutech market will grow to KRW481 trillion by 2020. It is expected that soon, students will learn through augmented reality or virtual reality technologies under the instruction of AI teachers. Korea should not lag behind the Edutech educational revolution that fosters creative top talents instead of relying on unilateral cramming method of education. Korea is equipped with the conditions to take the lead in Edutech because Korea has the world's best educational zeal and the world's highest-level IT infrastructure.

The stumbling blocks are the government's regulation, the college admission-oriented education system, and the people's perception of Edutech as being part of a shadow education. Korea should take notice that countries with advanced Edutech environment, such as Australia, the United States, Britain, and other countries are all guaranteeing the maximum autonomy of schools.

SOCIAL INFRASTRUCTURE IS BASED ON COMPETITIVENESS AND MOST BE CONSTANTLY REFORMED

Social infrastructures such as water supply, transportation and health care not only determine the standard of living, but they also determine national competitiveness. The winning or losing in the race among companies on the global stage directly affects the country's employment and tax revenues. It is natural that the government tries to create a more favorable energy, communication and logistics environment for domestic companies to win in the race. The government is called on to build new communication and logistics environment demanded by the Fourth Industrial Revolution, and overhaul dilapidated water supply and sewage facilities, but Korea's social overhead capital budget has been the target of cuts for some time.

SOCIAL OVERHEAD CAPITAL BUDGETS PUSHED OVER BY WELFARE BUDGETS

Korea has been cutting down its social overhead capital (SOC) budgets for several years since 2016 while increasing budget for welfare. The government's fiscal management plan, drawn up in 2018, calls for a 2% cut in the SOC budget every year until 2022. The SOC budget peaked at KRW25 trillion in 2010 when the Lee Myung-bak administration pushed forward with the Four Major Rivers Restoration Project, and it recorded a slight increase in 2015 to KRW25.8 trillion, but since then, it's been on a steady decline. Initially in 2019, the government sought to cut the SOC budget for four years straight, but the National Assembly increased it by KRW1.2 trillion and the final budget became KRW19.8 trillion, a slight increase from 2018.

As seen in the case where the New Deal policy absorbed the unemployed during the Great Depression of the U.S. in 1929, investment in SOC has a direct effect on job creation and narrowing the gap between rich and poor. If SOC investment is increased by KRW1 billion, the employment inducement effect in the construction industry is 13.9, which is higher than the entire industry's average of 12.9. In addition, the labor income share ratio in the construction industry is 0.89, far higher than the 0.54 in the manufacturing sector. That means, if added value is created in the construction industry, 89% of the value will go to the share of

Government's SOC Budgets

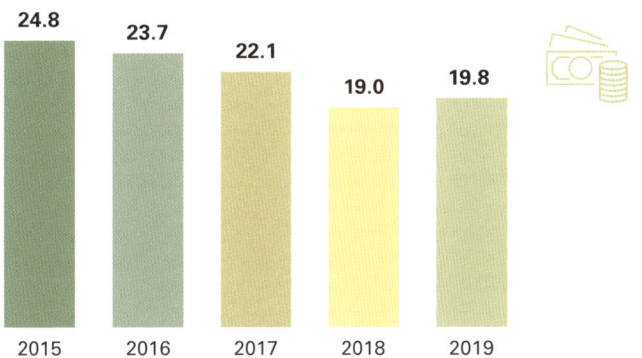

Source: Ministry of Economy and Finance

workers and help improve income distribution.

Reducing the SOC budget will not only have negatively effect on employment and income distribution, but it will also increase inefficiency at construction sites. Most of Korea's civil engineering projects are carried out within the secured budget each year, but if the budget is cut, the construction of roads and railroads that have already been under way will be stopped or the construction period will have to be expanded like a rubber band. The cost of maintaining the site is also likely to increase as a result.

KOREA WILL BE A COUNTRY WITH INSUFFICIENT INFRASTRUCTURE INVESTMENT BY 2040

Responding to the aging population and the dawning of the Fourth Industrial Revolution, advanced countries are also stepping up their efforts to invest in infrastructure. Korea was highly rated as the world's sixth most competitive country in infrastructure in the World Economic Forum's Global Competitiveness Index in 2018 by ranking first in the power supply ratio, third in the maritime transportation connections, fourth in the railway service, and ninth in the air service, but the problem is what the future holds for Korea. Although Singapore was also considered the world's second most competitive country with strong air and port infrastructures, Singapore is planning to increase its infrastructure investment further from 4.4% of GDP in 2017 to 6.0% in 2020. On the contrary, Korea is barely maintaining 2% of GDP in infrastructure investment.

The Global Infrastructure Hub (GI Hub), which was established under the G20 Summit Agreement, released a report in 2017 in which it diagnosed infrastructure demand and investment in 50 countries around the world. In this report, Korea was cited as a country with insufficient infrastructure investment. By 2040, Korea's demand for infrastructure investment is expected to reach $1.49 trillion, but at the current rate, investment will fall short by $41 billion. Germany and Singapore are categorized as countries where infrastructure demand and investment will be balanced by 2040,

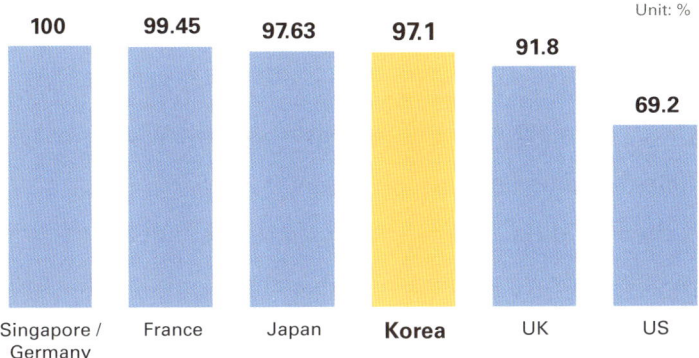

Ratio of Investment to Infrastructure Demand by 2040

Source: Global Infrastructure Hub (GI Hub)

while Japan, Korea, the United Kingdom and the United States are expected to have insufficient investment relative to the infrastructure demand.

In response, the Trump administration announced a plan in 2018 to invest more than $1.5 trillion in infrastructure over the next 10 years. Korean government also announced a plan to select KRW24 trillion scale SOC projects for balanced national development in early 2019, exempt them from preliminary feasibility studies, and allocate budget for these projects beginning from 2020. Though turning the focus to the SOC projects again is welcoming, there is a concern over the fairness, adequacy and reliability of the SOC budget if the preliminary feasibility study is exempt.

JAPAN IS IN THE MIDST OF A LOGISTICS REVOLUTION, BUT KOREA HAS BEEN IN STATUS QUO FOR MORE THAN 10 YEARS

Korea's competitiveness in the logistics industry has been stagnant for more than a decade.

In the World Bank's Logistics Performance Index (LPI), which is a biannual report that scores 167 countries, Korea backtracked from ranking 21st in 2014 to 25th in 2018. Since it ranked 25th in 2007, the company has regressed to its competitive position of 10 years ago.

On the contrary, Japan's logistics competitiveness jumped significantly from ranking10th in 2014 and 12th in 2016 to fifth in 2018. Singapore and Hong Kong turned out to be ahead of Korea in terms of customs clearance, logistics infrastructure and timely transportation by ranking seventh and 12th, respectively.

Recognizing the fact that rapid and accurate transportation increases the efficiency and competitiveness of the national economy, countries around the world are striving to realize "smart logistics" by mobilizing all the Fourth Industrial Revolution-related technologies such as artificial intelligence, big data, blockchain and drones. In 2018, the Japanese government decided to work with Yamato Holdings Co., the largest logistics company, to establish a data platform in which logistics companies, producers and retailers share logistics flows. It is an initiative that allows all companies to utilize big data while jointly managing product delivery data. The plan is

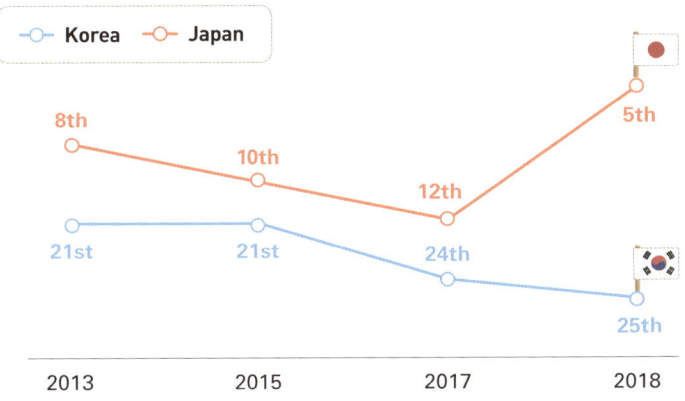

Korea and Japan's Rankings in the Logistics Performance Index

Source: World Bank

aimed at addressing the shortage of manpower in the logistics sector and increasing productivity.

Korea ranks 12th in terms of exports but only 25th in logistics competitiveness in the world, all because of a combination of the small scale of logistics companies, the restructuring of the shipping industry and government regulations. In Korea, the rate of use of third-party logistics (3PL) is about 68%, which is considerably lower than 80 to 90% in advanced countries. With the rapidly expanding online shopping market and logistics technology that is changing day by day, logistics innovation can no longer be delayed

SEJONG AND BUSAN SMART CITIES, THE TEST BEDS FOR WILDEST IMAGINATIONS

A few model smart cities with easy access to artificial intelligence, self-driving cars and big data in everyday activities will welcome residents by the end of 2021. The Presidential Committee on the Fourth Industrial Revolution announced a plan in 2019 to make two regions of "Sejong City 5-1 Living Zone" and "Busan Eco-Delta City" leading smart city models. These two regions were previously selected as test beds for the realization of smart cities in 2018. It can be considered as the realization of "Idea City: Strategy for Future Cities of Korea," which was proposed by Maeil Business Newspaper at the 2018 National Reporting Conference.

Countries around the world are already in an endless race to transform existing cities into smart cities. China and India have already started to build smart cities in a national level, while Google is currently carrying out its own Smart City project in Toronto, Canada, and Panasonic in Denver, the U.S. There are 152 regions around the world where some kind of smart city projects are underway.

In smart cities, imaginations turn to reality one by one. At the Amazon Go store on the first floor of the Amazon headquarters in Seattle, USA, customers can pick what they want and walk out the store without having to go through the payment process, because the sensors installed throughout the store can perfectly identify the customers' purchase items and submit the bills. Office workers in Seoul spend an average of 135 minutes a day to commute, which is the longest commuting time among OECD members. By comparison, 96% of the cars in the city are parked in parking lot almost the entire day. The idea of reducing traffic and smoke in the city by using car-sharing services is blocked by resistance from the taxi industry. In order to stay ahead of the competition in smart cities, the government needs to demonstrate leadership in adjusting conflicts of interest among the groups with vested interests and eliminate regulations.

A NEED TO BUILD SMART PORTS WHERE THE ENTIRE PROCESS FROM ENTRY TO CUSTOMS CLEARANCE IS AS EASY AS A SNAP

Maritime logistics account for 99.7% of Korea's trade volume. The cargo volume of Busan remained the fifth-largest among the ports of the world until 2013, but it is now ranked sixth due to an increase in the cargo volumes in ports in China. The Busan port recorded the highest cargo volume in history in 2018, but 53% of the shipments in Busan was transshipment cargo that changed ships in the port en route to third countries.

Global hub ports are also competing in a race to automate by using the latest technologies such as artificial intelligence and Internet of Things (IoT) in response to the advent of the Fourth Industrial Revolution. Long Beach port in the U.S. opened its first

Cargo Volumes in the World's Top 15 Container Ports, 2018

Unit: 10,000 TEU, %

Rank	Ports	Cargo Volume	Rate of Change
1	Shanghai	4,201	4.4
2	Singapore	3,660	8.7
3	Ningbo / Zhoushan	2,652	7.8
4	Shenzhen	2,574	2.1
5	Guangzhou	2,189	7.5
6	**Busan**	2,159	5.4
7	Hong Kong	1,964	-5.4
8	Qingdao	1,930	5.5
9	LA / Long Beach	1,740	3.1
10	Tianjin	1,602	6.3
11	Dubai	1,494	-2.8
12	Rotterdam	1,448	5.4
13	Port Klang	1,203	0.4
14	Antwerp	1,102	5.5
15	Xiamen	1,060	2.1

*The increase or decrease from 2017   Source: Alphaliner

fully automated container terminal in 2016, and in Asia, Qingdao Port of China became the first to open a fully automated container terminal in May 2017. The fully automated container terminal is where robots handle unloading and transporting containers, and it is in operation at the ports of Rotterdam in the Netherlands and Xiamen in China as well. In comparison, Busan New Port and Incheon New Port are still stuck at a semi-automated level.

Just as competition to develop self-driving cars on land is growing fiercer, there is a fierce race for the development of self-driving ships at sea as well. In the "2018 World Knowledge Forum Busan," some suggested that the city of Busan should focus its efforts on creating smart ports as well as smart cities by taking advantage of its geographical features such as its close vicinity to the ocean. Smart ports refer to ports built with optimized environments, where all facilities are built on automation and intelligence and information is exchanged between ships and ports in real time so that the entire process from entry to customs clearance is as easy as a snap. To help Busan catch up with the global trend of building smart ports, the government needs to loosen its regulations on the hinterland ports and revamp the law on the entry and exit of self-driving ships

THE BEST HYDROGEN CAR TECHNOLOGY SHOULDN'T BE HELD BACK BY FUELING STATION

During a state visit to France in 2018, President Moon Jae-in took a test drive in a hydrogen-powered car Nexo and watched a taxi driver fueling hydrogen by himself at a hydrogen fueling station with a view of the Eiffel Tower in the background. It was a scene he could not see in Korea, because in Korea, a hydrogen fueling station cannot be installed in residential and commercial areas, and it is illegal for drivers to fuel hydrogen on their own.

Hyundai Motor introduced the world's first dedicated hydrogen-powered car Tucson ix in 2013 and was going to export 5,000 units of hydrogen-powered vehicles to France in 2018, but in Korea,

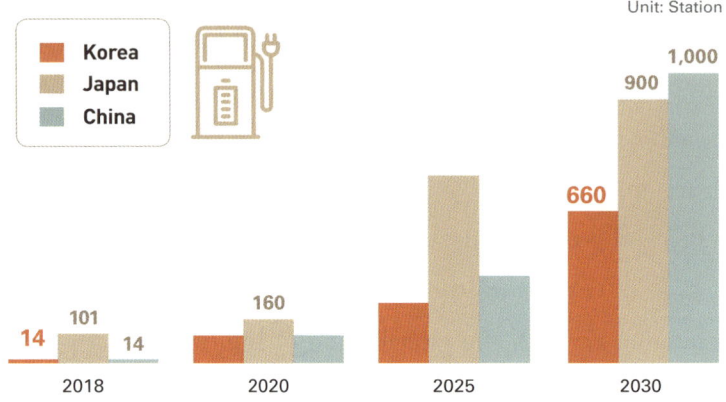

Plans to Build Hydrogen Fueling Stations in Korea, China, and Japan

Unit: Station

Source: H2stations.org, data collected from each country

numerous regulations allowed only 14 hydrogen charging stations to be built by the end of 2018. That is the background of the Korean government's special permission to build three small charging stations in the center of Seoul including the area near the National Assembly as exceptions as "the first project under regulatory sandbox" in 2019. If Korea is to lead the global hydrogen-fueled vehicle market, the government should continue its efforts to deregulate even after the two years of special permission period under regulatory sandbox expires.

At a time when companies are competing in the race of developing hydrogen-fueled cars and electric cars, national-level large scale investment in hydrogen-fueled cars is an important decision where the future food and employment are at stake. That is the reason the government has unveiled a "hydrogen economic road map" to distribute 65,000 hydrogen-fueled passenger cars by 2022.

Rival countries such as Japan, Germany and China are making moves that shouldn't be overlooked. Japan plans to supply 40,000 hydrogen cars and increase the number of charging stations to 160 by the opening of the 2020 Tokyo Olympics. China is pushing forward with a plan to supply one million hydrogen cars and increase the number of charging stations to 1,000 by 2030. Countries around the world are stepping up their efforts including funding to promote their hydrogen car industry because it is highly effective not only in creating jobs but also in improving the environment. The Korean government should also put its efforts in building infrastructure so that Hyundai's hydrogen cars can take the lead in the global market.

FIND KILLER AR AND VR CONTENT THAT WILL LEAD THE 5G MARKET

Three Korean mobile carriers began to offer live commercial 5G services in December 2018. The three mobile carriers made 5G available for purchase in Korea starting April 2019. The response time of 5G is less than 0.0001 second, which is faster than 0.01 seconds that humans respond to visual information. In other words, a self-driving car can recognize danger faster than humans and stop. Countries around the world are scrambling to take the lead in the 5G era because 5G is the foundation of all changes that will happen in

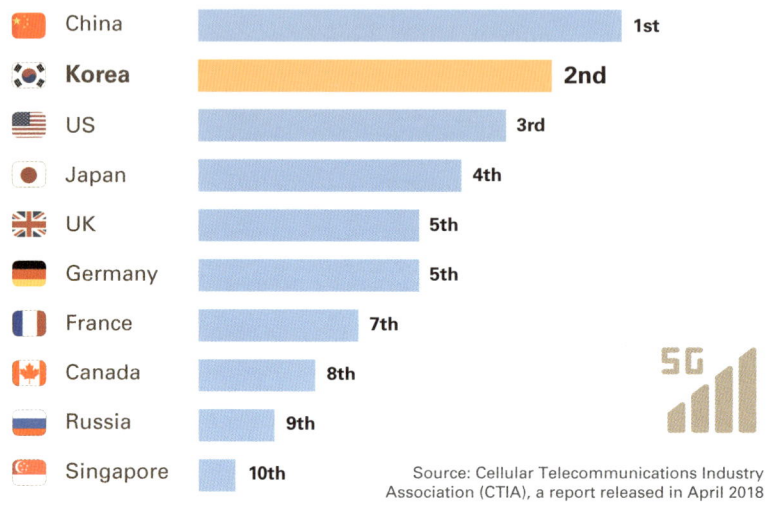

modern life, such as self-driving cars, the Internet of Things, virtual reality (VR) and smart cities.

In a report released in April 2018, the US-based Cellular Telecommunications Industry Association (CTIA) cited China as the country that is best prepared to commercialize 5G technology. China was followed by Korea, the United States, Japan, Britain, and Germany. However, there is only a slight difference between countries in the race of 5G that started in 2019. In the case of China, it is highly likely that commercialization of 5G will happen earlier than 2020 as was planned, considering how the Chinese government allowed Chinese carriers to use 5G frequencies in December 2018.

Some predict that China will unveil its 5G-Advanced technology via the 2022 Beijing Winter Olympics. Japanese telecommunication industry is also planning to move up the commercialization of 5G to September 2019, and AT&T, the second-largest U.S. telecommunication company, is also making moves to offer 5G services in 19 cities, including Dallas and Atlanta, in 2019.

Smartphone manufacturers such as Samsung Electronics, Japan's Sony, China's Huawei, Xiaomi, and Oppo are also releasing Smartphones for 5G beginning from the first half of 2019. It is predicted that virtual reality (VR) and augmented reality (AR) services will be the main stage of competition in the commercialization of 5G, and Korea is called on to make aggressive investment to explore killer 5G content products.

NUCLEAR PHASE-OUT? THE COST OF ENERGY IS THE BASIS OF NATIONAL COMPETITIVENESS

Korea officially announced its so-called "nuclear phase-out policy" in 2017 when it began to halt construction of nuclear power plants Shin-Kori Units 5 and 6. The Korean government dropped a series of plans to construct nuclear reactors under the plan to lower the share of nuclear power from 30% of the total electricity to 18% by 2030. Instead, the government would increase the share of renewable energy such as solar and wind power, which cost more to generate power. Considering the examples of other countries, the

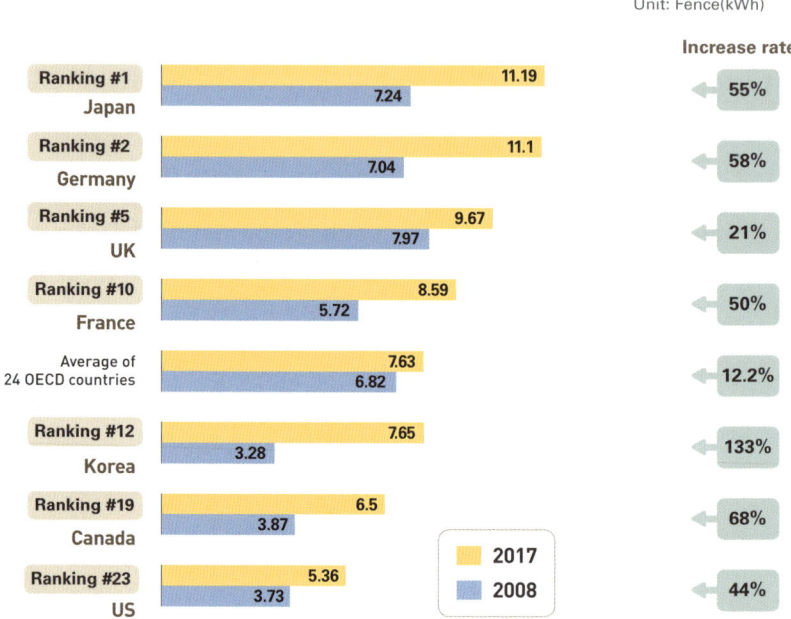

government's move is likely to result in the increase of electricity cost.

After suffering from the Fukushima nuclear crisis in 2011, Japan had declared "zero nuclear power plant," but it resulted in rising electricity cost for household that went up by 25% by 2014. The Japanese government started running nuclear reactors again in 2015 to reduce the burden of the electricity cost, and it plans to restore the share of nuclear power to the pre-Fukushima level of 22% by 2030. Taiwan also pushed forward with "no nuclear power policy" when

Tsai Ing-wen was elected President of Taiwan with the campaign promise of "no nuclear power policy" in 2016 but ended up scrapping it after a national referendum in 2018 due to rising electricity cost and unstable power supply.

Korea's electricity cost for industry is the 12th-highest level among 24 major OECD countries, according to a report published by the Department for Business, Energy and Industrial Strategy of the United Kingdom (BEIS) in 2018. Korea's electricity cost for industry was only 3.28 pence per kWh, just half of the OECD average of 6.82 pence, 10 years ago, but it rose to almost the same as the OECD average level after recording the highest increase rate within the last ten years. In a comparison of OECD and IEA data by the National Assembly's Budget Office in 2019, Korea's electricity cost for industry as of 2017 ranked 16th among 32 OECD countries, which placed Korea the middle-tier as well.

Korea is a globally recognized nuclear powerhouse because Korea is the sixth country in the world ever to export nuclear power plant. Given that, it is a pity that Korea is breaking down the eco-system of the nuclear power industry, causing a surge in the electricity cost and even pushing back its industrial competitiveness.

MID-TO-LONG-TERM BUDGET PLAN IS NECESSARY FOR AGING INFRASTRUCTURE

There are frequent accidents caused by old infrastructure. In

Seoul alone, there are an annual average of 800 road depreciation accidents. Water supply would get cut off due to the rupture of water supply pipes, and reservoir embankments would collapse during the rainy season. The number of government-managed facilities such as dams, bridges, tunnels, ports and water supply and sewage is pushing 90,000. Of these facilities, those that are older than 30 years were around 5% in 2018, but the number is about to surge to 36.9% by 2030.

By region, the old infrastructure problem is most serious in Seoul, and by type of facilities, it is most series with reservoir embankments and underground facilities. The percentage of water supply and sewage facilities that are older than 30 years has already reached 17% in 2018. As for the Seoul Metropolitan area alone, 48.4% of sewage pipes are over 30 years old, and 30.5% of them were installed over 50 years ago.

When old facilities became the cause of frequent safety problems, the U.S. and Japan have been preemptively increasing their budget for SOCs to maintain and repair the government-managed facilities, but Korea is still in a helpless state. Korea does not even have an integrated map of underground facilities because the government has been digging up the ground and laying pipes underground each time it becomes necessary. In Korea, all the utilities are maintained by different entities: the electric power lines by KEPCO; communication cables by telecommunication companies; gas pipes by utility companies; water supply and sewage by municipalities; and

Infrastructures Whose 30-Year Service Life will Expire

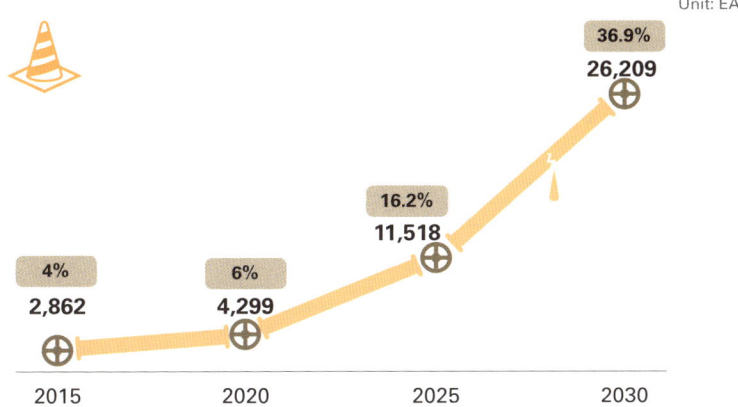

Based on Class 1 and 2 facilities such as bridge and tunnel
Source: Korea Infrastructure Safety Corporation

hot water pipes by regional heating corporations.

Fortunately, the "basic law on sustainable infrastructure management" took effect as of 2019, marking the beginning of the aging infrastructure management. The government is planning to put together standards for improvement in performance and maintenance of old facilities, but the problem is money. The Construction & Economy Research Institute of Korea examined to estimate how much it would cost to maintain and repair transportation infrastructure. According to the results, the budget shortage was nearly KRW500 billion a year until 2019, but it is expected to surge to KRW1 trillion in 2020 and KRW4 trillion in 2030. A systematic mid-to-long-term budget plan should be established to keep pace with the increasing number of aging infrastructure facilities.

NO MORE POLICIES THAT OVERTURN WHENEVER A NEW PRESIDENT TAKES OFFICE

SOC investment is something that needs to be pursued consistently while thinking about decades or hundreds of years ahead. In reality, however, policies over individual facilities such as airports and ports, as well as policies over national development plans and energy, change and overturn each time a new president takes office.

The Saemangeum project is a good example. The project kicked off in 1991 by President Roh Tae-woo, who was elected after making campaign promise that he would "build a massive reclaimed land on the west coast to ensure food sovereignty." But this project had been subject to a lawsuit over the environmental concern, and it was only 20 years later during the Roh Moo-hyun administration that the seawall to block the ocean water was constructed. Original plan was to use the entire reclaimed land for farming, but during the Roh Moo-hyun administration, the plan changed to use 70% of the land for farming, and the rest 30% for industry and tourism, but this plan changed again during the Lee Myung-bak administration to use only 30% of it for farming, and the rest 70% for industry. It reflected the situation in which the production of rice became less important following the opening of the rice market. The Park Geun-hye administration announced a plan to develop the land into a Korea-

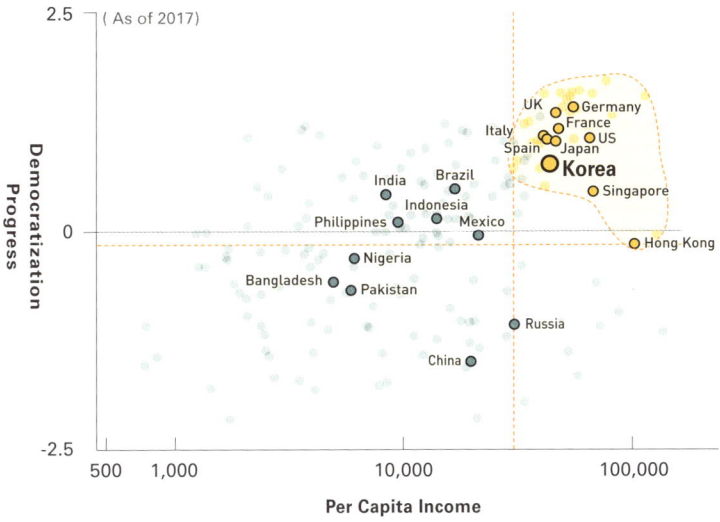

Per Capita GNI and the Level of Democratization of Countries Around the World

(Based on 2019 purchasing power indexa)   Source: Financial Times, World Bank, IMF

China free trade industrial complex, and the following Moon Jae-in administration announced that solar power generation facilities worth two nuclear reactors would be built on the land to turn it into the hub of solar power generation. While each president presented a new blueprint for the region for the last 30 years, the original objective of the project is completely gone.

Saemangeum is not the only case. The Wolseong No.1 nuclear power plant that cost a whopping KRW700 billion and whose service life was extended to 2022 was suddenly shut down in 2018. The Four Major Rivers Project that was carried out during the Lee

Myung-bak administration became subject to audit and investigation each time a new administration took office until it was decided in 2019 to dismantle some of the weirs on the Geum River and the Yeongsan River. In the international community, Korea is perceived as a country with a high level of national income and advanced democracy. Korea needs a system that ensure consistency in policy that is in line with such reputation. A system that prevents confusion caused by policies that overturn constantly is also part of the essential national infrastructures.

PURSUING A VISION OF UNIFIED KOREA DESPITE THE G2 COMPETITION

The situation on the Korean Peninsula is changing so fast that it is surprising the international community. The North Korean nuclear and missile crises had seemed heading toward the worst case scenarios, but the tension over the Korean Peninsula started to disappear since 2018 after the South and the North started to have dialogue instead confrontation. Then the first inter-Korean summit in 11 years took place, and in 2018 alone, there were as many as three inter-Korean summit meetings, not to mention the first-ever summit between the U.S. and North Korea in the same year. Meanwhile, the U.S. and China are openly waging a trade war, creating a fear over the possible economic crisis. A number of challenges lie ahead Korea amid such diplomatic, military and economic changes, but there can be no change in the fact that Korea should find a way out as a "middle power" and that the South and the North should pursue peaceful reunification.

AN ASIA-PACIFIC ECONOMIC COOPERATION ALLIES BORN AMID THE TRADE WAR BETWEEN THE US AND CHINA

The "Comprehensive and Progressive Agreement for Trans-Pacific Partnership (CPTPP)" went into effect in late 2018 when the U.S. and China engaged in a fierce trade war with each other using tariffs as the weapons. The CPTPP is spearheaded by Japan and joined by 11 countries in the Asia and the Pacific region, under the banner of "complete elimination of tariffs from automobiles to rice." CPTPP, which accounts for 14.9% of the world's trade volume, is also a variable in the U.S.-China trade war as it is a new free trade coalition against protectionism. Japan plans to use CPTPP as a shield against trade pressure from the U.S. over agricultural products

CPTPP Spearheaded by Japan in 2018

Title	Comprehensive and Progressive Agreement for Trans-Pacific Partnership
Participants	11 countries, including Japan, Canada, Australia, Brunei, Singapore, Mexico and Vietnam.
Enactment date	December 30, 2018
Population	690 million
GDP	12.9% worldwide
Trade	14.9% worldwide
Key contents	Elimination of tariffs on agricultural and fisheries products/ Promotion of data sharing such as e-commerce, and loosening regulations on finance/foreign investment

and services.

The CPTPP originated from TPP, which was initially promoted jointly by 12 countries including the U.S. Its influence has weakened since the withdrawal of the U.S. in 2017, but it is unleashing a formidable influence. It is spearheaded by Japan, the world's third-largest economy, and Britain, Indonesia and Thailand are hoping to join as new members. Colombia and Taiwan are also expected to join. If these countries join the coalition, CPTPP will be large enough to account for 20% of the world's GDP.

Korea's exports and imports to CPTPP members account for 23.3% and 26.2% of the total exports and imports, but Korea has been less than enthusiastic about joining CPTPP. It is because the Korean government believed there was little to gain for Korea to join CPTPP because Korea has signed free trade agreement with nine participating countries except for Japan and Mexico, and that joining it would only result in growing chronic trade deficits against Japan. Korea, however, is cited as the country that will suffer the most if the U.S.-China trade war spreads due to the high 46% export dependence on China and the U.S. Given the fact that the global trade trend is shifting toward economic blocs, the government should take a more proactive approach to CPTPP.

WTO SYSTEM IN CRISIS: KOREA SHOULD TAKE THE LEAD IN FINDING A BREAKTHROUGH

The G20 adopted a joint statement in support of World Trade Organization (WTO) reform at the Argentine Summit in late 2018. The WTO system is so broken that G20 countries, which account for 75%the world's trade, are calling for a reform.

Launched in 1995, the WTO has been playing a role in monitoring the promotion of free trade while coordinating trade disputes among 164 member states under the Uruguay Round (UR) agreement. The problem arose after China joined the WTO in 2001 but the organization failed to put strong sanctions against China even though China kept fostering its companies with government subsidies, curbing imports with all kinds of non-tariff barriers and infringing on intellectual property rights. The WTO was pushed to crisis when the U.S. started bilateral trade talks with China, expressing distrust in the roles the WTO was playing. Four of the seven seats for justices at the dispute-resolving Appellate Body of the World Trade Organization became vacant because the U.S. refused to appoint them. The Appellate Body needs at least three justices settle trade disputes, but when two more justices retire in 2019, the WTO will no longer be able to function.

To revive the WTO system, 13 countries including Korea held a separate trade ministers' meeting in October 2018, excluding the U.S. and China, which resulted in a joint G20 statement supporting

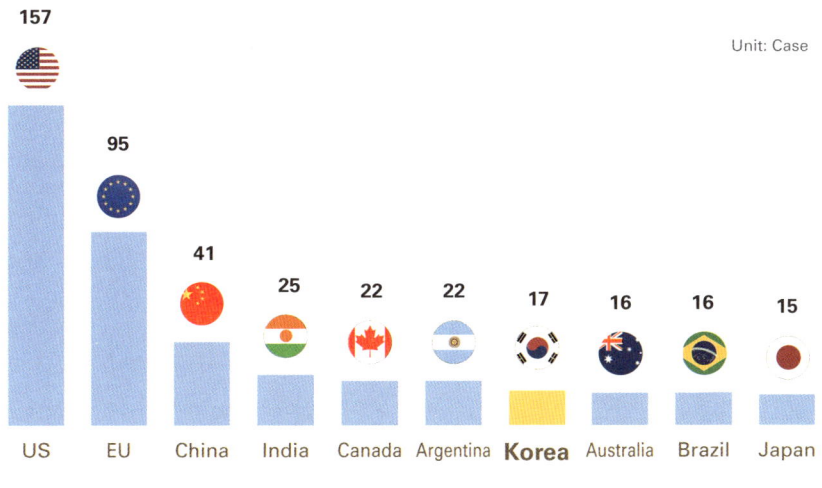

the reforms of WTO. Korea has the capacity to lead WTO reforms more than any other country, because Korea has extensive experience in international trade negotiations and accumulated expertise while signing FTAs with the United States, the EU and China. Korea is also the biggest beneficiary of the multilateral free trade order due to its heavy reliance on trade. In addition to existing tasks such as protecting intellectual property rights and removing non-tariff barriers, the WTO also has new tasks such as overcoming "digital protectionism" through promoting data use. Korea should take the initiative to find a breakthrough for the broken WTO system.

CENTERING ON THE MIDDLE POWERS OF 13 COUNTRIES THAT SUPPORT TO KEEP WTO

As the two superpowers of the U.S. and China are openly competing for for trade hegemony, the middle power countries are inevitably forced to scramble to find ways to protect their economies. Countries like Korea, Japan and Australia that have significant presence in the international stage but not powerful enough to change the world order by themselves must join forces to play a balancing role amidst the war of the G2. It was within this context that Australia named four countries -- Korea, Japan, Indonesia and India -- as targets for cooperation among middle powers.

Additionally, Korea and Australia have been operating a middle powers' consultative body called MIKTA along with Mexico, Indonesia and Turkey since 2013. Although the G20 has emerged as a new international cooperative body in the wake of the 2008 financial crisis, there are clear differences in interests among the G20 countries. It is like the G7, the old economic powerhouses including the US are confronting with BRICS, the emerging economic powerhouses including China. MIKTA is an organization of countries that are not included in either the G7 or the BRICS, but among the G20 countries, Saudi Arabia and Argentina are excluded even in MIKTA. The five MIKTA countries cited energy, terrorism and economic and trade as the main agendas for cooperation, but their actual diplomatic priorities vary. Since the economic, environmental and energy realities of each country are very different, their joint activities have been restricted on issuing declarative statements and exchanging scholars and officials.

For the middle powers union to function properly, the member countries must share common values and objectives. In this sense, it is a significant development that 13 countries, including Korea, Australia, Brazil, Canada, Chile, EU, Japan, Kenya, Mexico, New Zealand, Norway, Switzerland and Singapore, gathered in Ottawa, Canada in October 2018 with goal of finding ways to maintain the WTO system as a countermeasure against the U.S.-China trade war. It is indeed an alliance of middle powers that came together apart from either G7 or BRICS. Since the war of hegemony between the G2 will continue even after the U.S.-China trade war comes to an end, these middle powers allies must continue to strengthen their role.

UNIFICATION IS EXPECTED TO BRING AN OVER KRW3000 TRILLION WINDFALL TO THE ECONOMY

Unification of the Korean Peninsula is the dream come true for Koreans, but it is also expected to be a "big break" for the Korean economy. The globally-renowned investor Jim Rogers said, "Unified Germany could not afford to invest in its neighbors such as Hungary and Russia, but in the case of Korea, its neighbors such as China, Japan and the United States are waiting for an opportunity to make

Economic Benefits of Korean Unification

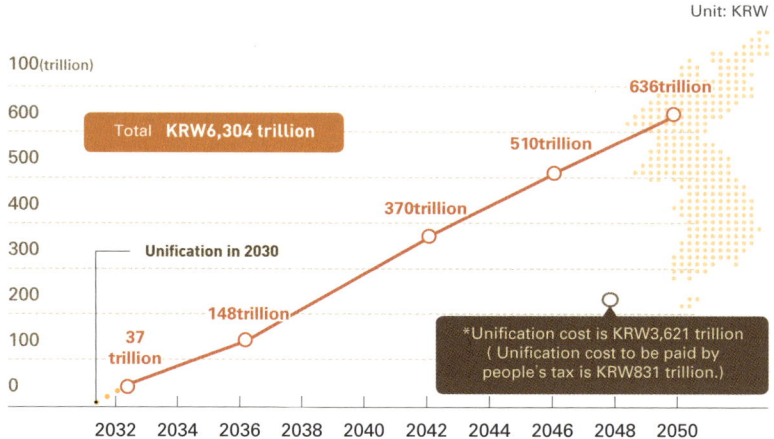

big investment in the unified Korean Peninsula. There is no need to worry about the cost of unification."

In its 2014 analysis, the Korea Institute for National Unification estimated that if unification takes place in 2030, the total political, social, and economical cost of unification will amount to KRW3,600 trillion by 2050. Of the total, the cost of unification in public sector that should be paid with tax revenues --- other than the amount invested by private sector for production activities --- is estimated at KRW831 trillion according to the same analysis. On the other hand, it estimated that the benefits generated by unification would total KRW6,800 trillion including KRW6,300 trillion in the economic sector and KRW300 trillion in political, diplomatic and security sectors. That means the net benefit generated by the unification is estimated to reach KRW3,200 trillion. Korea University's Asia-Pacific Research Institute also estimated that unification will cost between KRW3,100 - 4,700 trillion by 2050, but the benefits of unification will be around KRW4,900 trillion.

It is estimated that Germany had to spend about KRW1,800 - 2,800 trillion in the process of achieving unification. The unification of the Korean Peninsula is expected to cost more because the economic gap between the South and the North is larger than that of East and West Germany, but that depends on how and how fast Korea achieves unification. It means the actual costs and benefits of unification are hard to predict. Still, it is clear that if money saved from national defense is used for the increased SOC investment, and if the hundreds of thousands of South and North Korean soldiers enter the labor market, it will be a strong impetus for the Korean economy, which is losing its vitality due to low birth rates and aging population.

SOUTH-NORTH SPECIALIZATION STRUCTURE IS MORE ADVANTAGEOUS THAN THE KOREA-CHINA OR KOREA-VIETNAM STRUCTURE

During the 2018 inter-Korean summit at the truce village of Panmunjom, the North Korean leader Kim Jong-un was quoted as saying that he wanted to go with a "Vietnamese-style model" with regards to the desired future economic development model. There are about 100,000 Vietnamese employees working at Samsung Electronics' mobile phone plant, which is currently operating in Hanoi. Samsung Electronics is responsible for 20% of Vietnam's GDP and 25% of its total exports. "If the Samsung Electronics' mobile phone plant in Hanoi were in North Korea, North Korea's per capita GDP will jump directly to $3,120 from $1,215 in 2018," said Min Kyung-tae, the leader of the Future of Korean Peninsula Team at the Yeosijae Foundation, at the North Korea Policy Forum in 2018 which was hosted by the Maeil Business Newspaper and the Korea Development Bank (KDB).

There is little difference between China and Vietnam in that two countries achieved gradual reform and opening under the leadership of the Communist Party. While China, as a superpower, mostly used capital from Chinese expats and direct foreign investment, Vietnam, as a small power, mostly relied on foreign loans. Like China and Vietnam, North Korea would quickly and extensively build economically cooperating relationship with South Korea if it went for reform and openness policies.

Moreover, South Korea and North Korea speak the same language and are geographically close to each other, all of which conditions can offer more favorable business environment that cooperating relationships with China and Vietnam. It is attested by the fact that even though the Kaeseong Complex in North Korea was completely shut down in 2016, 97% of South Korean firms that had factories in

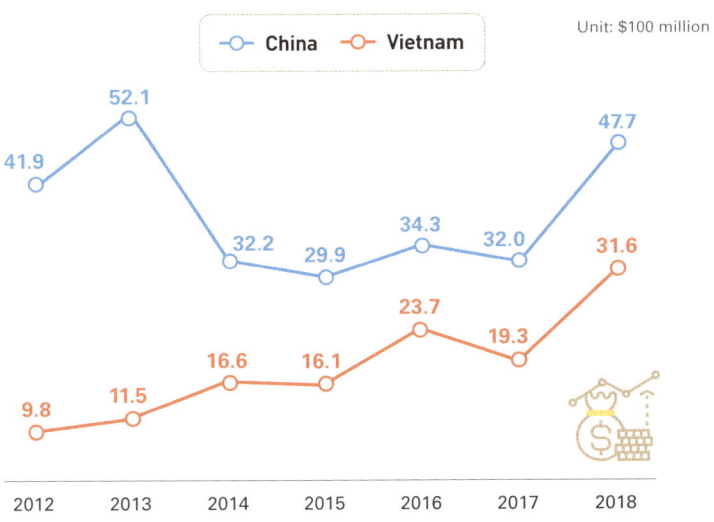

Korean Investments in Vietnam and China

Source: The Export-Import Bank of Korea

the complex expressed their willingness to move their factories back to the complex again. Korea is a peninsula that is connected to the Chinese continent, but it's been like an island that was isolated from the continent. If South Korea can build an economically cooperating system with North Korea, Korea is in an advantageous position to make inroads into China's three northeastern provinces and Russia in the Far East. However, the pace of inter-Korean economic cooperation will be adjusted depending on the wage level of North Korean workers, as we can see from the rapid movement of South Korean investment from China to Vietnam in response to the rapidly rising labor costs in China.

THE SPECIAL ECONOMIC ZONE IN NORTH KOREA COULD BECOME A SUCCESS MODEL OF A SMART CITY

Regarding inter-Korean economic cooperation, people often think about taking advantage of the low wage level of North Korea, but in fact, the inter-Korean economic cooperation can help Korea become the leader in the Fourth Industrial Revolution through a cooperation in the latest technology fields. Min Kyung-tae, the leader of the Future of Korean Peninsula Team at the Yeosijae Foundation who delivered a keynote speech on the subject of "a leap forward to co-prosperity on the Korean Peninsula through the smart revolution" at the 2018 North Korean policy forum, explained in detail the reason North Korea has ideal conditions to build a smart city, and suggested, "Let's find a model that is different from the Kaeseong Complex-type cooperation model."

Since North Koreas don't have the right to own private property, there is no burden on land expropriation and compensation, and there is no resistance from those with vested interests because there is nobody who had invested on anything. The fact that North Korea is a barren land when it comes to technology might also work for the better to spread new technologies faster. It has indeed a unique investment environment where the infrastructure construction costs are only one-third of those of South Korea. Analysts say that just as North Korea moved directly to wireless phone without going through a wired communication system, it is possible to introduce

Smart City, why North Korea has a better place

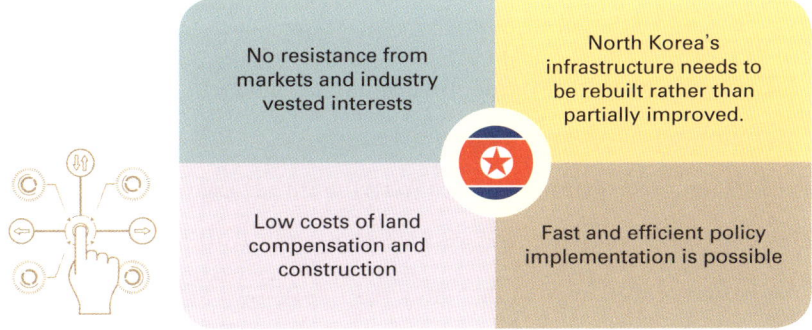

Source: Summary of the 2018 North Korean Policy Forum's keynote speech by Min Kyung-tae, the head of the Yeosijae Foundation, the Future of the Korean Peninsula Team.

mobile pay system without going through the credit card system in the finance and payment field, and even in the communication system, it is possible to introduce 5G directly without going through the 4G system. Of course, there are limits. Due to the very limited access to internet, it is difficult to build big data and distribute, and energy is another problem that needs to be resolved.

Nevertheless, if South Korea's leading IT technology is combined with the unique investment environment of North Korea's special economic zone, it could create a successful model for a smart city that will surprise the world. Advanced technologies and services such as the Internet of Things and self-driving cars that are made available through the Fourth Industrial Revolution could become a reality earlier in North Korea than in South Korea.

REDUCTION OF UNIFICATION COSTS BY USING IMF AND THE WORLD BANK

Cooperation with international financial institutions such as the International Monetary Fund (IMF), the World Bank, the Asian Infrastructure Investment Bank (AIIB) and the Asian Development Bank (ADB) could further reduce the cost of unification of the two Koreas. North Korea had sought to join the IMF and ADB in 1997, but it did not happen because the US objected it. Therefore, it is safe to say that its membership depends on the outcome of the denuclearization negotiations and the North's attitude toward terrorism.

If North Korea joins the IMF, it should first establish a statistical system and train its personnel to draw up economic and social statistics to be submitted to the international community. Usually, it takes about three years to apply for membership and join the organizations, but only after the establishment of a statistical system can an objective assessment of the North Korean society be possible.

At the 2018 North Korean Policy Forum, Yang Moon-soo, vice president of the University of North Korean Studies, said that if North Korea joins international financial organizations, it will be able to enjoy various membership benefits along with the possibility of reducing its foreign debt. First of all, it is likely that North Korea can receive a significant reduction in foreign debt within the range of $10-15 billion by becoming eligible to apply for the national debt

Effects of North Korea's membership to the International Financial Institutions

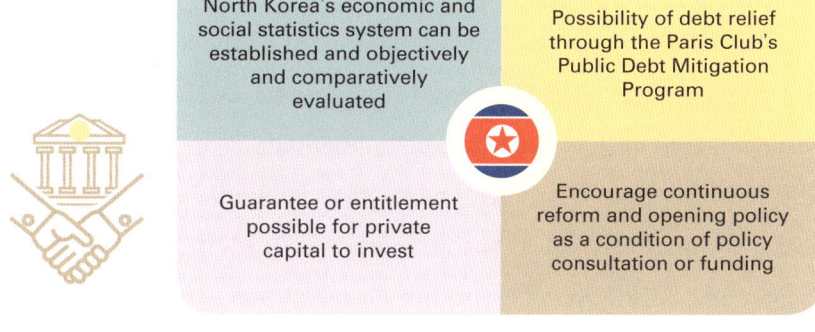

Source: Summary of the presentation made by Yang Moon-soo, Vice President of the University of North Korean Studies Graduate School, at the 2018 North Korean Policy Forum

relief program at the Paris Club which is a club of advanced creditor countries. While the amount of direct aid from international financial institutions is important, it also has a significant effect of becoming qualified for private funds from the international community to invest in North Korea with confidence.

International financial organizations will steadily demand reform and openness policies from the North as well as the condition Whenever they provide funds to the North. Just as South Korea stepped up restructuring at the demands from the IMF during the Asian financial crisis, the international financial organizations could play a role in pushing North Korea to reform and open its doors to a certain degree.

EXPECTATIONS ON THE JOINT HOSTING OF 2032 SOUTH-NORTH SUMMER OLYMPICS

The leaders of the two Koreas announced in the joint statement after the summit in Pyongyang in September 2018 that the two leaders agreed to "jointly participate in international events, including the 2020 Summer Olympics, and work together to jointly host the 2032 Summer Olympics" to the South-North Joint Declaration in September 2018." Sports events are a stage of non-scripted touching drama that helps people to understand each other better beyond politics and ideology.

Korea also began to communicate with the world in earnest only after hosting the 1988 Seoul Olympics and the 86 Seoul Asian Games. Until then, South Korea had not issued any tourist passports at all, but it began issuing them gradually in 1983, before completely liberalizing overseas travel in 1989 after gaining confidence with the successful hosting of the Seoul Olympics. If the two Koreas jointly host the Olympics, North Korea will have no choice but to open its doors to the world. Transportation, communication and tourism infrastructure will develop rapidly, and the North Koreans will develop the spirit of citizenship while kindly welcoming visitors and keeping order.

So far, Brisbane in Australia, Mumbai in India, Shanghai in China, and Jakarta in Indonesia are some of the cities that are hoping to host the 2032 Summer Olympics, and the final decision will be made at the IOC general assembly in 2025. If denuclearization of the Korean Peninsula becomes a reality and North Korea embraces reform and open door policies before that time, the IOC may be able to clear way for the unified Korea to host the Olympics. The IOC made an unusual decision in 2017 when Paris in France and Los Angeles in America clashed fiercely over the 2024 Summer Olympics. The IOC announced that Paris was selected as the host city of the 2024 Olympics and LA was selected as the host city of the 2028 Olympics simultaneously. If several cities compete to host the 2032 Games, it is possible that IOC might step in with an unusual decision. It would be difficult for the IOC to ignore the cause of joint-hosting of the Olympics by South Korea and North Korea as the two Koreas try to move beyond the Cold War era to an era of reconciliation.

WHEN UNITED, KOREA IS QUALIFIED TO JOIN EVEN THE 40-8-CLUB

At the beginning of the book, I introduced the fact that Korea joined the 30-50 club in 2018. This is a remarkable achievement made 70 years after the establishment of the Republic of Korea government. By the time the government celebrates its 100th anniversary, it is expected that Korea will have soared to a new height and become a member of the 40-80 clubs. If the Korean Peninsula is reunified, the population of the unified Korea will immediately become more than 75 million. When Korea joins the 40-80 Club, which is a group of countries with a per capita income of $40,000 and a population of more than 80 million, Korea will be able to manage a pretty stable domestic market-oriented economy instead of being at the mercy of the export market conditions. As of now, there are only three countries in the world capable of doing that: the U.S., Japan and Germany.

As for the future of the Korean Peninsula, the outlook of the international community is worthy of reference.

The OECD released a gloomy outlook for Korea in 2013 and said, "Korea's potential growth rate will fall to the 0% range after 2031, making it the lowest among OECD members." On the other hand, the global investment bank Goldman Sachs announced a rosy outlook for Korea in 2007 and said a unified Korea will see its per capita GDP exceeding $80,000 in 2015, making it the world's second-largest economy after the U.S.

There is variable that explains the completely opposite outlooks of these two reports: unification. The OECD report is based on an analysis of the economy of Korea as a divided country, while the Goldman Sachs report is based on the economy of Korea as a united country. The best way to predict the future is to invent it, said the U.S. computer scientist Alan Kay. Inventing a future in a way that is desirable for all of us is exactly what the Korean leaders are called for now.

EPILOGUE

A BRAINSTORM OF IDEAS FOR A REFORMED KOREA

In the process of compiling and editing references and data to write this book, The Republic of Korea That We Don't Know: a 70-Year Miracle, I received many words of advice and encouragement from the people around me. Most of them felt the same way about the objective of this book and were willing to share with me their ideas and advice on what needed to be done for the further development of the Republic of Korea. I could feel how deeply they cared about our society from the words that they were giving me. Some of their advises were already included in the manuscript I was writing for this book, but many of them were ideas that I couldn't think about.

Although I was inspired by my pride of being a Korean and that pride made me write this book with a hope for Korea to become a country that will be envied by the world, I'd experienced many a frustrating moment during the writing process--- such as the time when I could not keep up with all those new reports and statistics that continued to mill out , and the time when I knew I could not include every word advice and encouragement that I was given while I was writing. I wrote down all those ideas and words I was given by the people who are active in various fields of our society, and I am sharing them here to relieve that frustration.

ELIMINATION OF THE RANK AND JOB ROTATING SYSTEMS FOR GOVERNMENT EMPLOYEES

The current rank and job rotating systems for government employees are cited as the main reasons for low professionalism and irresponsible administration of civil servants. Civil servants are still considered to have the best job security. The government should transform the government employees into a group that is compensated according to ability and performance in order to develop their professionalism.

IMPROVING LABOR FLEXIBILITY AND STABILITY

The culture where super-powerful labor unions are constantly staging illegal structures should be abolished. Companies can become more competitive only when the rigid labor market is improved, and labor flexibility is increased. Of course, it has to be accompanied by efforts to improve labor safety to the level of advanced countries. Labor flexibility can take roots in society only when a minimum quality of life can be guaranteed even if people fail to find a job or get fired from their jobs.

ABOLITION OF CLOSED-DOOR PARTY-GOVERNMENT MEETING

With the significant part of the power to decide policies shifting from the government to the National Assembly, the closed-door party-government meeting is playing a major role in leaving the administration out of the policy-making process. The National Assembly members with ties to the party leadership and the Presidential office are becoming a means of putting pressure on the government and causing public officials to develop an apathetic attitude. It is natural for ruling party lawmakers to exert influence on state affairs, but it should be done through legislative activities within the National Assembly or persuasion in open occasions. For the sake of mutual checks between the administration and the legislature, the closed-door meetings between the ruling party and the government should be made open and public.

INTRODUCING AN ADVANCED COUNTRY-STYLE TAXATION SYSTEM

The taxation policy should be simplified based on low tax rates and wide range of tax revenues. The most desirable is to put a cap on all tax rates such as seen in Hong Kong. The inheritance tax rate, which is up to 65% under current policy, should be drastically lowered. Corporate taxes should be reduced to support companies to perform well in the global market.

CREATION OF THE KOREAN-STYLE "INDUSTRY 4.0" ENVIRONMENT

"Industry 4.0" is an industrial policy that has been in practice in Germany for several years. The policy entails the establishment of a communication system between production devices and products through the Internet of Things and optimizing the production process. One of the characteristics is that the discussion and debates started spontaneously among the associations of industries, or in the private sector. In the case of Korea, where a grand compromise between parties of interest is not easy, the government needs to create an open innovation induction system.

CREATING A NATION AND INDUSTRY-WIDE ADVISORY BODY

Currently, the government-affiliated think tanks are separated into several groups in economy (Korea Development Institute), industry (Korea Institute for Industrial Economics & Trade), labor (Korea Labor Institute) and health (Korea Institute for Health and Social Affairs). Since policy, industrial and labor issues are growing increasingly complicated, solutions to these issues need to be encompassing different fields. In order to carry out comprehensively encompassing research on policy and industry sectors and present a vision, a nation and industry-wide advisory body whose functions go beyond the existing Economics, Humanities and Social Research Council should be established. Market-oriented, profit-oriented, and innovation-oriented researches that are linked to businesses (industries) should also be carried out.

LABOR POLARIZATION WORSE THAN INCOME POLARIZATION..."DUALIZING OF THE DUAL" PROBLEM HAS TO BE RESOLVED

The dual structure of the labor market in Korea is in a serious situation and the problem is growing worse, as attested by various research reports and statistics. Korea's labor market is even criticized as being "dualizing of the dual." This is because the market is exposed to overlapping wage gaps between regular and non-regular employees and employees of large corporations and small businesses. In order to improve productivity, Korea has to put the solution to the labor market polarization as the priority. National Assembly Recall System should be introduced and the immunity for lawmakers should be abolished so that unqualified lawmakers can be replaced at any time even during their terms. Statistics on the average annual salary by occupation in Korea show that the lawmakers rank number one in the rank. Their annual salary should be drastically cut and the National Assembly should be reformed into an European-style working parliament.

IMPERIAL PRESIDENCY SHOULD BE REFORMED INTO AN ADVANCED COUNTRY-STYLE POLITICAL MODEL

The five-year, single-term presidency system, which was established during the era of democratization movements, needs to be amended by now. The wasteful political disputes can be reduced only when a power structure that corresponds to the new economic environment and the IT era is established. The government should choose to introduce a two four-year terms system or a parliamentary cabinet system.

THE KIM YOUNG-RAN ACT SHOULD BE ABOLISHED TO PROMOTE DOMESTIC CONSUMPTION

The Kim Young-ran Act, which was created at a time when Korea's per capita income was $20,000, runs counter to a time when Korea's per capita income is expected to reach $50,000. Domestic market and the national economy will become revitalized only when consumers are free to spend money. Even though regulations to crack down on corruption are clearly necessary, the regulations that broadly restrict the people's freedom should be eliminated.

MULTILATERAL TRADING SYSTEM SHOULD BE RE-ESTABLISHED AND THE SMART DIPLOMACY AS A MIDDLE POWER SHOULD BE PRACTICED THROUGH A "SEOUL ROUND"

Korea should proactively seek to establish multilateral trade alliances with middle-power countries to counter protectionism of the U.S. and China. Korea should shift from passive diplomacy, which simply arbitrates conflicts, to active diplomacy, which seeks clues for shared growth. For developing and developing countries, Korea should transplant its growth base through proactive aid, investment and knowledge transfer, and narrow the gap with advanced countries by forming knowledge and technology alliances.

INTER-KOREAN ECONOMIC COOPERATION IS THE NEW GROWTH ENGINE AND RESOLVING NORTH KOREA'S NUCLEAR WEAPONS PROGRAM IS THE FIRST STEP TOWARD PEACE AND COEXISTENCE ON THE KOREAN PENINSULA

Peace is the cornerstone of the economy. If the North Korean nuclear issue is resolved, inter-Korean economic cooperation will become a new growth engine. The North's aging population index stood at 49.9, half of South Korea's 110.5. That means there is a low-cost manpower is readily available. A unified Korea can connect by land with China, one of the largest consumer bases, and also with Russia's Far East economic bloc. If inter-Korean cooperation in economic development becomes a reality, aid from other countries, including the U.S. and China, is expected to increase significantly as well.

REALISTIC COLLEGE TUITION POLICY SHOULD ENSURE THE AUTONOMY OF UNIVERSITY MANAGEMENT

The college tuition and fees that have been frozen for more than a decade should be allowed to be readjusted to a realistic level to ensure improved the autonomy of university budget management. College insiders lament that "Tuition and fees that do not reflect the inflation rate make it difficult even to pay professors." Universities around the world are waging a scouting war to recruit prominent scholars, but Korean universities are left out in this war. In order to respond quickly to the era of the fourth industrial revolution, it should also be made easier for colleges to adjust the number of enrollments at each department. The government should drastically expand the autonomy of colleges in selecting students and professors to prepare for a rapidly changing demand for education. The future of the university is the future of the country and industry. The future of Korea is also bleak with the college management and system of the past industrialization era.

ELEMENTARY SCHOOL ENTERING AGE SHOULD BE LOWERED BY ONE YEAR

Korea's sharply decreasing population problem is a very bad factor that contributes to the weakening national competitiveness. It calls for revolutionary measures and a shift of ideas. In order to address the vicious circle of late college graduation age, delayed marriage, and low birth rates, the elementary school entering age should be lowered from seven to six. If kids enter school system one year earlier, they can graduate college one year earlier than they do now. The government also should consider changing the current 6-3-3 school year system to 5-3-3 school year system. If these measures allow students to graduate college and start career two years earlier than they do now, it could greatly reduce the cost of private education and help solve the problem of delayed marriage trend.

RELOCATING THE PRESIDENTIAL OFFICE AND THE NATIONAL ASSEMBLY TO SEJONG CITY

The Korean government is spending a significant amount of budget in administration because the Presidential office, Cheongwadae, and the National Assembly are located in Seoul while major government institutions are in Sejong City. The government should reduce administrative costs and achieve balanced national development by developing Sejong City as a political city and Seoul, an economic city.

ENGLISH SHOULD BECOME A COMMONLY-USED LANGUAGE AND THE DONATION-BASED COLLEGE ADMISSION SYSTEM SHOULD BE INTRODUCED

Korea should aim to become an open society by adopting English as a commonly-used language. Parents in Korea have to spend a significant amount of money for shadow education in order to send their children to good colleges. The government should introduce donation-based college admission system so that the money can go to colleges instead of private after-school academic institutions. The donation-based college admission system can also contribute to the stronger competitiveness of Korean colleges.

ADOPTING A SOLDIER RECRUITMENT SYSTEM CAN RESOLVE THE YOUTH UNEMPLOYMENT CRISIS

People say the army is not what it used to be. Soldiers are highly regarded and respected in the U.S. and other countries, but they are not in Korea. The government should adopt a soldier recruitment system for the sake of boosting morale among soldiers and resolve the youth unemployment crisis as well.

KOREA SHOULD TRY TO JOIN THE ASEAN

Korea should try to become the 11th member of the new economic growth engine, ASEAN. According to the ASEAN charter, countries are qualified to join the organization only when they meet the geographical requirement of being located in Southeast Asia, but Korea should find a way to join, such as an exceptional rule, to emphasize the fact that Korea is a key partner of ASEAN.

A SWEEPING TRANSITION INTO A HAVEN FOR STARTUPS AND UNIVERSITY SYSTEM REFORM

The limitations of large corporations and manufacturing industries are being exposed. Now, jobs should be found in startups and the college education system should be completely reformed. Colleges should transform themselves into startup incubators and establish incentive systems, and national and public universities should become the models.

KOREA MUST CATCH UP WITH THE TREND IN SHARING ECONOMY AND REALIZE A SOCIAL CONSENSUS

It is a pity that ride-sharing services are not allowed in Korea due to the objection of interest groups. Grab in Malaysia started as a car-sharing service provider and now, the company is dominating the Southeastern markets by expanding its businesses to travel, finance, education, and other platform-based businesses. The sharing economy of Korea is falling behind even the Southeastern countries, and Koreans who wish to tap into the sharing businesses have to find a business territory in overseas. The employment issue in existing industries is same in other countries. Korea needs to deregulate and allow sharing service providers to enter its market sooner than later.

AUTONOMOUS LOCAL GOVERNMENTS SHOULD BE RESTRUCTURED INTO EIGHT MEGA MUNICIPALITIES

The cost of maintaining 252 small and large local governments is significant. All those small city and country-level local governments should be restructured into eight mega municipalities for a more efficient local administration and balanced regional development.

THE SENIORITY-BASED WAGE STRUCTURE SHOULD BE CHANGED INTO JOB-BASED WAGE STRUCTURE

In order to achieve $50,000 per capita income, Koreans need to increase their income level by increasing years of being employed. Under the current pyramid-style and seniority-based employment structure, however, companies will the burden over the employees who have been working for many years. Changing into the job-based wage structure will reduce the burden on both employees and companies over long years of employment.

REFORMING EMPLOYMENT SYSTEM INTO AN ADVANCED COUNTRY-STYLE MARKED BY FLEXIBLE EMPLOYMENT AND LAYOFF

The essence of the employment system demanded by both companies and labor community is "flexibility" after all. From a corporate standpoint, organizations should be flexibly managed through the flexible layoff system, and from the employees' standpoint, they have to be able to find a new job immediately when they are let go from the existing jobs. In advanced countries, employment is just as flexible as layoff. For this reason, it is possible for them to build a corporate culture where a grand compromise is possible between management and labor. Korea's current system of hiring through open recruitment is also a stumbling block for the flexible labor market.

THE NEED FOR RE-SHORING FOR THE REVIVAL OF MANUFACTURING INDUSTRY

Many people claim that the U.S. economy was able to turn to a positive cycle thanks to the recovery in the manufacturing sector. They explain that the policy that started during the Obama administration to strengthen the US manufacturing sector was just what they needed. At the root of this is the "re-shoring" policy, which is about encouraging factories that have fled to developing countries and other countries to return to the homeland. Korean government needs to create an environment where big manufacturers such as Samsung and Hyundai Motor can build manufacturing facilities and produce products in Korea.

PROACTIVE APPROACH IN ECONOMIC EDUCATION

In order to instill a proper sense of economy, the government should offer practical economic education to students from the elementary education level. Education on savings, interest rates and long-term investments in stocks will not only transform an individual's life more economically logical, but also help the Korean economy grow and boost the capital market.

ELIMINATE THE REGULATIONS THAT HINDER THE ACTIVE USE OF BIG DATA, THE RAW MATERIAL FOR THE FOURTH INDUSTRIAL REVOLUTION

There are three regulations that hinder the proactive use of big data in Korea: the Personal Information Protection Act, the Information and Communication Network Act, and the Credit Information Act. Industry insiders mock these three regulations by dubbing them "three shameless regulations." Companies around the world are introducing innovative and revolutionary new big data-based services, but the Korean government is excessively regulating the commercial and industrial use of personal information. Some even point out that while the government is blocking the use of personal information, it is not really doing a good job in protecting information. The ministries in charge of the three laws are also divided into multiple public agencies including the Ministry of Public Administration and Security, the Ministry of Science and Technology, the Ministry of Information and Communication, the Broadcasting and Telecommunications Committee and the Financial Services Commission, making a swift reform an urgent task.

IS KOREA'S NATIONAL BRAND GOOD AS IT IS?

The Lee Myung-bak's administration envisioned a national brand under the slogan of "Considerate and Beloved Korea" by creating a Presidential Council on Nation Branding and picked five themes to focus to realize this vision: Korea's role in the international community; fostering the sense of global citizenship; consideration for multi culture and foreigners; promotion of culture and tourism; and development of high-tech technologies. However, the Council was eliminated during the Park Geun-hye administration. The catch phrase for the promotion of Korea also changed to "Dynamic Korea" and "Sparkling Korea," but even those are gone now. Koreas need to think about Korea's national brand and identity from the very bottom line again.

LET'S CHANGE THE IMAGE OF "MADE IN KOREA"

Although Korean products are perceived to have relatively good design and quality, their brand recognition is very low, according to KOTRA and other trade-related organizations. The image of the Republic of Korea as a nation perceived by foreign media is not as good as what Korea really is. So far, news about Korea has been mostly about North Korea-related summits or missile launching, as well as mass demonstrations, rallies and impeachment of the president. In particular, Korea was seen as a country heavily under the influence of Shamanism when the president was being impeached. Therefore, it is necessary for Koreans have an accurate diagnosis of Korea's national image and think about ways to improve it.

SEOUL, THE CENTER OF KOREA, AS A "YOUNG CITY"

Regulations on the height of buildings (35 floors) and the floor space rate should be loosened to promote the construction of high-rising landmark buildings that can represent Korea in the international community. Regulations for redevelopment and reconstruction should be loosened but the construction of landmark-level residential facilities should be allowed in Apgujeong-dong and Daechi-dong under practical construction plans. Yongsan, whose redevelopment is being delayed due to residents' conflicting interests and the administrative agencies trying to avoid responsibility, should be developed into a residential complex with a job-housing proximity to the Korean version of Silicon Valley, and measures should be introduced to allow the entire population to share the profits. Ten high-rise landmark buildings should be constructed in Seoul and about 10 residential complexes in Yongsan, Yeouido and Gangnam as cities with job-housing proximity.

THE NEED TO RESOLVE THE FACTION CONFLICT WITHIN LABOR UNIONS, THE FUNDAMENTAL CAUSE OF MAJOR INDUSTRIAL CRISES

Price competitiveness is still important in international competition among companies. If labor costs are high and productivity is low, it will inevitably result in the weak competitiveness of companies. Productivity increases when labor-management relations are cooperative, and it decreases when the labor-management relations are uncooperative, as testified many cases in countries around the world. The militant labor unions in the northern part of the United States are turning to be more cooperative, Japan has been maintaining cooperative labor-management relations since 1960, and labor unions in the UK and Spain have also changing their existing stance, but Korea is only going against the tide. In order to change the hard-lined Korean labor unions, factional strife within the labor unions must be resolved. There are so many factions that it is becoming an element that blocks new proposals and rational approaches within the union itself.

Some point out that the Korean labor unions cannot let go of their hard-liner approaches due to factional rivalry and struggle for political leadership. Currently in Korea, labor union leaders are elected once every two years, but the factional conflict can be resolved and changes can happen within labor unions if the term is changed into four years. In major countries around the world, the labor union leaders are elected once every four years as well.

MILITECH 4.0 ERA, AN URGENT NEED FOR CIVILIAN-MILITARY TECHNICAL COOPERATION

Under the fourth industrial revolution, the technological division between the private sector and the military sector has disappeared, and the defense industry market is rapidly expanding in a way that is completely different from the past. The Millitech 4.0 era has opened, but technological cooperation between the military and the private sectors has not been dynamic in Korea compared to advanced countries. Although Korea also has the Agency for Defense Development, which is in charge of R&D in military technology, its development goal is focused largely on replacing the existing imported weapons, and it does not have enough budget to develop future technologies. It is urgent to establish a defense R&D control tower, such as the U.S. Defense Advanced Research Projects Agency, DARPA. Through such tower, Korea has to start building a network of high-tech science and technology that encompasses the military, businesses, universities and research institutes. It should also open up the closed military community to apply telemedicine services as well as products such as AI-based robot soldiers and high-tech textile materials to military training sites to catch two birds of national security and innovation with one stone.

PLAYING FIELD THAT IS UNLEVELED IN FAVOR OF LABOR UNION SHOULD BE REPAIRED

Korea is in need of emergency measures to rectify badly distorted labor-management relations before full-fledged labor reform, including loosened regulation on layoff, can happen. The government should repair the unleveled playing field that is in favor of labor unions now by legislating the extension of the validity of collective agreements (from two to three years) and stronger sanctions when labor unions fail to correct illegal collective agreements such as passing down jobs to the children, punishing labor unions for unfair labor practices, prohibiting the seize of business facilities during strikes, and permitting the use temporary agency workers during strikes.

THE NEED TO GROW A GLOBAL BRAND AS A "LITTLE COUNTRY WITH BIG DREAMS"

Although the Israeli lunar probe spacecraft failed to land on the moon, the "Little Country, Big Dream," a slogan written on the spacecraft, has a significant implication for the Korean economy. In order to overcome the limitations of a small domestic market, Korea needs to make inroads into global markets. Instead of relying on just a few brands such as Samsung, Korea should also look into ways to grow global franchise businesses comparable to McDonald's, Burger King, Subway, and KFC. Instead of fighting over labor-management issues or the abuse of authority by the people in superior's positions, Koreans should think more about making forays into the global markets.

THE NEED TO RESPOND TO THE GLOBAL PARADIGM SHIFT

The future of Korean companies is uncertain due to the rising barriers to export industries, including stricter environmental regulations in Europe. For sustainable growth, a campaign to raise people's awareness of the environment and biodiversity is imperative.

FOSTER 5,000 AI GENIUS FOR THE FOURTH INDUSTRIAL REVOLUTION

Korea is in a serious shortage of talented human resources who can handle AI and big data for the era of the fourth industrial revolution. Korea needs to provide exceptional support to nurture such creative talent, while breaking away from the existing uniformed and cramming-type educational frameworks. Korea should build global-level, state-of-the-art education and super-special gifted programs to foster 5,000 AI geniuses who can support 10,000 people each.

All-out Reform of New Industry Regulations, Such as Ride Sharing

Exceptions to regulations should be applied until industries grow larger than a certain size instead of being killed due to regulations, such as in China. Regulatory sandbox should be applied to all industries instead of being applied only to the companies that have applied for it.

Labor-related Uniform Regulations Such as 52 Hours Per Week Should Become More Flexible

The U.S. does not sanction companies for having violating

regulations regarding working hour limit, although the statutory working hours is 40 hours a week. Companies can pay one and a half times surcharge for overtime. However in Korea, violations on labor-related regulations such as 52 hours per week working hour limit are subject to severe and uniformed punishments such as penalties for CEOs. The severity of punishment should vary depending on the degree of violation of the law. Flexible working hours and conditions should be applied broadly in the IT and gaming industries.

Create More Jobs and Improve Productivity Through the 5G Industry Revolution

With 5G marked by ultra-low latency and ultra-high speed network, current wired-based facilities will be replaced wireless facilities and manufacturing production lines will become more flexible. It can increase productivity by changing manufacturing processes frequently by linking them with cooperative robots, Clouds, and AIs to accommodate the demand for the variety and small quantity productions.

THE NEED TO GROW "THE OIL FOR THE FUTURE", DATA INDUSTRY

The commercialization of 5G is dawning the "super-connected age" where numerous sensors and devices are connected. Data production is surging across the economy and society, because a wide variety of devices such as cars, drones, robots, and CCTV are connected to 5G and produce big data. A significant volume of high-capacity data such as real-time streaming of high-resolution (4K, 8K) images, which were previously impossible, is also being generated due to 5G high-speed transmission, is also being generated. It is necessary to utilize data from industrial fields and innovate industrial structures by combining 5G's "ultra-fast, ultra-low-latency, and ultra-connectivity" features with AI and Cloud.

A CONTINUOUS REGULATORY REVOLUTION FOR THE REVIVAL OF CORPORATE VITALITY

Regulatory reforms ensure autonomy and creativity in private sector while making fair competition possible in markets. The situation is where the tendency to maintain vested interests within the existing boundaries, the complexity of interested parties, and the reform of civil service-related regulations are conflicting with each other. An all-out reformation is necessary in areas close to people's livelihoods, such as housing, childcare and education, in addition to the promising new industries. Institutional innovations should also follow, such as upgrading regulatory costs and strengthening screening of new regulations.

Since regulations are born in line with the reality of the time, efforts should be made to continuously identify unnecessary regulations and eliminate them. When it comes to the regulatory revolution, communication with the field are two important factors. Regulations should be reformed through communication with fields instead of armchair debates and theories. The government should reduce the cost of regulating the environment of small and medium businesses and reduce the burden of quasi-taxes on companies.

RESOLVE THE POLARIZATION BETWEEN LARGE AND SMALL-TO-MEDIUM COMPANIES

There is a growing polarization in productivity, profit ratio, employment and wages between large and small-to-medium companies. Unbalance growth resulted in the creation of an industrial structure that is skewed heavily towards a small number of large companies. The situation is creating a negative side effect in which any crisis that hit a large company is shaking the overall industrial ecosystem. The polarization between large and small-to-medium companies is causing social polarization in job market and welfare system as well. Co-prosperity of large and small-to-medium businesses is more important than ever in order to create a sustainable corporate ecosystem that can weather economic crises.

PROMOTE ENTREPRENEURSHIP... CREATE AN ECOSYSTEM FOR VENTURE STARTUPS

Entrepreneurial spirit can be revived only when a social foundation is created where anyone is encouraged to start a business and can make success. Startups and ventures bring dynamism to the economy. The Republic of Korea can change only when the society is willing to embrace failures and further, learn from failures. Korea needs to create a virtuous cycle in terms of the venture capital support, investment, and recovery ecosystem.

REDUCE THE NUMBER OF GOVERNMENT EMPLOYEES TO SAVE TAX REVENUES AND REDUCE REGULATIONS

Innovation in regulations is a must to become an advanced country. In order to make it happen, a number of unnecessary government jobs must be eliminated. Without reform in government employment system, there is no industrial renovation.

PRODUCTION OF TALENTED HUMAN RESOURCES TO MEET THE INDUSTRIAL DEMAND

Non-performing universities must be shut down since the number of school-age population continues to drop. At the same time, the government should strengthen vocational education in high school level and adjust the number of enrollments at colleges, while increasing government support to expand training of workers in areas with the shortage of human resources such as bio and AI industries.

RESEARCH IN ADVANCED COUNTRIES IS DIRECTED TOWARDS THE R&DB (BUSINESS)

In recent years, research and evaluation standards are shifting from pure academic excellence to socioeconomic ripple effect. The total amount of profits from royalties on commercializing research results and technologies is less than the amount of profits made by a single college in the United States. There are also many research achievements that have been remaining dormant after registering patents or publishing papers. However, since most researchers rely on government research funds, the there are many people in the Korean society who perceive startups by scientists as an attempt to profit off patents. There are also people who have negative opinions about "scientists who make money." On the other hand, other countries, such as China, are dreaming of creating a second Silicon Valley in their country and properly compensating researchers for their achievements and encouraging startups. Although there are projects in Korea that encourage technology startups such as VC (venture capital) pitching competition, they are very limited. There is a need for a change in the very foundation level to allow systematically support from the research stage to the commercialization stage instead of just an one-time promotional event.

A TIME WHEN ECO-FRIENDLY, HIGH-EFFICIENCY ENERGY IS NATIONAL POWER

Carbon regulations are on the rise due to climate change, while the electricity demand is expected to grow 2.7 times by 2050 as the world moves into a hyper-connected society. Korea is recording the fastest increase rate in in power demand in the world. If the government continues its nuclear phase-out policy, it runs the risk of collapsing the supply and demand system. The Korean government should let go of its nuclear phase-out policy, while expanding R&D of next-generation energy such as nuclear fusion energy and high-efficiency hydrogen batteries.

KOREA'S ECONOMIC FUTURE LIES IN THE DERIVATIVE INDUSTRIES OF THE SUPER-AGING POPULATION

In preparation for Korea's entry into the super-aged society in 2025, the government should make an intensive investment to nurture social welfare-related medical devices, regenerative medicine, and elderly medical-related industries. Super-aged population is resulting in the reduced consumer spending. In the case of Japan, 65% of the nation's total household loans are attributed to the people aged 60 or older. Korea needs to create an environment where the elderly citizens can make investment and spend money on consumption. Healthcare system should also be changed from treatment-oriented to prevention-oriented. Currently, people who frequent hospitals more than others get more benefits from the government, but in the future, the government should give more benefits to those who visit hospitals less than others. When people get older, they can remain healthier if they continue to work. When there are more senior citizens who work after retirement than those who stop working after retirement, it results in the increase per capita income nationwide, not to mention healthier elderly population and reduced social welfare costs.

INCREASED PRODUCTIVITY AND BIGGER PIES

Currently, Korea is faced with a situation where people can feel the marginal utility in which major industries such as semiconductors and automobiles becoming less and less competitive. Koreans have to proactively improve productivity and expand economic territory. Korea is sure to fall behind unless it tries to get bigger pies.

THE INTERNATIONALIZATION OF THE KOREAN CURRENCY

A number of limitations are exposed because the Korean currency, won, is not so internationalized considering Korea's economic power. The Korean government needs to put together big visions within a big frame and take actions so that the Korean currency will gradually become more internationalized eventually, if not now.

KOREAN SOCIETY SHOULD BREAK FREE FROM THE EXTREME ATTITUDE OF PERCEIVING OTHERS EITHER AS ENEMY OR COMRADE

Korea needs a Korean-style "tolerance." Korea needs to create a society where people acknowledge those who are different from Koreans. Koreans have to acknowledge the difference between Koreans and non-Koreans and be generous about the difference. Extremism is the cause of all sorts of conflicts in society, and this chronic conflicting structure is reducing productivity and adding the burden of costs. It is urgently necessary to reduce the conflicts between ideologies, classes, regions and various sectors of society.

THE NEED TO CHANGE EXCLUSIVE ATTITUDE

Koreans often show exclusive attitude. It is good to embrace what is uniquely ours, but Koreans can grow global competitiveness when they become hybrid with what are universal. Koreans have to change the attitude of exclusively insisting only on what is ours while crying for globalization and global competitiveness.

MAJOR OVERHAUL ON THE NATIONAL PENSION SERVICE, THE GOVERNMENT EMPLOYEES PENSION, AND THE MILITARY PENSION SCHEMES

The age of receiving pension should be older than it is now, and the share individuals have to contribute has to be more than it is now. The burden of pension should not be thoughtlessly passed on to future generations.

EXTENSION OF MANDATORY RETIREMENT AGE TO 65

In Korea, the rapidly aging population is a crisis in itself. Companies with a large number of employees over the age of 60 should be entitled for government-level support. The government should also establish a pool of highly skilled human resources over the age of 60.

REFORM IN PURSUIT OF A NEGATIVE-TYPE REGULATION SYSTEM

The framework of the existing domestic regulatory system is a positive type that lists permissible projects, thereby posing obstacles to the development of new businesses and industries. The government can ensure accelerated development of new technologies and industry only when the frame of regulations is changed into a negative type in which the government lists only the special prohibited conditions such as those associated with safety issues. Negative regulations are necessary to foster new industries such as the fourth industrial revolution.

REFORMATION OF AUDIT SYSTEM THAT HAMPERS REGULATORY REFORMS

Government employees are reluctant to loosen regulations because they fear the possibility of audit when problems arise, even if they want to loosen or eliminate regulations. As of now, government institutions are subject to multiple audits by the Board of Audit, the National Assembly, and the Prosecutors' Office, not to mention their own internal audits. This audit structure should be overhauled, and the policy audit by the Board of Audit should be abolished as well. Only then can the government employees will be willing to participate in the regulatory reforms.

FROM THE COMPETITION OF RISK AVOIDING TO THE COMPETITION OF CREATIVITY

People are flocking to jobs that offer security such as government jobs. They are entering a competition that is fierce but is all about avoiding risks for their lives. They don't want to join a competition of creativity where they compete with their creative skills. In order for Korea to grow into a society where people compete with their creativity, it is necessary to establish culture and system that embraces failure.

KOREA, THE LAND OF EXTREMISM, NEEDS A ROOM FOR THE MIDDLE GROUNDS

The conflicting structure of the Korean society is expanding along the growing voices of the extreme conservatives and progressives on social media channels such as YouTube. In the field of dialogue and negotiations, there are abundance of attacks but hardly any effort to communicate with each other, because nobody is willing to acknowledge differences, and everybody only insists on refusing them. It seems that the situation calls for a field of open meeting where the conservatives and the progressives from various fields come together to listen to each other's opinions and to narrow the gap in their extremist thoughts.

SEVEN DECADES OF
KOREAN ECONOMIC SUCCESS :
ISSUES FOR THE NEXT GENERATIONS

초판 1쇄 2019년 9월 30일

지은이　장대환
책임편집　권병규
마케팅　김선미 김형진
디자인　김보현

펴낸곳 매경출판㈜ **펴낸이** 전호림
등록 2003년 4월 24일(No. 2-3759)
주소 (04557) 서울시 중구 충무로 2(필동1가) 매일경제 별관 2층 매경출판㈜
홈페이지 www.mkbook.co.kr
전화 02)2000-2631(기획편집) 02)2000-2636(마케팅) 02)2000-2606(구입 문의)
팩스 02)2000-2609　**이메일** publish@mk.co.kr
인쇄·제본 ㈜M-print 031)8071-0961
ISBN 979-11-6484-020-5(03320)

책값은 뒤표지에 있습니다.
파본은 구입하신 서점에서 교환해 드립니다.

이 도서의 국립중앙도서관 출판예정도서목록(CIP)은 서지정보유통지원시스템 홈페이지(http://seoji.nl.go.kr)와
Country자료공동목록시스템(http://www.nl.go.kr/kolisnet)에서 이용하실 수 있습니다.
(CIP제어번호: CIP2019034767)